China's Economic Transformation Over 20 Years

Organized and Sponsored by
the China (Hainan) Institute of Reform and Development

Chief Editor: Wang Mengkui

Foreign Languages Press Beijing

First Edition 2000

Home Page:
http://www.flp.com.cn
Email Address:
Info@flp.com.cn
Sales@flp.com.cn

ISBN 7-119-02610-0

Published by Foreign Languages Press
24 Baiwanzhuang Road, Beijing 100037, China
Distributed by China International Book Trading Corporation
35 Chegongzhuang Xilu, Beijing 100044, China
P.O. Box 399, Beijing, China
Printed in the People's Republic of China

Contributors

Introduction

By **Chen Jinhua**, vice chairman of the National Committee of Chinese People's Political Consultation Conference and board chairman of China (Hainan) Institute of Reform and Development

Chapter I

By **Zhou Shulian**, research fellow of Institute of Industrial Economics under the Chinese Academy of Social Sciences, and Wang Yanzhong, Ph.D. in economics of the Institute of Industrial Economics under the Chinese Academy of Social Sciences

Chapter II

By **Zhang Zhuoyuan**, research fellow of Institute of Economics under the Chinese Academy of Social Sciences

Chapter III

By **Chen Xiwen**, chief and research fellow of Rural Department of Center of Development Studies under the State Council

Chapter IV

By **Gao Shangquan**, director-general of China Society for Reform of Economic Structure, and director and professor of China (Hainan) Institute of Reform and Development

Chapter V

By **Chi Fulin**, executive director and professor of China (Hainan) Institute of Reform and Development and vice chairman of China Society for Reform of Economic Structure

Chapter VI

By **Zheng Lixin**, vice secretary-general and research fellow of State Development and Planning Commission

Chapter VII

By **Lin Zhaomu**, executive deputy director and research fellow of Macro-economic Research Institute of State Development and Planning Commission, and Chang Xiuze, research fellow of Macro-economic Research Institute of State Development and Planning Commission

CONTENTS

FOREWORD

By Wang Mengqui

The on-going economic reform, which started in 1979, is undoubtedly one of the most important events of the twentieth century in China. With its profound social and economic impact, the reform has turned over a new leaf in the history of China and its influence has been felt worldwide. Over the past decades, a great number of books have been produced on China's economic reform both in and outside the country. This is especially so as China's economic reform is entering its 21st year.

Then, why have we taken the time and trouble writing this book on China's economic reform?

The purpose is to provide readers at home and abroad a concise yet comprehensive summary of the process and experience of China's economic reform over the past twenty years. As far as I know, such a book is not yet available. Out of such considerations, we have planned this book in the following structure: First, it includes a general introduction titled "Basic Experience of China's Economic Transition over the Past 20 Years." Then, it is followed by seven separate chapters expounding respectively on the reform of the ownership system as well as state-owned enterprises; reform of the price system reform; reform of the rural economic system; planning and market in China's reform drive; the open policy; the macroeconomic reform; and the relationship between the reform, development and social stability. I am of the opinion that this book will be sufficient for the general readership if they simply want to have a rough understanding of what is going on in China's reform. If they are too busy and even cannot find the time to read the whole book, they might as well just read the general introduction. The publication of the book in both Chinese and English is intended to meet the needs of both Chinese and foreign readers and to promote the understanding of China's economic reform in the international community.

The book is a retrospective summary of China's reform over the past two decades. With a critical attitude, the readers can draw their own conclusions about the current state of affairs and prospects of China's reform. As a rule, the more distant we are from a historical event, the better we can see its true essence and come to a better understanding of its historical significance. China's economic reform is no exception. It is our hope that this book will an understanding of the laws underlying China's economic reform, which is definitely indispensable in a full understanding of China's modernization drive.

The publication of the book was initiated by Mr. Chen Jinghua. Moreover, he himself contributed the insightful general introduction that is printed at the beginning of the book. China Institute for Reform and Development, on the other hand, took care of the day-to-day organizational job. As the chief editor, I only chaired two meetings attended by contributors and publishers, with the purpose of unifying styles of presentation and avoiding repetition, rather than seeking a consistency of views between different contributors. All the contributors to this book are, without exception, highly accomplished experts in the study of China's economic reform. Some of them have served at one time or another at leading posts for the reform practice. This certainly adds to the authority of their discussions. Although different contributors did not deliberately seek a complete congruency in their views, they shared wide consensus on the basic experience of China's economic reform. Therefore, chapters from different contributors will not cause any difficulty to the readers' understanding of China's economic reform as a whole.

Throughout the world, there have been different interpretations of the term "economic transition," some of them are drastically different from one another. The economic transition mentioned in the this refers precisely the economic reform going on in this country. In essence, it implies the transition from a traditional planned economy to a socialist market economy. To view it from the practical angle, it started in 1979, although the objective of establishing a socialist market economy was only identified in 1992. Obviously, such a profound transition in the economic system is not confined to the questions of planning and market. For instance, a mixed ownership structure with the public ownership as the dominant part is taken as the basis for the development of a socialist market economy. And opening to the outside world as well as rural reform are also necessary elements in the establishment of the market economy. These issues are all adequately addressed in this book.

August 5, 1999

INTRODUCTION

Basic Experience of China's Economic Transition over the Past 20 Years

Synopsis

The Third Plenary Session of the 11th Central Committee of the Communist Party of China marked the beginning of China's economic reform. Running through the course of the past two decades or more are two basic lines. The first one is the transition of the economic structure, that is, creating favorable institutional conditions that can effectively facilitate the development of productive forces through the implementation of the policy of opening to the outside world and reform. The second one is finding a road of industrialization and modernization that is compatible with the reality of China. Practice over the past two decades has proved that China has made quite a few historical breakthroughs in its economic transition and the achievements made so far have caught worldwide attention.

China has now arrived at a critical juncture in its economic transition. A study and summary of the experience gained in the reform drive over the past two decades is of great importance in both summing up the experience and making a comparison of the historical processes of economic transition in various countries, or affixing the historic position of reform in the entire course of China's development.

Proceeding from the perspectives of the establishment of the reform approach and basic economic structure, thc relations between reform, development and social stability and between planning and

market as well as the role of the government, this introduction reviews the 20-year historical course China has traversed in its economic transition, evaluates the achievements and experience, and ventures a number of strategic proposals for further pushing forward the economic transition.

The Third Plenary Session of the 11th Central Committee of the Communist Party of China, held in December 1978, ushered in a new era of reform, opening up to the outside world and modernization drive China. This historical process has lasted for 20-odd years now. Two basic lines run through this historical process. The first is the transition of economic system, i.e. the establishment of institutional conditions that can effectively facilitate the development of productive forces; and the second is to find a road to bring about industrialization and modernization in China. These two basic lines run side by side each other and are mutually complementary, with the latter being the principal connotation and goal of the former.

Looking back now, it can be concluded that China has made tremendous achievements in its economic transition. Over the past twenty years or more, China's economic structure has gradually shifted from the planned economy to the socialist market economy, from a semi-secluded model to a generally open model, and covers every spheres of social life. The reform and opening-up drive has fundamentally changed the rigid traditional economic system and brought about an unprecedented change in the outlook of the nation. China's economy has been developing by leaps and bounds. In a short span of ten years from 1979 to 1998, the country's GDP increased 6.4 fold, with the annual growth averaging 9.7 percent, ranking China among the fastest growing economies in the world during this period. Economic development has lifted the Chinese people out of poverty and backwardness. The "bottleneck" phenomenon that has long molested the Chinese economy has been gradually eliminated, thus putting an end to an era marked by "overall shortage." The country's economic vitality and economic strength have been markedly enhanced and the living standards of the people both in urban and rural areas have been greatly improved. According to the "three-step" strategy(1) chartered by Deng Xiaoping, China has accomplished the objective of the first step ahead of time and will accomplish that set for the second step before the end of this century, thus laying a solid foundation for attaining the objective set for the third step in the first half of next century.

Since the 1980s, many countries have successively launched economic reform or economic transition drives. Due to differences in natural conditions, market environment, economic foundation, historical and social background and human factors, the economic transition has displayed different characteristics in different countries. With regard to the big countries, China and Russia are rather typical. In his report titled "Where Should Reform Go? On Transition over the Past 10 Years," Mr. Stiglitze, vice president and a famous economist from the World Bank, pointed out that it was necessary to draw some lessons after the economic transition has gone on for ten years. He believed that up till now the transition in China proved to be more successful while that in Russia has turned out to be a failure. In his report, he focused on discussing the two extreme cases of success and failure, and claimed that the lessons were obvious. Compared with Russia, he believed, China had relatively low level of economic development and it was confronted with greater challenges – both the challenges of transition and development. He said that the transition in China was an economic transition from planned economy to market economy under the precondition of upholding the socialist system. Comparing the actual achievements made in both countries since from 1989, the GDP in China had nearly doubled while that of Russia had dropped by half. This meant, he pointed out, at the initial stage the GDP of Russia was more than twice as much as that of China, but now it was one third less. While the GDP of Russia was coming down, the economic imbalance had almost redoubled (calculated according to Gini's law).(2) From the perspective of practical results, China's reform is a success, just as Mr. Stiglitze claimed. Therefore, it is important to study and summarize the experience of China's reform over the past two decades, including issues yet to arise and remain to be tackled. This is of great significance by both making an international comparison of the progress of economic transition and studying the historical role played by the reform in the country's entire course of economic development.

China's reform has been going on under the guidance of Deng Xiaoping Theory. Deng Xiaoping was the chief architect of China's reform drive. His thoughts of reform, proceeding from the actual conditions of China and the needs of the time, had come into form gradually and had been continuously enriched. These thoughts include: (1) After the socialist system is basically established, it is necessary to fundamentally change the economic system that fetters the development of productive forces and establish a socialist economic system that is full of vigor. (2) Reform is a revolutionary transformation rather than making a few minor modifications of the original system. Therefore, reform should be regarded as the second revolution in China. (3) Reform is the self-perfection and self-development of the socialist system, and it is the only way to build socialism with Chinese characteristics. Under the historical condition today when socialism is confronted with a new technological revolution as well as various sorts of ideological and cultural challenges, there would be no way out for China if it does not persist in reform and opening up to the rest of the world. (4) The socialist reform is an comprehensive social reform. It does not only comprise the economic reform but also political reform as well as reform in other fields. All these reforms should be conducted in a coordinated manner. (5) Opening up to the world is also a form of reform. To ensure that socialism gains superiority over capitalism, it is necessary to be bold in assimilating and learning from the achievements of all civilizations in the world, and drawing on all the advanced experience and managerial expertise that reflect the laws of modernized production from all countries, including developed capitalist countries.

China has made great progress in its economic reform. Yet, there are still many problems that remain to be settled. For example, after the establishment of the macroeconomic control system which is conducive to the development of the socialist market economy, how should the corresponding microeconomic basis be consolidated, particularly with regard to the establishment of the modern enterprise system in big and medium-sized state-owned enterprises? How should such basic frameworks as the social insurance system be established to deepen the reform? All these problems remain to be studied and tackled in the course of future reform.

I. Deciding the Approach of Reform by Proceeding from China's Realities

(I) In View of China's National Conditions and Proceeding from Reality, the Gradual Reform Model Has Been Proved Successful

In carrying out the reform, China has chosen a road different from that taken by the former Soviet Union and other East European Countries. By this, I mean that China has adopted a step-by-step (gradual) approach for the reform, as vividly described by the saying "walking across the river by feeling the pebbles in the water," rather than the so-called "shock therapy," which intends to accomplish every task of the reform in one stroke. The gradual approach proved to be conducive to avoiding extensive social instability. By keeping the adjustment of interest relations caused by the reform within the limit the public can stand, thus handling in a more satisfactory manner the relations between the structural reform and the smooth progress of the transition. This is a key to the success of reform in China. In economic life, the gradual model of reform chosen by China has the following advantages:

1. Starting the Reform in the Rural Areas Where the Influence of the System of Planned Economy Is Relatively Weak, Then Carrying Out the Reform in the Urban Areas Step by Step. China's reform was first launched in the countryside where the influence of the system of planned economy is relatively weak. The household-based contract responsibility system with remuneration linked to output was first tried out in Anhui and Sichuan in 1979, and then was gradually introduced to other parts of the country. In 1982-83, it was put into effect across country. By the end of 1984, 180 million rural households (98 percent of the total) had adopted the system. As a result, noticeable progress had been achieved in rural reform, the rural economy had quickly turned vigorous, a rapid growth had been witnessed in the output of farm products and the farmers' incomes had increased greatly. This laid the most important material foundation and created the most favorable environment for the overall reform, and enabled China to feed 22 percent of the total population of the world with only 7 percent of the arable land. The rural reform had produced a satisfactory demonstrative impact for the reform in the urban areas. In 1984, reform was launched in all fields of economic life in the cities. Unlike the countryside, the reform in the urban areas cannot possibly be a smooth sailing, and it had undergone a process that is better expressed by the saying "walking across the river by feeling the stones." For instance, the reform of state-owned enterprises has experienced numerous stages of policy readjustments, including expanding the power of the enterprises to make their own decisions, the two-step policy to replace profits with taxes, the overall introduction of the contract responsibility system and the transformation of the management mechanism. Now, the urban reform has entered a new stage, that is, efforts are being made to establish a modern enterprise system and conduct a strategic restructure of the layout of the state-owned sector. The approach to making breakthroughs first in the easy and weak links and then proceeds to the "hard nuts" is conducive to accumulating experience, training personnel, maintaining social stability and avoiding major detours in the reform.

2. Implementing a "Double-track Price System" First for a Period of Time, then Replacing It with the Overall Introduction of the Market-Formulated Prices. In the price reform, China has gone through the process from a "double-track system" to a "single-track system" under the guiding principles of "combining control with decontrol, exercising control first and carrying out decontrol later, and decontrolling gradually." Prior to 1978, the prices of almost all commodities and services were unanimously determined by the government. In 1979, the State Council adopted the policy of purchasing the grain products above the fixed quotas at higher prices. At the same time, the purchasing prices were also raised correspondingly for animal by-products, aquatic products and forest by-products. In 1980, the retail prices of eight kinds of non-staple food were raised. In 1981, while adjusting the prices of some industrial products, the state introduced the market price mechanism for certain industrial products. As of 1985, the control over the prices of commodities and services has virtually been lifted. For example, the prices of rolled steel and other means of production proved above the state-fixed quotas, had been put to be regulated by the market exclusively. The control over the purchasing prices of pigs and vegetables had been removed. And the traditional system of monopolized purchase of principal farm products by the state, such as grain and cotton, had been replaced by purchase on the basis of contracts. As a result, a "double-track price system" came into being, i.e., the state-fixed prices for products covered in the state plan and market-regulated prices for products outside of the state plan existed side by side. Along with the rapid increase in the number of commodities whose prices were regulated through the market, the former State Price Bureau revised and made public a new "Catalogue of Commodities and Services under Price Control by the State" in the second half of 1992. According to the catalogue, the state had lifted control over the prices of great number of commodities. The variety of commodities whose prices were still put under direct control of the central government was reduced from 737 to 89. In 1993, control was lifted over the producer's prices of oil products, the overwhelming part of rolled steel, coal and cement, and the prices of cereals and cooking oil were also decontrolled nationwide. By then, the "double-track price system" gradually faded out to give way to the market price system. Now, market-regulated prices have been introduced for more than 90 percent of total retail sales of consumer goods and some 80 percent of total sales of the means of production as well as 80 percent of the total state purchases of farm and sideline products. This indicates that a market price system has basically been established for the prices of commodities in kind.

3. Carrying Out the Policy of Opening to the Outside World in the Southeast Coastal Regions First, Then Introducing the Policy to Other Coastal and Border Areas as well as the Inland Areas on the Basis of Experience Gained. Opening to the outside world, importing foreign investment and especially setting up special economic zones have played an important role in China's reform. Shortly after the Third Plenary Session of the 11th Party Central Committee, Mr. Deng Xiaoping put forward the idea of establishing special economic zones. He asked the special economic zones to follow the example of the Shaanxi-Ganshu-Ningxia border area in the Liberation War years to "break a bloody path." In August 1980, the proposal of establishing special economic zones in Shenzhen, Zhuhai and Xiamen was approved at the 15th Meeting of the Standing Committee of the Fifth National People's Congress. In May 1984, the Party Central Committee and the State Council again decided to open up 14 port cities, namely, Dalian, Qinhuangdao, Tianjin, Yantai, Lianyungang, Nantong, Shanghai, Ningbo, Wenzhou, Fuzhou, Guangzhou and Beihai (including the Fangchenggang District of the city), and to establish economic and techonoligical development zones in these cities. In early 1985, a decision was again made to turn the Yangtze River Delta, Zhujiang River Delta and the Xiamen-Zhangzhou-Quanzhou Delta in southern Fujian as well as the Jiaodong Peninsula and Liaodong Peninsula into open economic zones. In April 1988, Hainan was made another special economic zone. In April 1990, the Party Central Committee and the State Council made the important strategic decision to open up and develop Pudong of Shanghai. By early 1990s, a coastal open belt had taken shape along the country's coastal regions. It covers 410,000 square kilometers and has a population of over 200 million. To these regions and areas, the state granted preferential policies by different degrees in import and export, allowing them to retain part of their foreign exchange earnings and local tax revenues and encouraging them to take the lead in stepping into the international market. In the 1990s, to further expand the scope of opening to the outside world, the state extended the open policy from the coastal regions to areas along the country's major rivers, border areas as well as major cities in the inland areas. In succession, decisions were made to open up six cities along the Yangtze River, namely, Chongqing, Wuhan, Huangshi, Yueyang, Jiujiang and Wuhu, as well as all the provincial capital cities. In addition, a decision was also made for the establishment of the Yangtze Three Gorges open economic zone, where all the preferential policies introduced for the coastal cities and coastal open areas would be implemented. Again, the state made the decision to open up 13 cities along the country's borders to promote border trade. By the end of 1995, the open areas in China embraced 354 cities and counties, covered a total area of 550,000 square kilometers and had a population of 330 million. They included five special economic zones, 32 state-class economic and technological development areas and 13 areas for bonded trade, forming the basic framework to open to the outside world that comprises special economic zones, coastal open cities, coastal economic development zones and inland areas, which were required to play deferent roles.

4. In Ownership Reform, Readjusting and Improving the State Sector First, then Developing the Non-state Economic Elements in the Course of Readjustment. In the reform of the ownership structure, China has also followed the gradual approach. It is mainly manifested as the following: while readjusting and improving the state sector, vigorous efforts have been made to develop non-state sectors, including the privately owned sector, so as to develop a mixed economy in which diverse forms of ownership exist side by side while the public ownership is ensured a dominant position. Great changes have taken place in the ownership structure due to the rapid development of the non-publicly owned sectors, which are less affected by the fetters of the traditional planned economic system. Out of nothing, the individual and privately owned sectors have developed rapidly. Now, they have become an important part in the overall ownership structure. The mixed ownership economy, including the joint-stock and joint-stock partnership enterprises in all forms, have grown out of their embryonic stage and become a point of vigorous growth in the overall ownership structure of China. However, the proportion of the public sectors, though relatively reduced, still accounted for more than 70 percent of the aggregates of national economy (calculated according to GDP statistics produced). Partial readjustment has been conducted in the state-owned sector in line with the principle that "the state-owned sector must hold the dominant position in important industries and critical areas that have an important bearing on the lifeline of the national economy." The state-owned sector still enjoys a predominant position in finance, and energy, transport and communications, postal and telecommunications, civil aviation and war industries as well as in important infrastructure construction as well as high and new technology development.

5. In the Reform of State-owned Enterprises, First Making Policy Readjustments to Granting Them More Power and Profits, Then Proceeding to the Establishment of a Modern Enterprise System and the Readjustment of the Layout of the State-owned Sector. Prior to the 14th National Congress of the Chinese Communist Party, the reform of state-owned enterprises was basically carried out along the line of making policy readjustments to delegate more power to the enterprises so that they could make their own decisions and allow to retain a part of the profits earned. In May 1979, the former State Economic Commission, the Ministry of Finance and four other government departments selected eight enterprises in Beijing, Tianjin and Shanghai for experiment to enlarge the decision-making power of the enterprises. These enterprises included the Capital Iron and Steel Company, Tianjin Bicycle Factory and Shanghai Diesel Engine Plant. At the end of 1979, the number of enterprises trying out the reform increased to 4,200. In 1980, the number grew further to 6,000, accounting for 16 percent of the industrial enterprises covered in the state budget. At the time, they generated 60 percent of the output value and 70 percent of the profits of the industrial enterprises covered in state budget. The Third Plenary Session of the 12th Party Central Committee, held in October 1984, reestablished the objective model for the reform of state-owned enterprises—to turn the enterprises into relatively independent economic entities and socialist commodity producers and managers that operate independently, take sole responsibility for their and losses and have the capability for self-reform and self-development. In other words, the aim was to turn them into legal persons with corresponding rights and obligations. The 14th National Congress of the Communist Party of China, held in 1992, and particularly the Third Plenary Session of the 14th Party Central Committee, held in 1993, specified that the aim of the reform of state-owned enterprises was to establish a modern enterprise system characterized by "distinct property ownership, explicit powers and responsibilities, separation of functions between government and enterprise management and scientific management." Consequently, the reform of state-owned enterprises has shifted to the innovation of enterprise system and the strategic readjustment of the structure of the state-owned sector. The guidelines and principles for the reform are: orienting the reform of the state-owned enterprises towards the establishment of a modern enterprise system; striving for a sound development of the state-owned economic sector as a whole rather than giving protection to all state-owned enterprises; strategically restructuring the state-owned enterprises by placing the focus of work on big enterprises through the introduction of the corporate system and giving a free hand to small ones; lifting control over and invigorating the small enterprises in large numbers; combining reform with restructuring as well as the efforts to improve management; encouraging merger, codifying bankruptcy, laying off and repositioning redundant personnel to cut the size of payroll and improve efficiency, and launching reemployment projects; and making vigorous efforts in supporting reforms, which include the establishment of an effective mechanism in the management and operation of and supervision over state-owned assets, as well as the establishment and improvement of a social security system that covers the entire society, etc.

6. Taking Economic Reform as the Major Link and Pushing Forward Political Reform Gradually on the Basis of the Economic Reform. China did not plunge headlong into political reform. Instead, it first launched a reform in the economic field and adopted a gradual approach for political reform as well as reform in other fields. Proceeding from the countryside to the cities and from the micro aspect to the macro aspect, marked progress has been achieved in the economic reform and it has caught worldwide attention. The 15th National Congress of the Chinese Communist Party called to build a socialist political system with Chinese characteristics. In essence, this means to manage state affairs according to law and develop socialist democratic politics under the leadership of the Chinese Communist Party and on the basis that people are masters of the state. To accomplish this objective, it is necessary to uphold and improve the system of people's congress and the systems of multi-party co-operation and political consultation under the leadership of the Chinese Communist Party, as well as the system of regional autonomy for minority ethnic groups. In political reform, the immediate task in the near future is to develop democracy, strengthen the legal system, separate government administration from enterprise management, streamline the administrative structure, improve the system of democratic supervision, and uphold unity and stability. In March 1998, the National People's Congress approved the plan for organizational reshuffle of the State Council. As the first step of the plan, 19 ministries and commissions under the State Council would be abolished and the size of government employees in the remaining ministries and commissions would be reduced by 50 percent. The next step is to organizationally restructure the governments at the provincial, municipal and autonomous regional levels. The purpose of the reform is to establish an administrative control system featuring high efficiency, coordinated operation and standardized rules of behavior, and set up administrative organs that satisfy the needs of the market economy and are unified and efficient.

(II) Divorce from the Specific National Conditions and Over Haste for Success Would Surely Lead the Reform Astray

Some countries undergoing the economic transition have taken another approach – the radical model of reform, also known as the "shock therapy." The so-called "shock therapy," according to the explanation given by one of its advocators, includes the following major aspects: (1) Adopting strict tight money policies to control the volume of currency and credit in circulation; cutting down fiscal subsidies, reducing financial deficits and suppressing total social demand so as to forcibly eliminate the gap between the total supply and total demand and hold in check the expansion of inflation. (2) Lifting control over prices and calling off all price subsidies to form a pricing system through market supply and demand. (3) Carrying out free conversion of currency and removing all control over foreign trade to establish a free trade system by "importing" from abroad a genuine price system. (4) Lifting control over the economy, breaking as quickly as possible the monopoly over certain industries and abandoning all kinds of restrictions imposed on privately owned organizations. (5) Carrying out privatization as soon as possible in the transformation of the state-owned enterprises and establish a mixed economic structure based on private ownership. Practice has proved that the radical approach of reform characterized by "shock therapy" wishes to "uproot" the public ownership entirely. The result is nothing but "damages beyond repair."(3) Reality also has proved this point.

1. Lifting Control over Prices in a Single Step Has Led to Serious Inflation. According to the "shock therapy," all control over the prices of commodities and serves should be lifted overnight at one stroke in the price reform. In 1992, for example, Russia, Ukraine, Kazakhstan and Kyrgyzstan lifted at one stroke control over the prices, hoping to bring about a fundamental change in the industrial structure that would be compatible with the needs of the market. In one single effort, Russia removed control over the prices of some 90 percent of the consumer goods and 80 percent of the means of production. Following this move, it also gradually lifted control over housing rent and the prices of public services, as well as the prices of transport services and fuels. Kazakhstan lifted control over the prices of practically everything, except food, transport, energy and housing rent, which were still controlled and regulated by the state. In Poland, government control over the prices of all commodities was lifted in a short span of a few weeks from late 1989 to early 1990. Lifting the price control, however, had failed to produce the expected result, that is, making the economic structure change towards the needs of market. On the contrary, it had caused serious and even vicious inflation. Generally speaking, the annual average rate of inflation in East European countries exceeded 50 percent, and in a number of years it even ran as high as 200-500 percent. In Russia, the highest annual rate of inflation once shot up to 2,600 percent while in Poland it reached 2,000 percent in a peak year. According to statistics available, commodity prices in Russia rose by 6,188 fold from 1991 to 1996. The money some people formerly put in banks as savings for buying cars was barely enough to pay for three or four bus tickets. The harm caused by such a disaster, if it occurs in an underdeveloped country, would be beyond any imagination.

2. The Implementation of Tight Money Policy Has Thrown the Enterprises into a Fix. In the reform of fiscal and credit system, the former Soviet Union and most East European countries implemented the policy of tight finance and money policies to strictly limit the budgetary deficits, money supply and the volume of credit. When inflation occurred in the wake of lifting control over prices, the government adopted harsh measures to curb inflation by means of tight money at the cost of lowering the people's living standards and cutting down production. Although this had a temporary effect in reducing the rate of inflation and financial deficits, the chain debts between the enterprises, however, increasingly dramatically (which amounted to 1,160 billion rubles by May 1996 in Russia). Moreover, the problem of arrears with salary payment to the staff and workers became more and more serious (by the end of 1996, the total amount of salaries unpaid reached was 472 billion rubles and the total amount of unpaid pensions amounted to 110 billion rubles). The over-rigid tight money policy damaged the macroeconomic environment for the enterprises, and even posed a threat to their very existence. The results were a dramatic reduction in investment and a lack of funds for the enterprises to maintain normal production and operation. Not only that some enterprises could not expand reproduction, they were also unable to sustain simple reproduction. Some were even forced to close down.

3. All-round Drive of Privatization or Denationalization Have Resulted in Serious Polarization. At the early stage of the economic transition, the Russian government adopted the "shock therapy" and launched an all-round drive for privatization and denationalization, hoping to accelerate the transition to a market economy. The major policy measures included auctioning medium-sized and small state-owned enterprises and carrying out joint-stock transformation of large and medium-sized state-owned enterprises. The full-scaled transformation to establish the joint-stock mechanism in Russia underwent two stages. The first stage was known as the stage of "securities privatization" (July 1992-June 1994), that is, to transfer stocks of state-owned enterprises to the public without asking for any compensation by means of issuing privatized securities. The second stage was called "cash privatization" (July 1994-1996), that is, to transfer with some compensation the stocks of the state-owned enterprises by asking for payment in cash. The massive stock buying and selling had in a way promoted the establishment of the joint-stock system in state-owned enterprises. Yet, its purpose, its compulsive nature and the non-standardized steps adopted to make it happen had caused serious problems and grave consequences. First, none of the three goals set by the government was accomplished through the all-round promotion of the joint-stock system and privatization. In other words, it did not bring into being a so-called "massive class of private owners," nor did it help raise the productivity of the enterprises, let alone helping stabilize the financial situation. On the contrary, it caused a serious and long-lasting decrease in social production. Second, it led to serious losses of state-owned assets. According to statistics released at the various sessions of the Duma, the total losses caused by the privatization drive in these few years added up to 9,500,000 billion rubles (of which the economic losses amounted to 5,500,000 billion, and the social losses, 40,000,000 billion). The amount is 4.2 times the total GNP of Russia in 1996 and 2.5 times the total losses during the Second World War. Third, it gave rise to serious polarization in social distribution. Some 10 percent of the Russian population turned out to become a new elite class and they have made enormous fortunes by both legal and illegal means, while over 60 percent of the population suffered a big drop in their actual incomes and some 40 percent were plunged into dire poverty.

4. Opening the Market and Unifying Exchange Rate in a Blind Way Has Caused Continuous Deterioration of the Financial Situation. According to a decree adopted by Russia to liberalize economic activities related to other countries at the end of 1991, any enterprises registered in Russia would have the right to engage in foreign economic activities. Moreover, the decree lifted control over barter trade to reduce the varieties of commodities whose import was restricted or to be done by means of licenses and ordered to reduce or exempt customs duties, establish a foreign exchange reserve fund and develop foreign exchange markets. According to the decree, the exchange rates were unified to facilitate free conversion of the currency. Such methods adopted to open the market had led to serious reductions in domestic industrial production and a steady decline of the national economy. The premature implementation of free conversion of the currency caused the 1998 financial crisis in Russia. Moreover, in face of a serious shortage of foreign exchange reserves, Russia turned to the West for loans to stabilize its finance. The increase in foreign loans added to the country's burden of foreign debts. The increasingly heavy burden of debts has turned out to be a factor hindering its economic recovery and development.

5. Giving Up Macroeconomic Control on the Side of the Government Has Caused Disorder and Confusion in Reform. In the course of economic transition, Russia and some other East European countries went from one extreme to another – from a highly centralized planned economy to totally forfeiting the state's role in macroeconomic control. They took the state plans as the cause for their sluggish economic development and were determined to "turn out a new leaf." In their efforts to break away from the traditional system, they abandoned macroeconomic control that should be exercised by the state over foreign trade, exchange rate, investment and credit along with the rigid quotas set in mandatory plans, fixed prices and unified allocation of goods and equipment. Consequently, they had paid heavy costs that should have been avoided and thrown the reform into chaos.

(III) In Drawing Up the Plan for Reform, It Is Important Not to Indiscriminately Copy Western Economic Theory of Laissez-Faire

From the exorbitant prices Russia and some other East European countries paid in implementing the "shock therapy" we should learned a good lesson, that is, in making plans for the reform, it is important not to copy blindly the economic models from the West. In other words, we should not follow blindly the Western economic theory of laissez-faire without giving due consideration to the actual conditions of the country. Otherwise, the reform will be led astray.

The plan for radical economic reform in Russia was formulated and designed with the direct participation of Mr. Sacks, an economist from the United States, who served as an advisor to the Russian government. The gist of the "shock therapy" advocated by Sacks means in fact a one-stroke transition and the establishment of a market economic framework overnight. The famous "500-Day Program" Russia implemented was a radical approach of reform and it was obviously impractical for a big country with so large a territory and where the traditional economic system had taken deep root. At the best, it could be described as pedantic wishful thinking, if not castles in the air. Since January 1992 when the radical economic reform program was launched, production in Russia nosed down while inflation remained soared high and the living standards of the people dropped by wide margins. A comparison of the statistics of 1996 with that of 1991 indicated that the country's GDP dropped by 45 percent. This rate of drop far exceeded that in the war years (25 percent) and that in the 1929-33 Great Depression in the United States (33 percent). The national economy as a whole was pulled back by nearly 20 years. Because the architects of the Russian reform failed to take into consideration the specific conditions of Russia and its actual level of economic development and blindly copied the economic theories of the West, the country and its people have paid a heavy cost. Just as the former deputy speaker of Russian Duma said, one of the most serious drawbacks in the Russian reform was that phony theoreticians "always copied or tried to copy the experience of the International Monetary Fund (IMF), or endeavored to directly borrow the experience of other countries."

II. Setting Up the Basic Economic System for the Primary Stage of Socialism

The primary stage of socialism referred to here has a dual meaning. First, the transition or reform of the economic structure in China is a transition from a planned economy to a market economy under precondition of upholding the basic socialist economic system. Second, China's socialism is still at its primary stage. The formulation of strategies, plans and policies for development must proceed from the primary stage of socialism, and never should we try to bypass it. The basic economic system at the primary stage of socialism is an economic system suited to this particular stage. It is a system in which the economy under diverse forms of ownership develops side by side while the economic sector under public ownership is taken as the mainstay.

(I) Understanding of the Long-term Nature of the Primary Stage of Socialism and the Basic Economic System at This Stage

After the founding of the People's Republic of China, China entered socialism. As far as the development of the productive forces is concerned, the country lagged far behind the developed countries. This has determined that China has to undergo a rather long primary stage of socialism and it has to accomplish the objective of industrialization, marketization and modernization in this stage of socialism, and thus lay the foundation necessary for establishing and developing a socialism featuring a high degree of development of the productive forces and with great comprehensive national strength. This is an insurmountable historical stage to achieve socialist modernization under the conditions of backward economic and cultural development. However, such a understanding of the primary stage of socialism only dawned on us after the reform and opening-up drive was launched.

In 1981, the Sixth Plenary Session of the 11th Party Central Committee adopted the "Resolution on Certain Questions in the History of Our Party since the Founding of the People's Republic of China." For the first time in Chinese history, this document stated, "Our socialist system is still at its primary stage." The political report to the 12th National Congress of the Chinese Communist Party, held in 1982, once again said, "Our socialist society is still at its initial stage, it is not yet highly developed materially." In 1987, the report to the 13th National Party Congress gave a systematic account of the theory of the primary stage of socialism in China and clearly pointed out, "It is not the initial phase in a general sense, a phase that every country goes through in the process of building socialism. Rather, it is, in a particular sense, the specific stage China must necessarily go through while building socialism under conditions of backward productive forces and an underdeveloped commodity economy." While expounding the main contents of the theory of building socialism with Chinese characteristics, the report to the 14th National Party Congress stated that on the question of the development of socialism in stages, "According to our scientific thesis, China is still in the primary stage of socialism, which will last for at least a hundred years. All principles and policies must be based on this fundamental reality. We must not divorce ourselves from it or try to skip this stage." In 1997, the report to the 15th National Party Congress further expounded the Party's basic line and basic program at the primary stage of socialism, and explicitly and comprehensively summed up the basic objectives and basic policies in building socialism with Chinese characteristics politically, economically and culturally. The report pointed out, "Building a socialist economy with Chinese characteristics means developing a market economy under socialism and constantly emancipating and developing the productive forces. To be more specific, we should uphold and improve the basic economic system in which the socialist public ownership is dominant and different types of ownership develop side by side. We should uphold and improve the socialist market economic structure so that the market will play a basic role in the allocation of resources under state macro-control. We should uphold and improve different modes of distribution with distribution according to work remaining dominant, allowing some people and some areas to become prosperous first so that they can help others to become well-off and achieving common prosperity step by step. We should uphold and improve opening up and take an active part in international economic cooperation and competition. We should ensure that the national economy will develop in a sustained, rapid and sound way and that the people will share the fruits of economic prosperity."

From practice over the past two decades, the Chinese people have come to a relatively comprehensive understanding of the primary stage of socialism. To sum up, it includes the following aspects. (1) It is a historical stage to gradually rid off underdevelopment and basically bring about the socialist modernization. (2) It a historical stage of gradual transition from an agricultural country in which the rural population makes up the bulk and the production mainly relies on manual labor to an industrialized country with modern agriculture and modern service industries, in which non-rural population makes up the bulk. (3)

It is a historical period of gradual transition from a stage when natural and semi-natural economy accounts for a heavy proportion to a stage when the market economy is well developed. (4) It is a historical period of gradual transition from a stage featuring a great proportion of illiterates and semi-illiterates and backwardness in science, technology, education and culture to a stage with a high level of development in science, technology, education and culture. (5) It is a historical period of gradual transition from a stage characterized by a large proportion of the population suffering from poverty and have low living standards to a stage that features relative affluence for the entire population. (6) It is a historical period in which a vigorous socialist market economic system, a socialist democratic political system and other systems will be established and improved through reform and exploration. (7) It is a historical period for the Chinese people to firmly foster the common ideal of building socialism with Chinese characteristics through making unremitting efforts to improve their lots, becoming keenly determined in making progress, working hard and diligently in defiance of all hardships and practicing thrifty, so as to attain a high level of development of socialist culture and ethics while striving for a high level of economic development. (8) It is a historical period in which the gap between China and the advanced countries of the world will be gradually narrowed and the great cause to rejuvenate the Chinese nation will be accomplished. It will take at least one hundred years to complete such a great historical process. Just as Deng Xiaoping pointed out, "It will take a long historical period to develop and consolidate the socialist system; it requires unremitting efforts by several, a dozen of or even dozens of generations. We should by no means take a casual attitude to it."

(II) Making Active Efforts to Develop the Non-publicly Owned Sectors while Building Up the Strength of the Publicly Owned Sector

It is an important practical and theoretical question in our reform efforts how to correctly view China's basic economic structure of socialism at the present stage. In the past, the traditional theory of socialism held that the socialist economy should be an economy under sole and unitary public ownership. It excluded all the non-publicly owned economic sectors from the socialist system. Practice has proved that such a theory and all principles and policies formulated on the basis of it do not accord with the historical conditions at the primary stage of socialism. On the contrary, they have fettered the development of the productive forces. The political report to the 15th National Congress of the Chinese Communist Party clearly pointed out, "It is China's basic economic system for the primary stage of socialism to retain a dominant position for public ownership and to develop diverse forms of ownership side by side." This is a scientific generalization of the basic economic system at the primary stage of socialism made by the Chinese Communist Party on the basis of earnestly summing up past experience and lessons in relation to the question of ownership.

According to above scientific generalization, the content of the basic economic system at the primary stage of socialism covers two aspects: one is the dominant position of public ownership, and the other is the simultaneous development of the economic sectors under diverse forms of ownership. These two aspects are an integrated whole and are mutually complementary.

Practice has proved that this basic economic system in which the public sector of the economy takes the dominant position and the economic sectors under other forms of ownership develop side by side is determined by the country's socialist nature and the specific conditions at the primary stage of socialism.

First, China is a socialist country and it must take public ownership as the basis of its socialist economic system. Second, China is now at the primary stage of socialism. The development of its productive forces as a whole is low and uneven and assumes a multi-tiered structure. Only by promoting the development of the sectors under diverse forms of ownership under the precondition that the public sector takes the dominant position can the enthusiasm of people in various walks of life be brought into full play and different types of resources be brought into full use to facilitate the development of the productive forces. Third, at the primary stage of socialism, the principal contradiction in the society is still the contradiction between the ever-increasing material and cultural demand of the people and the backward social production. This principal contradiction is witnessed in every aspect of social life and runs through the entire primary stage of socialism. This compels China to take the development of productive forces as its major task. Any form of ownership, so long as it is conducive to the development of the productive forces, the strengthening of the comprehensive national strength and the improvement of the people's living standards, should and can be adopted to serve socialism.

The report to the 15th National Party Congress also made new definitions for public ownership. In the past, whenever the socialist public ownership is mentioned, it was only used to refer to the state and collectively owned economic sectors. According to the report to the 15th National Party Congress, the economy under public ownership not only embrace the state and collectively owned sectors but also the state and collectively owned elements in various forms of economy under mixed ownership. To ensure the dominant position of public ownership does not mean to ensure a dominant position of the state-owned sector, nor does it mean the greater the share of the sectors under public ownership in the entire economy the better. The dominant position of public ownership is mainly manifested in the following. Viewing the country as a whole, publicly owned assets occupy an advantageous position in the total assets of the society; and the state-owned sector holds control over the lifeline of the national economy and plays a dominant role in economic development. Since the reform and opening-up drive was launched, both the state and collective sectors of the economy have witnessed a marked development, and the development of the collectively owned and non-publicly owned sectors has turned out to be much faster than that of the state-owned sector for their previously low level of development and thanks to the support given by government. In the gross industrial output value of 1978, the contributions made by the state-owned enterprises and non-state-owned enterprises were 77.6 percent and 22.4 percent respectively. In 1997, however, they were altered to 26.5 percent and 73.5 percent. Such a change reflects truthfully the developmental level of productive forces at the primary stage of socialism. Despite the change, the state-owned sector still controls the lifeline of the national economy and plays a decisive role in the progress of industrial modernization. The economic sectors under state and collective ownership as well as the stocks held by the state and collectives in other forms of ownership are still ensured a dominant position.

The dominant position of the state-owned sector is mainly reflected in its power of control. Therefore, under the preconditions that the public ownership holds the dominant position, the state controls the lifeline of the national economy and the power of control and competitiveness of the state-owned sector are strengthened, their absolute quantity will still increase by wide margins despite a decrease in their proportion of contribution to the national economy. It is in view of such a state of affairs that the state renders energetic support, encouragement and help to the development of diverse forms of collective economy in both the urban and rural areas. In particular, the state advocates and encourages collective economy based on the association of laborers and capital union of the laborers. It is also necessary for the government to continuously encourage and guide the development of non-public sectors in order to meet the diversified needs of the people, extensively pool idle funds in the society, relieve the pressure of employment and increase public accumulation and state tax revenues.

The report to the 15th National Party Congress pointed out that, to ensure that the public ownership takes the dominant position, it is necessary to seek suitable forms for its materialization that can greatly promote the development of the productive forces. The ownership of the means of production should be a system that includes the forms materializing the rights of ownership, possession, disposal and use of properties. In the past, people only paid attention to "ownership" and ignored the question how it should be materialized. The report to the 15th National Party Congress pointed out, "Public ownership can and should take diversified forms. All management methods and organizational forms that mirror the laws governing socialized production may be utilized boldly." This represents an important breakthrough in the traditional economic theory. The joint-stock system is a form of capital organization of modern enterprises. It is favorable for separating ownership from management and raising the efficiency of the operation of enterprises and capital. It can be used both under capitalism and socialism. In addition, it also provides an effective choice for the reform of the state-owned enterprises, and it should be further explored and developed in practice.

The new generalization of the basic economic system at the primary stage of socialism has, on the one hand, stressed the need to ensure the dominant position of the public ownership and, on the other, listed the simultaneous development of the economic sectors under different types of ownership as an essential content of the basic economic system. In this way, the non-public sectors have been include in "the system," and turned into "an important component of the socialist market economy" from "a useful supplement to the socialist economy." To expound the necessity of ensure the dominant position of the public ownership and the common development of the sectors under diverse forms of ownership, the report to the 15th National Party Congress not only has presented its argument from "the practical conditions of China at the primary stage of socialism" but also approached the issue from the perspective of the "socialist market economy." This has opened up an even broader vista for the common development of the sectors under diverse forms of ownership in the future. Ensuring the dominant position of public ownership and striving for simultaneous development of the economy under diverse forms of ownership will be a long-term basic economic system in China.

In March 1999, the Second Meeting of the 9th National People's Congress made amendments to the Constitution of the People's Republic of China, which gave a new definition to China's basic economic system at the primary stage of socialism. Article 6 of the Constitution adopted in 1982 said, "The basis of the socialist economic system of the People's Republic of China is socialist public ownership of the means of production, namely, ownership by the whole people and collective ownership by the working people." In the 1999 amendments, it runs as follows: "In the primary stage of socialism, the state upholds the basic economic system with the dominance of the public ownership and the simultaneous development of an economy of diverse forms of ownership, and upholds the distribution system with the dominance of distribution according to work and the coexistence of diverse modes of distribution." After 20 years of practice and theoretical exploration in the reform, China's basic economic system at the primary stage of socialism had at long last been finalized in the form of law.

(III) Strategically Readjusting the General Layout of the State-owned Sector

The 15th National Party Congress decided to further readjust and improve the ownership structure and structure the layout of the state-owned economy by proceeding from a strategic perspective. In the future, it is only necessary for the state-owned sector to hold a dominant position in major industries and key areas that concern the lifeline of the national economy. In other industries and areas, encouragement will be given to the development of economy under mixed ownership and the non-state-owned sector. In line with market changes, it is necessary for the state to change the fields in which it makes investment and make active efforts to turn enterprises, including non-state-owned enterprises, into the major investors.

Strategically readjusting the pattern of the state-owned sector is important to do a good job in the reform of state-owned enterprises. The state-owned sector, particularly those big and medium-sized enterprises, amasses the bulk of China's skilled labor force. These enterprises have considerable advantages in terms of trained personnel, technology, equipment, product quality, labor productivity and enterprise management, etc., and are a major source for the state's financial revenue. At present, the strength of the state-owned sector is spread too thin. Moreover, it is also haunted by such problems as repeated construction, excessively scattered distribution of industry, small scale of the enterprises and poor product quality. These problems cause many difficulties for the management of state-owned enterprises, such as high input, low output, high consumption of energy and other resources and low efficiency. Such a structural pattern of the state-owned sector neither can keep up with the changes in supply-demand relations of the domestic market nor is it adapted to the increasingly fierce competition in the international market. With the development of reform and opening to the outside world, the domestic market is linked up more and more closely with global economic competition and cooperation, and transnational corporations in the world are taking active steps to enter the Chinese market, thus making the competition even fiercer. The state-owned enterprises would never be able to lift themselves out of the difficult plight if the overall pattern or structure of the national economy were not changed and the overall competitive edge of the state-owned sector were not sharpened. The excessively wide dispersion of state-owned capital has produced a very bad effect on the overall situation of modernization. If those industries that are important to the safety of the nation cannot develop or cannot develop in the shortest possible period, the progress of China's modernization drive will be adversely affected. Therefore, it is necessary to strategically readjust the overall pattern of the national economy by making advances in some industries, pulling out from others and investing the limited financial resources in those fields that need them the most, so as to bring to the state-owned enterprises an industrial, technological and product upgrading. In the future, the state-owned sector should mainly play a role in the so-called lifeline departments of the national economy, the construction and operation of major infrastructure and public utilities, basic industries as well as high and sophisticated technology development areas. Strategically readjusting the structure of the state-owned sector is bound to lead to further readjustment of the ownership structure and spur on the diversification of the forms for the materialization of the public ownership.

(IV) Developing Diverse Forms of Distribution on the Basis of Distribution According to Labor

The distribution system at the primary stage of socialism is an important aspect directly related to the basic economic system. At the primary stage of socialism, apart from the publicly owned sector, there are economic sectors under diverse forms of ownership. It is impossible for these economic elements under different types of ownership to enjoy an equal footing in the possession and utilization of the means of production. Those who are employed in non-public sectors can, apart from incomes in the form salaries, participate in distribution by their ownership right over the means of production. This has impelled people to study the question of distribution of personal income under the conditions of co-existence of various elements of the means of production.

After many years of exploration and practice, the 14th National Party Congress clearly put forward the objective of establishing the socialist market economic system and, correspondingly, the goal of establishing the personal income distribution and social security systems compatible with the market economy. The congress has clearly stipulated the principle of distribution, the wage or salary system, the issue of income regulation and so on. For the first time, the 15th National Party Congress generalized the personal income distribution system in the socialist market economy in the following, "We shall keep to the system in which distribution according to work is primary and in which a variety of modes of distribution coexist. By combining remuneration according to work and remuneration according to factors of production put in, and by giving priority to efficiency with due consideration to equity, such a system is conducive to optimizing the allocation of resources, promoting economic development and maintaining social stability. We shall protect lawful incomes according to law, allowing and encouraging some of the people to get wealthy first through honest labor and lawful operations, and allowing and encouraging the use of capital, technology and other factors of production to participate in the distribution of gains. Illegal earnings shall be banned and those who appropriate public property or seek gains by such illegal means as tax evasion or by striking deals between power and money shall be resolutely punished according to law. We shall take stock of irrational incomes and must correct the malpractice of individuals obtaining extra incomes by taking advantage of sectoral monopolies and some special privileges. We shall regulate the excessively high incomes, improve the individual income tax, and standardize income distribution so as to make the income gaps more reasonable and prevent polarization."

Based on such awareness, the amendments made to the Constitution at the Second Meeting of the Ninth National People's Congress in March 1999 clearly stipulated that, at the primary stage of socialism, the state "upholds the distribution system with the dominance of distribution according to work and the coexistence of diverse modes of distribution." Compared with the wording regarding this issue in the Constitution adopted in 1982 (The system of socialist public ownership supercedes the system of exploitation of man by man; it applies the principle of `from each according to his ability, to each according to his work'), this represents a great step forward. Of course, how to handle the relations between the statement "distribution according to work is primary" and the statement "a variety of modes of distribution coexist" and, in particular, how to "combine remuneration according to work and remuneration according to factors of production put in," further study is called in the future.

(V) Improving the Macro-control System Compatible with the Socialist Market Economy

The socialist market economy must have a well-established macro-control system. The major task of the macro-control system is to maintain basic balance in economic aggregates, promote the optimization of the economic structure, provide guidance to the national economy and ensure it a sustained, rapid and healthy development and, promote the overall progress of the society. In enforcing macro control, economic and legal means are employed mainly. Therefore, it is necessary to reshuffle the government departments and change the functions of the government to meet the requirements of the socialist market economy. It is necessary to deepen the reform of the monetary, financial and planning systems, improve the means for macro control and mechanism for coordination, establish an effective macro-control system and effectively prevent or dissolve various types of financial risks. It is necessary to carve up the power over economic control between the central government and local governments and bring the initiatives of both into full play.

III. Correctly Handling the Relations between Reform, Development and Stability

The 20 years of reform has been proved to be 20 years of rapid economic development and social stability in China. Correctly handing the relations between reform, development and stability is another major line running through entire course of China's reform over the past two decades. It is very important for a comprehensive understanding of the historical process and characteristics of the China's economic structural transition.

(I) To Correctly Handle the Relations between Reform, Development and Stability Is a Basic Experience Achieved in the Reform over the Past Two Decades.

China's economic transition, reform and opening to the outside world over the past 20 years have been going on under the guidance of Deng Xiaoping Theory. One strategic thinking in Deng Xiaoping theory is to correctly handle the relations between reform, development and stability. This strategic thinking includes the following aspects: First, it is necessary to take economic development as the key link and place development above everything else. Deng Xiaoping clearly pointed out, "The solution to all our (China's) problems lies in economic development," "Development is the absolute principle," and "if we are to seize opportunities to promote China's all-round development, it is crucial to expand the economy." Second, in order to achieve development, it is necessary to persist in reform as reform and development are closely related to each other. In March 1985, Deng Xiaoping stated explicitly, "All our reforms are aimed at one goal, that is, to remove obstacles that hinder the development of the productive forces," and "reform is the direct driving force for and technical basis of development." Third, to reform and develop, it is necessary to maintain political and social stability. Deng Xiaoping repeatedly stressed, "In China the overriding need is for stability. Without a stable environment, we can accomplish nothing and may even lose what we have gained," and "If there is no stability but political upheaval, it is impossible for us to conduct socialist construction, let alone anything else." After all, adherence to reform, development and stability is related to a whole lot of practical problems in bringing about China's institutional and structural transition, and it is of extremcly important theoretical and practical significance. Practice has proved that a correct handling of the relations between the three is tantamount to have a sound grasp of the overall situation, thus providing reform and development with the necessary social environment and ensuring a smooth development of the economy and society. If the relations are not handled well, there are bound to be social upheavals, which will adversely affect stability in every field of work and make it impossible to attain the objective of improving the people's living standards, thus lose their support.

(II) Development Is the Absolute Principle and It is Necessary to Take Economic Development as the Key Link in All Times.

Taking economic development as the key link and placing development above everything else were put forward by Deng Xiaoping in view of all sorts of the interference and harassment China had suffered in its economic development over the 20-odd years prior to reform. "In the 20 years from 1958 to 1978, the Chinese society was virtually at a standstill or in a lingering state, and the economy of the country as well as the living standards of the people did not achieve much development and improvement." Deng Xiaoping made a penetrating summary of historical experience and lessons and pointed out that the fundamental cause for this was the failure to put economic construction in the center of all work.

Besides, Deng Xiaoping raised the understanding of the development of the productive forces to the theoretical plane – bringing into play the superiority of socialism and giving expression to the nature of socialism. In 1978, he said, "The basic expression of the superiority of our socialist system is that it makes it possible for the productive forces of our society to grow at a rapid rate unknown in old China and for us to gradually satisfy our people's ever-increasing material and cultural needs."

The Third Plenary Session of the 11th Party Central Committee made the strategic decision to shift the focus of work of the Party and state to the socialist modernization. Over the past two decades, in view of the situation in economic construction as well as new problems arising in the course of development, China has launched reforms in its market system, microeconomic foundation, macroeconomic regulation and control, distribution system, social insurance system, etc. These reforms have opened up a broader vista for economic development. In early 1980s, Deng Xiaoping, on the basis of a comprehensive analysis of China reality as well as various subjective and objective factors, proposed clearly a "three-step" strategic plan for China's economic development. He said, "In this century we shall take two steps – to solve the problem of adequate food and clothing for our people and attain the better-off goal. In the next century, we will spend another 30 to 50 years to achieve the goal for another step -- to catch up with the level of moderately developed countries in the world." This strategic goal was put forward on the basis of summing up the past lessons, such as being over-anxious for success in economic development, and thoroughly analyzing the general trend of global economic development. It gives expression to Deng Xiaoping's lofty spirit and scientific attitude to seek truth from the facts and make steady progress.

(III) Linking Reform with Economic Development Closely and Making Them Promote Each Other.

To achievement development, it is imperative to conduct reform. In the two decades prior to the Third Plenary Session of the 11th Party Central Committee, China's economic development had undergone many twists and turns; it was not well coordinated. Despite political factors, a very important reason is that the rigid economic structure was proved to be a heavy shackle on the development of the productive forces. Confronted by a mountain of problems in political, economic and other areas, China had only one way out, that is, to carry out reform while persisting in taking economic construction as the central link of all work. Only in this way was it possible to promote the development of the productive forces and consolidate the socialist system. As Deng Xiaoping once pointed out, China was forced to make the decision for reform at the Third Plenary Session of the 11th Party Central Committee in December 1978. He said, "If we do not carry out reform now, our cause of modernization and socialism will be doomed."

Reform and development are closely related to each other. Deng

Xiaoping said that all the reforms China had carried out were aimed at one target, that is, to remove the obstacles that hinders the development of the productive forces. He gave a penetrating account of the intrinsic relations between reform and development: Reform is to remove those relations of production and superstructures that are not conducive to the development of the productive forces and remove the obstacles hindering the development of productive forces. In other words, it is to emancipate the productive forces. Reform is the direct driving force and solid foundation for development. Only through reform can it be possible for us to remove the obstacles hindering the development of production. Development, on the other hand, is the "objective" all the reform measures seek to accomplish. Without development, reform will be meaningless. "The essence of reform is to lay a sound foundation for sustained development in the next decade and the first 50 years of next century," he said.

Reform is an entirely new undertaking. What criteria should be taken to judge the success or failure of reform? This is a major question of theoretical and policy significance. At the early stage of China's reform, Deng Xiaoping proposed the "standard of productive forces," and it was included in the resolution of the Third Plenary Session of the 12th Party Central Committee and the report to the Thirteenth National Party Congress. In 1992, it was expanded into the principle of "three favorables," that is, whether it is favorable to the growth of the productive forces in a socialist society, favorable to increasing the overall strength of the socialist state and favorable to raising the people's living standards.

(IV) Maintaining Political, Economic and Social Stability and Creating the Basic Conditions for Reform and Development

Both reform and development call for a stable social environment. To bring about such a sound social environment, over the past two decades China has made efforts in the following three aspects:

First, to maintain a political stability. Of the stability in all fields of work, political stability is the most crucial. Despite short episodes of instability over the past 20 years, the political situation in China has been stable on the whole. Three major reasons contribute to this. (1) The political line is stable. The Chinese Communist Party has overcome interruptions from both "Right" and "Left," particularly those from the "Left," and upheld its basic line unswervingly. (2) The core of the leadership has remained stable. In particular, a smooth transition has been realized from the second generation to the third generation of the core of leadership. Moreover, major political problems have been properly dealt with. (3) The basic policies are stable. It is particularly so in regard to such major policies as household-based contract responsibility system in the rural areas and encouraging some people to get prosperous first. All these basic policies have remained unchanged.

Second, to maintain economic stability. According to China's experience over the past few years, to maintain economic stability, major attention should be paid to preventing the occurrence of the following three situations: (1) serious economic depression and high rate of unemployment arising in its wake; (2) rampant inflation; and (3) monetary disorder and even financial crisis. In order to prevent the occurrence of the three situations, much work has done over the past 20 years. When serious inflation occurred in 1988 and 1993 respectively in the national economy, government departments in charge of macro control and regulation made curbing inflation the major objective of the macro policies and adopted a moderately tight money policy to check inflation. When a downward trend appeared in the growth of the national economy in 1990 and 1998, they adopted such measures as stimulating the market and increasing investments to promote the growth of domestic demand and ensure economic growth. In 1997, the central government held a special national meeting on financial and monetary affairs to discuss ways to dissolve the potential monetary crisis and maintain monetary stability. When the financial crisis in Asia broke out, the government remained steady and adopted the policy decision not to devaluate RMB, thus succeeded in maintaining economic stability.

Third, besides political and economic stability, it is necessary to adopt appropriate countermeasures to tackle the employment problem, the problem of ethnic minorities as well as the problem of imbalanced economic development between different regions so as to maintain the social stability.

To ensure that the common folks get tangible benefits from the reform is an important basis to maintain social stability. Deng Xiaoping repeatedly stressed that the ultimate aim in developing the economy is to satisfy the ever-increasing material and cultural needs of the people. He also listed whether it is conducive to improving the living standards of the people one of the three major criteria to judge the success of failure of a reform measure. For instance, available statistics indicated that the annual per-capita income for living expense in urban areas had increased from 316 yuan in 1978 to 5,160 yuan in 1997 and the annual per-capita net income for residents in the rural areas had been up from 133.6 yuan in 1978 to 2,090 yuan in 1997. In addition, the total amount of people's bank savings rose from 21.1 billion yuan at the end of 1978 to 4,628 billion yuan by the end of 1997.

In China's economic structure transition in the future, not only the deep-rooted contradictions accumulated over a long period of time will come to the surface under new conditions, some new factors of instability and new contradictions will also emerge. It can be said that China's reform has reached its most difficult "fortification-storming" stage. At this stage, reforms that have more risks, such as the reform of state-owned enterprises, the reform of the employment system, the reform of the welfare system and financial reform, will all enter the most difficult phase. The markets of production factors will be developed in an all-round way, and the socialist market economic system will be further improved. Bankruptcy of some state-owned enterprises, unemployment of redundant workers and staff from bankrupt enterprises, chaos in the mobility of surplus rural labor force, polarization arising in the course of marketization and the spread of corruption – all these still remain major problems challenging the economic and social instability. Therefore, it is necessary to make continuous efforts to handle well the relations between reform, development and stability. On the one hand, it is necessary to make vigorous efforts to deepen the reform and promote the economic development and, on the other, full account should be given to the endurance of various sectors to the reforms. Only in this way, is it possible to ensure the social and economic stability.

IV. Properly Handling the Relations Between Planning and Market

Properly handling of the relations between planning and market is not only related to the fundamental guiding principles and objectives of the reform but also has an important bearing on some key issues in the practice of reform as well as in the establishment of new economic models.

(I) Planning and Market: Both Are the Means

A key problem encountered in China's reform is how to handle the relations between planning and market. In the practice of reform, the people are encouraged to emancipate their mind, break away from old concepts and explore for new theories. Deng Xiaoping made close observation of the course of reform, timely summed up new experiences and theoretical achievements appeared in practice and clearly put forward the thinking of the socialist market economy.

As early as 1979 when meeting with a delegation from the United States, Deng Xiaoping pointed out, "It is wrong to maintain that a market economy exists only in capitalist society and that there is only 'capitalist' market economy. Why can't we develop a market economy under socialism? Developing a market economy does not mean practicing capitalism." In fact, this was tantamount to acknowledging the rationality of the existence of market economy under socialism.

In 1985, he again pointed out, "There is no fundamental contradiction between socialism and a market economy." "The experience we have gained over the years shows that with former economic structure we cannot develop the productive forces. That is why we have been drawing on some useful capitalist methods. It is clear now that the right approach is to open to the outside world, combine a planned economy with a market economy and introduce structural reforms." In 1987, on the eve of the Thirteenth National Party Congress, he further stated, "Actually they are both means of developing the productive forces. So long as they serve that purpose, we should make use of them. If they serve socialism they are socialist; if they serve capitalism they are capitalist." According to his opinion, the report to the 13th National Party Congress for the first time dropped the wording of "take planned economy as the key."

From late 1990 to early 1991, Deng Xiaoping warned on two occasions not to always associate planned economy with socialism and market economy with capitalism. "There is not such a thing. They are both means," he said. In early 1992, he made an inspection tour in southern China and during the tour he delivered some important speeches. In more succinct language, he pointed out, "A planned economy is not equivalent to socialism, because there is planning under capitalism too; a market economy is not capitalism, because here are markets under socialism too." This represented a clear, penetrating and precise answer to the long-debated issue whether market economy could exist under socialism and thoroughly removed the ideological shackles on people's thinking to take the planned economy and market economy as the basic attribute of socialist system and capitalist system respectively. In October 1992, the 14th National Party Congress made it clear that the objective of China's economic reform was to establish a socialist market economic system, thus ultimately solving the fundamental issue regarding China's drive for socialist modernization.

In line with the thinking of Deng Xiaoping, the Chinese Communit Party and government have, in the course of reform, paid attention to tackling the following questions in handling the relations between planning and market. First, there is no fundamental contradiction between socialism and market economy. Planned economy and market economy are not landmarks distinguishing socialism from capitalism. There is market economy under socialism and planned control under capitalism. The proportion of planning to market forces is not the essential difference between socialism and capitalism. This represents a fundamental breakthrough in the traditional concept that identifies planned economy with socialism and market economy with capitalism.

Second, both planning and market are means of controlling economic activity. So long as they serve that purpose, they can and should be used. If they serve socialism they are socialist; if they serve capitalism they are capitalist.

Third, planning is used to concentrate resources for major accomplishments. While stressing the necessity of reforming the system of planned control and introducing the market forces, Deng Xiaoping affirmed the important role played by planning in key state construction projects and clarified the functions of planned control under the conditions of the socialist market economy. To be specific, in planning work the stress should be placed on formulating medium- and long-range objectives, direction and strategies for national economic and social development to display the macro, strategic and policy significance of the planning work, and amass the financial and material resources under the disposal of the state to ensure the construction of key projects that have an important bearing on the overall economic situation.

Fourth, it is necessary to ensure authority of macro control. In macro control, what the central government says must account. In other words, the various localities and departments must follow the guidelines of macroeconomic control and regulation adopted by the central government, respect the market and be good at making use of the market forces in regulating the economic operation. The phenomenon that "the higher-ups may have their policies but those below always find ways to get around them" is not allowed. Moreover, local and sectoral barriers should be removed.

(II) Constantly Refreshing the Contents of Planning as Well as Their Forms of Materialization in the Course of Reform

1. Along with Advance in Reform, Constant Changes Have Taken Place in the Functions of Planning

In the course of reform, constant changes have taken place in the functions of planning. On the one hand, these changes are necessary in the course of reform and, on the other, they are the inevitable results of reform. Looking back at these changes at different stages, those taking place prior to 1992 represented mainly efforts to break away from the traditional planned economic system, while those after 1992 are marked by efforts to establish the socialist market economy.

From 1978 to 1983, in line with the guiding principle of "making the planned economy play the dominant role and market regulation play the supplementary role" and in connection with experiments in rural and urban areas, an initial reform was carried out of the system of planning and guiding proposals were made for reforming the forms, contents and systems of planning. Consequently, market mechanisms were initially introduced in the realm of planned management, and attention was given to market regulation in the economic activities.

In 1984 the Third Plenary Session of the 12th Party Central Committee adopted the "Decision on Reform of the Economic Structure." The document pointed out that it was necessary for China to establish a planning system that facilitated the conscientious utilization of the law of value and the development of a socialist commodity economy. In October 1984, the State Council endorsed and transmitted throughout the country the "Interim Regulations on Improving the Planning System" drafted by the State Planning Commission. The document proposed to gradually take steps to make the five-year plans for national economic and social development as the major form of plans, simplify annual plans, formulate long-term plans and, at the same time, formulate plans for the development of different industries, regions and the use of land resources as well as some specific plans. The document put forward the demand to reduce the scope and proportion of mandatory planning and enlarge the scope of guidance plans and the regulation through market. It also included the decision to expand the power of the local governments and the enterprises with regard to investment in fixed assets. Meanwhile, it called to expand the power of the enterprises in production, sales, product pricing, utilization of funds, distribution of profits, wage and salary payment, labor and employment as well as the directors' rights and responsibilities. In 1987, the 13th National Party Congress further proposed to "gradually establish the basic framework for a planned commodity economy," saying that "the operating sphere of planning and the market covers the whole society. On the whole, under the new economic mechanism 'the state regulates the market, and the market guides enterprises'." In line with these requirements, big steps had been made in the reform of the system of planned control. On July 16, 1988, the State Council again transmitted throughout the country "Plan for Reform of the Investment Management System in the Near Future" drafted by the State Planning Commission. The document suggested to introduce level-by-level management over important and long-term investments in construction, increase the responsibility of the local governments for key construction projects and divide responsibilities between the central government on the one hand and provincial, autonomous regional and municipal governments on the other. It proposed to expand the power of the enterprises in making their own decisions with regard to affairs of investment, so as to make them the major investors for commonplace construction projects. It proposed to establish the capital construction foundation system to ensure a stable source for funds for key construction projects. It proposed to establish investment companies to enforce management over investment affairs by economic means. It suggested to streamline government and delegate more power to lower levels, improve planned control over investment affairs, strengthen the self-disciplinary mechanism for the investors and improve the macro regulatory mechanism. It called for the introduction of the system of public bidding to give a full play to the role of the market and the competition mechanism. Meanwhile, in order to meet the needs of the economic restructuring in urban areas and bring into better play the role of the enterprises and major cities, the state, step by step, gave a group of major cities and large enterprise groups with independent budgetary status in the overall state plan.

In 1989-91, major attention was devoted to consolidating and expanding the achievements already made in the reform. At the same time, no opportunities were lost in introducing new reform measures. In 1989, for example, the State Council issued "Decision of the State Council on Essential Points of the Current Industrial Policies." The decision clearly listed the key areas that should be supported or restricted in each sector of the national economy, decided the order or priority for industrial development in terms of production, capital construction, technological upgrading and foreign trade. This was nothing short of an expansion of the scope of functions of planning work. Again for example, in 1991 the State Council endorsed and transmitted throughout the country the "Circular on Interim Provisions to Work Out a Two-year Plan for

Economic and Social Development on a Trial Basis" prepared by the State Planning Commission. The circular called to carry out experiment on mapping two-year plans for economic and social development throughout the country so as to increase the predictability for economic work and ensure the stability of the macroeconomic policies.

2. Changes in Functions of Planning Should Give Expression to the Demands of the Socialist Market Economy

From 1978 to 1992, the reform made in the planning system had already broken away from the old concept of focusing only on readjusting the division of power between the central and local governments. Moreover, the introduction of the market mechanisms had been made the major content of the reform in the planning system. The reform at this stage had also succeeded to a certain degree in simplifying government administration and delegating more power to the local levels. It had also achieved success in substantially narrowing the scope of mandatory planning and, at the same time, enlarging the self decision-making power of the local governments and especially that of the enterprises. All this represented a fundamental breaking from the traditional planned economic system, which was characterized by a high degree of centralization and took mandatory plans as its major form, thus created the necessary conditions for the establishment of a socialist market economic system.

In 1992, the 14th National Congress of the Communist Party of China put forward the objective to establish a socialist market economic system. In the following year, the Third Plenary Session of the 14th Central Committee of the Communist Party of China made the "Decision on Some Issues Concerning the Establishment of a Socialist Market Economic structure," thus further chartered the road for China's reform of the economic structure.

The socialist market economic system should play the following essential functions:

First, giving full play to the positive role of both planning and market. Planning and market are both means and modes in allocating resources and regulating the economy. To establish a market economic system, it is necessary to give full play to the basic role of the market in allocating resources and make the economic activities comply with the law of supply and demand, the law of value and the law of competition. Only in this way the vitality and efficiency of the economy can be enhanced. Planning should be geared towards the market, serve the market and reflect changes in the market. At the same time, planning should guide the market, regulate and control the market, help the market system grow to maturity, reduce blindness and spontaneity of the market and remedy the shortcomings of the market. In developing the market economy, it is necessary to bring into play the role of the "invisible hand" (market) and "the visible hand" (planning) and make them mutually complementary so as to ensure a sustained, coordinated and sound development of the national economy.

Second, combining microeconomic decontrol with macroeconomic control and regulation. In reforming the highly centralized planned economic system, one basic aspect is to invigorate the enterprises and make them play the major role in market competition, and to enlarge the power of the local governments and make the local governments and enterprises fully display their enthusiasm and initiative. On the other hand, the market mechanism must play a full role to imbue the economy with vitality. On the other, the state must pay attention to macroeconomic control and regulation and create a sound social and economic environment for market competition and for the enterprises to maintain their vitality. While persisting in lifting control over and invigorating the economy in micro terms, it is necessary to strengthen and improve macroeconomic control and regulation by the state.

Third, combining direct control and regulation with indirect control and regulation in macroeconomic control and regulation by the state. Under the conditions of the socialist market economy, the strategy and objective for macroeconomic development should be mainly realized by indirect means of control and regulation. But, necessary modes of direct control and regulation are still needed under certain conditions. Likely, necessary supervisory and checking systems should not be overlooked.

Fourth, combining necessary centralization with appropriate decentralization, and combining uniformity with flexibility. China is a big country and the development in different parts of the country is uneven. To develop a socialist market economy, it would not do without necessary decentralization of power. Only by altering the past situation in which decision-making power as well as financial and material power were over-concentrated in the hands of the central government and appropriately sharing out the power can it be possible to fully mobilize the enthusiasm of the local governments and enterprises to enliven the economy and facilitate a quicker and sounder development of the productive forces. At the same time, China is a big developing country, its market system has not been well developed and the country in general suffers from a relative shortage of resources. Moreover, it is necessary for the country to distribute the productive forces in a planned way, to undertake necessary key construction projects, to concentrate strength to cope with fierce international competition, to strengthen national defense and ensure the safety of the state. Under such a situation, it will not do either without necessary centralization. Therefore, it is imperative to combine necessary centralization with appropriate decentralization of power.

(III) State Plans Are an Important Means to Enforce Macro Control and Regulation by the Government

The "Decision of the CPC Central Committee on Some Issues Concerning the Establishment of a Socialist Market Economic Structure," adopted in 1993 at the Third Plenary Session of the 14th Party Central Committee, decided to build a new macro control and regulation system suited to the socialist market economy and further defined the status, roles, scope and functions of planning in macro control and regulation. According to the document, the functions of control through planning should be geared towards the market, reflect the market, guide the market and regulate the market under the conditions of the socialist market economy. On the whole, state plans should be based on the market and they should be mainly in the form guidance plans. The tasks of planning are: to rationally define the strategies for national economic and social development, the objectives of macroeconomic control and industrial policies, make sound economic forecasts, and map out plans for major economic structures, distribution of productive forces, conservation of national territories and construction of key projects. Planning work should concentrate on the overall situation, strategies and policies, with emphasis being laid on drafting medium- and long-term plans, and on the comprehensive and coordinated implementation of macroeconomic policies and economic levers. The basic contents of planning covers strategies for national economic and social development, objective of macroeconomic control and important corresponding programs for economic regulation as well as plans for the mobilization and utilization of the public funds and resources of the state. The major forms of planning include comprehensive planning reports and policy documents as well as planning and policy documents for important specific projects. Medium-term and long-term plans should be ensured a dominant position while annual plans represent special measures for the implementation of the medium-term and long-term plans. The major regulatory means of planning are mainly comprehensive and coordinated use of macroeconomic policies and economic levers. At the same time, it is necessary to make use of the material and financial resources in the hands of the state to carry out prompt regulation when necessary, and bring into full play the guiding role of information. It is necessary to invite people from various circles of the society to participate in formulating the plans, while the implementation of the plans must rely on the market subjects and various types of intermediary organizations. The control through planning must be standardized and codified.

In order to meet the needs of the socialist market economy, since 1993 China has carried out a series of reforms in the planning control system.

First, the planning work acquired new contents and forms on the basis of new changes in the concept and functions of planning. In line with the nature and functions of socialist planning work, a massive reform was conducted in the contents of planning work:

(1) Giving prominence to strategies for economic and social development, which include the overall strategy for national economic and social development, the strategy to change the industrial structure, the

strategies for regional economic development, the strategy for scientific and technological progress, the strategy for natural resources utilization and environment and the strategy for international cooperation and competition.

(2) Reforming the planning index system, fixing goals for macroeconomic control and regulation and changing the targets of some important economic activities and social development into predictive targets. As of 1994, China has officially set the major indexes of macroeconomic control and regulation for its annual plans. These indexes include the rate of economic growth, rate of inflation, total investment in fixed assets, money supply, total volume of import and export in foreign trade, balance of financial revenue and expenditure, unemployment rate in urban areas and natural growth rate of the population. These indexes represented both the starting point and end-result in the formulation of macroeconomic policies and in the comprehensive use of various economic levers.

(3) Giving prominence to macroeconomic policies and working out important economic regulatory programs correspondingly. At present, macroeconomic policies covered in planning include mainly the policy of overall balance in economic aggregates, the policy regarding economic structure, the policy for income distribution and the policy for international economic cooperation, as well as the policies that are to ensure the attainment of the goals set for macroeconomic control and regulation, such as the financial policy, montary policy, investment policy, price policy and policy concerning foreign economic relations and trade. The important economic regulatory programs represent concrete measures to implement the various macroeconomic policies and make use of the various economic levers.

(4) Rationally determining the scope of mobilization and utilization of public funds and state resources and changing the mode of control by planning. In making plans for investment, efforts have been made to improve macro control over the general scale of investment in fixed assets of the whole society, enforce control and regulation over the total volume of investment starting from the sources of funds, lay particular emphasis on the readjustment of investment structure, step up efforts in

the construction of state key projects, and improve the investment information network. Further steps have taken to change the modes in pooling funds and classify the projects of investment into three types -- competitive, basic and public welfare – in line with the specific characteristics of investment activities, and separate policy-oriented loans of investment and loans for commercial purposes. In addition, efforts have been made to sort out the investment subjects, strengthen the self-disciplinary mechanism for them, establish the capital fund system for investment projects, investment responsibility system for legal persons, as well as the public bidding system and engineering supervisory system, and simplify investment approval procedures. In terms of foreign trade and import of foreign investment, mandatory plans have been removed for imports and exports and guidance plans have been only adopted regarding the total volume of import and export as well as the modes of trade. Moreover, the list of commodities whose import and export were controlled by way of fixed quotas and issuance of licenses has been reduced and the methods of management have been reformed to make room for bidding, auction and standardized allocation. An end was put to the "double-track exchange rates" practice and a controlled floating exchange rate system has been established. The system under which the exporters were allowed to retain certain proportions of their foreign exchange earnings and the quota system of foreign exchange have been abolished and a system has been established for the banks to settle foreign exchange accounts and sell foreign exchange. Overall planned management has been enforced over the borrowing of foreign loans and policies have been adopted to guide foreign investment, improve foreign investment structure and enhance the sense of risks. Active, rational and effective measures have been adopted to encourage the utilization of foreign capital.

Second, gradual steps have been taken to establish a network of economic situation analyzing, forecasting and monitoring systems to enforce comprehensive balance, coordination, analysis and macro control over the operation of the national economy. In line with the requirements of operation of the socialist market economy, China has step by step established an indcx system for monitoring and analyzing the operation of the national economy, an index system for analyzing the economic situation as well as monthly, seasonal and semi-annual and annual macroeconomic situation analyzing and forecasting report systems. In formulating state plans, China has gradually established a new system of comprehensive balance that takes the total amount of value as the core and macroeconomic aggregates and important economic structures as the major contents. In terms of comprehensive balance, it mainly refers to the balance and coordination of total social demand and total social supply, total amount of funds in the whole society, important economic structures, sources and use of disposable income of the residents, supply and demand of commodities that are important to the national economy and people's livelihood, social labor force, general price level of commodities and price structures. Taking into account the outstanding contradictions and problems arising in the implementation of the state plans and economic operation, follow-up analysis has been made and macro control and regulation have been enforced out to ensure the normal operation of the market and smooth attainment of the objectives of macro control and regulation by the state. Macro control measures adopted by the state in 1993-96 in view of the overheated economic development and rampant inflation as well as various policies adopted by the state to expand domestic consumption are indispensable in the establishment and continuous improvement of the above-mentioned systems.

Third, in planning work raising the level of democratization and legalization as well as the scientific level. First, in mapping out state plans, the level of social participation has been raised. Starting from the period of the "Eighth Five-Year Plan," great attention has been paid to soliciting opinions from various government departments and local governments in formulating both medium- and long-term plans and annual plans. At the same time, different methods have been devised to mobilize the various sectors of the society, particularly people from the Chinese Academy of Sciences, the Chinese Academy of Social Sciences, large enterprise groups, economic research institutions, information gathering and consultation organizations as well as important social organizations, to work together in the formulation of state plans.

Second, efforts have been made to bring planning work onto the orbit of legalization. Since 1993, the National People's Congress has examined and enacted the "Price Law" and the State Council also has enacted and promulgated more than a dozen laws and administrative decrees of various kinds. Moreover, a number of important laws and regulations, such as the "Investment Law" are now under consideration. All of these have played an important and positive role in regulating the economic activities in the market, codifying the behavior of economic subjects and standardizing planning work by legal means.

Compared with the situation in the starting stage of reform, the reform conducted in the system of control by planning since 1993 has effected fundamental changes in many important aspects of the planning work, such as the functions, contents, forms and regulatory means of planning. Reform in the early stage, which was characterized by "granting decision-making power to enterprises and allowing them to retain certain portions of the profits," fundamentally broke the framework of the traditional system of planned control and set in motion the transition from the old system to the new. And the reform carried out since 1993, which is characterized by innovation, has gradually brought into being the framework of a new-type system of control by planning that complies with the requirements of the socialist market economy on the basis of achievements made in the early stage of the reform.

V. Roles of the Government in Market Economy

The objective of China's economic reform is to establish a socialist market economic system. Compared with the traditional planned economic model, this represents a fundamental change. The market economic system China intends to establish is a market economy regulated by the government. It not only gives expression to the common law governing the market economy in modern times but also is an intrinsic requirement raised by China's economic development.

(I) Viewing the Roles of Government by Making a Comparison and

from the Perspective of Development

Based on the mode of the market in allocating resources, the modern market economy introduces at the same time government and other public institutions to regulate economic activities through plans and policies. Viewed from the perspective of government's control over the economy, each market economy in the world has its own unique features thanks to the different scopes, forms and degrees of government intervention. In general, the market economies throughout the world can be summarized into the following models:

The first is the free market economic model, as represented by Hongkong. Even this economic model is not absolutely free. Yet, due to various special conditions, the intervention by the government has been kept at the minimum, known as active non-intervention by the government.

The second is the relatively free model of market economy represented by the United States and Britain. Under this model, stress is given to free competition between the enterprises and individuals, while the government ensures free competition by means of enacting appropriate laws and policies. The government scarcely involves itself in the economic activities of the enterprises. Yet, it exerts a powerful influence on macroeconomic aggregates and a number of special industries. For example, the US government intervenes in economic activities through the ministry of finance, and makes direct investments in war and hi-tech industries through the "star war" program and other programs. The US government often claims that the economy in the United States is a "free economy" and denies its intervention in economic activities. In fact, this is not the case.

The third is the model represented by the former Federal Germany, which practiced a social market economy. Under this model, no state plans are formulated. Yet, it still exerts powerful intervention in the market by various means, with the focus of attention being placed on maintaining the market competition environment and social equality.

The fourth model is represented by Japan and the Republic of Korea, which is a kind of planned market economy. Under the model, the government plays quite a powerful guiding role by working out medium-

and long-term plans for economic development to decide the orientation, objectives, key projects and important policies. Moreover, the government has under it a very powerful planning department. For instance, the Ministry of International Trade and Industry under the Japanese government exerts very powerful intervention in the economic activities; it promotes the development of economic sectors that the governments encourages through enacting industrial policies and adopting corresponding means to support their development. In order to carry out its strategy of catching up with the developed countries, the government of the Republic of Korea directly intervenes in investment activities of the banks in large enterprises and large enterprise groups, thus building a very close relationship between the banks and enterprises by making them hold each other's shares.

The fifth model is represented by the newly emerging industrial countries in Asia, such as Thailand and Malaysia. Under the conditions of relative backwardness, these countries have seized each opportunity to develop themselves. One very important reason for their rapid development is the effective role played by the government. For this reason, some scholars named this economic model "government guided" economy. These emerging industrialized countries have aroused widespread attention among economists throughout the world. The 1997 a report issued by the World Bank on development in the world held that the roles played by the government were reconsidered all over the world. After the outbreak of the Asian financial crisis, however, some economists attributed the causes of the crisis to excessive intervention by the government. What are the relations between the sustained and rapid economic growth and the roles of the government in these newly emerging industrialized countries? This is a topic calling for further study.

China is a country in the transitional process. Under the traditional system of planned economy prior to the reform, the government played an omnipotent role, and the enterprises were no more than a machine operated by the government. Practice has proved that such a system is not conducive to the development of the productive forces. One of the most obvious landmarks of the transition of China's economic structure is the change in the role played by the government in economic activities. The government has shifted from direct intervention in economic activities and allocation of resources to indirect macroeconomic control and regulation to make the market play its role in resource allocation. This does not mean that the government sits idle or gives up all control to the economic activities, but withdraws from areas that it should intervene.

In the course of economic transition, the Chinese government has played an important role, particularly in promoting the development of the market, providing public products and services and exercising macro control and regulation in the economic operation. Of course, in the government's intervention in economic activities, there are both successes and failures. One example of successes is the macro regulatory effort made in the 1993-96 period, which succeeded in curbing inflation and bringing about a "soft landing" for the economy. In terms of failures, due to the limits imposed by the traditional investment system and the system of sectoral and regional segmentation, the phenomenon of repeated construction is still fairly serious, causing a great surplus in the productive capacity. The major reason for such failures is that the change of government's functions has lagged behind, that is to say, the government has done many things that it should not do and cannot do well but failed to do well in many things it should do.

(II) The Actual Conditions and Current Stage of Development in China Predestine the Particularly Important Roles Played by the Government

Generally speaking, the change in the roles played by the government are determined by many factors, such as the level of economic development, the rapid development of science and technology, social environment at home and international relations.

The complexity of the situation in China is unparalleled, so is the formidability of the tasks confronting the country in the economic transition. Such a unique situation and state of development in China has determined that the role played by the government is of particular importance.

First, in China the transition of the economic structure and the establishment of a socialist market economic system are bound to be very long historical process. It is impossible to accomplish these objectives in one step or overnight. In this process, due to the fact the market is not well developed, the pace of transition in different fields is impossible to be the same, thus giving up to serious "rent-seeking" problems. When the government is incapable to enforce effective macro control, there is bound to be chaos and instability.

Second, China is a large developing country with a population of 1.2 billion people. The level of development in different regions varies greatly. So, it is necessary for the government to render support to the development in those backward regions. Since the 1980s, the gap in economic development between the east part and the west part and between the coastal and inland areas has become increasingly wider. Obviously, it is impossible to solve the problem of economic disparity between different regions by relying on the market mechanisms alone. On the contrary, it may make the situation worse. To reduce the disparity, it is imperative to make the government, particularly the central government, play effective roles in strengthening the infrastructure construction in the backward areas to improve the environment for investment, increasing the transfer expenditure from the financial department of the central government to develop educational and cultural undertakings in these areas, and encouraging the developed areas to move industries and give technological support to them, so as to eventually establish an operational mechanism in which "the gap is narrowed through prosperous areas rendering help to the backward areas" while a relatively quick economic growth is maintained in the developed areas.

Third, the overall level of economic development is still low in China and backwardness in infrastructure proves to be the "bottleneck" factor in China's economic development. As the construction of infrastructure facilities calls for large sums of investment, involves great risks and needs longer periods to recover the investment, most enterprises find it hard or are reluctant to get involved. Therefore, the government has to make direct investments by pooling funds or guide and organize social funds to make investment according to government plans.

Fourth, China is a large agricultural country and also a large developing country with outstanding contradictions in the dual economic structures. The stability in China relies, to a large extent, on agriculture and the development of the rural economy. How to support the development of agriculture, and improve the living standards of the farmers, increase their purchasing power and expand the rural market for industrial products – all these are of vital importance for the steady development of the Chinese economy. To develop agriculture and raise the living standards of the farmers also need the government to give support to agriculture and other fragile industries and, at the same time, to promote urbanization in an orderly manner, so as to turn the dual economy into a unitary economy based on socialized mass production.

(III) Practice and Exploration in Ways to Bring the Roles of the Government into Play in the Course of Economic Transition

In the course of China's economic transition, how to bring the role of the government into better play is a process of continuous exploration, practice and summarization. At the same time, it is necessary to borrow from the advanced experience in the rest of the world.

1. Enforcing Effective Macro Control and Regulation while Making Efforts to Bringing the Role of Market Forces into Full Play

In 1992, China's economy has entered a new round of growth. The annual growth rate of GDP went up from 9.1 percent in 1991 to 14.2 percent; the growth of industrial increment value, from 14.4 percent to 21.2 percent; and the growth of investment in fixed assets, from 23.8 percent to 44.4 percent. In the first half of 1993, the national economy continued to grow rapidly. The GDP increased by 13.9 percent as compared with the corresponding period in the previous year, the demand for investment and consumption kept to expand quickly, the growth of investment in fixed assets in the whole society reached 61 percent, of which that in state-owned units it increased 70 percent, and the growth in total sales volume of consumer goods was 21.6 percent. Due to excessively rapid growth, the phenomenon of overheated development gradually became obvious in the economic life. The overall economic situation turned from bad to worse and the economic order was plunged into confusion. The major manifestations were that effective control was lost over the economic aggregates, as shown in the fact that total demand far exceeded total supply, and maladjustment appeared in the economic structure, as shown in the fact that markets of stocks, futures and real estates swelled rapidly – a typical phenomenon of a "bubble" economy. On the other hand, however, the development of infrastructure and basic industries lagged behind. The monetary order was chaotic. Under the interaction of the craze of fund raising, craze of inter-bank borrowing and lending, craze in the establishment of monetary institutions and economic development areas as well as over-heated development of the real estates industry, the total demand for funds swelled, further aggravating the imbalance between total demand and total supply and distorting economic structure. Moreover, an imbalance also appeared in foreign trade, with only a 4.4-percent increase in export but a 23.2-percent increase in import. The RMB was devalued by a large margin, increasing the pressure on the objective to keep a balance of payment. The direct consequences of these problems were the increase of currency issuance far exceeded the economic growth and the pressure of inflation markedly increased. The ratio of reserves of major specialized banks kept lingering around the warning line; some banks even met with difficulties in payments. And the issuance of government bonds was retarded. The country's foreign exchange reserves dropped, with the spot exchange rate going down by 25 percent as compared with the previous year; the exchange rate between RMB and the US dollar dropped from 8:1 to 10:1 in the foreign exchange regulation market. Market prices witnessed an all-round hike. As compared with the same period of the previous year, the prices of the means of production rose by 40 percent while the price index of necessities for urban residents went up by 17.4 percent in 35 large and medium-sized cities.

In order to stop further deterioration of the economic situation and maintain a sound momentum for economic development, the Chinese government took a series of important measures from March to June

1993. In particular, it issued a circular in late June, which laid down the measures to strengthen and improve macro control and regulation. These measures played a decisive role in altering the unhealthy trend in economic development. The major measures were as follows:

First, putting the financial and economic order straight. A ban was imposed on pooling of funds in violation of state stipulations. Strict control was imposed over the scale and categories of annual issuance of various kinds of bonds and over the issuance of bonds by local governments. A time limit was set to close down unapproved monetary institutions or merge them with approved ones. The People's Bank, the specialized banks as well as commercial banks were asked to completely separate themselves from their newly established non-monetary institutions or other economic entities. And black securities markets were banned.

Second, strengthening monetary control. Steps were taken to strictly control the issuance of currency. The People's Bank of China was asked to stop issuing loans to non-banking institutions and retrieve funds loaned out in violation of relevant stipulations. Strict measures were taken to control the scale of banking credit, making it clear that the annual credit plan should be in no way exceeded. The State Council demanded the banks to ensure the value of people's three-, five- and eight-year fixed deposits and a responsibility system was established on the payment of savings deposits. At the same time, the interest rates on bank savings were raised on two occasions, so were the interest rates on state treasury bonds. Measures were taken to enhance the macro regulatory capacity of the central bank and annulled the power of the provincial branches to adjust the total sum of loans by 7 percent. It was stipulated that the interest rate on funds pooled in any form should not be higher than that on the state treasury bonds so as to ensure that the issuance of state treasury bonds as well as bonds for key state construction projects receive priority.

Third, strengthening financial control. Measures were taken to strengthen tax collection and management and clear up tax reductions and exemptions approved by the local authorities overstepping their limits of power. All policies adopted by local governments on the exemption of energy and transport facilities construction funds and budgetary adjustment funds were claimed null and void. Time limits were set to fulfil the task of issuance of government debts. And efforts were made to control the excessively rapid growth of institutional purchasing power.

Fourth, strengthening control over foreign exchange. Measures were taken to make sure that all foreign exchange earnings were turned over to the state and strict procedures were adopted for the examination and approval of investment abroad and the flow of other foreign exchange capital. Hundreds of millions of US dollars were sold in the domestic foreign exchange markets to keep the exchange rate stable. A strict ban was imposed on the circulation of foreign currencies in the domestic market and on speculation in foreign exchange.

Fifth, controlling investment in fixed assets. Vigorous measures were adopted to control the scale of investment and sort out projects under construction. Strict procedures of approval were designed for new projects. Control was strengthened over the real estate markets.

Sixth, enforcing control over price rises. Strict control was enforced over lifting the prices of commodities and services under state control. A stop was put to price adjusting measures adopted by local governments over the prices of commodities and services under their control. A food grain risk fund and a non-staple food price adjustment fund were established.

The implementation of the above-mentioned policies, which were aimed at strengthening and improving macro control and regulation, had reaped marked results. It had alleviated some outstanding contradictions in the economic life and stabilized the economic situation as a whole. The problem of imbalance in the economic aggregates was brought under control. In the third quarter of 1993, the growth rate of investment made by state-owned units dropped by nine percentage point as compared with that in the first half of the year; in September, the drop reached 14 percentage point. The growth rate of industrial production dropped from 30.2 percent in June to 19.1 percent in September. The monetary order obviously turned for the better and the financial situation was stabilized. The confused situation caused by rampant raising of funds, wanton inter-bank borrowing and lending and willful establishment of monetary institutions was basically brought under control. Over half of the inter-bank loans were retrieved. The measures to straighten up the capital market, futures market and foreign exchange market as well as to tackle the problems in the development of the real estates industry and development areas had played an effective role in curbing speculation and "bubble" economy. As a result, the stock market became increasingly stable and the craze in the real estates business began to ebb. The downhill trend in bank savings by the people was basically halted, the rate of fund reserves returned to a normal level for the specialized banks, and the exchange rate of RMB against the US dollar was stabilized as 8.7:1.

In line with the "Decision on Some Issues Concerning the Establishment of a Socialist Market Economic Structure," which as adopted at the Third Plenary Session of the 14th Party Central Committee, the Chinese government adopted many important measures for reforms in the financial, taxation, monetary, foreign trade, foreign exchange control and price systems. Starting from 1995, the Chinese government had taken it its primary task of macro control to curb inflation. Keeping this mind, the government had adopted moderately stringent fiscal and monetary policies, and continued to enforce strict control over the scale of investment in fixed assets and new construction projects. Thanks to these unremitting efforts, the macroeconomic environment had improved continuously. By 1996, the annual growth rate of GDP was 9.7 percent, the hike of retail prices was 6.1 percent, and the foreign exchange reserves of the state reached US$105 billion at year end and regular RMB items became exchangeable. All these indicated that the Chinese economy had made a "soft landing." The efforts made by the Chinese government in macro control from 1993 to 1996 show that, in the course of economic transition, the effective role played by the government is extremely important in maintaining economic stability and growth. The success achieved played an important protective role in helping China alleviate the harms caused by the Asian financial crisis and ensured that the value of the RMB remains stable.

2. The Government Gives Expression to the Long-term Interests of the State through Formulating Medium- and Long-term Plans, Gives Expression to Its Strategic Intentions through Enacting Policies and Guarantees the Implementation of the Policies by Using Economic Levers and Necessary Administrative Means

Due to historical and practical reasons, China has encountered extremely outstanding contradictions as shown in the irrationalily of industrial structure and regional structure. As the government had often laid particular stress on short-term, local and after-event readjustment of the market and failed to play an effective role in formulating clear-cut long-term objectives for development and in making corresponding structural readjustments in the past, it is therefore required to pay more attention to formulating plans and objectives for medium- and long-term development and adopt correct strategies and industrial policies for economic development in line with the trend of economic development, so as to guide the structural readjustment. The "Outline of the Ninth Five-year Plan for National Economic and Social Development and the Long-range Objectives Through the Year 2010," formulated in 1996, was the first medium- and long-term plan for development under regulation through the market. Compared with the previous eight five-year plans, this new plan greatly reduced the coverage of mandatory planning and related quantitative quotas. It focused on the major objectives, basic principles, guidelines and strategic measures for the national economic and social development, including the predictive and guidance plan for the readjustment and optimization of the industrial structure. The outline stated that the objectives of macro control and regulation should play a guiding role for the management and operation decisions of the enterprises and the microeconomic activities, but did not have any direct restrictive effects. The state would render financial assistance and policy loans to ensure the implementation of the industrial policies, structural readjustment programs as well as key construction projects listed in the outline and, taking into account the competition in the market and changes in the supply-demand relations, employ various economic levers and economic policies to ensure their accomplishment.

3. Establishing a Legal System Necessary for the Market Economic System

In a certain sense, market economy is a legal and credit economy. To develop a market economy, it is necessary to establish a corresponding legal system. In the course of China's economic transition, much effort has been made to enact and improve laws and regulations related to the market economy. The Amendments to the Constitution of the People's Republic of China adopted the First Session of the Eighth National People's Congress stipulated, "The state practices socialist market economy," and "The state shall enhance economic legislation and improve macro-control of the economy." This has provided the constitutional basis for the establishment and development of a socialist market economy. The Amendments to the Constitution adopted at the Second Session of the Ninth National People's Congress stipulated, "The non-public sector of the economy comprising self-employed and private businesses within the domain stipulated by law is an important component of the country's socialist market economy," and "The state protects the legitimate rights and interests of the self-employed and private businesses." These stipulations further clarified the legal status and rights of individual and private sectors of the economy.

China has taken as its primary task to accelerate the enactment of economic legislation in the building of the legal system. Since the early 1990s, it has made much effort in putting up the legal framework for the socialist market economy by focusing on the major links of the market economic system. To provide legal codes to standardize the behavior of the market subjects, the National People's Congress has enacted, among other laws, the corporate law, partnership enterprise law and the commercial bank law. To establish rules for market operation and maintain the market order, it has enacted the price law, law against competition by inappropriate means, law on the protection of consumers' rights and interests, law on urban real estate management, advertising law, auction law, guarantee law, negotiable instrument law, insurance law and arbitration law, and amended the economic contract law. To improve macroeconomic control and regulation, it has enacted budget law, audit law, law on the People's Bank of China and price law, and amended the statistics law and individual income tax law. For the establishment of the social security system, it has enacted the labor law and some other related laws. To facilitate the drive to open to the outside world, it has enacted the foreign trade law and other related laws. To promote the development of basic and pillar industries, it has enacted the agriculture law, civil aviation law, electric energy law, highway law, coal mining law, law on energy conservation and construction law, and amended mineral resources law and some other related laws. These laws, together with those related to the market economy previously enacted, represent a big progress in the establishment of the legal system of the socialist market economy and have provided the important legal environment for the transition towards a market economic system.

4. The Role Played by the Government Must Be in Conformity with the Laws of the Market Economy

The existence of the laws of the market economy is an objective reality independent of man's will. They include the law of value, the law governing the relations between supply and demand and the law of competition. What people do is to understand and use them rather than going against it. Violation of the laws of the market economy might turn the role of the government into unnecessary administrative intervention, which in turn will hinder the economic development and retard the development of the market. Therefore, in the course of economic transition, it is necessary to study, understand and make use of the laws of the market economy. It is necessary to protect the pioneering spirit of the enterprises and individuals who are the microeconomic subjects of the market economy, improve the market environment and promote fair and orderly competition. More importantly, it is necessary to study the particularities of the operation of the Chinese market in connection with the actual conditions in China now -- the market is still growing, its operation is not yet standardized and the market rules are far from being perfect. Viewing the whole world as a whole, the system models of different market economies are also in a process of development and change. Along with the gradual establishment of the market economic system in China, the roles played by the government are also changing.

Generally speaking, the government is now withdrawing itself from those areas where the market forces should be made to play a full role, in other words, withdrawing from areas the government should not intervene, to make sure that it does a better job in areas where its responsibilities lie.

Notes:

(1) To fulfill the arduous historical task of modernization for China, Deng Xiaoping put forward an overall strategy for economic development that involves three steps. The first extends from 1981 to 1990. During this period, the aim is to double the GNP of 1980 and basically solve the problem of adequate food and clothing for the people. The second step runs from 1991 to 2000, and the aim is to double again the GNP and to enable the people to live a better-off life. The third step is from 2001 to the mid-21st century, and the aim is to reach the per-capita GNP level of moderately developed countries, which means by then China will basically achieve its goal of modernization and the people will enjoy a relatively affluent life. In 1995, China successfully fulfilled, five years ahead of schedule, the goal of quadrupling the 1980 GNP. In 1997, the per-capita GNP amounted to 5941.5 yuan. Calculated according to constant price of RMB, this figure also quadrupled that in 1980.

(2) Stiglitze: "Where Should Reform Go? On Transition over the Past 10 Years," carried in Issue No. 44 of *Reports on Research and Analysis of China's National Conditions.*

(3) Stiglitze, "Where Should Reform Go? On Transition over the Past 10 Years," carried in Issue No. 44 of *Reports on Research and Analysis of China's National Conditions.*

CHAPTER 1
REFORM OF OWNERSHIP SYSTEM ANDSTATE-OWNED ENTERPRISES IN CHINA

Synopsis

China's economic restructuring started with reform in the ownership system. The success in the reform of the land system and land allocation system in the rural areas promoted the reform of the enterprise system in the urban areas and created an increasingly relaxed environment for the development of the non-state-owned sectors, particularly those sectors that are not publicly owned. The ownership reform has boosted the development of diversified economic elements and the readjustment of the ownership structure, brought forth a large number of market subjects, ensured the continuous development and improvement of the market system, accelerated the formation of market mechanisms, brought about changes in the means of macroeconomic control by the government, and expedited the development of the market legal system and social security system. Reform in the ownership system has laid the foundation for the socialist market economy in China and served as a prerequisite for the transition of China's economic structure. The report to the 15th National Party Congress summarized the experience and objectives of the ownership reform in the country, which proved to be an important breakthrough in the Marxist theory regarding the ownership system.

State-owned enterprises are the basis on which the traditional economic system stand. Reform in the ownership system is bound to raise an urgent demand for the reform of state-owned enter-

prises. As of the mid-1980's, China has made the reform of state-owned enterprises a central link in the overall economic restructuring and has made active efforts in blazing a new road and creating new forms for the reform. Over the past two decades, China has made great achievements and accumulated much experience in the reform of state-owned enterprises. On the whole, however, no fundamental breakthrough has been achieved in the reform. The continuous deterioration of the plight of the state-owned enterprises has dawned on the government and people of various circles the urgency to speed up the reform of the state-owned enterprises.

This chapter reviews the course China has traversed over the past two decades in its reform of ownership structure and state-owned enterprises, describes the achievements and experience gained so far and, in the meantime, analyzes the major problems confronting the reform and ventures some suggestions and policy choices for the reform in the period to come.

Section 1
Course of Ownership Reform and Changes in Ownership Structure in China

I. Course of Ownership Reform

1. Background of Ownership Reform

China's ownership system prior to the reform was the product of the traditional theory of socialist ownership, which held that socialism was precisely aimed at eliminating private ownership and establishing an economy under absolute public ownership. According to this theory, the socialist public ownership consists of the state-owned sector (economy owned by the whole people) and the collective sector. The state-owned sector represents a higher level of the socialist public ownership while the collective sector is at a lower level, and the lower level would gradually shift to the higher level.

Table 1-1. Changes of Land Policy in China from 1953 to 1978

Year	Major Contents of Land Policy
1953-1954	Mutual-aid agricultural production groups under private ownership of land
1955-1956	Elementary agricultural production co-ops comprising a number of households and individually owned land
1957	Establishment of advanced agricultural production co-ops, the ownership right of Land was given to the collectives while allowing the individual households remain Small plots of land for private needs
1958-1959	Introduction of the People's Commune System, the ownership right of land was turned to the state, the small plots of land remained by the individual households were taken away, and a rationing system was applied
1963-1978	Restructuring the People's Communes, introducing the three-level ownership of land, i.e., the communes, production brigades and production teams, and allowing the existence of household small plots of land
After 1978	Introducing the production responsibility system and gradually eliminating the remnants of the system of people's communes

Source of Data: David W. Zhang, *China under the Leadership of Deng Xiaoping*, p. 125, Law Press, 1991)

Under the guidance of the above-mentioned theory, New China launched its drive to continuously eliminate private ownership and establish the public ownership, which took the state-owned sector as its mainstay. In times of war and during the early days of the People's Republic, the Communist Party distributed land to the farmers in the countryside. But soon after, it took back the land from the farmers and put it in the hands of the agricultural co-operatives or communes (See Table 1-1). In the cities, foreign capital and bureaucrat capital was confiscated, industrial construction was launched in full scale and socialist transformation was carried out for the individually owned handicraft businesses. As a result, the proportion of the public sector, particularly that of the state-owned sector, rapidly swelled. During the so-called "Great Leap Forward" and "great cultural revolution" movements, individual and private economy in both the cities and countryside, including even the rural fairs, were considered "capitalist tails" that should be cut. Moreover, the collective economy was continuously transformed into state-run economy. Consequently, the economic sector under public ownership boomed throughout the country and it was attributed with an overwhelmingly dominant position in the Chinese economy (see Table 1-2). In 1978, the number of individual handicraftsmen and business owners was no more than 150,000 in the urban areas, and their lines of business were strictly limited to handicrafts, including repairing and other services.

Table 1-2. Proportional Change of Various Economic Elements in the Total Economic Composition in Cities and Towns from 1952-1978

Economic Sector	Proportion of Total Industrial Output Value (percent)			Number of Employees (in thousand)		
	1952	1957	1978	1952	1957	1978
State-run Economy	41.5	53.6	77.6	15,800	24,510	74,510
Economy under Private Ownership & Joint Public and Private Ownership	34.6	26.4	0	-	-	0
Individual Economy	20.6	0.8	0.5	8,830	1,040	150
Collective Economy	3.3	19.0	21.8	230	6,500	20,480

Source of Data: *China Statistical Almanac (1981)*, p.107

The system of ownership prior to the reform, although compatible with the traditional ownership theory and had helped the country build a relatively comprehensive national economic system and industrial system through nationalization and massive industrialization, had caused many serious problems to the sound and sustained development of the national economy. (1) Under the conditions of poor productivity, the single-faceted pursuit of public ownership, especially the universal domination of the state-owned sector, in the ownership relations and ownership structure, represented in fact a divorce from the practical development level of productive forces and retarded the development of production and services much needed by different circles of the society. (2) It is ideologically unrealistic to expect the general public to abandon personal interests for the sake of public interests at the current stage. The absolute denial of the people's rights in possession, use and exchange as well as getting benefits from the factors and means of production has greatly dampened their enthusiasm for production. (3) In socialist countries, such as the former Soviet Union and China, the pursuit of a unitary public ownership brought at one time or another harm rather benefit to the development of productive forces. This phenomenon was particularly obvious in the rural areas. Viewed from the perspective of management, the individual household has been proved to be an organizational set-up most suitable for agricultural production at the current stage, while the collective generates low efficiency because of high cost incurred for exercising supervision and management.(1) According to calculations, from 1952 to 1957 when the farmers were nominal or titular owners of the land, the labor productivity in the rural areas could still grow by 1.7 percent each year while the productivity generated by all the production elements increased by 0.63 percent. From 1957 to 1978, however, the annual average growth rate of labor productivity dropped to 0.2 percent, along with a general trend of decrease in the productivity generated by all the production elements. Even in industrial production, it also failed to maintain the enthusiasm of the workers by solely depending on ideological encouragement while totally denying their personal interests. (4) Due to the harsh controlling measures enforced on productive activities and commodity circulation, a phenomenon of "shortage economy" prevailed, which was featured by a serious lack of commodities in the market. Most of the commodities were rationed by issuing dozens and even more than a hundred kinds of coupons. This made people's life extremely inconvenient. (5) The people's income remained low and their living standards had not witness any improvement for a long time and even deteriorated in certain periods of time. From 1957 to 1978, the average annual net income of the farmers increased from 73.37 yuan to 133.57 yuan, with an annual average increase of only three yuan. Moreover, there were still 200 million people who could barely get enough to clothe and feed themselves. In state-owned units, the average annual salary of the workers and staff only increased from 637 yuan in 1957 to 644 yuan in 1978. The period from 1963 to 1965 was even more typical. The annual income for the urban workers and staff during this period dropped as compared with that in 1957.

From the description above, it can be concluded that the one-sided pursuit for a higher degree and a wider scope of public ownership, particularly state ownership, is not necessarily conducive to the improvement of economic efficiency and people's living standards. On the contrary, it impoverished the farmers to the point of desperation. In time of natural disasters, many farmers had to leave their homes begging. After Mao Zedong passed away and Deng Xiaoping took over the helm, a political environment favorable for reform gradually took shape in the wake of a drive to emancipate the mind. The Third Plenary Session of the 11th Central Committee of the Chinese Communist Party was held in December 1978. The session reinstated the ideological line of "seeking truths from facts," which marked the prelude of China's reform and open-up drive. Also in December 1978, the 20 farmer households in Xiaogang Village, Fengyang County, Anhui Province decided to share out the village's land. As a result, they reaped a bumper harvest the next year, increasing the total grain output from the original 15,000 kilograms to 60,000 kilograms in a single year. The breakthrough made by the village produced a tremendous demonstrative effect and aroused intense dispute as well. Nevertheless, the event marked the initiation of China's rural reform, especially the reform of land ownership system in the rural areas. In the urban areas, meanwhile, in order to tackle the problem of reemployment for large numbers of urban educated youths, who were sent to the countryside previously and were allowed to return to the cities, the government gradually lifted control over non-state-owned economic sectors, allowing people to set up individually owned businesses. In August 1980, the Central Committee of the Chinese Communist Party put forward the employment policy characterized by "employment via introduction of labor departments, employment in organizations formed on a voluntary basis and self-sought employment." This policy cut a new path for the development of a diversified economy and represented a breakthrough in the monolithic system of public ownership.

2. The Course and Stages in the Reform of the Ownership System

Reform in the ownership system involves many aspects. But, the basic trend has been to gradually lift control over non-state-owned economic sectors, especially the non-publicly owned sectors, so as to enable the privately owned sectors to acquire a lawful status and grow steadily. In view of the policy changes regarding the non-public sectors since the launch of the reform drive, China's reform of the ownership system from 1978 to 1999 can be roughly divided into four stages.

The first stage extended from the Third Plenary Session of the 11th Party Central Committee in 1978 to the Third Plenary Session of the 12th Party Central Committee in 1984. During this period, the focus was to give the survival and development of the individual sector a lawful status. The Third Plenary Session of the 11th Central Committee of the Chinese Communist Party rehabilitated the ideological line of seeking truths from facts, shifted the focus of work from class struggle to economic construction and established principle of reform and opening to the outside world. In August 1980, the Party Central Committee, in the "Circular on Transmitting the Document of the National Meeting on Labor and Employment," criticized the defects of the traditional concept about ownership, pointing out, "For many years, we have given undue stress to the `massive and public nature' in the production relations, overstressed the transition of collective economy to state-run economy, suppressed and eliminated the individual economy." On the basis of such criticism, the document pointed out that it was necessary to "encourage and support the development of the individual cconomy in cities and towns." In June1981, the Sixth Session of the 11th Party

Central Committee approved the "Resolution on Certain Questions in the History of Our Party since the Founding of the People's Republic of China." The document pointed out, "The state economy and the collective economy are the basic forms of the Chinese economy. The working people's individual economy within certain prescribed limits is a necessary complement to the public economy." The "Constitution of the People's Republic of China" adopted at the Fifth Meeting of the Fifth National People's Congress held in December 1982 stipulated, "The individual economy of urban and rural working people, operating within the limits prescribed by law, is a complement to the socialist public economy. The state protects the lawful rights and interests of the individual economy." Since then, the individual economy has been ensured a legal status, which in turn promoted its restoration and development.

From 1978 to 1984, the number of individual laborers in urban and rural areas increased from 150,000 to 3.39 million, and the number of employees in foreign-funded enterprises and other non-publicly owned sectors also amounted to 370,000. Meanwhile, much progress was also made in rural reform. On the one hand, in terms of land relationship, the collective mode of management, featured by "ownership at three levels (people's communes, production brigades and production teams) with the production teams as the base," was gradually abandoned to give way to the household-based management system by fixing output quotas to individual households or production groups. The No. 1 document of the Party Central Committee in 1982 ratified the various forms of responsibility system as "production responsibility system of the socialist collective economy" and this made it possible for the adoption of the household responsibility system nationwide. By 1983, some 98 percent of the production teams throughout the country had adopted the household responsibility system based on fixed output quotas. In the same year, the system of people's commune fell apart. In 1983, the number of communes disintegrated was 12,702; in 1984, it amounted to 39830; and in 1985, it was 249. To replace the people's communes and production teams, 61,766 towns and townships and 847,894 villagers' committees were established. On the other hand, while conducting a reform of the land system, control over the farmers engaging in non-agricultural trades was relaxed, "enterprises of the people's communes and production brigades" under the people's commune system were turned into "township enterprises" while the rural individual economy and economy operated on the basis of association of individual households became an integral part of the township enterprise economy. Statistics collected by the Ministry of Agriculture on township enterprises indicated that in 1984 the number of township enterprises reached 6.065 million, whose payroll added up to 52.08 million and whose total income amounted to 153.7 billion yuan. Of them, the number of individual enterprises and enterprises set up by associations of individual households reached 5.415 million, their number of employees grew to 13.6 million and their total income was 26.8 billion yuan.

The second stage covered the period from 1984 when the Third Plenary Session of the 12th Central Committee of the Chinese Communist Party was held to 1987 when the 13th National Party Congress was held. In terms of policy changes, the focus was to give permission to the existence and development of private economy. Along with the development of individual economy, businesses operated with hired laborers began to arise. In 1983, the Party Central Committee put forward a "three-don'ts" policy with regard to this sector of the economy, that is, "don't advocate, don't publicize and don't ban in haste." In 1984, Deng Xiaoping's attitude toward the economy with hired laborers was to "wait for two years and see." The Third Plenary Session of the 12th Party Central Committee held in October 1984 adopted the "Decision on Reform of the Economic Structure." The document gave a comprehensive account of the status and role of the sector under the ownership of the whole people, the collective sector, the individual sector and foreign-invested sector in the entire socialist economic structure, and proposed that it was necessary to "uphold the development of diversified economic forms and diversified modes of economic operation." As a result, this turned out to be an encouragement to the development of the individual sector, private sector and the sector operated with foreign investment. In January 1987, in a document titled "Intensifying the Reform in Rural Areas," the Party Central Committee pointed out, "For a considerably long period to come, the presence of individual economy and a small number of privately owned enterprises is unavoidable." Regarding the privately owned enterprises, the document said, "The principle of allowing them to exist, strengthening control, bringing into play what is good and doing away with what is harmful should be adopted." In September 1987, the report to the 13th National Party Congress advanced the theory of primary stage of socialism. This proved to be an important milestone in the theoretical exploration about socialism. With regard to the privately owned economy, the report pointed out that the development of different types of ownership, with the public ownership remaining dominant, and even allowing the private sector to exist and development "are determined by the actual condition of productive forces at the primary stage of socialism, and it is the only way to promote their development." The report maintained, "Public ownership should remain predominant in the primary stage of socialist society. However, others sectors of the economy that are not owned by the whole people are far from adequately developed. Co-operative, individual and private sectors of the economy in both urban and rural areas should all be encouraged to expand."

The third stage extended from the First Meeting of the Seventh National People's Congress, held in 1988, to 1997, prior to the convention of the 15th National Party Congress. The major feature of this period was that the private economy, having acquired the "legitimate status," gradually got the right to compete with other economic sectors on an equal footing along with the continuous deepening of China's reform and opening to the outside world. Of course, due to the constantly changing political and economic situation inside and outside China, the course for the private economy to obtain such legitimate status and equality was a tenuous one.

In line with the suggestion included in the report to the 13th National Party Congress, the First Meeting of the Seventh National People's Congress was held in April 1988 to adopt "Amendments to the Constitution of the People's Republic of China." The amended Article 11 of the Constitution stipulates, "The state permits the private sector of the economy to exist and develop within the limits prescribed by law. Private sector of the economy is a complement to the socialist public economy. The state protects the lawful rights and interest of the private sector of the economy, and exercises guidance, supervision and control over the private sector of the economy." The amendment affirmed the legality of the existence and development of the private sector of the economy. Shortly afterwards, the State Council issued some specific regulations and decrees concerning the private sector of the economy. One of the example was the "Interim Provisions Regarding Privately Owned Enterprises in the People's Republic of China." The State Administration of Industry and Commerce Bureau also began to accept registration applications turned in by the privately owned enterprises according to law.

However, the campaign launched in China to consolidate the economic order in the second half of 1988 somewhat held back the development of the private sector, which had just acquired a legitimate status. In the nationwide tax check-up conducted in 1989, the phenomenon occurred to mete out over-serious punishment to privately owned enterprises. The general public described this situation as "pinning flowers over the chest in the first half of the year and putting on the fetters in the second." Furthermore, the No.9 document of the Central Committee of the Chinese Communist Party in 1989 stipulated, "Owners of privately owned enterprises cannot be Communist Party members." This produced a very bad influence on the development of the private sector of the economy. When the consolidation campaign came to an end, the No.15 document issued by the Party Central Committee in 1991 terminated the implementation of the principle of "utilization, restriction and transformation" towards the private sector, and clearly specified, "The owners of privately owned enterprises now should not be analogized and equated to industrialists and businessmen of the past in an oversimplified manner, and still less should they be forced to undergo the socialist transformation as did in the 1950s."

In October 1992, the report to the 14th National Party Congress stated the objective of China's economic reform is to set up a socialist market economic system. It broke through the traditional mode of thinking that everything must be considered in the terms of "socialism" or "capitalism." Consequently, the report turned out to be the manifesto for the second round of mind emancipation since the launching of the reform and opening drive. It again confirmed the necessity to establish an ownership structure in which diverse economic elements could exist side by side. In November 1993, the Third Plenary Session of the 14th Central Committee of the Chinese Communist Party approved the "Decision on Some Issues Concerning the Establishment of a Socialist Market Economic Structure." With regard to the ownership reform, the decision pointed out, "It is necessary to uphold the principle of taking the public owned sector as the mainstay, while striving for simultaneous development of all economic sectors." It said, "The state should create conditions for economic sectors under different kinds of ownership to compete in the market on equal terms, and should deal with various types of enterprises without discrimination." The document also specified that it was necessary to accelerate the pace of the reform of state-owned enterprises in line with the requirements of the modern enterprise system. As for small state-owned enterprises, they could even be sold to collectives and individuals. In general, the Third Plenary Session of the 14th Party Central Committee outlined the basic framework of the socialist market economic system in China and changed the traditional concepts that the state only cared about the development of the public sector of the economy but not that of the non-public sectors, and even adopting restrictive policies for the non-public sectors. Since then, the non-public sectors have acquired the status to participate in market competition on equal terms with the publicly owned sector. The time from 1988 to 1997 was a historical period of simultaneous development of diversified economic elements in China. During this period, rapid development was witnessed in the individual sector of the economy in both urban and rural areas, in the private sector, in the foreign-invested sector as well as in various other economic sectors with a mixed ownership. For instance, from 1989 to 1997 the number of privately owned enterprises, their payroll and their annual growth of output value increased by 34.3 percent, 30.1 percent and 58.8 percent, respectively.

The fourth stage runs from the 15th National Party Congress to the present. The main feature of this stage is to clarify the important status and role of the various non-public sectors in the socialist market economy. The report to the 15th National Party Congress, which was adopted in September 1997, summarized the experience gained in the ownership reform over the previous 20 years, clearly pointing out, "It is China's basic economic system for the primary stage of socialism to retain a dominant position for public ownership and to develop diverse forms of ownership side by side." The report also said, "The non-public sector is an important component part of China's socialist market economy. We should continue to encourage and guide the non-public sector comprising self-employed and private businesses to facilitate its sound development. This is of great importance to satisfy the diverse needs of the people, increasing employment and promoting the development of the national economy." The report is the most comprehensive document to expound the ownership reform ever since the time when policy of reform and opening to the outside world was put into effect.

The "Amendments to the Constitution of the People's Republic of China" adopted at the Second Meeting of the Ninth National People's Congress in March 1999 stipulates, "In the primary stage of socialism, the state upholds the basic economic system with the dominance of the public ownership and the simultaneous development of an economy of diverse forms of ownership, and upholds the distribution system with the dominance of distribution according to work and the coexistence of diverse of modes of distribution." It also states, "The non-public sector of the economy comprising self-employed and private businesses within the domain stipulated by law is an important component of the country's socialist market economy," and "The state protects the legitimate rights and interests of the self-employed and private businesses."

II. Changes in Ownership Structure

The ownership reform not only has promoted the readjustment of the ownership relations but also brought about changes in the ownership structure. At present, in collecting economic statistics, China divides the various elements of ownership into nine sectors, namely, state-owned sector, collective sector, private sector, individual sector, jointly operated sector, the sector under the joint-stock system, foreign-funded sector, the sector with investment from Hongkong, Macao and Taiwan and the sector operated under other forms of ownership. Of them, the publicly owned sector covers the state-owned sector, the collective sector and the state and collectively owned elements under mixed ownership. The non-publicly owned sector consists of the private sector, the individual sector, the sector under other forms of ownership as well as the privately and individually owned elements under mixed ownership. And the sector under mixed ownership includes joint partnership sector, the joint sector under the joint-stock system, foreign-funded sector and the sector with investment from Hongkong, Macao and Taiwan.

Since the adoption of the reform policy, marked changes have taken place in China's ownership structure. The most noticeable change is that the dominant position of the public sector has been maintained while a continuous growth has been achieved in absolute amount despite its proportional decline in the total of the national economy. The growth rate and proportion of the state-owned sector have gone down but its leading position has remained. The non-publiclt owned sector has witnessed a rapid growth. But, the development of the individual sector, the private sector, the foreign-funded sector and the sector operating under various forms of mixed ownership has shown different features.

1. The Proportion of Publicly Owned Sector Has Declined, Yet Its Dominant Position in the National Economy Has Maintained.

Since the adoption of the reform policy, the biggest change in China's ownership structure is that the proportion of the publicly owned sector has declined while that of the non-publicly owned sector has been on the rise. According to recent calculations by the State Statistical Bureau, from 1978 to 1997 the proportion of GDP generated by the publicly owned sector (including the state-owned sector and the collective sector) dropped from 94.7 percent to 75.8 percent in the national total, down by 18.9 percentage point in a span of 20 years, or down by one percentage point in each year. By contrast, the proportion of GDP generated by the non-public sector went up from 5.3 percent to 24.2 percent, accounting for nearly one-fourth of the total GDP of the country. The non-publicly owned sector has become an important component part of China's national economy (see Table 1-3).

Table 1-3. Structural Changes of GDP Generated by Publicly Owned Sector and Non-Publicly Owned Sector from 1978 to 1997

(Unit: 100 million yuan)

Year	Publicly Owned Sector				Non-Publicly Owned Sector	
	Total GDP by State-owned Sector	Proportion of GDP by State-owned Sector (%)	Total GDP by Collective Sector	Proportion of GDP by Collective Sector (%)	Total GDP by Non-Public Sector	Proportion of GDP by Non-Public Sector (%)
1978	2,092	57.7	1,342	37.0	190	5.3
1985	4,288	47.8	3,632	40.5	1,044	11.6
1990	9,039	48.6	7,105	38.2	2,436	13.1
1995	22,222	38.0	23,274	39.8	12,988	22.2
1997	30,777	41.9	24,900	33.9	17,776	24.2

Source of Data: *Statistical Data* by State Statistical Bureau, Issue No. 9, 1999.

Industry holds a leading position in the national economy. In terms of the structure of total industrial GDP, the gross industrial output value generated by state-owned and collectively owned industry dropped from 100 percent in 1978 to 67.1 percent in 1998, down by about 37 percentage point. Meanwhile, the proportion of gross industrial output value produced by non-publicly owned economy exceeded one-third of the national total (see Table 1-4).

From the perspective of capital input, the proportion of investment in the public sector of the economy had steadily dropped from 81.5 percent in 1981 to 68.1 percent in 1998 in the composite of investment in fixed assets, down by 13.4 percentage point. At the same time, however, the proportion of invèstment in the non-publicly owned sector reached one-third of the total invested in fixed assets by 1998 (see Table 1-5). From the perspective of the ratio between the gross industrial assets and industrial fixed assets, the dominant position of the public sector is even more obvious, with the industrial assets in the non-public sector of the economy accounting only for about 16 percent of the total industrial fixed assets (see Table 1-6).

Table 1-4. Composite Structure of China's Gross Industrial Output Value from 1978 to 1998 (%)

Year	State-owned Industry and Industry with Shares Held by the State	Collective Industry	Individually Operated Industry in Urban and Rural Areas	Industry under Other Forms of Ownership
1978	77.6	22.4	--	--
1980	76.0	23.5	--	0.5
1985	64.9	32.1	1.8	1.2
1990	54.6	35.6	5.4	4.4
1995	34.0	36.6	12.9	16.5
1998	28.5	38.3	18.9	19.9

Source of Data: *China Statistical Synopsis (1999)* by State Statistical Bureau, p. 100.

Note: Some of the statistics on the gross output value of state-owned industry and industry with shares held by the state and the statistics on various forms of industry are repeatedly calculated. That is why the add-up total exceeds more than 100 percent.

Table 1-5. Composite of Investment in Fixed Assets in Various Economic Sectors (%)

Type of Investment	1981	1985	1990	1995	1997	1998
State-owned Sector	69.5	66.1	66.1	54.4	52.5	55.0
Collective Sector	12.0	12.9	11.7	16.4	15.4	13.1
Individual Sector	18.5	21.0	22.2	12.8	13.8	12.8
Other Types of Economy				16.4	18.3	19.1

Data source: *China Statistical Synopsis 1999* by State Statistical Bureau, p. 8.

Table 1-6. Structural Changes of Investment by Industrial Units Practicing Independent Accounting in Various Economic Sectors (%)

Type of Investment	1980	1985	1990	1995	1997	1998
Percentage in Gross Industrial Assets						
State-owned Industry	87.3	80.9	75.8	58.9	57.2	69.2
Collective Industry	12.3	18.1	20.6	19.1	16.0	14.1
Other Types of Industry	0.4	1.0	3.7	22.0	26.8	16.7
Percentage in Industrial Fixed Assets						
State-owned Industry	90.3	85.2	79.8	63.7	63.5	72.0
Collective Industry	9.4	14.0	16.5	15.7	12.8	12.2
Other Types of Industry	0.6	0.8	3.7	21.6	33.7	15.8

Source of Data: *Study on the Quality of Industrial Growth* by Guo Kesha, et al., p. 193; *China Statistical Almanac (1998)* by the State Statistical Bureau, p. 445; *China Statistical Synopsis (1999)* by the State Statistical Bureau, p. 109. Of the statistics for 1998, the statistics of state-owned industry include those from the industrial enterprises with shares controlled by the state, while the collection of the statistics covered all state-owned enterprises and enterprises under non-public ownership with an annual income of no less than 5 million yuan from sales of their products.

2. The State-Owned Economic Sector Still Holds a Leading Position despite a Rapid Decline in Its Proportion in the National Economy.

An important objective of China's ownership reform is to alter the situation in which the state-owned economy comprised the sole economic sector formed under the system of planned economy and gradually reduce the proportion of state-owned sector while making sure to maintain its leading position in the national economy.

The leading role of the state-owned economic sector is largely reflected in its strength of control. Under the conditions of the socialist market economy, the strength of control of the state-owned sector means that the state-owned sector can become the dominant force in the overall economic development and operation. The strength of control is manifested in terms of quantity. More importantly, it should be reflected in terms of quality (that is, whether the state-owned sector can really play a leading role in the national economy).

Since the launching of the reform, the absolute amount of GDP produced by the state-owned sector has kept increasing. From 1978 to 1998, the gross industrial output value turned out by the state-owned sector witnessed an annual average growth of 8.7 percent as calculated in comparable prices. The net value of fixed assets of state-owned industry increased by 14.5 percent each year. The total amount of profits and taxes of the state-owned industry was up 11.8 percent annually. Calculated in current prices, the total inventory of the state-owned economic sector amounted to 2916.2 billion yuan in 1998 as compared with 209.2 billion yuan in 1978, representing a 14-fold increase. The gross output value of state-owned industry increased from 328.9 billion yuan to 2902.8 billion yuan, a 9-fold increase. The net value of fixed assets of state-owned enterprises that practiced independent accounting jumped from 320.1 billion yuan to 2451.4 billion yuan, representing an increase of nearly 8-fold.

Compared with the economic sectors under other forms of ownership, the growth of the state-owned sector has been relatively slow, which explains the obvious decline of its proportion in the total national economy. The proportion of GDP generated by the state-owned sector dropped by 15.8 percentage point from 1978 to 1997, while the proportion of the output value generated by the state-owned industry in the country's total industrial output value dived by 52.1 percentage point, the proportion of investment in the state-owned sector dropped by 17 percentage point and that of fixed assets of state-owned industry dipped by 29.9 percentage point.

Viewing the national economy as a whole, however, the state-owned sector still makes the largest proportion and holds a dominant position in various key industries. Now, the state-owned sector still holds a control and even monopolist position in basic, naturally monopolist and special industries, such as infrastructure development, which includes resource exploitation, raw materials production, transport and communications, energy, water conservancy, post and telecommunications facilities, as well as such special industries as national defense and tobacco processing. It also exercises a rather tight control in some important key industries that are vital to the national socio-economic development and people's livelihood, such as the petroleum, metallurgical, machine-building, medicinal, chemical engineering, electric power, aeronautics as well as post and telecommunications industries. In these industries, the state-owned sector not only occupies a higher proportion, but also, through controlling the large enterprises, plays a regulatory role in the entire industries.

3. Rapid Development of the Non-public Sector Has Promoted the Deepening of the Economic Restructuring and Rapid Growth of the National Economy.

The individual sector, private sector and foreign-funded sector are the three major types of non-public economy that have developed rapidly since China launched its reform drive. In the course of the economic restructuring, the economic sector under various forms of mixed ownership has also witnessed fairly rapid development.

Due to its previous low and uneven level of development, the individual sector enjoys a bright prospect for development. With control over it being increasingly relaxed, the individual sector has experienced continuous development in both amount and scope (see Table 1-7). By the end of 1997, the number of individually owned units throughout the country had only been next to that of farm-households; their total output value had accounted for 17.9 percent of the national total; and their number of employees had increased by 361-fold as compared with 1978. The individual sector has become an imp ortant channel to tackle the problem of employment in China.

On the basis of the development of the individual sector, the private sector also began to grow. In 1988, the number of privately owned enterprises registered exceeded 40,000, and they hired a total of more than 700,000 people. During the period of "economic consolidation" (1989-1991), the pace of development of the private sector slowed down. Yet, they had continuously expanded in size. As of 1990, the private sector has been developing by leaps and bounds, becoming the most rapidly growing economic sector in China (see Table 1-8).

Table 1-7. Statistical Survey on Development of the Individual Sector of China's Economy from 1978 to 1997

Year	Number of Households (thousand)	Number of Employees (thousand)	Turnover (100 m yuan)	Gross Output Value (100 m yuan)
1978	140a	150a	--	1b
1988	14,550	23,000	--	516
1990	13,280	20,930	--	1,290
1995	25,280	46,139	8,972.5	11,821
1997	28,509	54,410	11,554.2c	20,376

Source of Data: *China Statistical Almanac (1998)*, edited by the State Statistical Bureau, p. 433.

Note: In the table, "a" stands for the number of individually owned economic units in cities and towns, "b" stands for statistics collected in 1980, while "c" stands for statistics collected in 1996.

The foreign-funded sector has also witnessed development in the course of reform and opening to the outside world. From 1979 to 1997, China managed to bring in a total amount of US$220.162 billion of foreign investment. Since 1993, China has ranked the second in the import of foreign investment for five years in a run. By the end of 1997, some 235,681 foreign-funded enterprises had been registered in China. Of them, 145,000 had gone into operation, employing 1.75 million people. The utilization of foreign capital not only solved China's problem of lack of funds for domestic construction, promoted its economic growth, brought in advanced technology, equipment and management expertise, accelerated the readjustment of the industrial mix and technological upgrading, trained personnel much needed by the country, altered the situation of seclusion and brought forth a new open-type economic system, it also helped facilitate the reform of the economic structure and change people's minds. Facts have proved that utilizing foreign capital and opening to the outside world are indispensable in our efforts to expedite the country's modernization drive.

Table 1-8. Development of the Private Sector from 1989 to 1997

Year	Units		Employees		Registered Capital		Output Value		Retail Sales of Consumer Goods	
	Number	Increase over the previous year(%)	Number (thousand)	Increase over the previous year(%)	Amount (billion yuan)	Increase over the previous year(%)	Amount (billion yuan)	Increase over the previous year(%)	Amount (billion yuan)	Increase over the previous year(%)
1989	90,581		1,640		8.4		9.7		3.4	
1990	98,141	8.3	1,700	3.7	9.5	13.1	12.2	25.8	4.3	26.5
1991	107,843	9.9	1,840	8.2	12.3	29.5	14.7	20.5	5.7	32.6
1992	139,633	29.5	2,320	26.1	22.1	79.7	20.5	39.5	9.1	59.6
1993	237,919	70.4	3,730	60.8	68.1	208.1	42.2	105.9	19	109.8
1994	432,240	81.7	6,480	73.7	144.8	112.6	114	170.1	75.9	299.5
1995	654,531	51.4	9,560	47.5	262.2	81.1	229.5	101.3	100.6	32.5
[illegible]	819,252	25.2	11,710	22.5	375.2	43.1	322.7	40.6	145.9	45.0
[illegible]	960,726	17.3	13,490	15.2	514	37.0	392.3	21.6	185.5	27.1
[illegible]	[illegible]4.3		30.1		67.2		58.8		64.9	

[illegible]*ence*, February 10, 1999.

Table 1- 9. Position of Foreign-funded Enterprises in China's National Economy

Year	1996	1997
Amount of Foreign Investment Actually Used (billion US dollars)	54.8	64.4
Proportion of Foreign Investment in Total Investment in Fixed Assets (%)	11.7	10.8
Number of People Employed by Foreign-Invested Enterprises (thousand people)	--	17,500
Total Volume of Import and Export by Foreign-Invested Enterprises (billion US dollars)	137.1	152.6
Proportion of Import-Export Volume of Foreign-Invested Enterprises in National Total (%)	47.3	46.9
Total Tax Levy from Foreign-Invested Enterprises (billion US dollars)	87.0	99.3
Proportion of Tax Collected from Foreign-Invested Enterprises in National Total Tax Revenue(%)	14.26	13.16

Source of Data: *China Statistical Almanac (1998)*, by State Statistical Bureau, p.
...*a (1998)* by the Institute of Indus-
...cial Sciences, p. 90.

...as Laid the ...Market Economy

...nt factors in the production
... the relations of distribution
...at the same time, exerts an
...y big social change or revo-
...bout changes in the original

ownership relations. China's reform of the traditional economic structure since the launching of the reform and opening-up drive started with the reform in ownership. With people's understanding of the ownership system enhanced, China's reform of the economic structure has been further deepened, thus laying the foundation for the development of a socialist market economy.

I. The Reform in Ownership Has Created a Diversified Variety of Market Subjects Compatible with the Socialist Market Economy.

Under the traditional planned economy, the public sector held a monopolistic position in almost every field of production and management. This was a situation that was further complicated by using mandatory plans as the major means in allocating resources. Under this situation, the state-owned and collective enterprises, and even economic units under the people's communes and production brigades, were actually not independent economic entities. At the most, they were production workshops or accounting units under the system of planned economy, without any initiative and enthusiasm for optimal economic returns. Because of the lack of vitality in the micro-economic units, the country had to rely on the mobilization of the government to achieve economic growth by massively increasing the input of manpower, funds and other resources, even at cost of the deterioration of the ecological environment.

Thanks to the reform in the relations of allocation of resources, such as the means of production and various other factors of production, a diversified variety of micro-economic entities have come into being. In the countryside, as the farmers have acquired three forms of property rights, they have become independent interest subjects;(2) as a dark horse, the rural (or township-run) enterprises have turned out to be the forerunner in breaking the state's monopoly in industry and commerce and in bringing into effect the market forces. With regard to individually and privately owned enterprises, enterprises operating solely with foreign investment, Sino-foreign joint ventures and Sino-foreign partnership enterprises as well as enterprises under various forms of mixed ownership, they all are by definition micro-economic entities that take part in market competition and work for their independent economic interests. In 1997, there were 234.06 million rural households, over 28 million urban and rural individual enterprises, more than 1 million privately owned enterprises and 240,000 foreign-invested enterprises.

The vigorous development of economic units in the non-publicly owned sector has spurred on the reform of state-owned enterprises as well as the urban and rural collectively owned enterprises. Competition from the non-state enterprises has put an end to the monopoly of state-owned enterprises, gradually compelled them to develop towards the direction featured by autonomous management and operation, taking sole responsibility for their own profits and losses, seeking self-development and enforcing self-control. Moreover, it has also represented the objective of the reform of the state-owned enterprises — to become independent commodity producers and managers, which is also the most important feature of true enterprises under the conditions of market economy. Although China's reform of state-owned enterprises still has long road to go from attaining its desired goal, yet compared with the situation at the early stage of the reform, the state-owned enterprises have become more market-orientated. In particular, since 1990, as China has adopted various flexible measures in the ownership reform in the state-owned and collectively owned enterprises, including the introduction of the joint-stock system and joint-stock partnership, many small and medium-sized state-owned enterprises, particularly those collectively owned enterprises, have turned into privately owned ones or ones operating under a mixed ownership. In other words, they have gradually become completely independent commodity producers and managers. Thanks to the emergence of a huge number of independent commodity producers and managers as well as other types of economic units in the course of the ownership reform, a solid micro-economic foundation has been laid for China's market economy.

II. Ownership Reform Has Spu tinuous Improvement of the Mar

Modern market economy is an e sources are mainly allocated by me preconditions for the market force developed and sound market system. organic composite formed by various kinds of markets. The maturity of the market system is inseparable from ownership reform. Not only that the emergence of a diversified variety of market subjects is closely related to the ownership reform, the transactions between the various market subjects as well as the formulation and improvement of rules for transaction are also inseparable from the market environment and rules that are conducive to fair competition created by the ownership reform. The state-owned sector and the collective sector are two different types of public economy, that is, they represent two different levels of public ownership. In the past, even these two sectors did not enjoy equal conditions and positions in obtaining resources, not to mention that the non-public sector was subject to suppression and discrimination. If the rules for market transactions were not fair, it would be impossible to establish a well-developed market system. It is in the course of the ownership reform that China has brought into being the market system and, at the same time, continuously improved the rules for market transactions.

Prior to the reform, China practiced a rigid planned economic system. At that time, harsh measures were taken to restrict the role of the market and even ban traditional market fairs. Of the total sales of farm products in 1978, that part with prices fixed by the state accounted for 94.4 percent; and of the total sales of industrial products, that part with prices fixed by the state made up for 97.95 percent. Moreover, almost all the service products were placed under state control. The overwhelming part of the exchange of products and services was not done through the market. So there is nothing to be said about the existence of markets for products and services. As the factors of production (such as land, capital, labor and technology) were not considered "commodities"

ays, there was no point to talk about the existence and devel-
t of markets for production factors.

The ownership reform has promoted the establishment and improvement of a market system in China. First, the markets for agricultural produce and industrial consumer goods have been restored and developed. Thanks to the development of the market system over the past 20 years, the rate of agricultural products transacted in the market increased from 5.6 percent in 1978 to 77.20 percent in 1997, while that of industrial products went up from 2.5 percent to 68.30 percent and that of service products was up from practically zero to 41.1 percent. Generally speaking, the rate of marketization for all products had risen from 2.56 percent in 1978 to 61.71 percent in 1997.(3)

Second, the market for production means has witnessed development. Prior to the reform, the means of production were not considered commodities and their exchanges were banned in the market; they were distributed by means of allocation as ordinary products. In 1978, for example, 256 products were earmarked for unified allocation by the central government, 316 were allocated by the various state departments, and the rest were allocated by the local governments according to pre-set plans. Since the launching of the reform drive, planned allocation of production means by the government has gradually faded out along with the establishment of the market for the means of production. By the mid-1990s, China had set up over 1,000 wholesale markets, each with an annual business volume of more than 100 million yuan and over 3,000 wholesale markets for agricultural and sideline products, in addition to some 20 futures markets. Meanwhile, 82,982 market fairs and several million retail enterprises had cropped up throughout the country.

The emergence and development of markets for various production factors are a major indicator of the establishment of the market system in China. Now, the financial market in China already comprises various kinds of securities markets and stock markets. Markets for different production factors, such as labor, technology and information, land and real estates, have taken shape. According to calculations by some scholars, by 1997 the rate of marketization for capital reached 17.2 percent, that for land was 22.5 percent, and that for labor, 70 percent. In total, the marketization rate for production factors had reached 36.57 percent.

The ownership reform had made it possible for commodities and production factors to enter the market and be exchanged there. Moreover, it has also created the condition conducive to the maturity of the market. The 14th National Party Congress, held in 1992, again confirmed the objective of China's economic reform, that is, to shift from the planned economy to the socialist market economy. It means that market would replace planning as the basic means in the allocation of resources -- an extremely crucial step in the country's transition from planned economy to market economy.

III. The Ownership Reform Has Promoted the Formation of the Market Mechanism.

The market-orientated reform of the economic structure has made it possible for China's market mechanism to continuously grow to maturity. The participation in market competition by economic entities under different forms of ownership has promoted the establishment of the market system.

By market mechanism, it refers to the mechanism of economic operation according to which the market subjects readjust their allocation of resources through market competition, the changes in supply, demand and prices. It mainly comprises of the price mechanism, supply-demand mechanism, competition mechanism, risk mechanism and the mechanism of letting the successful ones survive and the unsuccessful ones parish. Of them, the price mechanism is the most important, because in market competition the fluctuation of prices will lead to changes in market supply and demand. Consequently, resources will flow from production units whose products are in surplus to those whose products fall short of demand, and from poorly operated enterprises to soundly operated ones, thus realizing the rational allocation of resources.

Through reform over the past 20 years, China has basically formed a market pricing system under the state's macro control. In 1996, the proportion of market-regulated prices in total retail sales jumped from 3 percent in 1978 to 92.5 percent, with the proportion of state-fixed prices dropping to 6.3 percent. Virtually all control has been lifted over the prices of all kinds of services in competitive trades. Agent prices have been adopted for over 95 percent of import commodities. So, it can be said that market prices are playing a leading role with regard to commodities and services. In the market of production factors, a market mechanism has gradually been established and grown to maturity for salaries and wages as a labor prices and interest as capital price as well as for the prices of land and technology. Non-publicly owned enterprises, foreign-funded enterprises in particular, have been acquiring various production factors by the market price system. This has posed a serious challenge to enterprises in the public sector. Along with the progress in marketization, the role played by the price mechanism has become increasingly obvious in readjusting the allocation of resources.

IV. The Ownership Reform Has Compelled the Government to Change Its Mode of Macro Control.

The reform in the ownership system and the diversification of the economic structure have strengthened increasingly the independence of the market subjects. The government has gradually reduced its direct intervention in micro-economic organizations as well as direct control over the allocation of resources. This has helped make the market mechanism the basic means in the allocation of resources. The government has shifted its focus of work from intervening in the operation of micro-economic organizations to reinforcing macro-economic regulation and control. And the basic concept of "the market guiding the enterprises and the government regulating the market" has been gradually formed in the course of reform.

In order to bring macro control into better play, the Chinese government has continuously reshuffled its departments, gradually shifted from direct intervention in the allocation of resources and the operation of concrete macro-economic organizations to exercising macro control over the national economy by indirect means. To do this, it has step by step repealed those government departments that exercised direct control over micro-economic units and strengthened those that are responsible for comprehensive coordination. In addition, more attention has been paid to regulating the economic operation by such economic means as financial, tax, currency, interest and industrial policies. Without the reform in the ownership system, it would not be possible for the government to make use of such economic measures, because under the condition that public sector alone held the dominant position it would not be possible for the market mechanism to develop as it would be much easier and less costly for the government to allocate the resources by administrative means. Thanks to the diversification of the economic subjects and the development of the market mechanism, direct administrative means have gradually lost their effect. Only by regulating the market with the economic means could it be possible for the government to play a positive guiding role.

V. The Ownership Reform Has Promoted the Development of the Market Legal System and the Establishment of the Social Security System.

The sound operation of the market economy depends on a well-established legal framework that provides the guarantee for the formulation and implementation of market rules. It also calls for a social security system that covers the whole society.

Market economy is a law-based economy. Law plays the guiding, standardizing, guaranteeing and restricting roles in a market economy.

Laws are an important means for the government to enforce macro control. They also guarantee that the market mechanism plays its role and the market subjects compete on equal terms. The progress of the ownership reform has gradually clarified that economic entities under different forms of ownership should enjoy see to it that their property and other legitimate rights are protected. For instance, China has amended on three occasions the Constitution of the People's Republic of China since the launching of the reform drive. The 15th National

Congress of Communist Party, in particular, made it clear that, "It is necessary to improve the legal system concerning property and protect the legitimate rights and interests of, and fair competition among, all types of enterprises." This has provided the legal basis for fair competition between the various economic elements in the market. Since the launching of reform in 1978, the National People's Congress has enacted and promulgated more than 400 laws and regulations. Thousands of administrative rules and regulations have been enacted by the State Council, the various ministries and commissions and the local governments at various levels. A legal framework that is compatible with the socialist market economy has taken shape.

In order to ensure the sound operation of the market economy, it is also necessary to establish a social security system that covers the whole society, because the social insurance serves as a "network of safety" for market economy in modern times. Under China's traditional planned economy, the social security system only covered the workers and staff in state-owned enterprises and part of the workers and staff in collective enterprises in both urban and rural areas. Despite the limited coverage, it was also unfair to some extent. Along with the development of an economy under diversified ownership, China has carried out reform of its traditional social security system. Now, the basic framework of a modern social security system, which is designed to cover the whole society, has been set up in the urban areas.

The practice in China's reform of the economic structure shows that the adjustment in the relations of ownership and breakthroughs made in the ownership reform are an important guarantee for the success of the reform. The success of the reform in the rural areas is mainly attributed to the success of the reform in the ownership. And the reform in the urban areas, particularly the reform of the large and medium-sized enterprises, has also developed in depth and reached the stage of reform in the ownership system. The ownership reform has promoted the diversification of economic subjects, gradually brought into being a basic framework of the market economic system and made it possible for the market forces to play the basic role in the allocation of resources. "The reform in ownership and the development of the non-state sector of economy are both the institutional causes for the tremendous achievements in China's economic reform and development and the institutional precondition for further success in China's economic reform and development."(4)

Section 3
Theoretical Breakthroughs Made in China's Ownership Reform

Over the past two decades, the ownership reform in China has kept developing in depth. The generalization of the ownership reform in the report to the 15th National Congress of the Chinese Communist Party serves as a summary of the experience gained in the reform over the past 20 years; it also represents a great leap forward in the understanding of the theory of ownership under socialism.

I. At the Primary Stage of Socialism, China's Basic Economic System is to Maintain the Dominant Position of Public Ownership while Ensuring a Simultaneous Development of Diverse Forms of Ownership.

The report to the 15th National Party Congress pointed out, "It is China's basic economic system for the primary stage of socialism to retain a dominant position for public ownership and to develop diverse forms of ownership side by side." This is fundamentally different from the traditional theory of socialism that excludes non-public sectors outside of the socialist economic system. It shows that the Chinese Communist Party has turned away from its traditional concept that only public ownership is socialism and brought the diverse forms of ownership together with the nature of socialism. This is an important breakthrough in the theory of socialism and a great leap forward in the history of socialist ideology.

This new definition is of extremely great significance to evaluating the nature of the Chinese society at present. Since the launching of the reform drive, the Chinese Communist Party has put forward quite a many new ideas regarding the nature of the Chinese society at the current stage, which are different from those popular in the period of planned economy. The most important ones include the following: First, the 13th National Party Congress ventured the theory of the primary stage of socialism, that is, China is now at the stage of socialism, but the primary stage of socialism. The fundamental task at the primary stage of socialism is to develop productive forces. At the primary stage of socialism, it is necessary to adopt whatever production relations and ownership structure that can best promote the development of the productive forces. Selecting the form of production relations and ownership structure from the perspective of promoting the development of productive forces is compatible with the fundamental goal of socialism. Second, the report to the 14th National Party Congress put forward the theory of socialist market economy, saying that market and planning are not the criteria in judging the nature of a society and they are both tools and means for the allocation of the resources. This concept has connected market economy with the socialist system. Third, the report to the 15th National Party Congress put forward the theory of "retaining the dominant position of public ownership while striving for a side-by-side development of diverse forms of ownership," that is to say, the diverse forms of ownership, including the non-public sectors, are included in the basic economic system of socialism at the current stage. According to this theory, the non-public sectors are no longer the opposition of socialism and, on the contrary, the development of the economy under diverse forms of ownership based on the maintenance of the dominant position of public ownership is a bright road for the construction of socialism. This represents yet another important breakthrough in the traditional theory of socialism.

II. Ownership System Should Not Be Treated the Same as the Forms of Materialization of Ownership

Ownership should not be equated to the forms materializing it is an important thesis put forward in the report to the 15th National Party Congress. The report pointed out that the forms to materialize the public ownership can and should be diversified, all management methods and organizational forms that mirror the laws governing socialized production may be utilized boldly. And it is necessary to seek various forms for the materialization of the public ownership that can greatly promote the growth of the productive forces.

Ownership and its materializing forms are never one thing. Ownership mainly refers to the right to own the means of production and it is mainly a kind of legal relationship. The ownership materializing forms, however, refer to the organizational form, the enterprise system and the operational ways of the property relations under a given type of ownership of the means of production. A given ownership must materialize in a given form. However, a given type of ownership does not always correspond to its materializing form. Ownership of the same nature can take different materializing forms in different enterprises, and a state-owned enterprise can be managed by the state or by some individuals. Conversely, ownership of different natures can adopt the same materializing form in different enterprises. For example, state-owned, collectively owned and privately owned enterprises can all adopted the forms of sole proprietorship, joint-stock system, consigned management, etc. Reviewing the traditional materializing forms of China's public ownership prior to the reform, the state-owned owned enterprises were owned and managed by the state, while the collectively owned ones were owned and managed by the collectives that owned them in a "quasi form of state management." These traditional materializing forms were compatible with the system of planned economy. Since the launching of the reform drive, China has embarked on the road of gradual transition from the planned economy to the socialist market economy. The traditional materializing forms of the public ownership had a poor adaptability to the operation of the market economy. Therefore, it is necessary to seek diverse forms of materialization for the public ownership that can better cater to the requirements of the market economy.

In this way, the materializing forms of the public ownership will gradually diversify. Now, such forms as profit-sharing, contractual management, leased management, corporate enterprises and joint-stock partnership enterprises are found in the state-owned sector, and collective management, contract with remuneration linked to output, cooperatives and joint-stock partnership have adopted in the collective sector.

The report to the 15th National Party Congress approved of the diversification of forms of materialization for the public ownership. This has opened up a new vista to develop new forms that can greatly promote the development of the productive forces, because different materializing forms of the public ownership can produce different and even vastly different results in the development of the productive forces, in the development of the market economy, in the operation and productivity of the enterprises, as well as in the relations between the owners, managers and workers. The result is determined, to a great extent, by the materializing form. Therefore, each enterprise should look for the best ownership materializing form that is most favorable for its own development in line with its own specific conditions.

The diversification of the materializing forms of public ownership has brought to an end the debate in the theoretical circles over the issue whether the transformation of state-owned and collectively owned enterprises in line with the requirements of joint-stock system and joint-stock partnership means "privatization." Once, heated debate erupted over the issue of the joint-stock system and joint-stock partnership. Some people insisted that joint-stock system was nothing but private ownership; it was "capitalist" in nature rather than "socialist"; and the introduction of the joint-stock system was tantamount to practicing privatization. There were similar views regarding the joint-stock partnership. To prove that the joint-stock system and joint-stock partnership could be adopted under public ownership, some people in the theoretical circles raised the idea that ownership and its materializing form were two different concepts. They argued that the joint-stock system and joint-stock partnership were only materializing forms of ownership and they themselves were neither "socialist' nor "capitalist." This view was affirmed in the report to the 15th National Party Congress. The report scientifically analyzed the joint-stock system, saying that it was an form of capital organization for modern enterprises; it was conducive to separating ownership from management and raising the efficiency of operation and capital; it could be adopted under both capitalism and socialism; it was not simply not right to say in general terms that the joint-stock system is public or private, for the key lies in who holds the controlling share. These views are of great practical significance for the corporate-orientated transformation of large and medium-sized enterprises as well as the establishment of a modern enterprise system, because the joint-stock system, judging by its nature and function, can be used as a more general and appropriate form for China's large and medium-sized state-owned enterprises who are making efforts to establish a modern enterprise system. Of course, the state-owned and collectively owned enterprises can also actively explore for other forms to materialize the ownership. Guided by the theory that the materializing forms of ownership can and should be diversified, major breakthroughs are bound to be made in the materializing forms of the public economy, thus bringing forth more new ways to invigorate the state-owned and collective enterprises.

III. It Is Necessary to Correctly Understand the Status and Role of State-owned Economy

With regard to the state-owned economy, the report to the 15th National Party Congress said that the state-owned sector of the economy should maintain a dominant position. The leading role of the state-owned sector manifests itself mainly in its control power. In the past, the leading role was mainly defined in terms of quantity and proportion the state-owned sector. Now, the focus of attention has been shifted to the control power and quality of the state-owned sector. The role or control power of the state-owned sector is mainly demonstrated in the following aspects: (1) controlling the lifeline of the national economy;

(2) playing a leading role in economic development by holding controlling shares in big enterprises or conglomerates of big enterprises and becoming a shareholder in some other enterprises; (3) doing things that the non-public sectors are unwilling, cannot or are not allowed to do; (4) seeing to it that the social reproduction goes on smoothly and that the socialist nature and orientation of development of the national economy are kept; and (5) exercising macro control and regulation over the economy and maintaining socio-economic stability.

It represents a re-understanding of the status and role of the state-owned economic sector and state-owned enterprises to maintain the dominant position of the state-owned sector and at the same time to interpret its leading role from the perspective of control power. It also gives rise to a new, correct and feasible approach for the reform of state-owned enterprises. According to the report to the 15th National Party Congress, it is imperative to readjust strategically the general layout of the state-owned sector. The state-owned sector must occupy a dominant position in major industries and key areas that are related to the lifeline of the national economy. In other areas, efforts should be made to reorganize assets and readjust the structure to strengthen the focal points and improve the quality of the state assets as a whole. At the same time, it is necessary to create better basic conditions, market conditions and an external environment for the development of the non-state-owned sectors so as to achieve a sound, sustained and efficient development of the entire national economy.

So long as the state controls the lifeline of the national economy and the state-owned sector exercises greater power of control and becomes more competitive, even if the state-owned sector makes up for a smaller proportion, the socialist nature of the country will not be affected. This can relieve people of their misgivings and better spur on the reform and development of the state-owned enterprises.

IV. Collectively Owned Sector Is an Important Integral Part of the Public Sector

At the stage of planned economy, the collective sector was regarded as an elementary and transitional form of the public sector. Constant efforts had been made to "upgrade" it to the level of ownership by the whole people, carry out the so-called "poverty" transition and take away from the laboring masses their right of property. It was not until the launching of the reform drive that a breakthrough was made in this traditional concept and the collective sector achieved great development. This indicates that the collective economy enjoys vigorous vitality and extensive popularity in China. At the same time, restrictive stipulations for the collective economy have been gradually removed from relevant laws and the nature of the collective economy has been more clearly defined. The Chinese Constitution stipulates that the various forms of cooperative economy in the urban and rural areas all belong to socialist economy under the collective ownership by the working people; both the collective ownership and ownership by the whole people are independent economic forms, and there is not the question which is superior and which is inferior and the question that the collective economy must be lifted to the level of ownership by the whole people. The report to the 15th National Party Congress clearly pointed out that collective economy is an important component of the public sector, and the diverse forms of joint-stock partnership cropping up in the process of the reform fall into the category of collective economy, which are mainly based on the association of the laborers and pooling together of the laborers' capital. Special support and encouragement should be given them.

The idea that collective economy is an important component of the public sector has laid down the foundation and rendered support that are necessary for the development of diverse forms of collective economy. The traditional forms of collective ownership of the means of production are the collective economy and public economy. The large numbers of cooperative enterprises and joint-stock partnerships emerged since the reform also belong to collective economy and public economy. This has made it possible for the collectively owned sector to break through its excessively unitary form of materialization and spurred on the development of the collective economy and the diversification of its materializing forms. Besides, it has also blazed a new trail for the reform of the state-owned and collectively owned enterprises. For example, the change of state-owned enterprises into collective ones according to the needs of the market economy is no longer regarded as privatization. It is neither regarded as privatization when the traditional collective enterprises reorganize their property right and become enterprises of new types based on the association of labor and assets. The diverse forms of cooperative enterprises and enterprises under mixed ownership recently emerged are considered collective enterprises in new forms. Generally speaking, it has removed the ideological obstacle for the deepening of the enterprise reform and the development of collective economy in both urban and rural areas.

V. The Non-public Sector Is an Important Component of the Socialist Market Economy

In China, the non-public sector of the economy has appeared and developed in the course of reform and opening to the outside world. How to describe the nature and role of the non-public sector had remained a major issue of controversy in China's socio-economic development. The report to the 15th National Party Congress clearly stated that the non-public sector is an important component of the socialist market economy. This is an important breakthrough in the traditional concept of socialist ownership. First, it represents a breakthrough in terms of the nature of non-public sector. Being considered an important component of the socialist market economy, the non-public sector has been brought into the socialist economic system whereas it was excluded from it formerly. Second, it is a breakthrough with regard to its status and role. This means the status of the non-public sector has been raised from being a supplement to being an important component of the socialist market economy and from playing only the role of making good deficiencies to playing an important role in the development of the national economy. Third, it is a breakthrough with regard to its scope of development. The reduction in the scope of the state-owned sector has made room for the development of the non-public sector. Fourth, it is a breakthrough in the development of the legal system featuring by the fact that the property right of individuals are further protected. The report to the 15th National Party Congress pointed out, "It is necessary to improve the legal system concerning property and protect the legitimate rights and interests of, and fair competition among, all types of enterprises." This actually implies that legal protection is also provided to legitimate private property.[(5)]

Re-understanding of the status and role of the non-public sector is bound to open up a broader vista for its development. Now, the proportion held by the non-public sector in China is not too great but too small. Judging by the fact that the non-public sector still survived despite repeated bans from the government and judging by the marked progress it had achieved, the non-public sector is of great vitality and enjoys a bright prospect of development. Karl Marx pointed out that any social pattern would not perish before the productive forces it could accommodate were fully developed, and the new relations of production at a higher level could never emerge before the material conditions needed for its existence become ripe in the embryo of the old society. The fact that it is difficult to ban the non-public sector despite repeated attempts to do so in a socialist country is perhaps due to the reason that there is a natural internal logic for its existence. The 15th National Congress of the Chinese Communist Party redefined the role of the non-public sector, considering it an important component of the socialist economic system and one of the ownership foundations for the socialist market economy. This is a correct understanding acquired from the experience and lessons learned over dozens of years of efforts in the socialist construction. In other words, it represents another round of emancipation of the mind as well as a new development of Marxism.

VI. It Is Necessary to Make Judgement of Any Form of Ownership by Following the Principle of "Three Favorables"

There are two major types of criterion to evaluate or judge any system of ownership: one is to take the ownership system itself as a criterion, and the other is to judge it by the principle of "three favorables." People following the former criterion hold that the ownership by the whole people is superior to collective ownership and still more to non-public ownership. In fact, this is to mainly make judgement of different types of ownership by moral and ethical standards. Proceeding from the moral standards, it is natural to conclude that "private ownership is the source of all evils" and exploitation is immoral, thus it is necessary to eliminate private ownership and the relations between bosses and hired laborers. Thus, efforts are made to establish the public ownership, which is "large in size, public and pure in nature." Facts have proved that this understanding is in violation of the basic principles of Marxism and are very harmful in practice. China was seriously affected by this understanding during the period of planned economy.

Since the reform drive was launched, the Chinese Communist Party has gradually come to realize the danger caused by the above understanding and brought into being a new criterion based on the principle of "three favorables" put forward by Deng Xiaoping. By "three favorables," it means that the ownership structure must be favorable to the development of the productive forces, to the enhancement of the comprehensive strength of the socialist state and to the improvement of the people's living standards. As the existence of productive forces is an objective reality, the criterion of "three favorables" is thus the objective criterion in evaluating the system of ownership. One basic principle of Marxism is that productive forces determine the relations of production and the relations of production must be catered to the development of the productive forces. Obviously, the criterion of "three favorables" is in agreement with this basic principle of Marxism.

Thanks to this new criterion, China has succeeded in overcoming interference from various kinds of "Leftist" and "Rightist" ideas. It has persisted in taking economic construction as central link of all work and persisted in taking the development of the productive forces as the fundamental criterion in adjusting the relations and structure of ownership, and succeeded in maintaining a fairly high rate of growth of the national economy. From 1978 to 1998, the annual average growth rates of China's GDP and per-capita GDP reached 9.7 percent and 8.3 percent respectively, much higher than the 4.4 percent and 2.3 percent growth rates for the 1952-78 period.(6) The country's GDP, calculated according to the par value of the purchasing power, rose from No. 4 place in 1978 to No. 2 by mid-1990s in the world. Thanks to the development of the productive forces, the Chinese economy has extracted itself from the long-lasting problem of "shortage" and turned into a seller's market from a buyer's market. Marked improvement has also been witnessed in the levels of income and consumption of both urban and rural residents. Without the development of the diversified relations and structure of ownership, it would not be possible for the Chinese economy to reap such a sustained, high-speed development over the past 20 years.

In short, to maintain the dominant position of the public ownership and strive for a side-by-side development of diverse forms of ownership have been made China's basic economic system at the primary stage of socialism. This represents a great leap forward in the understanding acquired from both positive experience and negative lessons over dozens of years of practice in socialist construction, and a downright negation of the Stalin dogma that had long remained predominant in the international communist movement.(7) It is also a new development of the Marxist theory concerning ownership.

Section 4
Exploring Ways for Reform of State-owned Enterprises

The reform of state-owned enterprises is the central link in China's reform of the economic structure as well as a basic content of the ownership reform. To do good job in the reform of the state-owned enterprises is of extremely important significance for bringing into better play the leading of the state-owned sector, for the development of the socialist market economy and for the consolidation of the socialist system.

I. Reform of State-owned Enterprises: Course of Development and Current Situation

1. Course of Development

Starting from the end of 1978, the course of China's reform of the state-owned enterprises can be divided roughly into three stages, that is, the stage of granting more power and profits to the enterprises (1978-1984); the stage of separating the right of ownership from the power of management (1985-1993); and the stage of establishing the modern enterprise system (1994 onward).

(1) The First Stage

Under the system of planned economy, enterprises were affiliates to government organs. Virtually, all power, including that regarding manpower, finance, materials, production, supply and marketing, rested in the hands of the government, and the enterprises were devoid of any vitality. In order to enhance the vitality of the enterprises, in 1978 the Sichuan provincial authorities selected six enterprises, including Ninjiang Machine Tool Plant, to try out the reform featuring delegation of more power to enterprises. The following year, the former State Economic Commission selected the Capital Iron and Steel Corporation and seven other enterprises for experiment. The trial reform won widespread support and acclaim. In July 1979, the State Council issued five documents, calling for expanding the autonomous power of state-owned industrial enterprises with regard to management and operation and asking the local governments to select more enterprises for the experiment. By 1980, the number of enterprises trying out the reform had reached 6,000, accounting for some 16 percent of all industrial enterprises covered in the state budget; the output value generated by these enterprises accounted for 60 percent of the national total and their profits accounted for 70 percent. Meanwhile, granting more power to enterprises also meant to increase their responsibility, that is, to compel them to gradually adopt the economic responsibility system. In December 1981, the State Council endorsed and transmitted throughout the country "Proposals Regarding Problems in the Implementation of Economic Responsibility System in Industrial Enterprises" prepared by the former State Economic Commission, thus greatly quickened the pace of the introduction of the production and management responsibility system in enterprises. Towards the end of 1981, more than 42,000 industrial enterprises had adopted the economic responsibility system.

The reform, characterized by replacing delivery of profits to the state by tax payment, was launched in 1983. It was in fact a continuation of the reform to grant more power to the enterprises. In April 1983, the State Council again endorsed and transmitted throughout the country "Circular on Measures to Try Out Replacement of Profit Delivery by Tax Payment in State-owned Enterprises" drafted by the Ministry of Finance. According to this circular, all large and medium-sized state-owned enterprises that make profits should pay a 50-percent income tax to the state on the profits they reap. As for the post-tax profits, part should be turned over to the state and the rest was to be kept by the enterprises. All small state-owned enterprises that make profits should pay income taxes to the state in line with the eight-grade progressive tax rates on the profits they reap. So long as they pay the tax, the enterprises shall be left to take sole responsibility for their own profits and losses. In 1984, a second step was taken in the reform and appropriate readjustments were made in the tax categories and rates.

In May 1984, the State Council issued the "Interim Regulations on Further Expanding the Decision-Making Power of State-owned Industrial Enterprises." The document listed ten areas in which the power of the enterprises should be expanded -- power to map out plans for their own production and management, power to market their own products, power to set the prices for their own products, power to purchase raw materials and equipment for their own use, power to make use of their own funds, power in production management, power to decide on their organizational setup, power over personnel affairs, power in salary and bonus payment and power in cooperative operations. In September 1985, the State Council again approved and transmitted the "Interim Provisions on Questions to Invigorate Large and Medium-sized State-owned Industrial Enterprises." The document included 14 provisions regarding the decision-making power of the enterprises. Granting more power and profits to state-owned enterprises achieved initial success in breaking the old system in which state planning covered everything, enabled the state-owned enterprises to have more power over their own production and management and, to a certain extent, promoted their development. Yet, such efforts were made under the framework of planned economy and failed to bring into being a comprehensive system in which responsibility, power and interests are organically linked and in which the successful ones survive while the poorly operated die out. At this stage, the state-owned enterprises had not yet become market subjects and independent commodity producers in the real sense.

(2) The Second Stage

The second stage of the reform of state-owned enterprises began with the Third Plenary Session of the 12th Party Central Committee. The objective of the reform was to turn the enterprises into relatively independent entities in management as well as socialist commodity producers and managers that make their own decisions for their own operation, are responsible for their own profits and losses, are capable to seek self-transformation and self-development, and become legal persons that enjoy certain rights and shoulder certain obligations. The major guideline for the reform was to separate the right of ownership and the right of management. The main methods adopted for the reform were the leasing system and contract system, i.e. to lease out small enterprises and introducing the contract system in large and medium-sized ones.

As of 1987, various forms of contract management responsibility system were introduced in large and medium-sized enterprises. By the end of 1987, 70 percent of the enterprises covered in the state budget adopted the system. In 1988, the State Council issued the "Interim Regulations Regarding Contract Management Responsibility System in Industrial Enterprises Owned by the Whole People." The document provided the legal basis for the contract system. The first round of contract management expired in 1990. In this round, 33,000 industrial enterprises adopted the system, accounting for 90 percent of all enterprises. The second round followed immediately. By the end of March 1991, more than 90 percent of the enterprises that adopted the system in the first round had had their contracts renewed for the second round.

In order to encourage the enterprises to change their management mechanism, while making efforts to establish and improve the contract responsibility system, experiments were made in separating profits and taxes and the joint-stock system. The experiments on the separation of profits and taxes began in 1988, with more than 2,000 enterprises involved by 1991. An initial success was achieved. The joint-stock system was tried out in 1984. Yet, as there had been continuous arguments over the nature of the joint-stock system, the experiments had been going on intermittently. Towards the first half of 1993, the number of joint-stock enterprises exceeded 3,200, most of which issued internal stocks to their workers and staff. In May 1992, the former State Commission of Economic Restructuring and some other government departments jointly issued "Methods on Experiment in Joint-Stock Enterprises," which pushed the development of the joint-stock system towards institutionalization.

In line with the spirit of a working conference of the Party Central Committee, which was held in 1991 and laid stress on the necessity to transform the management mechanism in enterprises, the State Council issued the "Regulations on Transforming Management Mechanism in Industrial Enterprises Owned by the Whole People." The document included specific stipulations concerning such issues as the management power of the enterprises, the responsibility of the enterprises for their own profits and losses, as well as the relations between the enterprises and the government as well as their legal responsibilities. But, due to the rapid change in the overall situation, not much progress had been achieved in transforming the management mechanism of the enterprises. Even when the demand to establish a modern enterprise system became very obvious, the contract responsibility system, which laid stress on the separation of the right of ownership and the right of management, still remained as the major form of management in state-owned enterprises in this period.

The reform featuring the separation of the right of ownership and the right of management in enterprises greatly increased the enterprises' autonomy in management, brought into being a more direct interest incentive system and, to some extent, promoted the development of the enterprises. However, the "bargaining mechanism" in contract management had left some loopholes for the enterprises, particularly those who had contracted to manage the enterprises, to pocket the larger part of the benefits reaped from the development of the enterprises, while the government and the society gained little. Besides, the short-term behavior of the contractors had adversely affected the stamina for long-term development. When the power of the enterprises to make their own decisions concerning management was expanded, there lacked a corresponding restrictive mechanism, hence the widespread phenomenon that the enterprises that had adopted the contract management responsibility system were only responsible for their profits but not for their losses. In the final analysis, the contract management responsibility system only touched the surface of the property right relations rather than the real problem regarding the separation of government administration from enterprise management. Therefore, the separation of the right of ownership from the right of management was far from being complete and the objective of the enterprise reform was far from being achieved. At the same time, some sew problems that cropped up had made the operation of the enterprises going from bad to worse. A new way must be found to tackle the problem.

(3) The Third Stage

The 14th National Party Congress held in 1992 made the development of the socialist market economy the objective of the reform of the economic structure. The Third Plenary Session of the 14th Party Central Committee, held in November 1993, clearly pointed out that the goal of China's reform of state-owned enterprises was to establish a modern enterprise system, which meets the requirements of the market economy and socialized mass production, and under this system the property rights as well as the rights and responsibilities of the enterprises are clearly defined, government administration and enterprise management are separated and scientific management is adopted. This system refers, in fact, to the modern corporate system, particularly that of joint-stock companies. The aim of the establishment of the modern enterprise system is to turn the enterprises into legal entities that make their own decisions regarding management, shoulder sole responsibility for their own profits and losses, and can seek self-development and discipline themselves.

To implement the "Decision of the CPC Central Committee on Some Issues Concerning the Establishment of a Socialist Market

Economic Structure," adopted at the Third Plenary Session of the 14th Party Central Committee, the former State Economic Commission began to organize for experiment in the establishment of the modern enterprise system in 1994. In 1995, the experiment was focused on four areas. The first was the experiment to establish a modern enterprise system in 100 selected state-owned enterprises. The second was experiment to "optimize the capital structure" in 18 cities (this experiment was extended to 111 cities in 1997). The third was trying out setting up enterprise groups and three state stock-controlling companies (The number of enterprise groups was increased to 120 in 1997). The fourth was to spur on the overall reform of small enterprises in line with the principle of "focusing on large enterprises and giving a free hand to small ones" adopted at the Fifth Plenary Session of the 14th Party Central Committee in 1995.

In 1997, the 15th National Congress of Chinese Communist Party pointed out that, to conduct reform of the state-owned enterprises, it was necessary to focus attention on doing a good job in the entire national economy and carry out strategic reorganization of the state-owned enterprises. In 1995, the State Council decided to concentrate attention on 1,000 key state-owned enterprises. In 1997, the number increased to 1,212, of which 512 were enterprises that were granted special government support. Meanwhile, greater efforts were made to give support to the reform of 120 enterprise groups. In accordance with the principle of "lifting control over and invigorating small enterprises," the local governments accelerated the pace of the reform of small enterprises. By the end of 1997, more than 50 percent state-owned small enterprises in quite a few provinces and cities had undergone transformation and restructuring in various ways.

Starting from 1998, the Party Central Committee suggested to spend three years to lift the majority of large and medium-sized state-owned enterprises out of their difficult plight and initially introduce in them the modern enterprise system by means of reform, reorganization, transformation and improved management. Consequently, the reform of the state-owned enterprises has developed in further depth. New progress has been achieved in the readjustment and reorganization of the textile, coal mining, petroleum and petrochemical and metallurgical industries as well as defense industries. To strengthen supervision and control over the state-owned enterprises, the State Council has dispatched special inspectors to key state-owned enterprises. A number of enterprises have introduced the corporate system through transformation in line with the demands of the modern enterprise system. Institutional procedures have established in view of the problems arising in the reform of small state-owned enterprises and, meanwhile, efforts have been intensified to give support to small enterprises. Along with the organizational restructure of departments under the State Council, some government departments no longer exercise direct control over the enterprises, and steady progress has been made in separating government administration from enterprise management.

2. Major Achievements in the Reform of State-owned Enterprises

Most of the state-owned enterprises have changed or are changing their management mechanism. The market-oriented reform of the Chinese economy has compelled the state-owned enterprises to gear their production and management towards the market and participate in market competition, whereas in the past they only carried out production and management according to state plans. "All work should center around the market." This has become the consensus among the managers and workers in most state-owned enterprises.

Some state-owned enterprises have enhanced their vitality and developed into key state-owned enterprises with sharper competitive edge. Technological surveys and market investigations conducted at random show that the average quality of products turned out by state-owned enterprises is better than those made by other types of enterprises. Most of the brand-name products in China are produced by state-owned enterprises. In most of the Chinese industries, particularly those capital- and technology-intensive ones, the enterprises that enjoy the largest market share are still state-owned ones. This means large and medium-sized state-owned enterprises are still rather competitive in the market. Key state-owned enterprises are an important force to participate in international competition.

In China, the major proportion of large and medium-sized enterprises is still state-owned. Compared with enterprises under other forms of ownership, they still hold an advantageous position in terms of scale and size.

State-owned enterprises have borne most of the cost for China's economic transition. Although the non-state-owned sectors have made 80 percent of the contribution to China's economic growth in the 1990s and their contribution to the state financial income has also increased constantly, yet, viewed as a whole, the state-owned enterprises still constitute the major source for the country's financial revenue and public spending (the contribution made by the state-owned sector has remained at around 70 percent). So, it can be said that state-owned enterprises have borne the bulk of cost for China's economic reform. Besides, they still bear the major responsibility with regard to employment, social security and so on.

Certain progress has been made in supporting reforms of state-owned enterprises, which included cutting down the size of staff to increase efficiency, launching of reemployment projects and establishing a social security system. In 1998, the number of workers and staff in state-owned units dropped by nearly 25 million as compared with that in 1995, which was the peak year. A socialized social security system has taken initial shape.

A clearer understanding has been acquired regarding the status and role of state-owned enterprises. Now, people have come to realize that there must be state-owned enterprises, but their number should not be too large. Studies have been going on to look for new ways for the reform of state-owned enterprises.

3. Major Problems Encountered by State-owned Enterprises

First, the state-owned enterprises are large in number and are scattered in too many trades. One of the serious problems is their irrational distribution and composition – in those trades that have nothing or little to do with the function of state-owned economy state-owned enterprises make up too large a proportion. For instance, there were 291,000 state-owned enterprises in 1995 and they spread in almost all industries, including agriculture, forestry, animal husbandry, sideline occupations, fishery, industry, architecture, transport and communications, commerce and services. State-owned enterprises could be found in all 39 major industries. In 1997, of the 608 industrial sub-branches, state-owned enterprises were found in 599 of them. Moreover, state-owned enterprises still accounted for a fairly large proportion in most of the industrial sub-branches. In terms of incomes from sales, total assets and number of employees, the proportion of state-owned sector exceeded 50 percent in 169 of these industrial sub-branches; 20 to 50 percent in 249; 10 to 20 percent in 108; and below 10 percent in 73. Yet, when viewed from the demand that the state-owned sector should hold a dominant role, obviously state-owned enterprises were stretched too thin in too many industries, most of which were not important trades and key areas in the national economy. For example, nearly 50 percent of the state-owned enterprises were found in 13 of the 39 major industries. These 13 industries had a low content of technology, faced with intense competition in the market and produced little effect in the entire national economy. Of them, 12 were running at losses, and the only exception was the "beverage industry." Judging by this situation, it can be concluded that over spreading of the state-owned sector results in the excessively small size and low technological level of each single industry. It not only has reduced the strength of competition of the state-owned enterprises and made it impossible to concentrate state financial resources in important industries, but also used up that part of the resources and market share that should be given to non-state-owned enterprises and hindered the simultaneous development of the diverse economic elements. In those industries that were not suitable for the state-owned sector to get involved, not only was the state incapable to run so many enterprises (it has been proved that the cost incurred by enforcing direct control over micro-economic operation by the government departments is too high), the efficiency of resource allocation in the whole society was also affected. This "not only causes failure in strengthening the power of influence and control of the state-owned sector but also turns out, to some extent, to be a burden on the state and the society."

Second, the overwhelming majority of state-owned enterprises have not yet adopted the modern enterprise system that is compatible with the socialist market economy. In 1994, the Chinese government clearly laid down the objective of the reform of large and medium-sized state-owned enterprises, and it is to establish a modern enterprise system in which "the property right relations as well as the rights and responsibilities are clearly defined; government administration and enterprise management are separated; and the management is scientific." Meanwhile, it has taken a series of reform measures to ensure the attainment of this objective. Up till now, however, the goal has not been accomplished. First, the reform in property right has lagged behind. On the one hand, the property right of the enterprises as legal persons are hard to materialize, and the government departments in charge still meddle directly in the internal production and operation of the enterprises. On the other, it is difficult for the enterprises under interference from the government departments to fully participate in the market competition in line with the requirements of the market economy. The ultimate outcome is that both the meddlers and the enterprise managers are unable to take responsibility for the operation of the state-owned enterprises as well as for maintaining and increasing the value of state-owned assets, because the responsibility cannot be attributed to any particular natural person. Second, no fundamental change has been achieved in separating the roles of the government from those of the enterprises. The Chinese government has come to see the necessity to separate the roles of the government and those of the enterprises in the course of the reform of state-owned enterprises. It has also made various attempts to separate government administration from enterprise management. However, due to various factors, such as the delayed reform in property right, the phenomenon still exists that the functions of the government and those of the enterprises are not separated or the rights and responsibilities of the government and the enterprises are not clearly defined. So, there is still a long way to go before the functions government administration and enterprise management are truly separated (see Table 1-10). Without a clear line drawn between the functions of the government and enterprises, it would be impossible for the enterprises to enjoy full rights in their management and operation, and also would it be unlikely for them to have real vitality and get the power for competition. Lastly, it is difficult to establish state-owned assets management system in which rights and responsibilities are clearly stated. The management of state-owned assets is confronted with a series of problems. For example, who should represent the investors in state-owned assets? How should the supervision over state-owned assets be enforced and what incentives should be given to the managers of state-owned assets? And what measures should be taken to guarantee the independence of the enterprises and prevent insiders to harm and control the rights and interests of the owners of state assets? If these problems were not tackled properly in the reform of state-owned enterprises, separating the functions of the government and the enterprises would remain empty talk.

Third, when the market competition turns increasingly fiercer, the numerous difficulties and problems encountered by the state-owned enterprises caused their returns going down continuously. First, their assets-liabilities ratio was too high, and they were under an excessively heavy a debt burden. For them, the assets-liabilities ratio had risen from 18.1 percent in 1980 to 79 percent in 1994. In 1997, of the 15,000 large and medium-sized state-owned industrial enterprises, the debt rate for 40.5 percent of them exceeded 80 percent. Of these enterprises, 2166 (accounting for 14.6 percent) had not enough assets to offset their debts. Of the more than 50,000 small state-owned industrial enterprises that practiced independent accounting, the total loss added up to 6.6 billion yuan. Besides, the state-owned enterprises suffered from heavy historical and social burdens. Their production equipment and technology were obsolete. In addition, they also encountered many problems in management. In face of fierce market competition, the returns of the state-owned enterprises dropped sharply. Since the launching of the reform drive, the proportion of assets in state-owned enterprises had been down by 20-30 percentage point. Although it still accounted for over 60 percent of the total industrial assets of the country, their proportion of output had dropped rapidly from 77.6 percent in 1978 to 28.5 percent, a decrease of 49 percentage point. That the ratio between input and output fell seriously out step indicated a decline in the state-owned

Table 1-10. Statistics Collected in a Sample Survey on the Power of State-owned Enterprises to Make Their Own Decisions

Power Distribution	Production Plan	Personnel Affairs	Decision Over Employment	Decision to Fire Workers	Level of Bonus	Gap in Salary	Scope of Production Expansion	Merger
Decision-Making Power over Management under Limits Set by Owners								
Departments in Charge	25.7	80.1	30.9	13.8	15.9	34.0	28.6	56.1
Consulted with Departments in Charge	47.5	19.9	51.8	50.9	15.9	16.6	57.1	37.1
Enterprises	26.8	0	17.4	35.3	68.3	49.4	14.4	6.8
Decision-Making Power under Limits Set by Workers and Staff in Enterprises								
Independently by Management	4.3	3.4	5.2	1.7	4.0	1.8	2.0	1.8
Consulted between Leaders at Factory Level	76.3	9.7	73.1	31.3	62.1	48.4	63.3	37.6
Consulted with Party Committee	8.8	84.9	13.8	14.6	9.3	16.2	23.4	36.1
Decided by Workers' Congress	10.6	1.9	7.9	52.4	24.6	33.6	11.4	24.5

Source of Data: Liu Xiaoxuan, "State-owned Enterprises and Non-state-owned Enterprises, & Property Right and its Influence on Efficiency," carried in *Economic Research*, No. 7, 1995, pp. 14-15.

enterprises' level of output and level of profit. The rate of losses (total amount of profits of profit-making enterprises divided by total amount of losses of loss-incurring enterprises) rocketed from 10 percent in the 1980s to 67.6 percent in 1998 (see Table 1-11).

Table 1-11. Balance Sheet of Profits and Losses of Stated-owned Industrial Enterprises under Independent Accounting

Year	Total Loss Billion yuan (1)	Total Profit Billion yuan (2)	Rate of Loss (1) divided by (2) %
1978	4.206	55.086	7.64
1980	3.430	61.970	5.53
1985	3.244	77.064	4.21
1990	34.876	73.687	47.33
1995	54.041	120.601	44.81
1998	102.330	151.370	67.60

Source of Data: *China Statistical Almanac (1998)*, p. 461 and *China Statistical Synopsis (1999)*, p. 108.

II. Experience and Lessons Learned from the Reform of the State-owned Enterprises

The reform of the state-owned enterprises is the central link and a hard nut to crack in China's economic structuring. Certain experience has been accumulated and some lessons have been learned from the reform over the past two decades.

First, China's reform of the state-owned enterprises has taken a typical step-by-step gradual approach. This is a road chosen in view of the country's own actual conditions. There are two major modes in the economic restructuring of socialist countries -- the "shock therapy" adopted in the former Soviet Union and some other countries, and the "gradual approach" adopted in China and some other countries. As China's reform started in the countryside and the reform of the state-owned enterprises was only launched when most of them operated well and produced good economic returns, and the call for reform was not as urgent as in the former Soviet Union. At the same time, China's state-owned enterprises were and still are the main contributors to the country's financial revenue; they controlled a massive amount or proportion of assets; and it was extremely hard to reposition the large numbers of redundant workers and staff if drastic reform measures were adopted. In addition, political, ideological and even state security considerations made it difficult for China to adopt the "shock therapy" in its reform of the state-owned enterprises. So, China could only choose the easiest link where there was the least resistance as the point for a breakthrough and follow the procedure of "the relatively easy aspects first and the difficult ones later" for the reform in a step-by-step manner. Certainly, this is a fairly long course of treatment and the effect of the treatment would not be obvious in a short period of time. Over the past two decades, however, China's reform of the state-owned enterprises has never been interrupted, and this has enabled the organizational structure of the state-owned enterprises to gradually cater to the needs of the market economic system. More importantly, in view of the numerous tasks of the economic transition, the state-owned enterprises, while being the objects of reform, must at the same time provide the material guarantee to reforms in other fields. They have been and are the major force that bears most of the cost for the reform, which has ensured the progress and breakthrough in other aspects of China's economic reform.

Second, China's reform of the state-owned enterprises has never been carried out in the enterprises only. One more important task of the reform is to create conditions for the development of the non-state-owned sectors, particularly the non-publicly owned sector. As it is relatively easier to seek development of new economic elements than to alter the old system and, moreover, as there are important differences between the non-state-owned economic sector and the state-owned enterprises in terms of system, the development of the non-publicly owned sector can give better expression to the demands of the market economy – consistent with the market-oriented objective of the reform. The rapid development of the non-state-owned sectors has fundamentally changed the external environment of competition for the state-owned economy and created new favorable conditions for the reform of the state-owned enterprises. First, it has brought about a rapid economic growth and increased their contributions to the country's financial revenue, resulting in gradually reducing the financial burden on the state-owned enterprises. Second, it has created more chances of employment as well as the necessary conditions for repositioning the workers and staff laid off from the state-owned enterprises. Since the early 1990s, the number of workers and workers in state-owned enterprises has kept decreasing, and the newly increased population for employment together with the workers laid off from state-owned enterprises mostly obtained job opportunities in the non-state, particularly non-public, sectors. Third, it has brought into being a large number of non-state enterprises and entrepreneurs, thus laying the practical foundation for the transformation of the state-owned enterprises. Fourth, it has compelled the state-owned enterprises to adapt to market competition and played an "exemplary role" for the reform of the state-owned enterprises. In particular, competition in the domestic market together with external competition from foreign enterprises have produced the pressure, motivation and opportunities to push the reform of state-owned enterprises to a substantial stage. Since the mid-1990s, China's reform of the state-owned enterprises has entered a crucial stage that is marked by strategic reorganization, which will undoubtedly enable the reform to advance in still bigger steps.

Third, correctly handle the relations between reform, stability and development and combine the continuous deepening of the reform with the reorganization, transformation and the efforts to improve management. The reform of the state-owned enterprises is an extremely complicated and difficult undertaking. China's reform of the state-owned enterprises is not just for the sake of reform. The ultimate objective is to promote the development of the state-owned enterprises as well as the development of the productive forces. To bring about this objective, China has all along made efforts to handle well the relations between reform, stability and development. Development is the absolute principle, reform is the motive power and stability is the key. Therefore, while reforming the state-owned enterprises, China has done its best to coordinate well the efforts for reform, the pace of development and the forbearance of the society -- pushing forward the reform and development under the precondition of maintaining social and political stability and securing social and political stability through reform and development. In order to make a breakthrough in the reform of the state-owned enterprises, it was decided to combine enterprise reform with efforts made in enterprise reorganization and transformation as well as strengthening enterprise management. To run the enterprises well, it is imperative to focus on the development of the national economy as a whole and reorganize the state-owned enterprises and restructure the state-owned sector strategically. At the same time, it is necessary to combine efforts to deepen the reform with efforts to promote development and raise the quality of economic growth, and combine the efforts for enterprise reform with efforts to strengthen enterprise management. The 20 years of China's reform of the state-owned enterprises are also 20 years in which efforts have been made to continuously strengthen enterprise management. In this process, a large group of enterprises, including the Shanghai Baoshan Iron and Steel Corp., the Handan Iron and Steel Corp. and the Northeast China Pharmaceutical Group, have emerged as enterprises with modern management.

Fourth, China has, in practice, formulated a series of important principles to promote the reform and development of the state-owned enterprises and made active efforts in effecting the separation of government administration from enterprise management and carrying out various supporting reforms. For instance, the objective for the reform of the state-owned enterprises is defined as establishing a modern enterprise system. The focus of work is to do a good job in the development of the national economy as a whole, to readjust the distribution and structure of the state-owned sector of the economy, to do well in the development of the large enterprises and invigorate the small ones, and to strategically reorganize the state-owned enterprises. Encouragement is given to the merger of enterprises and procedures to declare bankruptcy have been codified so as to bring into play the mechanism of competition to let the successful enterprises survive and the unsuccessful ones parish.

At the same time, the request is raised to improve leading bodies and management systems of the enterprises in accordance with the laws of the market economy and the actual conditions in China; to wholeheartedly rely on the working class and bring into play the role of Party organizations in the enterprises as the political core; to promote the separation of government administration from enterprise management and coordinate various supporting reforms; to continuously improve laws and legal regulations that are conducive to the reform and development of the enterprises; and so on.

Although China's reform of the state-owned enterprises has been going on for 20 years, there are still many problems. For instance, the reform is conducted in an excessively extensive range, the property right relations still remain unclear, the functions of the government and the enterprises have not yet been completely separated, the rights and responsibilities of the government and enterprises in terms of enterprise management have not been clearly differentiated, management in the enterprises still lags behind and the economic returns of the enterprises have kept declining. All these indicate that up until now, no fundamental breakthrough has been made in the reform of the state-owned enterprises. On the one hand, the reason is that China has adopted the "gradual approach" in the reform, and the guidelines for the reform have taken shape gradually. The objective of the reform was not clear at the start and the measures adopted have to be modified from time to time. On the other hand, the subject of the reform has been the government rather than the enterprises. This not only hurts the enthusiasm of the enterprises but also makes it possible for the government to push forward the market-oriented reform of the state-owned enterprises with methods used under the planned economy. Besides, due to the restriction by various factors, the government has from time to time moved away from the issue of reform of property rights either intentionally or unintentionally while making efforts to expedite the reform. This has made it difficult for the large numbers of medium-sized and small enterprises that are inappropriate to retain their state-owned nature to "quit." Moreover, this situation also has made it impossible to carry out the desired strategic reorganization of the state-owned sector.

III. Tasks for Reform of Large and Medium-sized State-owned Enterprises

1. Further Clarifying the Role and Tasks of State-owned Enterprises

The 15th National Congress of the Chinese Communist Party defined the status and role of state-owned sector as the "dominant," which mainly referred to its control power over the national economy. Compared with the past situation, this represents a big step forward. It shows that China has decided to cut down the scope and size of and shorten the battle line for the state-owned sector to effect a strategic reorganization of it in line with the demands to develop a market economy. The way adopted for the reorganization is to introduce in the overwhelming majority of large and medium-sized state-owned enterprises the modern enterprise system and make them pull themselves out from their difficult plight in about three years.

To be more specific, the status and role of the state-owned enterprises should be manifested in the following three aspects. First, they should serve as a means for direct intervention in the economy, offset the defects of the market and play an active and positive role in areas where the market mechanism cannot play a role or cannot play an obvious role, such as in infrastructure facilities and the supply of public products. Second, they should serve as a tool or means for the post-industrialized countries to carry out their economic "catch-up" strategies and play a leading role in the basic industries as well as high and new technology industries of the national economy. Third, they should be used to show the control power of the state-owned economy. As China is now still in the transitional process from the planned economy to the market economy, state-owned enterprises also shoulder the responsibility to reflect the leading role of the state-owned sector in the national economy, i.e., displaying the function of the strategic control power. Considerable numbers of state-owned enterprises of certain scales should be kept in important industries and key areas that are vital to the national economy and the people's livelihood and represent the lifeline of the national economy. In the first two aspects, the condition in China is basically the same as in most of the countries practicing the market economy, particularly the developed countries. Yet, in terms of scale of state-owned enterprises, it should not be too large. Otherwise, they would produce a bad impact on the development of the non-state-owned sector and on the operational efficiency of the national economy as a whole. Along with the improvement of the market system, the number of state-owned enterprises should gradually reduce, as it is too large now.

2. Interpretations of the Modern Enterprise System

The objective of China's reform of large and medium-sized state-owned enterprises has been defined as the establishment of a modern enterprise system featuring "clear-cut property rights, distinctive rights and responsibilities in enterprise management, separation of government administration from enterprise management, and scientific management." Modern enterprise system is a concept with a very broad sense and can be interpreted in many different ways. In countries practicing market economy, state-owned enterprise is often used as a concept opposite to non-state-owned enterprise. As what enterprise organizational forms the state-owned enterprises and various kinds of non-state-owned enterprises should adopt, it is determined by various factors, such as the composite structure of investment and enterprise scale. The most common forms of organization are single-proprietor enterprises, partnerships, limited-liability companies and joint-stock companies with limited liabilities.

Apparently, it is imperative for the state-owned enterprises to adopt one of the organizational forms mentioned above. In the theoretical circles of China, people tend to regard the corporate system as the modern enterprise system, and hold that it should be the main organizational form that should be adopted for the state-owned enterprises through the reform of the economic restructure. According to a survey conducted by the State Statistical Bureau on 2,562 major enterprises in 1998, 1,943 (75.8 percent) of them had undergone the transformation towards the corporate system. Among them, 768 had been changed into limited-liability companies, accounting for 39.5 percent; 612 were turned into joint-stock companies with limited liabilities, accounting for 31.5 percent; and 563 remained as single-proprietor (the state as the sole investor) companies, accounting for 29.0 percent.

However, even for these state-owned enterprises that had undergone the reform to adopt the corporate system, there was still a long way for them to go to meet the demands of "clear-cut property rights, distinctive rights and responsibilities in enterprise management, separation of government administration and enterprise management, and scientific management." The reason is that there are still many problems that have remained unsolved. These problems include how to manage state-owned assets in the state-owned enterprises that had undergone the transformation, how to bring about a real separation of the functions of the government from those of the enterprises, how to ensure the property right of the enterprises as legal persons, and how to establish a structure for management by the legal persons. Inevitably, these unsolved problems make it difficult for the reform of the state-owned enterprises to deepen. To make the establishment of a modern enterprise system the primary objective of the reform appears to be too general a demand. Greater efforts are still called for to seek practical "bridges and ways" to introduce the modern enterprise system in the state-owned enterprises.

3. Comprehensively Materializing the Demand of "Clear-cut Property Rights, Distinctive Rights and Responsibilities in Enterprise Management, Separation of Government Administration from Enterprise Management, and Scientific Management," and Making Active Exploration for New "Bridges and Ways" to Introduce the Modern Enterprise System in State-owned Enterprises

First, resolutely promoting the property right reform in state-owned enterprises and materializing the property right of enterprises as legal persons. It is necessary to separate clearly the ownership right with management right. The state, as the owner of state-owned enterprises, enjoys the right to returns from its investment and shoulders part of the responsibilities. The enterprises possess all property rights entitled to the legal persons, enforce management independently and shoulder the responsibility to maintain and increase the value of the capital invested by the state.

Second, establishing standard structures to manage corporations in line with the requirements of the "Corporation Law." Now, the government administration is not separated from enterprise management in state-owned enterprises. This is because, on the one hand, the change of the functions of the government departments is slow and the government departments are unwilling to delegate more power to the enterprises and, on the other, the enterprises are devoid of standard structures for management of corporations. The government is unwilling to delegate power to the enterprises for fear that there might be control by insiders and chaos. In fact, a corporation management structure that can ensure a check-balance relationship between the owner and the manager is the core of the modern enterprise system. First, it is essential to ensure that the owner occupies a proper position. Second, it is necessary to guarantee that the board of directors can carry out its responsibilities entrusted by the owner. Third, it is imperative to ensure that the board of directors can exercise supervision over the high-ranking management personnel and provide them with sufficient incentives. In addition, it is necessary to standardize the stock market to enforce its supervision over the operation of the corporations from outside.

Third, accelerating the pace of change in the government's functions and introducing a multi-level ownership and management systems for state-owned assets. Party organizations and government administrative departments must all separate themselves from the management organizations of state-owned assets. In this respect, it is necessary to take resolute actions to separate the functions of the government from those of the enterprises.

4. Working Hard to Promote the Establishment of a Social Security System, Improving the Capital Market and Developing the Non-Public Sectors to Create a Better Environment for the Strategic Readjustment of the State-owned Sector

By "shock therapy." It means to bring out thorough transformation in property rights. Yet, the results are not as obvious as expected. The reasons are as follows: first, the transformation of property rights is not realized through market exchange. It is, therefore, difficult to achieve a quick development of the market system. Second, as it is devoid of support from a well-developed non-state-owned sector, it is difficult for the mechanism of competition to take shape, to say nothing of efficiency. It is necessary for China to be fully aware of the urgent need to carry out the strategic reorganization of the state-owned enterprises and to establish the modern enterprise system in large and medium-sized state-owned enterprises, and to push forward the reform unswervingly. Meanwhile, it is necessary to conscientiously sum up the experience and lessons leanrned in implementing the "gradual reform" approach, vigorously foster the development of the market system and the non-state-owned sectors, particularly the non-publicly owned sectors, make active efforts to establish a social security system and be ready to accept new ideas. It is necessary to take precautions against the frequent use of terminology as "privatization" and "loss of state-owned assets," which have a strong political tone, and against taking liberty to put various sorts of labels on measures taken for the reform and strategic reorganization of the state-owned enterprises. It is necessary to create an economic, social and political environment favorable to reform and make those state-funded enterprises, which cannot play their due role, quit from the public sector, so as to accomplish the objective set for the strategic reorganization of the state-owned capital. In view of the special position occupied by the state-owned enterprises, it is also necessary to handle well the relations between reform, stability and development while making efforts to deepen the reform of the state-owned enterprises, so as to maintain a social and political stability.

Section 5
Speeding up Reform and Development of Medium-sized and Small Enterprises

I. Position and Role of Medium-sized and Small Enterprises in China's Reform and Development

Over 99 percent of the medium-sized and small enterprises in China are non-state-owned. Their rapid development has turned out to be a major driving force in China's endeavor to adjust the ownership structure since the reform drive was launched in 1978. At the same time, thanks to the "gradual reform" approach adopted for the reform of the state-owned enterprises, the medium-sized and small enterprises have turned out to be the area in which a breakthrough can be made the most easily. Medium-sized and small enterprises play a unique role in China's reform and development.

1. The Development of the Medium-sized and Small Enterprises Has Facilitated the Readjustment of China's Ownership Structure

Prior to reform, medium-sized and small enterprises in China fell roughly into two categories – those owned by the whole people and those owned collectively. According to the statistics collected in 1978, of the 348,000 industrial enterprises (excluding village-run ones and individually established workshops), small enterprises accounted for 99.94 percent. Thanks to the development over the past 20 years, the number of medium-sized and small enterprises in China has increased by a wide margin. Towards the end of 1995, the total number of industrial enterprises had reached 7.26 million, of which medium-sized and small ones accounted for 99.9 percent, while the number of the large ones was only 6,416, making up less than 0.1 percent of the total (see Table 1-12). It should be pointed out that most of the newly established medium-sized and small enterprises were non-state-owned ones (state-owned enterprises accounted only for 12 percent of the total in 1995). Moreover, most of these newly established medium-sized and small enterprises are non-publicly owned. The medium-sized and small enterprises in the non-state-owned and non-publicly owned categories have undergone very quick development and grown into a major force in China's ownership structure.

2. Medium-sized and Small Enterprises Are an Important Force to Promote China's Economic Growth

In the period of the planned economy, China's economic growth was mainly achieved through investments by the government. But, the result was there was a long-standing shortage in all the sectors of the economy. Since the reform was launched, the investment subjects have diversified and this has greatly promoted the development of medium-sized and small enterprises. Not only that these enterprises have played the role of "making good omissions and deficiencies," they also turned out to be a new point for economic growth. In 1994, China's industrial growth rate reached 18 percent, while that for the large and medium-sized enterprises was only 5-8 percent. Yet, the growth of the medium-sized and small enterprises reached as high as 30 percent. Making up for the overwhelming majority of the medium-sized and small enterprises, the township- and village-run enterprises have reaped an average annual growth rate of over 20 percent since the reform was launched. The medium-sized and small enterprises have directly satisfied the market needs and at the same time constantly created new market demands. The development of small hi-tech companies in different forms has contributed to the technological progress in the country. In addition, the medium-sized and small enterprises have helped expand exports, which in turn has spurred on the growth of the domestic economy.

Since the mid-1990s, the total volume of exports made by the medium-sized and small enterprises has accounted for more than 50 percent of the national total. The rapid growth of the medium-sized and small enterprises has become an important force driving the economic development and has created conditions for China's economy to turn from the situation of overall shortage into a buyers' market.

3. Medium-sized and Small Enterprises Provide the Basic Channel for Increasing Job Opportunities

The medium-sized and small enterprises are mostly in the labor-intensive industries. Therefore, they play a decisive role in solving the country's employment problem. China has a large population and the employment pressure has always remained heavy. Since the reform, More importance has been attached to solving the employment problem through developing medium-sized and small enterprises. From the early stage of reform to the mid-1990s, some 75 percent of the newly added

Table 1-12. Scale and Structure of Industrial Enterprises in China in 1995 (%)

	Number of Industrial Enterprises		Industrial Output Value (billion yuan)		Number of Employees (thousand)		Capital Actually Amassed (billion yuan)	
	Absolute number	%	Absolute number	%	Absolute number	%	Absolute number	%
National Total	**7,259,822**	**100**	**8,051.961**	**100**	**143,672.3**	**100**	**2,481.599**	**100**
Large Enterprises	6,416	0.09	2,182.62	27.10	24,093.1	16.76	933.558	37.62
Medium-sized Enterprises	16,591	0.23	907.753	11.27	14,819.7	10.31	312.858	12.61
Small Enterprises	7,236,815	99.68	4,961.446	61.61	104,759.5	72.91	1,235.184	49.77
State-owned Enterprises	**87,905**	**100**	**2,588.993**	**100**	**66,100**	**100**	**4,747.206**	**100**
Large Enterprises	4,685	5.33	1,590.727	61.44			2,989.565	62.98
Medium-sized Enterprises	10,983	12.49	530.235	20.48			954.072	20.10
Small Enterprises	72,237	82.18	468.031	18.08			806.431	16.99

Source of Data: *Synopsis of Statistics Collected in the Third National Industrial Survey of the People's Republic of China in 1995*, by State Statistical Bureau, p. 4.

labor force in urban areas were employed in the medium-sized and small enterprises. In the countryside, over 100 million people redundant in agricultural production have turned to non-agricultural trades in the township- and village-run enterprises. After the mid-1990s, the large and medium-sized state-owned enterprises were asked to cut down their employees to increase efficiency and transfer of the labor force in agriculture was accelerated. Again, the medium-sized and small enterprises, particularly the non-publicly owned ones, have turned out as the main channels in tackling the employment problem (see Table 1-13 and Table 1–14). Toward the end of 1998, employees of individually and privately enterprises as well as enterprises in mixed ownership throughout the country had accounted for 13.6 percent of the total employed population, exceeding the proportion of people employed in the state-owned and collectively owned economic units. It so happened that these enterprises have become the economic elements that are the fastest in providing jobs to the jobless, and they will become the major choice for China to solve its problem regarding employment.

Table 1-13. Ownership Structure Nationwide in Terms of Employees (%)

Type of Ownership	1978	1985	1990	1995	1996	1997	1998
State-owned sector	18.6	18.0	18.2	16.6	16.3	15.9	12.9
Collective sector	81.4	20.7	22.6	23.5	24.0	22.9	13.5
Sector in Mixed Ownership	--	0.1	0.3	1.3	1.4	1.6	2.4
Private sector	--	09	4.0	8.4	9.0	9.8	11.2
Farm-household Economy	--	60.3	54.9	47.6	46.9	46.3	--

Source of Data: *Structural Transformation of the Chinese Economy and Economic Growth in China*, by Shen Kunrong, p. 57; *China Statistical Synopsis (1999)*, by the State Statistical Bureau, p. 8.

4. Medium-sized and Small Enterprises Are a Shock Force in China's Economic Reform and an Important Support for the Reform of the Large Enterprises

Before the reform, the medium-sized and small enterprises in China could only survive in the narrow crevices left under the system of the planned economy. Since the reform drive was launched, these enterprises, as represented by the township- and village-run, individual and private enterprises as well as foreign-funded enterprises, have witnessed a rapid development. Their quick development has keyed up the readjustment of the ownership structure, promoted the market, shook the monopoly position of the state-owned sector and compelled the state-owned enterprises, which were operating under the traditional rigid system, to pull back step by step. This not only has raised the efficiency in the allocation of resources but also created the necessary conditions for the market-orientated reform of China's economic structure and the establishment of the socialist market economic system. At the same time, they have also rendered important support to the large enterprises in their efforts to cut down the size of their employees to increase efficiency and in their market-orientated reform by buying their products and absorbing their redundant personnel.

The above is but a brief summary of the roles played by the medium-sized and small enterprises in China's reform and development. In fact, both in China and elsewhere, the status and roles of the medium-sized and small enterprises are becoming more and more profound. "Medium-sized and small enterprises have become increasingly the focus of attention for their flexible mechanisms, low-cost management, their pioneering spirit in technological innovation, their great ability in earning foreign exchange and their vitality in economic crises. They have been winning more and more acclaim and compliments from the public for their status and roles in developing production, increasing employment, turning out brand-name products, expanding export, invigorating the economy of backward areas, fostering the innovative spirit and training entrepreneurs."(8) But, any coin has two sides. It is true that the medium-sized and small enterprises have many merits and advantages. Yet, they have also encountered many problems and difficulties when compared with the large enterprises that have abundant financial resources, are advanced technologically and possess a larger share of the market.

Table 1-14. Ownership Structures in Urban and Rural Areas in Terms of Employees

	1978		1990		1995		1998	
	Number (million)	Rate (%)	Number (million)	Rate (%)	Number (million)	Rate (%)	Number (million)	Rate (%)
Urban Areas	**95.14**	**100**	**166.16**	**100**	**190.93**	**100**	**206.78**	**100**
State-owned Sector	74.51	78.3	103.46	62.3	112.61	59.0	90.58	43.8
Collective Sector	20.48	21.5	35.49	21.4	31.47	16.5	19.63	9.5
Individual/Private Sector	--	--	67.1	0.4	20.45	10.7	32.32	15.6
Other Economic Sectors	--	--		0.1	88.3	4.6	16.65	8.1
Rural Areas	**306.38**	**100**	**472.93**	**100**	**488.54**	**100**	**492.79**	**100**
Township Enterprises	28.27	9.2	92.65	19.6	128.62	26.0	74.47	15.2
Private Enterprises	--	--	11.3	0.24	47.1	--	73.7	1.5
Individually Employed	--	--	14.91	3.15	30.54	--	38.55	7.8

Source of Data: *China Statistical Synopsis (1999)*, by State Statistical Bureau, p. 33.

II. Major Problems and Difficulties Encountered by Medium-sized and Small Enterprises

There are two major types of problems that the medium-sized and small enterprises in China have so far encountered. One is the type of problems in development, and the other the problems in the reform of the enterprise system in the transitional period of economy.

1. Major Difficulties and Problems of the Medium-sized and Small Enterprises in Development

The difficulties confronting the medium-sized and small enterprises in the course of development come from two aspects -- the enterprises themselves and the external environment. With regard to the first aspect, the major obstacles they have encountered in their development are related to their own limits, such as the low level of technology and equipment, shortage of trained technological and managerial personnel, difficulties in raising funds, lack of stable avenues to market their products, low technological content in most of the products, fierce market competition and low rate of profit. With these disadvantages, bankruptcy will frequently occur in time of economic depression or crisis. Of the 468,506 industrial enterprises that practiced independent accounting in 1997, the average of capital fund for each small enterprise was less than 240,000 yuan, some one-10th of that of a medium-sized enterprise or one-74th of that of a large enterprise. The average annual output value of each of them was 7.08 million yuan, one-eighth of that of a medium-sized enterprise or one-53rd of that of a large one. The limits in "scale" of the medium-sized and small enterprises have placed them, generally speaking, at the bottom strata in the industrial division of labor, making them engage in production and operation with low added value. In fact, many household-based individual businesses are only operated as a means to sustain a living.

In China, the external environment has also been very poor for the development of the medium-sized and small enterprises. Over a long time in the past, there had been no laws or regulations that supported or encouraged the development of medium-sized and small enterprises. As a result, their development was devoid of the protection by law. Moreover, the management system of the medium-sized and small enterprises was not well established and enterprises in different industries and trades were put under the care of different government departments. Such a situation remained until 1998 when a special department – Department of Medium-sized and Small Enterprises – was established under the State Economic and Trade Commission to deal with affairs related to the medium-sized and small enterprises across the country. To date, not much improvement has been seen in this confused situation, as evidenced by the lack of nationwide unitary basic statistical data on the overall scope, industrial structure and financial conditions of the medium-sized and small enterprises. Moreover, not sufficient support has been given to these enterprises. For example, rural township enterprises, which make up the bulk of the medium-sized and small enterprises, generate 40-50 percent of the total industrial output value of the country. Yet, the bank loans granted to them accounted for less than 10 percent. For those individually and privately owned enterprises, it is even more difficult to obtain loans. Because of their small scale, there is little chance for the medium-sized and small enterprises to pool funds in the capital market. This explains the widespread phenomenon of capital shortage among the medium-sized and small enterprises. The support given by the government to the medium-sized and small enterprises in fund, technology, information and finance has remained seriously insufficient and the socialized service system has not yet come into shape. On the one hand, there are few intermediaries. On the other, the high service fees charged by the intermediaries scare away most of the medium-sized and small enterprises as they can hardly afford them. In this way, it is certainly difficult for most of them to get help and support.

The problems and difficulties encountered by the medium-sized and small enterprises in both their own development and the external environment easily subject them to the influence of economic fluctuations. In time of economic boom, they will see fast development. In time of economic contraction when tight money policy is implemented and the market demand goes down, large enterprises would automatically shift their difficulties to the medium-sized and small enterprises, making them the victims threatened by closedown, suspended operation, merger and switch to other lines of business. Prior to the mid-1990s, due to the overall shortage of products in the market, poor quality operation and economic fluctuations produced little influence on the survival of the medium-sized and small enterprises. Now, the general situation featuring more supply than demand has appeared in China and market competition has turned into a competition between brand-names and in quality, the medium-sized and small enterprises, which have been operating at a low quality, are faced with greater difficulties. The occurrences of bankruptcy have increased, which have produced an adverse affect on the overall economic growth and the efforts to solve the employment problem.

2. For Medium-sized and Small State-owned Enterprises, the Effect of Structural Reform Is Not Obvious

The reform of the medium-sized and small enterprises is a component of the overall reform of enterprises. Before the 14th National Party Congress (1992), there was no substantial difference between the reform of the medium-sized and small enterprises and that of the large and medium-sized ones in terms of content and means. The major forms adopted were granting more power and profits to the enterprises, management based on contract and leased management. Similar to the situation in the large and medium-sized enterprises, the reform in the above-mentioned forms failed to effect a change in the management mechanism of the state-owned and collectively owned medium-sized and small enterprises. On the contrary, losses were incurred extensively when the market competition has become increasingly fierce. In 1994, 24,000 state-owned industrial enterprises, which practiced independent accounting, found their balance sheet in the red. Of them, over 95 percent were medium-sized and small enterprises. Net deficits were also seen in the small state-owned enterprises after their gains were used to offset their losses.

Most of the state-owned medium-sized and small enterprises belong to the local governments at the city and county level. Losses incurred by these enterprises would directly affected the local financial revenue and increase the burden of fiscal subsidies. After the 14th National Party Congress, the Party Central Committee has step by step adopted flexible policies regarding the reform of small state-owned enterprises. In 1995, it put forward the policy of "doing a good job with regard to the large enterprises and giving a free reign to the small ones," allowing the local governments to adopt various flexible ways to speed up the pace of "freeing and invigorating" small state-owned enterprises, including selling them out to individuals. In fact, prior the adoption of this policy, some local governments had already made efforts to reform the medium-sized and small enterprises, mainly taking the form of selling them to individuals. After 1995, all localities have accelerated their tempo of reform of the medium-sized and small enterprises and the forms of reform have become more diversified. By August 1998, throughout the country 47,631 state-owned medium-sized and small enterprises practicing independent accounting had undergone transformation. They accounted for 64.1 percent of the total of their kind. Some provinces claimed that they had already had 80 percent or even over 90 percent of their state-owned medium-sized and small enterprises transformed. There are still some places that had carried out transformation of all the medium-sized and small enterprises under their jurisdiction. Now, there is only a small number of state-owned small enterprises that have not undergone the transformation. Most of them are ones whose assets are not enough to offset their debts or ones whose assets are in extremely poor quality. Beset with great difficulties, they cannot be easily invigorated. Yet, it is also hard to make them claim bankruptcy or have them sold out, because few people would have the interest to buy them. Also, there are a few enterprises for which the transformation is hard to be carried out, because they possess a considerably large amount of assets. In addition, there are still some others that are reluctant to be transformed for the results of their operation is rather satisfactory at the moment.

So far, most state-owned medium-sized and small enterprises have completed the initial stage of reform. There are some state-owned small enterprises whose management has been strengthened and whose financial situation has been proved after the transformation. On the whole, however, the reform and development of the state-owned medium-sized and small enterprises are far from being satisfactory. For example, a net deficit still appeared in 1997 when the gains of China's state-owned small industrial enterprises practicing independent accounting were used to offset their expenditure. In the reform and development of the state-owned medium-sized and small enterprises, there are the following major problems: First, no major steps have been taken in the reform of the property right relations in the medium-sized and small enterprises. In the reform conducted over the years, more than ten forms have been tried out. Of these forms, such as management based on contract, management on lease and consigned management, most have failed to touch the question regarding the property right relations. Lack of change in the property right relations means, in essence, to maintain the state-owned nature in ownership of the medium-sized and small enterprises. It is not conducive to the desired strategic reorganization of the state-owned sector, nor is it conducive to truly improving the management and operation of the state-owned small enterprises. The reform practice over the past two decades or more has proved that management based on contract without reforming the property right relations means, in fact, to make the enterprises only answerable to gains but not losses. It cannot possibly bring about a real transformation of the management mechanism in the enterprises and the state cannot possibly shirk its responsibility for financial losses at the end. Judging by the criterion of property right reform, the coverage of structural reform of the medium-sized and small enterprises is not yet wide enough and the task in the future is still very arduous. Second, there still lacks a unified, standard and easily operational program for property right reform in the state-owned enterprises. The reform of the state-owned small enterprises is mainly put under the leadership of the local governments. The forms and programs for the reform vary greatly in different places. There are no clearly defined and unified standards that are applicable throughout the country. This situation has caused some ambiguity in the objective of the reform. In the reform of the state-owned large and medium-sized enterprises, the objective is set as establishing a modern enterprise system while that for the reform of the small enterprises is to "give a free reign to and invigorate" them. But, with regard to such questions as how the objective can bc achieved, the specific measures are not clearly stated. Some localities have been over-anxious for quick results and resorted to methods usually adopted in political movements to carry out the reform, without paying sufficient attention to protecting the legitimate rights of the workers and debtors. Some other places worked out extremely complicated formalities for the reform and made the cost of reform exceptionally high, thus stifling the enthusiasm of the enterprises for the structural reform. Third, supporting reforms have not been carried out or lagged behind. Along with the reform, the functions of the government are supposed to be separated from those of the enterprises, which should turn into independent economic entities not affiliated to any administrative authorities. In fact, however, the traditional methods of control have still existed. For example, the enterprises now still have to look after their retirees and been the responsible for family planning, social welfare affairs, as well as activities of the Party and Communist Youth League organizations. Many enterprises are even compelled to provide jobs to a certain number of demobilized army people and new school graduates. The enterprises are still pressed by a high rate of debt as well as various other burdens, and the social security system has not been established. Judging by all this, it can be concluded that, even after the reform, the state-owned small enterprises are still not independent market subjects in the real sense and it is still difficult for them to make decisions regarding their own management like those privately owned ones. Besides, property right reform in the medium-sized and small enterprises has met with a very strong ideological resistance. More often than not, any reform involving property right relations will likely be labeled as "privatization" or "loss of state-owned assets." Fourth, the external environment is not yet satisfactory for the small enterprises after reform – they have not received sufficient support for their development and are faced with many difficulties in their operation. These are the common problems encountered by the medium-sized and small enterprises. Up to now, China has not yet established an effective policy and supporting system for the development of the medium-sized and small enterprises. Consequently, all these enterprises find it extremely difficult to raise funds. Some government departments have even set some restrictions on them, such as the restriction on the export of their products and their participation in competition in the international market, which will certainly hinder their efforts to seek opportunities for development in the global market.

III. Policy Suggestions to Accelerate the Reform and Development of the Medium-sized and Small Enterprises

1. Policy Suggestions to Accelerate the Reform of the Medium-sized and Small Enterprises

First, stop setting up new state-owned medium-sized and small enterprises. The state-owned sector should mainly pool its strength and resources in undertakings that have an important bearing on the overall national economic and social development, constitute the lifeline of the national economy, can only and must be accomplished by the state and cannot possibly be left to the non-public sectors. Other than these undertakings, there is virtually no need for the state to set up state-owned enterprises. It is necessary to resolutely stop establishing new state-owned medium-sized and small state-owned enterprises so as to concentrate the resources to strengthen the key areas, shorten the line of the state-owned sector, make a bigger room for the development of non-state-owned sectors and create a better social environment.

Second, take the opportunity of the strategic reorganization of the state-owned sector to the state-owned medium-sized and small enterprises to "quit" more quickly. Except for a small number of state-owned large and medium-sized enterprises whose nature of "state ownership" has to be upheld, the large numbers of state-owned medium-sized and small enterprises, for which it is inappropriate to retain the "state-owned" status, should be "denationalized" or be turned into commonplace enterprises – to have their "state-owned" nature removed. The measures and efforts taken to "give a free reign to small enterprises" should be resolute and thorough. Those enterprises that are operating in difficulties should be denationalized. Even the few state-owned medium-sized and small enterprises, which are still making profits now, should also be let free. Only in this way is it possible to cut off the umbilical cord of capital between the enterprises and the government and can the problem in ownership be solved for the state-owned medium-sized and small enterprises.

Third, center around the reform to change the property right and quicken the pace to turn state-owned medium-sized and small enterprises into individually operated ones. It is necessary to reduce the scope of or abolish the contract management system, the leased management system and the system of consigned management, all of which cannot effect any change in the property right relations. It is necessary to solve the problem regarding the nature of the medium-sized and small enterprises, which are still considered "state-owned" even after their property right relations are changed, through such means as establishing the corporate system or the joint-stock partnership system, bankruptcy, merger and, in particular, sales (or sales in "symbolic" sense). After such a structural change, these enterprises will become ones owned by the people rather than ones owned by the state.

Fourth, enact and improve laws and regulations regarding the property right reform of the state-owned medium-sized and small enterprises, and institutionalize the procedures for sales of these enterprises. It is necessary to enact strict standards for evaluation of assets, clarify the property right of the enterprises, rationally decide on and distribute stock rights and effect the change of property right according to law. In this aspect, the methods of work should be open, fair and just, and they should be subjected to supervision from the society, the employees as well as the public opinion. In order to protect the legitimate rights of the debtors and employees, the accumulated amount of state-owned assets can be converted into debts or social security deposits for the workers and staff (it should be allowed and encouraged to buy out the workers and staff in accordance with their different terms of service with a lump sum of money). For enterprises whose assets are not enough to offset their debts, the state can set aside part of the income from selling those enterprises that operated more successfully as "reserve fund for property right reform" to pay back the bank loans and arrears owed to the workers and staff.

Fifth, strengthening supporting reforms, including the reform of government departments aimed at changing their functions, the reform of social security system, the reform of the financial system, the reform of the investment system, and the development of the capital market. At the same time, efforts should be made to create a sound social environment for the property right reform of the state-owned medium-sized and small enterprises.

2. Policy Suggestions to Promote the Sound Development of the Medium-sized and Small Enterprises

After the property right reform, the state-owned medium-sized and small enterprises are bound to encounter the problem of how to develop. On the part of the government, it is necessary to divert attention from enforcing supervision over their internal micro-economic operation to establishing a macro supporting policy systems. At the same time, the government should adopt an unbiased attitude in promoting a sound development of all kinds of medium-sized and small enterprises.

First, active efforts should be made to establish an organizational supporting system to give support to the development of the medium-sized and small enterprises. Such organizations should comprise both governmental and non-governmental ones. At present, primary attention should be given to establishing a government-backed organizational supporting system and, at the same time, encouraging the establishment and development of non-government organizations, and in this way, bringing into being an organizational control and service network that is formed by official, semi-official, popular and private institutions and caters to the needs of the medium-sized and small enterprises.

Second, it is necessary to strengthen and improve support rendered to the small enterprises in terms of finance and taxation. It is imperative to institutionalize the collection of taxes and various levies from the medium-sized and small enterprises so as to reduce their burden. Preferential treatments, such as tax reduction or exemption for a certain period of time, should be given to enterprises that comply with the state's industrial policies, engage in production of handicraft articles and possess high and new technology. At the same time, financial departments should provide the medium-sized and small enterprises with financial support and preferential treatment in such areas as operation, personnel training, import of new technology, export of products, and development of new products.

Third, give support to the medium-sized and small enterprises by strengthening and improving the legal system. It is necessary to, under the precondition of gradually improving the socialist market economic legal system, enact as soon as possible the "Basic Law Concerning Medium-sized and Small Enterprises" in line with the actual conditions and special needs of the medium-sized and small enterprises, and enact and improve laws and regulations for protecting competition, providing these enterprises with various kinds of guarantee and support in credit, fund raising and export, promoting their technological advance and expediting local development.

Fourth, increasing financial support to the development of the medium-sized and small enterprises and open more reliable fund-raising channels for them. It is necessary to set up special financial institutions that can provide these enterprises with fund-raising services, increase loans granted to them, establish loan-guarantee foundations with subsidies from the state and develop risk investment foundations for the development of hi-tech enterprises. At the same time, it is necessary to make active efforts to create conditions for the medium-sized and small enterprise to enter the capital market and have more direct channels for them to raise funds.

Fifth, establish socialized service systems for the medium-sized and small enterprises. Government departments and training institutions subsidized by the government should pay more attention to bring into full play the role of non-governmental social organizations in undertaking various training tasks and providing consultation, information and technological services to the medium-sized and small enterprises, so as to enable these enterprises to make better use of their human resources.

Sixth, strengthen cooperation between medium-sized and small enterprises on the one hand and large enterprises on the other in spite of their division of work, encourage the urban and rural enterprises as well as the small, medium-sized and large enterprises to enter into various forms of alliance, as so to form well-coordinated industrial organizational structure, which is led by the large enterprises and supported by large numbers of medium-sized and small ones. It is necessary to actively render guidance to the medium-sized and small enterprises in their development by means of industrial policies, open more areas for them and encourage them to take the road of being "small but special," "small but proficient," "small but unique" and "small but allied," and improve their economic efficiency.

Notes:

(1) The "complete collectivization" movement launched in the former Soviet Union was strongly opposed by the farmers, who were so indignant that they damaged farm tools, killed livestock and rebelled against the government. It is estimated that 6-14.5 million people during the collectivization movement from 1929 to 1936. At the end of the 19th century, Russia was one of the two largest cereal producing countries in the world. Yet, it had to import grain from abroad after collectivization. Its agricultural output had not even reached the 1913 level util the death of J. Stalin. (See *Common Problems of Modernization* by Yin Baoyun, Tianjin People's Publishing House, 1998, pp. 93-95). During China's collectivization movement, the cereal output dropped by 15 percent in 1959 and 10 percent in 1960, and this caused the lives of thousands upon thousands of people. (See *China's Economic Reform in Modern Times: Strategies and Implementation* by Wu Jinglian, Shanghai Far East Press, 1999, p. 107). Mr. Lin Yifu described many of the defects of the people's commune system. Apart from stifling the farmers' enthusiasm in production, these defects also serve as the causes for the problems of high cost of management and low efficiency of production, both of which can be attributed to the lack of a supervisory mechanism and an incentive mechanism. (See *System, Technology and Agricultural Development in China* by Lin Yifu, Shanghai People's Press, 1994, pp. 44-75.)

(2) Wu Jinglian listed the three kinds of property rights obtained by the farmers after reform -- the right to private property, which comprises mainly bank savings, houses, the means of production for domestic use and means of subsistence; right to use land, which is a kind of property right never enjoyed by the farmers since the collectivization movement; and right to the growing human capital of the farmers. See *China's Economic Reform in Modern Times: Strategies and Implementation,* p. 125, Shanghai Far East Press, 1999.

(3) Chang Xiuze, et al., "Marketization of China's National Economy: the Level Reached and Thinking for Its Development," carried in *Institutional Effects of*

China's Reform and Development edited by Han Zhiguo, et al., Economic Science Press, 1998, p .81.

(4) Liu Wei, "Development of Marketization and Evolution of the Property System," carried in *Institutional Effects of China's Reform and Development* edited by Han Zhiguo, et al., Economic Science Press, p. 67.

(5) See *A Perspective of Private Enterprises* by Li Zhenjie, Economic Management Press, 1999, pp. 4-5.

(6) For the average annual growth rates of GDP and per-capita GDP in China in the 1978-98 period, see *China Statistical Synopsis (1999)*, pp. 14-15.

(7) Wu, Jinglina, *China's Economic Reform in Modern Times: Strategies and Implementation*, p. 441, Shanghai Far East Press, 1999.

(8) Department of Industry and Transport, State Statistical Bureau: "On the Orientation of Development of State-owned Industry in the Transitional Process of Economic Structure," *Statistical Reference*, Issue No. 3, 1999.

CHAPTER 2
PRICE REFORM IN CHINA

Synopsis

To promote the reform of the economic structure, China has always attached great importance to price reform. The rural reform was launched in 1979. One of the two important measures adopted in the rural reform was to increase by a large margin the purchasing prices of agricultural products (the other was to introduce the household-based responsibility system with remuneration linked to output). The "Decision of the Central Committee of the Communist Party of China on Reform of the Economic Structure," adopted on October 20, 1984, clearly described the importance and position of price reform in China's economic restructuring. It pointed out that price was the most effective regulatory means and the reform of the price system is the key to the success or failure of the overall reform of the economic structure. In October 1992, the report to the 14th National Party Congress reiterated this view, pointing out that price reform was the key to the development of the market and the reform of the economic structure, and it was necessary to us to accelerate the pace of the reform, so as to straighten out the price relations and establish a pricing system based on prices formed in the market while taking into account the capacity of endurance of people in all walks of life. Over the past two decades, China's price reform has been conducted under this guideline. Thanks to the efforts by governments of all levels and the support from the public, the reform has gradually gone into full swing and substantial progress has achieved. Now, a market pricing system has basically come into shape with regard to the prices of

goods and services, and the marketization of the prices of factors of production has also been underway. From the time when initial success was achieved in the rural reform in the early 1980s to the 1990s, the price reform has always played a leading role. It is of great importance in enriching the science of economics and spurring on the practice of reform to conscientiously sum up the experience of the price reform, find the laws governing the price reform and make a theoretical expounding of them.

This chapter reviews the course China has traversed over the past 20 years in its price reform, makes comments on the achievements and experience gained and ventures some proposals and policy suggestions for the future price reform.

Section 1

Price Reform Has Taken the Lead in China's Reform Drive after Initial Success Was Achieved in the Rural Reform

Since the Third Plenary Session of the 11th Party Central Committee at the end of 1978 adopted the policy of reform and opening to the outside world, one outstanding feature of China's economic reform is that price reform, which is considered the key to the success or failure of the overall reform of the economic structure, has had a clearly defined objective all along (which is, gradually establishing a price system with the prices mainly formulated in the market, straightening out the price relations through price readjustments and lifting all control over prices). Steady progress has been made in the reform (making short steps forward without stopping at ordinary times and taking long strides forward once the macro-economic environment is appropriate). Generally speaking, in the course of the reform, there have been no serious twists and turns (the two instances of moderate inflation were timely brought under control due to consolidation measures timely adopted without causing serious regression in economic development). Neither has the reform suffered from serious shocks (over the 20 years, the annual average hike of retail price is 6.91 percent, which is within the range the society and the public could stand). Because of these reasons, the price reform has all along played a leading role and reaped great success over the past 15 years after initial success was achieved in the rural reform.

1. The Pricing Mechanism for Goods and Services Has Been Basically Changed and a Market Price-Formulating System Has Been Basically Established.

Prior to the adoption of the policy of reform and opening to the outside world, the prices of most commodities in China were decided by the government. In 1978, prices set by the government covered 97 percent of all the commodities sold in society by retail, 100 percent of the income from the sales of industrial production means and 92.6 percent of total purchases of agricultural and sideline products. In 1997, after nearly 20 years of price reform, the coverage of market prices rose to 93.2 percent of all commodity retails while the proportion of government-set prices dropped to 5.5 percent, with the remaining 1.3 percent adopting the state-guided prices. In terms of total income from sales of industrial production means, the proportion covered by market prices increased to 81.6 percent while that covered by government-set prices reduced to 13.6 percent, with the remaining 4.8 percent adopting state-guided prices. Of the total volume of purchases of agricultural and sideline products, the proportion of market prices rose to 80.5 percent while that of government-set prices fell to 16.1 percent, with the remaining 3.4 percent adopting state-guided prices. In 1998, the coverage of prices under the control of the department in charge of prices and other relevant departments under the State Council, including state-set prices and state-guided prices, reduced from 1,336 kinds in 1978 to 58 kinds. It can thus be concluded that, in the field of material goods, a market price system has basically taken shape. At the same time, control over the prices of services in a few competitive trades was also lifted, making the prices be regulated by markets.

2. Great Improvement Has Been Witnessed in the Price Struc-

ture, the Price Differences Have Become Relatively Reasonable and the Market Signals Have Become Relatively Accurate.

With regard to the differences between the prices of industrial and agricultural products, the purchasing prices of agricultural produces had increased by 425,4 percent from 1978 to 1997 while the retail prices of industrial products for agricultural use had increased by 194.8 percent. In 1997, the amount of industrial goods that could be exchanged with agricultural products increased by over 50 percent as compared with 1978, indicating that the price scissors between industrial products and agricultural products had been narrowed. In terms of the price differences between different agricultural products, the purchasing prices for grain had risen by a total of 574.7 percent in 1997 as against 1978, 149.3 percentage point higher than the overall level of price rise for all agricultural prices, bringing about change in the situation that the prices of grain was a bit too low. Regarding the price differences for different kinds of industrial products, from 1978 to 1997 the prices of mining industrial products had risen by 712 percent in all, the prices of industrial raw materials had increased by a total of 411 percent, and the prices of manufactured industrial products had gone up by 201 percent. It shows a great improvement had been achieved in the situation in which the prices of manufactured industrial products were a bit too high while that of basic industrial products were a bit too low.

Quality price differences, seasonal price differences as well as the price differences for wholesale and retail have all become grown more reasonable gradually. The national working conference on reform of the circulation system for grain and cotton, called in May and June 1998, proposed to widen the quality and variety price differences in the purchasing of grain and cotton so as to promote a rational readjustment in the structure of acreage sown to grain crops and cotton. This is of great importance for establishing rational price difference relations.

3. Important Progress Has Been Made in Linking Domestic Market Prices up with International Market Prices.

As China has opened its door wider and wider to the outside world, its dependence on foreign trade has increased. Hence, it is natural tendency to link up the domestic price system with that in the international market. Since 1988 when China carried out the reform of its foreign trade system, which featured "each taking sole responsibility for its own profits or losses, free management, combination of industrial production with trade, and the introduction of the agency system," the effect to link up the domestic price system with the international market price system has enhanced, resulting in the gradual introduction of the agency pricing principle for imported and exported commodities. As of 1993, China has called off subsidies to import of grain, chemical products as well as three other major products, and also adopted the agency prices for these commodities. Now, the import agency system has been established for all commodities imported with foreign exchange, and the prices of these imported goods in the domestic market are now decided by the market, meaning that these prices have been linked up with international prices. Due to the increase in the number of tradable commodities, all circles of the society (local governments, government departments, enterprises and individuals) have come to show more concern for and attach greater importance to the price differences between domestic and overseas markets. According to a follow-up comparison between the overall average prices of 17 major kinds of production means and agricultural products in 1993, the prices of soybeans, peanut oil and zinc-plated boards were 10-15 percent higher than the average prices in the international market; the prices of crude oil, timber, cotton, rice and wheat were 14-15 percent lower; and the prices of steel wire, steel plate in medium thickness, copper, aluminum, lead, zinc, soybean oil, rapeseed oil and corn were on a par with the international market prices.

In 1998, some changes had taken place. Some related departments selected 48 kinds of commodities that were representative for a comparison between the domestic market prices and the international market prices in line with exchange rates announced by the state (see the attached table). Of the 48 kinds of commodities, the prices of 35 were higher than average international prices, accounting for 73 percent (13 kinds were 20 percent higher or lower, accounting for 27 percent; seven kinds were 21-40 percent higher, accounting for 15 percent; and 15

Table: Comparison of Prices in Domestic Market and International Market

Serial Number & Category		Name of Commodity	Specifications	Unit	International Market Price		Domestic Market Price in RMB	Domestic & Overseas Prices (International Market Price = 100)
					Price Condition	Price in RMB		
Farm Products		Wheat	Medium	500 g.	Futures price (Chicago)	0.44	0.63	143
		Rice		500 g.	FOB, futures (Bangladesh)	1.12	1.13	101
		Corn	Medium	500 g.	Futures price (Chicago)	0.36	0.56	180
		Soybean	Medium	500 g.		0.98	1.76	179
		Soybean oil	First-class, bulk	500 g.		2.52	3.94	156
		Peanut oil		500 g.	CIF, futures (Rotterdam)	3.73	5.70	153
		Live pig	First class	500 g.	Futures price (Chicago)	5.57	3.81	68
		Sugar		500 g.	Spot price (New York)	0.90	1.65	183
		Cotton	Grade 229	50 kg.	Futures price (New York)	745	800	107
Textiles	0	Cotton yarn	32 count	Ton	Futures price (Japan)	26,000	24,500	94
	1	Cotton cloth	30, 30, 68, 68	Ton	Hongkong	440	420	95
	2	Hexo-lactam		Ton	CIF	11,530	15,000	130
	3	Polyester slice	Filament class	ton	CIF	5,617	8,500	150

	4	Acrylic fiber wool	1.5D. 38	Ton	CIF	12,400	14,000	113
	5	Acrylic wool top	Standard	Ton	CIF	13,248	14,100	106
	6	Glued short fiber	1.5 D 38	Ton	CIF	11,592	14,300	113
Chemical Products	7	Rubber	Natural rubber, No. 2 piece	ton	Futures price (Singapore)	6,310	88,999	141
	8	High-pressure polythene	1st class for film	Ton	CIF	5,040	7,340	146
	9	Polypropylene	Wire-drawing Grade 2401	Ton	CIF	4,750	5,500	116
	0	Sulphur acid	98.5%	Ton	CIF	370	650	176
	1	Hydrochloric acid	31-32%	Ton	CIF	650	750	116
	2	Soda ash	>98.5%	Ton	CIF	1,323	1,400	106
	3	Caustic soda	Solid, >98%	Ton	CIF	3,475	2,500	79
	4	Urea	N 46%	Ton	FOB, futures, bulk (East Europe)	749	1,,530	193
	5	Diamine phosphate		Ton	FOB, futures, bulk (U.S.)	1,,664	2,,500	150
	6	Potassium chloride		Ton	FOB, futures, bulk (Canada)	1,035	1,450	140
Energy Products	7	Crude oil	Minas crude oil	Ton	FOB (Singapore)	662	678	102
	8	Gasoline	Lead-free 95#	ton		977	1,607	164

	9	Diesel oil	light diesel 0#	ton		764	1,506	197
Metall-urgical Pro-ducts	0	Copper		ton	London	13,898	19,681	142
	1	Aluminum ingot	AOO, 1#	Ton	Spot (London)	11,758	13,700	117
	2	Zinc		Ton	London	9,130	11,690	121
	3	Pig iron	For steel-making	Ton	FOB (CIS)	1076	1210	112
	4	Cast billet	120 square billet	Ton	FOB (CIS)	1,656	2,000	121
	5	cold- rolled steel sheet	1 MM	Ton	Hongkong	4,113	4,329	105
	6	hot-rolled steel sheet	0.5 Q235A	Ton	Cash, wholesale (Japan)	3,400	3,808	112
	7	Wire	Drawn	Ton	FOB (Europe)	2,274	2,551	112
Build-ing Mater-ials	8	Plate glass	3 mm	Sq. m.	Made in Thailand (Hongkong)	25.5	10	39
	9	Cement	525#, packed	Ton	Japan	750	384	51
Drugs	0	Vitamin C	Powder	Kg	CIF (North Korea)	439	49	12
	1	Penicillin sodium	Raw powder	1 bil. unit	India, North Korea	95.22	160	168
	2	Penicillin kainite		Kg	Hongkong	240.7	183.6	76

aside considerably large reserves of important commodities, including grain, cotton and rolled steel, and established price-regulating funds. In summary, it can be said that the government has accumulated much successful experience in regulating the prices, mainly the general level of prices, by economic and legal means as well as necessary administrative means.

5. The "Price Law" and Other Relevant Laws Have Provided the Legal Foundation for Price Work.

"The Price Law of the People's Republic of China" was promulgated on December 29, 1997 and has been put into effect since May 1, 1998. Some supporting laws and regulations are being enacted and improved. Apart from them, there were other major laws and regulations that are related to prices and were issued before the end of 1997. They included "Law Against Competition by Inappropriate Means" (issued on September 2, 1993), "Regulations on Clearly Stating Prices of Commodities and Services" (issued on February 28, 1994), "Provisional Regulations on Stopping Activities to Seek Unlawfully Exorbitant Profits" (issued on January 25, 1995), "Interim Regulations on the Price Management of Commercial Housing" (issued on July 20, 1992), "Interim Rules on Management of Prices in Urban Real Estate Deals" (issued on November 11, 1994), "Interim Regulations on Management of Prices for Utilization of State-owned Land in Cities" (issued on October 24, 1995) and "Rules on Management of Price Evaluation" (issued on November 18, 1996). Meanwhile, many provinces and municipalities have enacted some local regulations and rules in line with their specific conditions.

6. The Success of the Price Reform Has Greatly Enhanced the Vitality of the Economy and Ensured the Prosperity of the Market, and Turned Socio-economic Development from the Orbit Featuring Guidance by Planning to the Orbit Mainly Guided by the Market.

Due to the implementation of the traditional socialist economic system prior to the reform, China's economy was in an overall shortage – shortage of all commodities and services. Because of the short supply in the market, control was imposed on the prices of many important commodities, which were usually rationed by coupons. There were often instances that people queued in long lines for panic buying of some commodities. Sometimes, black market ran rampant because of the shortage. Not only that the level of consumption was generally low, people also suffered from many inconveniences. In the early 1980s, some provinces and municipalities took the lead to lift the control over the prices of some goods, such as fruit, aquatic products and vegetables. A miracle soon appeared. After a short period of price rise when the control was initially lifted, the output of some commodities greatly increased and the market flourished thanks to the role played by the market mechanism. Consequently, the prices had gradually come down. This enabled the officials and the broad masses see and personally experience the miraculous power of the market mechanism. Following this, control was further lifted over the prices of some agricultural products and industrial consumer goods, also reaping satisfactory results. Therefore, the biggest advantage to shift from setting prices by government to setting prices by the market is manifested as the greater vitality of the economy and the prosperity of the market. It enabled the Chinese people to bid farewell to various kinds of coupons that were used in buying rationed commodities in the early 1990s and later to the period of economic shortage, and achieve great improvement in their material life..

Price is the core in the allocation of resources through the market. The efforts to lift control over prices and shift to a market price system have made it possible for prices to better reflect the law of value as well as the relations between supply and demand, helped bring into being a more rational price structure and provided the producers and managers with more accurate market signals. In other words, the prices formulated in the market told the producers and managers what commodities to produce. In this way, the prices thus formulated have helped optimize the allocation of materials, improved economic efficiency and brought about a sustained, rapid and sound socio-economic development. *The World Development Report of 1983* prepared by the World Bank once analyzed the relations between price deviations (distortions) and

trol over the prices of those means of production that were not covered in state plans as well as those production means that were allowed to be marketed by the enterprises themselves (accounting for 2 percent of such products covered in the state plans). It is since then that markets for production began to emerge. Markets of production means have quickly mushroomed as the number of commodities whose prices are formulated in the market has increased. It is particularly so since the early 1990s when the double-track price system for production means were basically abolished to give way to unitary market prices. Up to date, over 1,000 wholesale markets for production means have been established throughout the country, with a total annual sales volume of over 3,600 billion yuan.

Thanks to the earnest efforts made in the price reform, both the markets for consumer goods and the markets for production means have gradually matured, along with the quick development of a production elements market at the initial stage. The development of these markets has enabled the Chinese economy to turn from the model characterized by planning to the model dominated by the market, hence the transition in the economic operation mechanism.

Moreover, the success of the price reform has posed a great challenge to the enterprise reform, especially the reform of the state-owned enterprises. Because of the price reform, the enterprises, including the state-owned enterprises, are required to become true market subjects or, in other words, subjects for competition that can quickly adapt to price changes in the market. Only when this is achieved can China accomplish its transition from the traditional system of planned economy to the system of socialist market economy. So far, the enterprise reform has not yet attained its objective and the state-owned enterprises have not yet become true legal entities and market subjects that can make their own decisions for management and take sole responsibility for their own gains and losses. The reform of the state-owned enterprises has now become the priority among priorities and the key link in the overall reform of the economic structure. In the coming few years, China will concentrate its efforts on promoting the reform of the state-owned enterprises, in the hope to make the economic operation keep in step with the development of the socialist market economy not only in operational mechanism but also in operational subjects.

Section 2

Combining Regulation with Decontrolling, First Regulate then Decontrol, and Decontrol Step by Step

Since the adoption of the reform and open policy, China has made marked progress in its price reform. There are many reasons accounting for this. Among them, two are the most important. One is to persist in orientating the reform towards market, and the other is to follow the model of gradual advance.

China has persisted in orientating the price reform towards the market. In the reform, no serious twists and turns have occurred, thus fundamentally guaranteeing its smooth progress. The objective of China's price reform is to replace the traditional government pricing system with the market pricing system and bring about a transition in the pricing model. At the initial stage, this idea was not clearly defined and accepted by all. In the early 1980s, only a small number of economists clearly pointed out that the aim of China's price reform was to get rid off the pricing system according to plan and replace it with the market pricing system. Yet, from the very beginning people were clearly aware that, in China's price reform, it was necessary to introduce the market mechanism, enhance its role and make price formation and control shift from seriously violating the law of value to respecting the law of value. In other words, this means that China's price reform has, in fact, always followed the market-orientated direction from the very beginning. In October 1984, the Central Committee of the Chinese Communist Party adopted a decision on the reform of the economic structure. The decision stated that the socialist economy was a planned commodity economy. Even since then, particularly since the early 1980s when some progress had been achieved in the market-orientated price reform, government control has been lifted over the prices of more and more com-

All along, it has been the central link in China's reform of the economic structure. It is also the key in carrying out and deepening the enterprise reform to make the enterprises true commodity producers and managers as well as market subjects that make their own decisions regarding management and take sole responsibility for their own gains and losses. Only in this way is it possible to rebuild an microeconomic foundation with great vitality for the socialist commodity economy and market economy. Moreover, when the enterprises step into the market, participate in the competition on a fair basis and seek their own development through competition, it is necessary to have relatively institutionalized and reasonable standards to evaluate the results of the enterprises' economic activities and necessary to establish a relatively rational price structure. Therefore, it is imperative to conduct the price reform to establish a market price system and smooth out the price relations. Moreover, it is an indispensable right for the independent commodity producers and market subjects to decide and adjust the prices of their own products. This right is an important component of the enterprises' autonomous rights. Such right can only be materialized by changing the price formation system, that is, to replace the government pricing system with the market pricing system.

4. The price reform is a necessity for the establishment of the socialist market economic system and the improvement of the market rules and order. To enable the products steer clear of the control by planned allocation and enter the market, it is necessary to lift all control over prices and make it possible for the products to be bought and sold in the market freely. To open up more market avenues, it is necessary to give permission to competition on an equal footing, encourage fair trade and exchange of equal values, oppose monopoly, sectoral segmentation and local protectionism and eliminate interference from non-market factors. This also requires the government to refrain from intervening into and exercising control over the prices of particular products and services, that is to say, let prices be formed freely in the course of exchange and make the prices truly reflect the amount of social labor spent in making the products, the changes in the supply and demand relations as well as the amount of resources consumed. So, energeti-

cally promoting the market-orientated price reform can be said as the key link in invigorating the market and making the market operate in an orderly manner.

It Must Be Pointed Out the Market Price System China Wishes to Set up Is Not Laissez-faire but a Market Price System under the Macro Regulation and Control by the Government.

1. Efforts to establish such a price system does not mean to lift control over the prices of all commodities and services but to remove control over the prices of most commodities and services. As for a small number of products under natural monopoly, important public products and services as well as a few particularly important products that have been in short supply for a long time and have an important bearing on the national economy and the people's livelihood, their prices must be decided by the government. In terms of the sales volume, the products whose prices are decided by the government should probably account for 15-20 percent, while the prices of the remaining 80-85 percent should be regulated by the market.(3)

2. As for those prices over which the control is lifted, they should not let go on their own either. In other words, there should still be some necessary restrictions, such as those on opposing monopoly and blockage and protecting equal competition. Such restrictions should be enforced by means of enacting necessary laws and regulations that reflect the law of commodity exchange, such as legal stipulations demanding clearly labeling the prices of commodities, opposing price cheating and seeking exorbitant profits, and opposing unfair competition.

3. The state should mainly resort to economic means to regulate and control the macro prices, primarily the overall price level, as well as some strategic prices, such as interest rate, exchange rate and salary, so as to avoid sharp rises and falls in the overall price level, which might adversely affect the economic stability and people's thinking. Therefore, the new price system to be established should still manifest the combination between planning and the market.

China has achieved substantial progress in the price reform. The reason is, apart from upholding the market orientation, China has all along implemented the principle of gradual advance, that is, to carry out readjustment first and decontrolling later, combine readjustment with decontrolling and lift price gradually. It also has followed the gradual approach in linking up the prices in the domestic market with that in the international market. It has never attempted to accomplish the goal at one stroke.(4)

The so-called making gradual advance in price reform is mainly reflected in the following facts. Prior to 1984, major attention was placed on readjusting the prices while efforts were made to lift control over them. After 1984, however, the focus of attention was shifted to lifting control (with the later 1980s and first three years of economic consolidation in the 1990s as an exception) while consideration was also given to readjusting the prices. To combine readjustment with decontrolling, China has also made efforts to gradually link up the prices in the domestic market with the prices in the global market. Efforts to readjust the prices are aimed at initially smoothing out the relations between the price structure, price parity and price differences to enable the various trades and industries get roughly on a par in their level of profit. By lifting control over the prices, the aim is to make prices give a relatively more accurate expression to the relations between the supply and demand in the market and to the overall condition of the resources. To make the domestic market prices link up with the international market prices is to make the prices better reflect the relations between the supply and demand in the international market so as to enable the enterprises to participate competition in the international market in a more efficient way.

Why Must China, in Its Price Reform, Follow the Principle of Readjustment First and Decontrolling Later, Combining Readjustment with Decontrolling and Getting the Domestic Market Prices Linked Up with the International Market Prices Gradually?

1. To uphold the principle of readjustment first and decontrolling later and combining the readjustment with decontrolling, the aim is to keep the price rises caused by the price reform within certain limits. This is conducive to the economic stability and can ensure the

economic development and reform to proceed smoothly. The traditional economic system had nurtured in it latent inflation. The price reform, regardless efforts to readjust the prices or efforts to lift control over them, would inevitably set off the latent inflation and cause the prices to go up. At the early stage of the reform, some people estimated that the efforts to smooth out the price relations and correct the distorted price structure would, when no new inflation occurs, cause the overall price level to go up double. If this price hike was divided in a 15-year period, the annual price rise would only be 4.7 percent, which was acceptable to people in all walks of life. If the latent inflation were to be released at once, the situation of low prices for all products were to be corrected at one stroke and the overall price level were to let go up double, it would inevitably cause damage to the economic stability. China's practice has proved that excessive price hikes would cause instability in the economy, which is detrimental to both the smooth development of the economy and the successful progress of reform. Thus, such a situation is unacceptable. Compared with 1978 when China's reform drive was launched, the overall retail price index in 1998 increased by 280.7 percent, with an annual average of 6.9 percent in a span of 20 years. Although it was a bit too high, it had not produced a serious adverse effect on the economic stability. Hence, China's price reform should be considered successful.

2. By following the principle of readjustment first and decontrolling later, combining readjustment with decontrolling and gradually linking up the domestic market prices with that in the global market, China has managed to minimize the adverse impact produced by the price reform on changes in people's economic benefits. The price reform is also a course in which the prices of all commodities and services change relatively. Despite the rigid nature of prices, it is easy to make them go up than make them go down. Yet, the rises in prices for different commodities and services are different. The different changes in the prices directly affect the economic interests of different areas, different departments, different enterprises and different individuals. Those areas and departments where the price rises are high would get greater profits, and those where the price rises are low get less or even suffer losses.

The drastic the steps taken in the reform, the greater the gaps in economic interests for different localities and different social groups. If the steps for the reform are too drastic, or when attempts are made to accomplish the reform in one step, some localities and social groups would get huge benefits while others are bound to reap minimal benefits and even suffer losses. When this happens, there would bound to be dissatisfaction with the reform or opposition to it. The principle to make gradual advance in the price reform can ease the contradictions in economic interests, mitigate resistance to reform, get wider support for it, avoid unnecessary social shocks and reduce the costs of reform. Thus, it is conducive to the smooth transition to the new system.

3. The principle of readjustment first and decontrolling later and combining readjustment with decontrolling is conductive to the establishment of a new price system along with the development of the market. China is a country where the commodity and market economy is underdeveloped. For a long time after the founding of the People's Republic, the country had adopted the traditional socialist economic system and repelled the commodity and market relations. In 1978 when the reform was launched, there was only a fragmented market for consumer goods. Although various market relations have been developing quickly since the reform, the government has been confronted with a heavy task in fostering and establishing the market because of the extremely poor foundation left over from the past. The development of the market is a long course and the market can only grow mature along with the gradual expansion of the commodity-money relations. Although the reform has been going for 20 years, China has not yet set up a well-structured nationwide open market system where competition can be proceed orderly, whereas the institutionalized market price system must be formed and put in operation in a nationwide open and orderly market system. It will take some time for the market to grow to maturity. This has set the precondition for the formation and sound operation of the market price system, which will also take time. In other words, the new price model can only be established step by step. Therefore, the price reform can only be carried out gradually. Under no conditions should one believe that lifting price control would naturally lead to market-oriented prices

even when the market is not well developed.

4. China's price system should also be linked up with that in the international market in steps. China's economic reform has been conducted alongside the country's efforts to open up to the world. When China's economic and trade relations with other countries expand, the dependence of its economy on foreign trade is increasing, exceeding 30 percent now.(5) The dependence on export went up to 19 percent and that on import, 15 percent. After many years' reform in the foreign trade system, now the enterprises turning out products for export now no longer receive subsidies and they are asked to assume sole responsibility for their own profits or losses. Moreover, the agency system has been introduced for almost all import commodities. This indicates that the relations between the domestic market prices and the global market prices have become increasingly closer. The selling prices of commodities imported under the agency system have been directly linked up with the prices in the international market. In the future, China is bound to open its door wider, its economy will naturally integrated more closely with the global economy (including joining the WTO), and its price system will be linked up with the international market prices in a wider range. Yet, because the old price system in China was divorced from the prices in the international market and the gaps were enormous, the process to link up the domestic prices with that in the international market can only be a gradual one. Otherwise, the prices of basic products would go up suddenly, beyond the limits the processing enterprises could bear. For instance, we can first try linking up the prices of tradable commodities and enlarge the scope gradually later. It is not necessary to complete the process in one step.

Proceeding from the reform in the prices of goods and services, that is, price reform in the narrow sense, to the overall price reform, or price reform in the broad sense – this is also an important characteristic of the gradual approach in conducting the price reform. This point will be discussed separately in other part of this book.

Traditional socialist economic theory rejects the concept of price in a broad sense, because it does not acknowledge the possibility and inevitability of the commercialization of such factors of production as funds, labor and land. It holds that interest rate, salary, land price and rent should all be decided and regulated by the state, neglecting the role of the market system. In 1985, the meeting called on board of passenger liner "Bashan" put forward the concept of strategic prices, that is, the prices of major factors of production.(6) Thanks to the progress made in the theoretical study of the socialist commodity economy, it has been generally acknowledged that the factors of production would be gradually commercialized and enter the market to realize their value. Consequently, the concepts of price in the broad sense and its materializing reform have been proposed and received widespread attention. Fairly great progress has been made in the research of this field.

In practice, China's price reform has undergone the following two stages since 1979: (1) the stage to mainly readjust the prices of all kinds of products and services prior to 1984; (2), the stage to mainly lift control over the prices of all kinds of products and services since 1985. The first 10 years can be considered mainly a stage for price readjustment, or reform in the narrow sense. As of the beginning of the 1990s, China's price reform has entered a new stage, which can also be called reform in the broad sense. The major characteristics of this stage were to readjust and reform the commodity prices, salary, interest rates and exchange rates in a comprehensive manner and extend the scope of reform from the marketization of prices of material goods and services to the marketization of the prices of factors of production. Only by going through this stage can the market mechanism be really established, can the basic role of the market in the allocation of resources be truly brought into play, and can the marked-orientated reform achieve real success.

It is a logical development in the course of the price reform to transit from price reform in the narrow sense to price reform in the broad sense.

Developing or rejecting the commodity-money relations constitutes the fundamental difference between the new and old systems. In widening the scope of the commodity-money relations, China has twice shaken off the fetters of the traditional economic theory and formulated new views about the socialist commodity economy and market economy. The first time was at the end of the 1970s, which resulted in acknowledging that the means of production were also commodities. The second time was after 1984, which led to the affirmation that the factors of production, such as funds, labor and land would be commercialized or possess the forms of commodities. In modern time, commodity economy is nothing but market economy. Along with the expansion of the scope of the commodity relations, not only the means of production will be exchanged in the market, so will the factors of production, thus giving rise to the formation of a comprehensive market system. As a result, to rely on the market to optimize the allocation of resources will become a practical economic process. This is a concentrated expression of the continuous development of China's reform of the economic structure.

Expansion of the scope of commodities and market has broadened people's view regarding the price reform. The price reform not only covers the reform of the price system and price-formation mechanism for material goods and services but also the reform of the price system and price-formation mechanism for all kinds of factors of production. In other words, it covers both the price reform in the narrow sense and the price reform in the broad sense. The process of the price reform in the broad sense is identical with process of the development of the comprehensive market system, and this is marked characteristic of the price reform in the new period. It signals both the deepening of the reform and the enhancement of people's understanding about the reform.

Section 3

The Double-Track Price System for the Means of Production Is China's Invention

In the mid-1980s, China adopted a double-track system for the prices of the means of industrial production. In the early 1990s, the double-track system had been smoothly replaced by a unitary market price system. In fact, this can serve as a successful example of the gradual approach China has adopted in promoting its market-orientated price reform.

In September 1985 when the double-track system was still implemented over the prices of the means of production, the well-known meeting on board the liner "Bashan" was held. At the meeting, Mr. Bruce, a Polish economist, spoke highly of the system and praised it as a useful invention by China. He said, "It is an invention of China to adopt dual prices on the means of production. In the transition from the rationing system to commercialization, other socialist countries have once carried out dual prices in the consumer goods market. But I have never heard of dual prices for the means of production. It is a useful invention. It is useful in that it can serve as a bridge for the transition from one price system to another price system, that is, from the administrative- or government-set prices to market prices. With this bridge, the transition will be smoother. But there is one important condition and that is the dual prices cannot last too long."(7)

More than 10 years later, Mr. Stiglitze, an American economist, again lauded highly the double-track system China adopted for the means of production. He likened it to an invention by a genius. He said that some 20 years before Chinese economists and government tried hard to work out a plan for the transition into the socialist market economy with Chinese characteristics. How could the transition be realized from a seriously abnormal price system into a price system that could more accurately reflect the shortage degree of economic resources? Maybe people could invent a set of economic models to balance the prices. But even if people did the theoretical research work, even they knew the balanced prices, still they could not know when to carry out the transition. Nevertheless, he said, China had been successful. It had settled the problem wisely: the implementation of a double-track price system, thus giving appropriate encouragement to the unplanned parts.(8)

Evidently, something should be written separately about the double-track system for the prices of the means of production.

Starting from 1984, planned prices and non-planned prices began to exist in China for same industrial means of production in the same place and at the same time. On May 20, 1984, the State Council stipulated: For that part of the means of industrial production the enterprises were allowed to sell by themselves (about 2 percent of the planned output) and that part produced by the enterprises above the state planned output, the enterprises had the right to set the prices; the prices set by the enterprises should be kept within a certain range — 20 percent higher or lower than the state-fixed prices; or the prices could be settled between the suppliers and buyers within the above stipulated range. On January 24, 1985, the State Administration of Commodity Prices and the State Bureau of Materials and Equipment again notified that the ex-factory prices of that part of industrial means of production, which was allowed to be marketed by the enterprises themselves, and that part the enterprises produced above the state planned quotas, did not need to follow the former state regulation that they should be no higher than 20 percent over the state-set prices, and that it would do if their prices were a little bit lower than the prices in the local markets and be subjected to regulation by the market. Since then, the double-track prices had been legalized and become open.

The double-track price system was a concentrated expression of the coexistence of dual economic systems, particularly the coexistence of the two kinds of economic operational mechanisms under the conditions of a shortage economy. As the reform of the planning system was aimed at reducing the scope covered by state mandatory plans and granting more power to the enterprises in making decisions regarding what to produce and how much to produce, and as the reform of the commodity circulation system was aimed at reducing the variety of goods and materials universally allocated by the state, it would only be of practical significance to give the enterprises right to sell part of their own products and buy part of the materials they need, and adopt free prices for this part of the free production as well as free purchases and sales. Without free prices, the so-called free production as well as free purchases and sales could never be truly implemented and would remain empty talk. It was under such conditions that the double-track price system came into being. The double-track price system for the industrial means of production was of the greatest importance, because it had been in existence all along for the agricultural products. Over a long period of time, the farmers had been allowed to sell their agricul-

(reaching 4,053 yuan per ton) was 310 percent over the state-set allocation price; the market price of steel rods, 220 percent higher; the market price of gasoline, 210 percent higher; the market price of diesel oil, 430 percent higher; and the market price of soft coal, 670 percent higher. Consequently, the market was plunged into confusion. Lots of people turned crazy and engaged in fraudulent purchases and sales of production means for exorbitant profits. Some people even abused power in their hands to loan such goods from the enterprises for personal gains. Because of such problems, people in all circles showed blames on the double-track price system, demanding the government to call off the double-track prices for industrial means of production. In 1990-91, as the government implemented the policy of consolidation, readjustment and retrenchment to improve the macro-economic environment, the contradiction between market supply and market demand was alleviated, the prices of production means dropped and the gaps between the two kinds of prices were reduced. Viewing the national market as a whole, the prices of most production means fell back to the level of 100-50 percent over the state-set allocation prices, while the prices of certain products dropped even below the state-set prices. This situation indicated that the conditions were ripe to merge the two kinds of prices.(9) In addition, the deepening of the price reform also demanded to replace the double-track prices with unitary market prices for the means of production.

Once again, the merger of the double-track prices met opposition from government departments in charge. For example, in 1991 the supply-demand relations remained harmonious for cement, glass and some other building materials and the gaps between the double-track prices became very narrow. People from various circles held that the opportunity had come to shift to the single-track market price system. However, the departments in charge devised every excuse to oppose this idea and some even suggested to turn back to the single-track planned prices. In 1992, the State Administration of Commodity Prices revised and made public a catalogue of prices, over which control was strengthened by various central government departments according to their division of power. Among them, prices of the means of production for heavy industry as well as transport and communications industry was reduced from 737 in 47 categories in 1991 to 89 (33 were state-set prices and 56 were prices under the guidance of the state). This means control was lifted over the prices of almost 600 kinds of production means in one attempt to give way to the single-track market prices for the overwhelming majority of industrial means of production. This was obviously a wise act.

China's practice indicates that it is necessary to uphold the market orientation in tackling the problem of the double-track pricing system for industrial means of production. This is very important. In this process, the focus of attention should not be placed on simply calculating the price level. Of course, for a small number of products for which the planned prices must be adopted, there is indeed the question to re-decide a reasonable price level for them, such as setting for them average prices on the basis of planned prices and the market prices. Yet, the single-track market prices should be adopted for the majority of products. For these products there is no such question as fixing the so-called reasonable prices. On the contrary, control should be lifted to make their prices be regulated by the market. Thanks to the sound solution China has found to tackle this problem, a satisfactory end has been put to the double-track price system for the industrial means of production.

Section 4
Correct Tactics for Reform: Keeping the Overall Price Level Basically Stable and Missing No Opportunity to Decontrol Prices

China's practice has proved that whether effective tactics are adopted is also very important in the development of the reform. With regard to the tactics for reform, the most important point is to seize every favorable opportunity to make substantial steps forward, and by favorable opportunity it refers to the period when the macro-economic environment is sound and the pressure caused by inflation is not very heavy.

overall economic situation and the pressure caused by inflation had gradually relieved. Taken the past 20 years of reform and opening to the outside world as a whole, the annual average price rise (in terms of rise in the retail prices of commodities) was kept under 7 percent, which was within the limits of sustainability of the society. Although moderate inflation had occurred twice over the two decades from 1978 to 1998, it did not cause much damage as it lasted for a short time and was brought under control soon. This had provided China's price reform with a sound environment, which ensured its success.

Why can't the price reform achieve success when there is inflation and a big rise in commodity prices? It is because when the commodity prices keep rising by a large margin, it will produce some sort of psychological pressure on people. When the commodity prices go up quickly, the enterprises and other institutions will not devote their major efforts to improving their returns through upgrading technology and improving management. Rather, they will turn their attention to hoarding, speculation and profiteering and compete with one another to raise prices to seek exorbitant profits from commodity circulation through such means of monopoly, their advantageous status and cheating in price. This will mislead the public and make the public anticipate that another round of inflation will come, which in turn can dampen the masses' enthusiasm to save money and lead to panic purchasing. There will be greater confusion in the price relations or the price relations will get distorted again. Excessively rapid price rises can also adversely affect the ongoing price reform and make it impossible to stage plans already worked out for the reform, such as the program to readjust the price of rolled steel in 1987 (a document had already been printed for the readjustment) and the plan for price and salary reform in 1988 (to crack the "hard nut" in the price reform). These steps of reform had to be slowed down because the risk was too great because the social stability could be affected. In 1993-94, soaring prices led to excessively wide gaps in the two kinds of prices under the double-track price system, with the interest rate in the market being more than 100 percent higher than that in state-owned banks. This posed a serious threat to the ongoing reform of the financial system and to the separation of policy finance from commercial finance, thus seriously hindering the process of commercialization of the specialized banks. Judging by China's reform practice over the past 20 years or more, it can be concluded that the price reform is inseparable from an overall well-coordinated macro-economy and the difficulties encountered in its course of development come mainly from overheated economic development and inflation. By the so-called overall well-coordinated macro-economy, it refers to the rough balance between the total supply and total demand in the society, that is, the gap between the supply and demand cannot be too great. According to China's experience, the gap between the supply and demand should not be over 5 percent.(10) When the total supply falls 5 percent short of the total demand, there might be high rises in the market prices, which might even be in double digits. Once such a situation occurs, it will be difficult for the reform to go on, because all attention will be given to controlling the high price rises, even by adopting administrative means. This, of course, runs counter to the objective of the reform—to lift control over the prices.

In general, the macro-economic environment in China has been favorable for the country's efforts for price reform over the past two decades. Yet, the situation varied each year, besides the moderate inflation that had occurred in a number of years. In a few years, the situation was favorable for an overall price reform, while in others it was only appropriate to carry out reform of the prices of some commodities and services. Besides, China has a large territory and the conditions in different places are also different. In some places, the reform was launched sooner and, therefore, these places were made to take lead in lifting control over the prices of some products to test out the effects. All these point to one question, that is, whether the favorable opportunities were seized. China has seized the opportunities, thus it has achieved one success after another in its efforts for price reform.

As early as in August 1978, the authorities in Guangzhou, a large city in southern China, made the decision to alter its 20-year practice of setting vegetable prices by the government to setting the prices within a prescribed range through negotiations between purchasers and vegetable growers. When the market mechanism was introduced, the vege-

Deng Xiaoping, the chief architect of China's drive of reform and opening to the outside world, once pointed out that China's reform of the economic structure must fight through several "passes," and we may have more "passes" to go through and more "enemy generals" to behead than Guangong (Lord Guan Yu, a famous general in the Kingdom of Shu in the Three Kingdoms Period), did. He said that the price reform would be the hardest nut to crack and it involved greater risks, but it must be cracked. "If we don't, there will be no foundation for sustained development."(13) China planned to "crack this hard nut" in 1988. The decision was made, the call was issued and the concrete program for action was worked out. But, as the economic environment at that time was not very favorable—as evidenced by overheated economic development and excessively high price hikes, the efforts failed. Starting from the 4th quarter of 1988, the government had implemented the principle of improving the economic environment and rectifying the economic order, focusing mainly on curbing continuous upward trend of inflation and high rises in price. Because the macroeconomic environment was unfavorable that year, not only did the government failed to launch any new programs for the price reform, it had to adopt some temporary measures to enforce control over commodity prices. Markets that had been opened had to be closed again and prices over which the control had been lifted had to be brought under control once more. Now, the situation is different. Control over the prices of more than 80 percent of the commodities and services has been removed and the market price system has been initially established. In this sense, it can be said that the "hard nut" in the price reform has been cracked. Yet, the "hard nut" in the price reform has not been cracked completely, mainly because the price reform for production factors has not yet completed. China is still confronted with the arduous task of market-orientated reform for the prices of factors of production, the price regulatory mechanism and system call for further improvement, and the laws and regulations regarding prices still need to be improved and enacted. In other words, the price reform has not yet accomplished all its objectives. It is generally estimated that a relatively comprehhensive market price system is only able to take form in the first decade of the next century.

First, It Is Necessary to Work Hard to Promote the Price Reform for Factors of Production

This is the key in China's price reform in the later 1990s and beginning of the next century. The price reform for factors of production is market-oriented and people must have a clear understanding about this. Some people have opposed the market-orientated price reform for the factors of production under the excuse that, as factors of production are extremely important in the economic activities, they should be put under control by the government. This is a "Chinese characteristic," they argued. However, this argument is not convincing, because, to shift from the system of planned economy to the system of socialist market economy and to bring into full play the role of the market in the allocation of resources, the key lies in the development of the market of production factors and the marketization of the prices of production factors. If the factors of production are not allowed to circulate in the market and flow freely from departments and enterprises that generate little returns to those that generate more, the allocation of resources will not be optimized. To allow the factors of production to enter the market means to allow their to be decided by the market. Only when the control over the prices of the factors of production is lifted will it be possible to make them to circulate in the market. Therefore, it is imperative to speed up the development of the factors of production market and bring about the marketization of the prices of the factors of production if China wants to set up the socialist market economic system and make the market guide the allocation of resources. This is logically clear. Negation of the marketization of the prices of the factors of production is tantamount to negation of the socialist market economic system.

The prices of production factors mainly include interest (the price of funds), salary (the price of labor), rent and price of land (the price of land resources) and exchange price (exchange rate between RMB and foreign currencies). According to the demands to establish the socialist market economy, all these prices should be formed and regulated through the market so as to avoid any distortion of the most important market signals, because any distortion of these market signals can produce an adverse effect on the efficiency in the allocation of resources.

Of all the prices of production factors, interest (the price of funds or capital) is the most important, because fund is the most important economic resource always in short supply in each market economy. To marketize the prices of the factors of production, it is necessary first and foremost to marketize the interest rates. Now, China still adopts unitary interest rates for bank savings and loans. In the past few years, negative interest rates were even adopted. This resulted in a serious distortion in the price of funds and widened the gap between the bank interest rates and that in market (sometimes over 100 percent). Such a situation is not conducive to the rational utilization and optimized allocation of funds; neither is it favorable to encourage people to put their money in the banks. Conversely, it will cause a more serious shortage of funds and abet corruption and rent-seeking activities. Therefore, it is necessary for the government or the central bank to regulate mainly the minimum lending rate and use it to influence the interest rates in the market, rather than directly decide the interest rates in the financial market. The government should not interfere with the interest rates of bank savings deposits and loans granted by the commercial banks and other financial institutions. Rather, it should lift control over them and let them be regulated by the market. Neither should the government interfere with the interest rates of funds pooled directly by the enterprises and companies, but let the creditors decide the interest rates on their own. It is necessary for the government to issue loans on favorable terms for the construction of infrastructure facilities and the development of frontier industries by such means of financial discount. The marketization of interest rates will serve as an important landmark for the initial development of the socialist market economic system at the end of this century.

Wage and salary are the prices of labor. Marketization should also be taken as the orientation of the reform of the wage system. This means wages and salaries should be decided through competition in the labor market. The marketization of wages and salaries as the price of labor is a precondition for the enterprises to become market subjects. If labor is not allowed to freely circulate and all workers and staff are given "iron bowls" and paid the same regardless how well and bad they perform their duties, the enterprises would not be able to compete in the market but are bound to fail in the competition. If the law of the jungle, that is, the fittest survives, is not applied to the workers and staff, it cannot be applied to the enterprises either. If so, it will be impossible for the market mechanism to produce any effect. Therefore, the marketization of the prices of labor is an important link for the enterprises to introduce the modern enterprise system and enter the market. Of course, the marketization of the prices of labor and the establishment and development of labor market must be closely coordinated with the establishment and gradual improvement of the social security system so as to relieve uneasiness among the people and ensure social stability.

In order to improve the currently chaotic situation in land prices, particularly the prices for the transference of land utilization right in urban areas, it is necessary to strengthen land price evaluation in the future. The transference of land utilization right for commercial purposes must all be conduced through public bidding or auction to strengthen competition and improve transparency in the work. Considerations can be made to establish a set of "public-notice price" systems to guide and standardize the land prices and be taken as the standards in the collection of land taxes. It is necessary to prevent the loss of state revenue in the transference or transaction of land utilization right and crack down on illegal speculation on land as well as activities to willfully driving up the land prices for exorbitant profits.

In 1994, China stopped implementing the double-track policy regarding exchange rates and introduced the system of conditional free exchange between RMB and foreign currencies for permanent RMB accounts. In the future, the exchange rates shall fluctuate along with changes in the supply and demand of foreign currencies and be readjusted in line with changes of exchange rates in the international market. When the conditions are ripe, free conversion between RMB and foreign currencies shall be introduced for capital accounts. In no way should free conversion for the capital accounts be introduced when the conditions are not yet ripe. It is necessary for China to learn from the lessons of the recent Asian financial crisis.

Second, Appropriately Readjust the Government-Set Prices and Charges

The socialist market economy is by no means a complete laissez-faire economy. It is under the guidance and macro regulation of the government. Correspondingly, it is impossible to lift control over the prices of all commodities and services in the new market price system to be established. No doubt, control will be removed over the prices of most commodities and services. Government-set prices will remain for some commodities and services, mainly those that are naturally monopolized as well as those important public products and services. These commodities and services will not be put in the competitive market. In terms of volume of transactions, the proportion of government-set prices may cover 15-20 percent. But, when the government-set and government-regulated prices are maintained, it is also necessary to show due respect to the law of value (with only few exceptions), and to take into full account the supply-demand relations in the market. To do so, the aim is to make ensure that the social cost for various commodities and services is appropriately compensated and an average fund-profit rate is reaped. With regard to the small number of prices that are taken as exceptions, they mainly include the price and rent of welfare housing provided to the poor, charges of urban public transport services, including subway ticket fares, and changes of other welfare facilities (museums, libraries and so on). These prices and charges should remain low, even lower than costs, and the differences should be subsidized by state.

Apart from them, there are two problems with regard to other commodities and services upon which government-set prices, which should be readjusted and made more rational, are adopted.

The first problem is that the prices of commodities and services produced or provided by the monopolized industries are a bit too high. It is particularly so regarding the charges collected for telecommunication services. For instance, the charge for installing a telephone was notoriously high in the past few years. In Beijing, the installation charge for one telephone set was as high as 5,000 yuan. Although it dropped a bit later on, the charges for services, however, have remained very high. The charges for international long-distance calls are 3-4 times higher than foreign standards. In addition, the department in charge has permitted the telecommunication enterprises to retain part of such monopolist profits, thus greatly widening the gaps in income between different industries. This has aroused much criticism from the public. Again for example, the toll for the 18.5-kilometer Beijing Airport Expressway was raised from 10 yuan to 15 yuan in early 1999. A hike of 50 percent, it has turned out be much higher than the average toll standard for all other expressways.

The other problem is that the prices of quite a few public products and services are a bit too low. At present, the most outstanding problem is that the rent for publicly owned residential housing in urban areas is abnormally low. In some big cities like Beijing, the monthly per-meter rent for such housing is less than 1 yuan, much lower than the 4-yuan monthly rent for commercial housing. This has produced an adverse effect on the efforts to commercialize residential housing. It will hurt the interests of many and encounters great difficulties to raise the rent. Great care must be taken and active efforts must be made to tackle this problem. Besides, tap water toll, fees for subway and other public transport services, postage and hospital registration fee in the urban areas are all much too low and should be raised appropriately. The growth rate of these charges, however, should be kept in step with the affordability of the residents. Generally speaking, the prices can be readjusted more frequently and the range of the readjustment can be somewhat larger when the overall price level is stable. Otherwise, the readjustment should be less frequent and the range should be limited, so as to avoid causing damage to the market and economic stability.

Third, Improve the Price Legal System and Institutionalize Pricing Activities of the Government and Enterprises

The "Price Law of the People's Republic of China" is the major legal document on the administration of prices. It is necessary for China to further improve its legal system concerning prices on the basis of the

haps explains the unfeasibility of such self-disciplinary prices. From this example, it can be seen that it is necessary to make more detailed and clear-cut stipulations to institutionalize the enterprises' pricing activities according to the "Price Law" and on the basis of the rich experience gained in practice.

Fourth, Further Improve the Price Regulatory System

Under the conditions of the socialist market economy, the regulatory role played by the government over prices is mainly manifested in controlling the overall price level and maintaining its overall stability (with the annual rate of rise remaining at 5-7 percent, never reaching two digits) and basic stability (with the annual rate of rise being 3-5 percent). Prices are a comprehensive reflection of the situation of the national economy. A basic stability of the overall price level is the most important landmark indicating market and economic stability.

What standards should be used in judging the fluctuations of the overall price level? In the past, China had for long time made use of standard of retail prices of the commodities in the society. Thanks to the development of the economy, the people's incomes have kept rising and their living standards have been improved continuously. At the same time, tertiary industries have developed quickly and their contribution to the total economy has also been on the rise. Money paid by people on various kinds of services has taken an increasingly larger proportion in their total expenditure. Under such conditions, the drawbacks of using the standards of social retail prices of commodities to judge the overall price level have become more and more obvious. The reason is that the social retail prices of commodities do not include the service prices and therefore cannot manifest the changes in service prices. Therefore, it seems more appropriate to judge the overall price level by the people's overall level of consumption prices than by the overall level of retail prices of commodities. To do so, the statistical departments must have rich experience. Of course, it is possibly more authentic and accurate to use the GDP parity index to judge the overall price level. But, it is not easy to calculate this index and the statistical departments have not yet acquired sufficient experience to do so. So, as the first step, the people's overall consumption price level can be used.

Under the conditions of the socialist market economy, economic and legal means should be used mainly to regulate the overall price level, while administrative means can only be used as unconventional and temporary measures. It is particularly so when the transition to the market economy has begun. The experience China has acquired in curbing inflation and the excessively high price rises in 1994-95 has testified to this point. At that time, China mainly adopted moderately tight finance and money policies to curb the overheated trend in total demand and coordinate the supply-demand relations. As a result, the country succeeded to make the price rises gradually fall back. In addition, some administrative measures were also used, such as setting a ceiling for the price rise, enforcing control over price differences and temporarily giving up making price readjustments. However, these measures either failed or produced effect for a very short period of time (such as the measure to limit the range of price rises). This indicates that, in the future, it is necessary for the government to resort mainly to economic and legal means, monetary and financial policies (including financial subsidies), the price regulation fund as well as the reserves of goods to regulate and control the prices.

From 1978 when the drive of reform and opening to the outside world was launched to 1997, it had remained a major problem for the government to decide whether the range of price rises was too high. For a certain period of time, the government was even compelled to take curbing inflation and checking price rises its first and foremost task in the efforts to enforce macro regulation and control. Starting from October 1997, the commodity retail prices began to drop as compared with that in October 1996. By June 1999, the prices had kept dropping for 21 months in a run. Starting from April 1998, people's consumption prices began to drop as compared with that in April 1997, and by June 1999, they had kept going down for 16 months consecutively. Since June 1996, the ex-factory prices of industrial products also dropped as against that in June 1995, and this trend has remained for three years till now. In view of this situation, quite many economists hold that China has apparently encountered a situation of deflation and they proposed

(8) "China's Second-Step Strategy for Reform," by Mr. Stiglitz (USA), carried in *People's Daily* (overseas edition), November 13, 1998.

(9) For statistics cited here, see *Price Reform and Price Problem in China* by Zhang Zhuoyuan, pp. 92, 151 and 152, published by Economic Management Press, February 1995.

(10) See *China: Towards 2020*, p. 377, edited by the Policy Research Office under the State Planning Commission and published by China Planning Publishing House, September 1997.

(11) See "Guangzhou Lifts Control over Prices of Agricultural Products — China's Price Reform Sets off Here," carried in *Guangdong-Hongkong Information Daily*, July 5, 1998.

(12) See "Historical Course and Basic Experience of China's Price Reform over the Past 20 Years" by Ma Kai, carried in *Price Theory and Practice*, Issue No. 1, 1999.

(13) See *Selected Works of Deng Xiaoping (Vol. III)*, pp. 132 and 262, People's Publishing House, October 1993.

(14) See *Statistical Synopses of China, 1999*, p. 72, China Statistics Publishing House, May 1999.

CHAPTER 3
REFORM OF ECONOMIC STRUCTURE IN CHINA'S RURAL AREAS

Synopsis

China's reform of economic structure made the first breakthrough in the countryside, whereas the rural reform started with the reform of the management system of the people's communes and the introduction of the household-based contract responsibility system in agricultural production. After the status of the household was established in the contract responsibility system for agricultural production, the rural reform went a step further. Step by step, the reform advanced from changing the management system to transforming the property relations in the rural areas, from reforming the system of unified and fixed state purchase of major agricultural and sideline products to making full use of the role of the market mechanism in the entire rural economy, and from reform in the economic domain to the reform of all social systems in the rural areas as well as the establishment of the democratic system at the grass-roots level. Spurred on by the reform, the factors of production began to be circulated and reorganized in the countryside, which gave rise to a major transformation in the rural economic structure and resulted in marked growth in the rural productive forces. China's agricultural production and rural economy have quickened their pace of transition from a closed model to an open one and from the traditional model to a modern one.

The rural reform has taken a course of gradual progress—from the relatively easy links to the more difficult ones. One of the most fundamental reasons for the success of the rural form is to

show respect to the farmers' wishes and uphold the market orientation of the reform. A number of important achievements have been made in the rural reform and they are all great inventions made by the farmers under the leadership of the Communist Party of China. Of these, the major ones include the establishment of the basic management system featured by the household-based contract operation and the integration of centralization with decentralization, the quick rise and development of the township-run enterprises and the establishment of the basic democratic system at the rural grassroots level. The consolidation of the three creations by the farmers not only means to consolidate the achievements so far made in the rural reform but also constitutes a basic precondition for carrying on the rural reform further and bringing about new innovations in the rural economic system.

This chapter tries to review the course of China's rural reform over the past 20 years and summarize the major achievements and basic experience. At the same time, it ventures an analysis of the major problems still existent in the rural economic reform and raises some proposals for future reform efforts in light of these problems.

Section 1

Background of the Rural Economic Reform

I. Evolution of the Rural Economic System Prior to the Reform

After the founding of New China, the broad masses of the Chinese farmers launched a vigorous movement of land reform under the leadership of the Chinese Communist Party. By the end of 1952, the land reform, which took as its major tasks to uproot the feudal landlord ownership of land and "distribute land to the tillers," had been basically completed. Shortly afterwards, agricultural producers' mutual-aid groups and elementary agricultural producers' cooperatives came into being in different places successively. As the mutual aid groups and elementary agricultural producers' cooperatives, established on the basis of the private ownership of small plots of land, could help the farmers solve some of their problems, such as shortage of labor hands and draught animals, they were thus welcomed by the overwhelming majority of the farmers. However, a major change took place since the movement was launched to set up advanced agricultural producers' cooperatives.

1. Establishment of Advanced Agricultural Producers' Cooperatives

On July 31, 1955, Chairman Mao Zedong delivered a report entitled "On the Cooperative Transformation of Agriculture" to a conference of leaders of various provinces, municipalities under the direct leadership of the central government and autonomous regions called by the Central Committee of the Chinese Communist Party. In the report, he criticized those who advocated that the development of agricultural producers' cooperative movement should be carried forward in a stead and slower pace, likened them to women tottering along with bound feet and accused them of committing the "Right" deviation mistake. Mao Zedong also believed that a nationwide upsurge of socialist transformation would soon appear in the countryside. In December the same year, he wrote the "Prefaces to Socialist Upsurge in China's Countryside." In these prefaces, he said that the situation in China underwent a fundamental change in the second half of 1955, and of China's 110 million farmer households, more than 70 million had joined semi-socialist agricultural producers' cooperatives. He also held that fundamental changes had taken place in rural situation. He hailed this as a tremendous event and said that the event had made it clear that China needed only the calendar year 1956 in order to basically complete the semi-socialist cooperative transformation of agriculture, and by 1959 or 1960 China could in the main complete the transformation from semi-socialist cooperatives into fully socialist ones.

However, due to the widespread impact of the "upsurge of socialism," the agricultural cooperative transformation, particularly the establishment of the advanced agricultural producers' cooperatives (or "fully socialist cooperatives"), developed at a speed much faster than Mao Zedong had anticipated. According to relevant records, before the spring plowing season in 1956, 85 percent of the farmer households had joined the agricultural cooperatives throughout the country. Of them, 48 percent had joined the advanced cooperatives. By the end of 1956, the percentage of farmer households having joined the cooperatives amounted to 96.3 percent, and 88 percent of them had joined the advanced ones. Therefore, it actually took only one year and a half -- from the summer of 1955 to the end of 1956, for China to complete the cooperative transformation of its agriculture and establish advanced agricultural producers' cooperatives throughout the country.

According to the stipulations in "Demonstrative Program for Agricultural Producers' Cooperatives (Draft)" adopted by the Standing Committee of the National People's Congress on November 9, 1955, "the cooperatives in the advanced stage are completely socialist in nature. In this kind of cooperatives, all the land of the cooperatives' members and all the other means of production needed by the cooperatives have become publicly owned." Regarding the characteristics of the advanced cooperatives, they can be summarized as follows: unified operation, joint labor, unified accounting and distribution on the basis of collective ownership of the means of production. This basic model of rural management system had actually been implemented up until the eve of the reform.

2. The Establishment of the People's Commune System Characterized by "Bigger in Size and of More a Developed Socialist Nature"

In March 1958, the Central Committee of the Communist Party of China called a meeting in Chengdu and adopted the "Proposals on Appropriately Merging Small Agricultural Cooperatives into Big Ones." Immediately afterward, a nationwide campaign was launched to merge the cooperatives. An article entitled "Merger of Agricultural Cooperatives in Liaoning Province" carried in *Bulletin on Agricultural Work*, No. 7, 1958, revealed that, thanks to the efforts made in May, the 9,600 agricultural cooperatives in the province had been merged into 1,461 bigger ones, which comprised on average 2,000 households each. Of these cooperatives, there were nine that had more than 10,000 households each, and the biggest had in it 18,000 households. At the same time, efforts were made to adjust the size of the townships. As a result, the 2,854 townships in the province were merged into 1,226, of which 83 percent were townships with a single cooperative. On July 1 the same year, Chen Boda made public the remarks of Chairman Mao in his speech at a meeting in Beijing University to mark the founding of the Communist Party of China. According to him, Mao Zedong said, "Our direction is to take steps to gradually merge industry, agriculture, trade, education and army (militia) into a huge commune so as to make it the basic unit of our socialism in an orderly manner." This was the first time that Mao's thinking about the establishment of the people's communes and his visualization to make the people's communes the basic units of China's socialism were made public. On August 31, the *People's Daily* published Mao Zedong's remarks made on August 9 when he was on inspection tour in the countryside in Shandong. "It is good to establish the people's communes. The advantage in doing so is that we can tie industry, agriculture, trade, education and military affairs together and put them under unified leadership." On September 1, the *People's Daily* carried a report covering the enlarged meeting of the Political Bureau of the CPC Central Committee held in Beidaihe, which had adopted the "Resolution of the Central Committee of the Communist Party of China on the Establishment of People's Communes in the Countryside." The report said, "The meeting held a heated discussion on the question of establishing people's communes in the countryside throughout the country. The meeting pointed out that to merge and transform the relatively small-scaled agricultural producers' cooperatives into comparatively larger people's communes was an inevitable trend under the conditions when the rural production has been developing at very rapid speed and the consciousness of the peasants has been quickly awakened. The people's commune represents a high degree of collectivization and in them industry, agriculture, trade, education and military affairs can be put together, and township management can be combined with government administration. The people's commune is the best organizational form to accelerate the socialist construction and spur on the transition to communism. Eventually, it will develop into the grass-roots unit of the communist society in the future." On the same day, *Red Flag* carried an editorial entitled "Greeting the Upsurge of People's Commune Movement." On September 10, the *People's Daily* also carried an editorial with the title "Let's Put Up the Framework of the People's Commune First." It was precisely in such a clamorous and exciting atmosphere that people's communes quickly sprang up throughout the country in September. Issue No.4 of the *Bulletin on the People's Commune Movement* released by the former Rural Work Department of the CPC Central Committee on September 30 made the following description: "The movement was first launched in July, underwent the stage of planning and widespread experiments in August, and reached the climax in September. On the whole, it lasted only a little more than one month." Then, the bulletin went on to say, "According to statistics collected by September 29, altogether 23,384 people's communes had been established throughout the country, involving 112,174,651 farmer households, accounting for 90.4 percent of the national total. On average, each commune comprises 4,797 households. In 13 provinces, including Henan and Jilin, 94 counties had established county-level people's communes or county-level joint communes." It is true that the people's commune system was set up in a short span of two to three months.

The basic characteristics of the people's commune system are "bigger in size and of a more developed socialist nature" and the "integration of government administration with commune management." According to an initial plan for the establishment of the people's communes, a commune would be taken as one single economic accounting unit, and the original advanced agricultural cooperatives would just become working areas of production and would not enjoy the status of independent economic accounting. The means of production and labor could be freely allocated within the commune. However, the commune, as an "economic accounting unit," was actually under the direct leadership of the township government. This system, together with the general social mood inspired by the "Great Leap Forward" movement, gave rise to many serious problems in the countryside. These problems were then summarized as "five winds," namely, the "wind of communism (extreme egalitarianism), wind of exaggeration, wind of commandism, wind among the rural cadres to seek privileges and wind of giving blind instructions." As a result, these "five winds" had brought great damage to the rural productive forces and seriously stifled the enthusiasm of the farmers. In the first two years after the people's commune system was established, a serious setback was witnessed in agricultural production. In 1960, the total output of grain, cotton and oil-bearing crops dropped by 26.4 percent, 35.2 percent and 53.7 percent respectively as compared with that in 1957. The entire rural economy was brought to the brink of collapse.

3. Readjusting the People's Commune System: Establishing the System of "Three-level Ownership with the Production Team as the Base"

Witnessing the chaotic situation and setback in the rural economy, people were forced to make some readjustment of the people's commune system by proceeding from the perspectives of property system and relations of distribution.

In November 1960, the CPC Central Committee issued "A Letter of Urgent Directive on Current Policies Regarding People's Communes in Rural Areas." The letter criticized the problem of "egalitarianism and indiscriminate transfer of manpower, land, draught animals, farm tools and funds," which was then quite common in the countryside. It stressed, "The three-level ownership with the production team as the base is the basic system of the people's communes at the current stage." But, the production team, which was taken as the base of the system here, actually referred to the production brigade. So, the letter stressed that the production brigade was the owner of the means of production and the basic accounting unit of the collective economic organizations in the rural areas. The production team, on the other hand, was but an operational group for which the brigade set output quotas. The brigade, on its part, assigned some land, labor force, draught animals and farm tools to the production team and fixed for it the output quotas, amount of work and costs. As the distribution of income among the members was carried out in a unified manner in the entire production brigade, the various production teams under a production brigade would get the same benefits, except for the little difference in the bonus. In a production brigade, the phenomenon of everyone eating from the same "big pot" remained very serious. In view of this situation, the CPC Central Committee again issued the "Directive Regarding the Issue of Basic Accounting Units in the People's Communes" in February 1962. The directive clearly pointed out the problem of incompatibility between distribution and production when the production brigade was taken as the basic accounting unit. It explained that it was contradictory to make the production team the basic unit to do the organizational work for agricultural production while distribution was carried out within the production brigade in a unified manner. Therefore, the Central Committee of the Party held that the production team, instead of the production brigade, should be made the basic accounting unit and it was necessary to give it both the power of production management and the power of distribution, so as to combine production with distribution. The CPC Central Committee believed that this was conducive to overcoming the egalitarian tendency between different production teams in the same production brigade, ensuring the power of production teams to make their own decisions and arousing their enthusiasm. Along with the issuance of this directive, the internal organizational structure of the people's commune was basically fixed in the three levels -- the commune, the production brigade and the production team, and the system with the production team as the basic accounting unit was basically established. Moreover, the directive also stressed that this readjustment of the people's commune system was by no means an expedient measure. Rather, it was a policy that would remain unchanged in at least 30 years.

To make the production team the basic accounting unit represented not only an important readjustment of the internal management system of the people's commune but also an important change in the distribution system introduced since the establishment of the advanced cooperatives. This is because that, the production team, when made the new basic accounting unit, was, in fact, roughly the same size as the elementary agricultural producers' cooperative prior to 1956. When the advanced cooperatives were established, the power of income distribution was concentrated in the advanced cooperatives and the problem of egalitarianism actually occurred among the formerly elementary cooperatives that were merged into the same advanced cooperative. As the advanced cooperatives existed only for a short period of time, the problem did not reveal itself fully. Therefore, the act to make the production team the basic accounting unit in 1962 was actually meant to lower the level of unified accounting and unified distribution to the level of the former elementary cooperatives. When the decision was made public, the farmers described the practice as "under the name of the people's commune, possessing the nature of the advanced cooperative, and in the scope of the elementary cooperative." What they meant was, although the name of the people's commune was not changed, the "wind of communism," which was characterized by the system of free supply, the wage system and big public canteens, had stopped blowing. Meanwhile, as land had already been put under the collective ownership, "dividend on land" had no longer existed. In addition, the collectives also owned all other means of production, and this had already been put into practice in the period of advanced cooperative system. Yet, the productive operation, economic accounting and income distribution were still kept at the level of the production team, which was roughly equivalent to the former elementary cooperative. In this sense, it can be said that the people's commune system, which was envisioned in summer 1958 to facilitate the transition to communism, was by then failed. Even since, the rural economic system, which was characterized by the "three-level ownership with the production team as the basic accounting unit," had been implemented continuously until the launching of the reform drive.

II. Position of Rural Economy in the Overall Structure of the National Economy Prior to Reform

The evolution of the economic system in the rural areas prior to reform was not an isolated process, but a process dominated by the country's overall strategy of development and the overall structure of the national economy.

Old China was backward in industry. In the early years after the founding of the People's Republic, the country was forced to face a serious situation caused by the cold war after World War II as well as the economic blockade and embargo imposed on it by the Western powers. To speed up the process of industrialization against such a background, New China had to depend on a quick accumulation of capital domestically. As the structure of GNP in 1952 shows, agriculture accounted for 45.42 percent; industry, 34.38 percent; building industry, 5.6 percent; transport and communications, 3.45 percent; and commerce, 11.13 percent. Naturally, agriculture had to shoulder the major responsibility to accumulate capital for the country's industrialization because it held so large a share in the national economy.

However, China's agriculture had its own unique characteristics. First, there is a very large rural population. In 1952, the rural population accounted for 87.54 percent of national total. Second, agricultural production was extremely scattered, and the some 1 billion *mu* (one *mu* equals one-fifteenth of a hectare) of farmland were tilled by 110 million farmer households. Third, the production was basically autarkic or semi-autarkic, each farmer household could only supply a very limited surplus of products and its savings was even less. So, industrialization turned out to be a nut that was hard to crack but had to be cracked. It was imperative to find a way to collect the limited surplus of funds from each of the 110 million widely scattered farmer households when it was clear that agriculture had to supply the needed funds for the country's industrialization. It was against this background that the state adopted the policies of unified purchase and marketing for grain, cotton and oil-bearing crops in the early 1950s.

Regarding the unified purchase and marketing of grain, Comrade Chen Yun said then, "The farmers can no longer be allowed to freely dispose of the grain they have produced. Although the state pays for the grain, they should not be allowed to wait for the best prices. Most probably this will affect their enthusiasm for production." He continued to say, "On second thought, however, what else could we do? The only possible alternative is to use all our foreign exchange to import grain. In that case, we would have no money to buy the needed machines and equipment, and we would not be able to conduct either economic construction or industrialization."(1) So, it can be concluded that unified purchase and marketing of grain was a policy the government was forced to adopt at that time to accelerate the pace of construction and industrialization.

However, the implementation of the policy of unified purchase and marketing of grain by the state needed a precondition and would also produce some aftereffect.

The precondition was that the cooperative transformation of agriculture must be accelerated and a well-knit system of rural collective economic organizations must be established. Only by bringing all the farmer households into a certain kind of organizations and making them give up their own say in the productive operation could planned plantation, planned distribution and planned purchase be guaranteed. There were, of course, various reasons for launching in such a hurry the cooperative transformation and establishing the people's communes in the countryside. However, one of the most important one was to establish as soon as possible an organizational framework to guarantee the fulfillment of the unified purchase and marketing of agricultural products. As for the aftereffect of the policy, it was mainly reflected in the slowdown of agricultural and rural economic development. First, the implementation of the policy of unified purchase and marketing by the state meant closedown of markets. This would naturally lead to distortion of the prices of farm products, not only making it impossible to optimize the allocation of agricultural resources but also artificially driving down the prices of farm produce. Moreover, the policy was responsible for the low economic efficiency of agriculture. All these explained the *de facto* slow growth in the output of agricultural products. In the 21 years from 1957 to 1978, China's average per-capita grain output only increased 4.15 percent, while that of cotton and oil-bearing crops dropped by 11.5 percent and 16.6 percent respectively. Second, it led to the highly centralized control over the entire industry of agriculture and the whole rural economy. Plans drafted by the various government departments in charge must be carried out strictly. These plans covered the sowing areas of crops, the use of labor force, the buyers and prices of all the products and even the internal income distribution of the rural collective economic organizations. Consequently, this had seriously affected the development of various trades along special lines and made hundreds of millions of farmers depend primarily on the limited billions of *mu* of farmland for subsistence. Third, in order to control the marketing scope and amount of such daily necessities as grain, cotton and oil at low prices, it was imperative to enforce strict control over the flow of rural population into the cities and towns. This not only had made the problem of insufficient employment for the rural population more serious but also retarded the normal progress of urbanization in China, resulting in the increasingly sharp structural contradictions in the development of the national economy.

Although the implementation of the policy of unified purchase and marketing of agricultural products was the only choice China could make under the historical conditions at that time, the farmers nevertheless had paid heavily. From 1957 when unified accounting and distribution were introduced in the advanced agricultural producers' cooperatives to 1978, the per-capita annual income for rural residents from the collective organizations had only increased from 40.5 yuan to 73.8 yuan, with only an annual increase of 1.67 yuan. As for the per-capita annual cash income got from the collective organizations, it had only increased from 14.2 yuan to 18.97 yuan, with an average annual growth of 0.24 yuan. The *Outline of Rural Economy in China,* edited by the Policy Research Office under the Ministry of Agriculture, revealed that, in 1977, the per-capita average consumption of commodity grain by the rural residents was 204.5 kg and that of cooking oil, 1.0 kg, down by 8.3 percent and 45.9 percent respectively as compared with 1957 (Agriculture Press, 1982, pp. 202-211). From this, it is not hard to conclude that the unitary public ownership and the unified management and distribution over the previous 20-odd years had seriously retarded the development of agriculture and that of the rural economy as a whole. The broad masses of farmers could not be expected to put up with such a situation any more. Hence, when the Third Plenary Session of the 11th Party Central Committee decided to relax to a limited extent the rural policies, a drastic transformation of the rural economic system had taken place naturally and with unprecedented momentum, because the farmers had long waited for such a moment.

Section 2

Course and Basic Experience of Reform of the Rural Economic Structure

I. Proceeding Gradually from the Reform of Management System to a Revolutionary Transformation of the Property Relations

At the end of 1978, the total value of productive fixed assets in the rural areas was about 90 billion yuan (excluding land). Of the sum, that owned by collective economic organizations at the three levels – people's commune, production brigade and production team, was 84.9 billion yuan and that owned by the farmer households was over 4 billion yuan. Now, the total value of productive fixed assets in China's rural areas has exceeded 2,000 billion yuan, of which more than 1,100 billion yuan is owned by the collective economic organizations and 910 billion yuan by the individual farmer households. No doubt, the reform of the economic structure in the rural areas is, in fact, also a massive revolutionary transformation in the rural property relations. Apart from the continuous and steady growth of the collectively owned public assets, the assets owned by the individual farmer households have also increased rapidly, thus bringing forth a new situation in which the publicly owned economic sector takes the dominant position while those sectors under diverse forms of ownership achieve a simultaneous development. It is also true that, when the reform was launched in the countryside more than 20 years ago, nobody had thought about or demanded to extend the reform to the field of ownership of the means of production, particularly in regard to the development of the non-public economic sectors. Honestly, in the early stage nobody envisioned that the rural reform would involve a change in the property relations. Rather, people only wished to limit the reform to rural management system. But, everything develops according to its inherent law. A thorough reform of the management system would ultimately come down to a revolutionary transformation of the property relations.

1. From "Fixing Farm Output Quotas on a Household Basis" to "All-round Contract System"

As people all know, the rural reform started with "fixing farm output quotas on a household basis." What does "fixing farm output quotas on a household basis" mean? It means to contract the collectively owned land to the individual farmer households and change the unified organization of labor and unified management of production by the collective into separated labor and management by the individual farmer households over the plots of land contracted to them. Yet, the economic accounting and income distribution are still conducted under the unified organization by the collective. The farmer households must see to it that the output produced on their plots of land reach the amounts as stimulated in the contracts they signed with the collective and hand to the collective their products. Only then can they get their rewards from the distribution conducted by the collective. If their output exceeds the quotas as fixed in the contracts, they can share the parts above the fixed quotas together with the collective according to pre-set percentages. Therefore, under the conditions of "fixing farm output quotas on a household basis," what the farmer households get is only the freedom in deploying their own labor. The produce from their contracted plots of land is still owned by the collective organization. So, it is obvious that, under the policy of "fixing farm output quotas on a household basis," the farmer households do not enjoy the status of independent economic accounting. Hence, "fixing farm output quotas on a household basis" can only be taken a partial reform of the production management system within the framework of the people's commune.

In reality, the practice of "fixing farm output quotas on a household basis" did not last for a long time after the rural reform was launched. In some places, it had never been put into effect, because soon after the reform the farmers had quickly replaced it with the "all-round contract system." "All-round contract" is so called because the farmer households no longer needed to turn over their produce from their contracted plots of land to the collective for unified accounting and distribution. What they are required to do was to pay certain amounts of taxes to the state and meet the set selling quotas of the produce to the state on their contracted land, in addition to paying certain amount of land contract fees in kind to the collective. Having "paid the sufficient amount to the state and set aside enough for the collective," all the rest would belong to the farmer households themselves. The change from "fixing farm output quotas on a household basis" to "all-round contract" is by no means a change only in form. Its real essence lies in the fact that it has returned the right regarding agricultural production to the farmer households and turned the farmer households into real independent subjects in agricultural production. Viewed from this perspective, the "all-round contract system" represents a reform in the real sense and a fundamental breakaway from the people's commune system that boasted "bigger in size and of a more developed socialist nature." Moreover, the "all-round contract system" did not change the collective ownership of land in the countryside. Yet, it has done away with the so-called system of joint labor, unified accounting and unified distribution, which engendered egalitarianism and the "big-pot" practice in agricultural production. Moreover, it has also made it possible to give the fullest play to the farmer households' power in making their own decisions regarding agricultural production under the conditions of public ownership of land and the socialist market economy. As a result, the enthusiasm of the farmers in production has been greatly aroused. To stress the "all-round contract system" does not completely deny the system of joint labor, unified accounting and unified distribution in all forms. I only intend to stress one point, that is, agriculture in China, as an industry with the most unique characteristics, is by nature most suited to management by individual households. Although there are many reasons answerable to the setbacks China had suffered in its agricultural production prior to the drive of reform, the attempt to eliminate household management in agricultural production can be taken as the most important one. The fact that the "all-round contract system" has restored agricultural production to household management is tantamount, in fact, to making China's system of agricultural management embark again on the right track that is compatible with the inherent law of agricultural production. This also serves one major reason why such significant changes could have taken place over the past 20 years in the country's agriculture and rural economy.

2. The Unique Law Governing Agricultural Production and the Household-based Operation in Agricultural Production

Compared with other sectors of the economy, agricultural production displays different features. Not only that agricultural production depends more on such natural forces as light, water, heat and air, it also relies on the biological processes of the animals and plants. Apparently, the natural forces and the biological processes of the animals and plants cannot be completely controlled by man at will. People can only make efforts to understand the laws governing the natural forces and the biological processes of the animals and plants in their practice of production and then make use of these laws for the development of agricultural production, rather than to change these laws at will. Therefore, as far as agricultural production is concerned, the most important issue is to understand, grasp and make use of the laws of these natural forces and the biological processes of the animals and plants. Conversely, the form of agricultural management apparently exerts a great influence on people's understanding, grasp and use of these laws. In other words, agricultural production has its own unique characteristics and, therefore, raises special requirements for the form of organization in the management of agricultural production.

Lenin clearly pointed out that agriculture had many characteristics that could never be obliterated and, due to these characteristics, large-scale mechanized production in agriculture could never attain all the characteristics of mechanized mass production in industry. This indicates that Lenin held that the managerial and organizational models for industry were not necessarily adaptable to thc objective requirements of agriculture. In the reproduction process of the economy, no matter what its social nature, agriculture is always intermingled with the same natural reproduction process. This is a major characteristic of agriculture. Natural laws play an obviously important role in agricultural production. Therefore, it is necessary to respect the natural laws in agricultural production in the following two aspects. One is the law of natural changes. For instance, the changes in light, heat, water and air can produce a direct influence on the growth of agricultural crops. The agricultural producers must take corresponding measures to reduce the possible negative influence produced by the changes of natural forces on agricultural crops. The second is the law of the biological growth of animals and plants. The different stages in the growth of the animals and plants pose different requirements for the external environment. The agricultural producers must therefore closely observe the laws and do whatever they can to meet these requirements at any time. The interaction of these two sets of natural laws actually make the work of the agricultural producers very complicated. They must do whatever possible to catch the most accurate signals from the changes in the natural forces and in the growth of the animals and plants so as to make timely decisions in line with them. Therefore, in agriculture it is necessary to make decisions on the spot as soon as possible. Otherwise, either that the information obtained is not accurate enough, or that the opportunity is lost. So, in agricultural production, the most ideal decision-makers are the producers. It is only them who can have the best understanding of the growth of the crops and animals and can make the timely and correct decisions.

What type of agricultural management organizations can ensure that the decision-makers in production are at the same time the direct producers? No doubt, the farmer households. Although in the agricultural management organizations composed of many households, the decision-makers can also participate in labor directly. But, such organizations encounter two problems very difficult to solve. One is the problem to evaluate the work of the laborers. As the life cycle of plants and animals is a continuous process. The quantity and quality of the work done by the laborers in any point of time in their life cycle will ultimately be manifested in their output. Therefore, if the work done by the laborers is not evaluated in relation to the ultimate output, or in other words, if the work done by each laborer is made to act on the entire life cycle of the animals and plants, it will be impossible to accurately assess how much labor a particular laborer has actually spent. But, if the labor contributed by each laborer is evaluated in relation to the ultimate output, the *de facto* basic unit of management will be the farmer households, regardless how large a nominal size the organization of agricultural management has. The other problem is the control over the cost incurred in the course of production, particularly the management cost of the laborers. Generally speaking, the bigger the size a management organization, the greater the cost for personnel management (absolute amount). This is particularly true in agricultural production, because it is characterized by many different kinds of work, scattered operation and distinct seasonal differences. If the labor is carried out collectively, it will take a great deal of time and energy to fix the quotas, check how well the work has been performed and determine the standards for payment. This problem, if tackled by the household, will be much simpler, because a household is the most closely knit unit in terms of interest, and the members of the same household have the least frictions in interest and objectives of work. Therefore, there is no need to calculate and compare how much each of the family members has done in pure economic terms and they can most easily form a collaborative organization without any additional management cost.

Under what conditions will the agricultural producers show continuous concern for changes in the natural forces and the growth of the plants and animals? It is when the changes in the natural forces and the growth of the plants and animals are most directly related to their personal interest. Only when the whole business is put under the care of the household will the producers be free from any worry to share the benefits from the their efforts with others. Agriculture, however, is precisely an industry in which the scale of production can be easily partitioned without affecting the life cycle of the plants and animals. Therefore, agriculture is appropriate for household-based operations. This is not directly related with the nature of the society and the ownership of the means of production. Another distinctive feature of agriculture is the inconsistency between the time of production and the time of work. This feature provides the natural basis to make sideline production a supplement to agriculture. No doubt, the household is the most effective unit to use its spare time to engage in sideline production.

For quite a long time after the cooperative transformation in the countryside, all household operations had been viewed as an opposition to the collective economy. It seemed that, to consolidate and develop the collective economy, household operations must be eliminated. Here, the question was how the collective economy could demonstrate its worth. It was only a form of organization in which the farmers worked together. This form of organization could not guarantee the efficiency of labor. Therefore, it was necessary to find a form of organization that could make the labor more productive. Otherwise, it would be impossible to consolidate and develop the collective economy.

In fact, from the time when the cooperative system was established, the collective economic organizations had been looking for an efficient form to organize labor. It should be said such a form was found a long time ago, and it is nothing else but the responsibility system. The responsibility system in agricultural production is a form of labor organization within the economic collectives in the rural areas. It has undergone a universal course of development, that is, from the responsibility system that did not link remuneration with output to one that linked remuneration with output, and from the responsibility system that only liked remuneration with output at the level of production groups to one that linked remuneration with output to individual farmer households. This course of development and change is in fact a process to gradually improve the traditional model of the collective economy and create a new, vigorous and efficient form to materialize the collective economy. The responsibility system that did not link remuneration with output came into being along with the old collective economic organizations. On November 9, 1955, the 24th meeting of the of the NPC Standing Committee adopted the "Regulations on Examples of Agricultural Producers' Cooperatives (Draft)." The document stated, "In order to carry out organized joint labor in the collectives, the agricultural producers' cooperatives must divide the work, establish certain labor organizations according to the needs of production and the specific conditions of the cooperative members, so as to gradually introduce the responsibility system in production." It also said, "In order to put into effect the responsibility system in production, the cooperatives should organize their members into several production teams. The production team should be taken as the basic form of labor organization and the various production teams should be allowed to make arrangements on their own for production for a period of time or on a daily basis under the guidance of the production plan of the whole cooperative." Again, it said, "Whenever possible, the production team leader or the production group leader should assign each member the responsibility to look after a particular piece of land or to do a particular piece of job, so as to really carry out the responsibility system." It continued, "The production team leader or the production group leader should, when a day's work draws to an end, check what has been done by each team or group member and note down the workdays in accordance with the stipulated quotas of work. For those cooperatives that have not yet set the quotas of work, the production team or group leaders should assemble the team or group members at regular intervals to, in a democratic manner, set the standard of reward for each member in line with his or her performance in work." This indicates that, at the very beginning when the system of unified collective management was introduced, people had come to the understanding that, to organize agricultural production more efficiently, it was necessary to divide the human resources in the collective organizations into smaller units of labor. The collective economic organizations that carry out unified management not only should enforce the production responsibility system in all the smaller units of labor under them, but also make these units to introduce the responsibility system for each of their individual laborers.

However, as "unified accounting and unified distribution" must be performed, the production responsibility system adopted in the rural collective economic organizations had encountered, from the very beginning, problems that they could not possibly tackle by themselves.

Problem No. 1: The production teams under the cooperatives were only units to organize labor among their members but not units given the duty to be responsible for management and distribution. This characteristic of the cooperatives determined that the agricultural producers' cooperative could only contract out labor but not output to the production teams under them. If contracts based on output were made to give reward to the production teams in line with the amount of produce supplied by the production teams, some problems would crop up. First, such contracts must cover the entire cycle of agricultural production; otherwise, it would be impossible to make such contracts valid. Second, how should the output above the agreed quotas be handled? If it were given to the production teams completely as reward, the production teams would then have, to a certain extent, the power in distribution. Moreover, the production teams would naturally obtain certain right to make their own decisions regarding production in order to produce more above the agreed quotas. They would have to see whether what they got would be sufficient to cover the increased input that were needed to overfull the set quotas and where the increased input should be invested to get better returns -- summer crops or autumn crops, cereal crops or cash crops, or even farmland capital construction and irrigation projects. Anyway, once the production teams began to have the right to make their own decisions and the right to handle their own distribution, it would naturally lead to a weakening in the position of the agricultural producers' cooperatives in terms of "unified accounting and distribution" and probably make the basic economic accounting units become smaller in the end. This was exactly what the designers of the model of the agricultural cooperatives would not like to see. If the cooperatives and the production teams under them shared out proportionally the above-quota products, why should the production teams report truthfully to the cooperatives the output they had reaped above the agreed quotas? Then, the problem of "concealing the output and distributing it without authorization" would arise. Again, this was not allowed by the cooperatives that exercised "unified accounting and unified distribution" either. Hence, the production responsibility system for the production teams at the time of the agricultural producers' cooperatives fell into a dilemma from the very beginning. If the production responsibility system in real sense, i.e., the "output contract" responsibility system, was implemented in real earnest, the decision-making power regarding production and management and the power of distribution would gradually go to the production teams. This was tantamount to denying the position of the agricultural cooperatives in "unified accounting and distribution." But, if the responsibility system in the incomplete sense, i.e., "contracting out labor" but not "contracting out output," is implemented, it would be impossible to correctly evaluate the contribution of each production link that was contracted out to the final output of agricultural production. In other words, it was impossible for the labor-based contract responsibility system to get rid of the egalitarian "big pot" practice. If the problem of egalitarian "big pot" practice was not done away with, it would be impossible to fully arouse the farmers' enthusiasm in production and the sustained development of production would be out of the question. In a way, this explains the self-denial of the model of "unified management, unified accounting and unified distribution."

Problem No. 2: The real difficulty confronted by the production teams in implementing the responsibility system among their members was identical with the difficulty encountered by the agricultural cooperatives in enforcing the responsibility system among the production teams under them. The only difference was that the problems cropping up were more serious. To carry out the labor-based responsibility system among the cooperative members, the "labor" referred to here could only be "probable amount of labor." As the labor-based responsibility system introduced by the cooperatives for the production teams under them resulted in egalitarianism among the production teams, the labor-based responsibility system adopted by the production teams for their members also gave rise to egalitarianism among the members. These two types of egalitarianism, when combined together, virtually made it impossible for the agricultural production to develop. To introduce output-based responsibility system among the cooperative members would unavoidably lead to returning the management power of agricultural production to the individual farmer households. Viewed from the perspective of the traditional theory about the collective economy, this was nothing short of "a restoration of the small-farmer economy and a negation of the collective economy." Hence, the emergence of a comprised form of responsibility system, i.e., responsibility system based on "fixing output quotas to labor hands." The theoretical base for its emergence seemed to be that the labor hands belonged to the production teams anyway. So, "fixing output quotas to labor hands" constituted only a change in the organizational mode of production within the production teams. What was overlooked here was that the labor hands belonged naturally to the households. Besides, there was not yet a clear definition as to what people could be considered as labor hands. But in the individual households, particularly in terms of agricultural production, such a definition was in fact superfluous. If one was not considered a full labor hand, he or she could be a semi labor hand. Even if he or she could not be counted as a semi labor hand, he or she still could give some sort of help at certain stages of the production. In fact, "fixing output quotas to labor hands" would ultimately lead to "fixing farm output quotas to households."

These two problems indicate that, for the collective economic organizations in agricultural production, it is absolutely necessary to implement a responsibility system. But, it would not do if the responsibility system was introduced without linking remuneration to output and being based on the households. Without fixing output quotas to households, the responsibility system would only be in name, because such a responsibility system could not provide any solution to problems arising in the management and evaluation of labor as well as the supervision over labor in agricultural production. Such a responsibility system could not provide any incentive to the laborers.

The responsibility system in agriculture must be linked with output and based on the households. Does this mean that it was unnecessary at all to develop a collective economy in agriculture? The answer is absolutely "no." Before we proceed with the discussion, there is a precondition that must be mentioned. This precondition is that collective economy is not equal to unified management by collective organizations. The attribute of the collective economy is largely manifested in the nature of ownership. For instance, land is public property of the collective. So are the big and medium-sized farmland irrigation facilities, big farm machinery and tools, processing machines and means of transport, etc. Yet, that the collective owns the assets does not necessarily mean that it must manage all these assets in a unified manner. The nature of ownership of assets can be defined in law, whereas the form of management of the assets may be established in line with the specific conditions and factors of a particular industry or trade. The household-based responsibility system with remuneration linked to output is, in fact, a specific form of management of the collectively owned assets (such as land). Therefore, the form of household-based management was not in any sense opposed to the nature of the collective economy in agricultural production.

No matter who owns the assets, the operation and management of the assets would always involve a choice between centralized management and decentralized management. More often than not, the choice is determined by the particular characteristics of a specific industry or trade. Just as it is not feasible to adopt the same organizational form of management for both railway transport and urban taxi services, it is impossible to adopt the same organizational form of management for industry and agriculture. To stress that unified management must be implemented in agriculture was, to some extent, tantamount to overlooking the special characteristics of agricultural production and mechanically copying management model of industry. Regarding agriculture, a debate once broke out within the Chinese Communist Party after the completion of the land reform over the issue whether China should carry out collectivization first or mechanization first. In essence, the debate was one over how to choose the organizational form of management for agriculture in view of its special characteristics. In deciding that China should carry out collectivization first and in determining the operational model of agriculture after the collectivization, the following idea of Mao Zedong's played a decisive role. He held: Now that the Western capitalism had, in its course of development, undergone a stage of handicraft industry, a stage in which steam engines were not yet put to use and the handicraft workshops alone created new productive forces through a division of work, it would then be feasible for China to shake the foundation of the private ownership by relying on the new productive forces generated through unified management in the agricultural cooperatives.(2) This was exactly where the problem rested. Indeed, the handicraft workshops generated new productive forces when they were put under unified management and shared out work along special lines. But was the example applicable to agricultural production? In China, changes in the forms of agricultural management organizations have indicated that in most cases the principle embodied in the above example was not applicable to agriculture. This is because the objects of labor in agriculture differed from that in handicraft industry. The objects of labor in agriculture are living animals and plants. Sure, in agriculture it is possible to divide up the farmland. But, the life cycle of the animals and plants is a continuous and inseparable process. In other words, agriculture can be divided in terms of space but not in terms of time. An agricultural producer must be responsible for the entire life cycle of his objects of labor. Otherwise, it would be impossible to evaluate accurately the quantity and quality of labor he or she has spent in each stage of the agricultural production activity. The objects of labor in the handicraft industry, however, are different. In the production process of the handicraft industry, the objects of labor can be separated into different independent forms at different stages, and on the basis of the independent forms of semi-products turned out at these states it would be possible to evaluate accurately the quantity and quality of labor a worker has spent in each link of the chain of production. Besides, the life activities of the animals and plants have an irreversible or non-reciprocal nature, which does not exist in the objects of labor of the handicraft industry. This is because no matter at which stage of the handicraft industry a problem arises, there is always the possibility to remedy it. In agricultural production, however, regardless whether the responsibility system is based on "contact for work by segments" or based on "payment with fixed quotas," so long as the subjects of management are not given the responsibility to look after the entire process of production, or in other words, so along as the labor of the subjects of management is not linked directly with ultimate output of agriculture, it

calls for 'contract.' The implementation of the system with remuneration linked to output quotas can better balance the interests of the collective and that of the individual and can bring into play simultaneously both the initiative of the collective in unified management and the initiative of the laborers in making their own decisions for production. So, it can be applied widely and is warmly greeted by the masses.... To contract the work quotas to production groups, to households and to individual laborers only indicates changes in the size of the labor organizations, and it does not necessarily signify the level of production.... Contract for jobs, contract for output quotas or overall contract mainly show differences in distribution methods of the labor gains. Regarding the contract responsibility system, the form of "delivering to the state and collective a certain amount and keeping the remaining part" has been adopted in most cases; it has done away with distribution by work-points and was easy to operate, thus much acclaimed by the masses." This provided the policy basis for the existence and development of the household-based contract responsibility system in which remuneration is linked to output. The document further pointed out that the contract responsibility system linking remuneration with output "is a great creation of the Chinese farmers under the leadership of the Party and a new development of the Marxist theory regarding agricultural collectivization in the practice of China." This comment further put the minds of the farmers at ease.

The responsibility system in the agricultural economic collectives has undergone several stages of transformation—not linked to output—linked to output—only linked to output at the level of production teams—linked to output at the level of production groups—linked to output on a household basis. In fact, it reflected the progress in people's understanding about the materializing form of the collective economy in agriculture. Wherever the farmers were allowed to choose at their own will the form of agricultural production, the overwhelming majority of them would select the household contract responsibility system. In no way should this phenomenon be simply dubbed as "the mentality of small-farmer economy." In fact, it has shown the objective needs of the agricultural production, which is unique in itself in many ways, for its organizational form of management. The re-establishment of the status of household-based operation in agriculture is a manifestation of the law of agricultural production as reflected in the management system of agriculture. So, it is not hard to understand why China can achieve such marked progress in agricultural production since the introduction of the household-based contract responsibility system.

But, to introduce the household into the collective economy as the management subject, the significance is not restricted to the fact it has made the form of agricultural management more adapted to the law of agricultural production. This is because when the household goes into action as a relatively independent management subject, profound changes have taken place actually in the rules governing the accumulation of rural property, division of labor and specialization of work as well as the flow and reorganization of productive factors. The household serves, in fact, as the foundation for rural economy to really go from a closed model to an open one and from the traditional model to a modernized one. That is to why some people say the significance of the reestablishment of household economy in the rural areas can never be overstressed. Without the contract responsibility system linking remuneration with output and without the household-based management, all subsequent changes in the rural economic reform and development would not be possible. These changes include the rapid emergence and development of the township enterprises in rural areas and the industrialization of agriculture. Therefore, the two-tiered management system, which takes the household-based contract management as the base and combines centralization with decentralization, must be taken as a basic system of management in the rural economy and be implemented for a long time to come.

3. Household-based Contract Management and Changes of Property Relations in Rural Areas

Prior to the rural reform, the public ownership of the means of production had been implemented for 23 years under the systems of the advanced agricultural producers' cooperatives and the people's communes. In the countryside, land and other fixed assets for productive purposes had long been turned into public property under the care of the collectives. What the farmer households had in their possession were simple tools that were of a cheap value and easily damageable, such as hoes and sickles. Taking the countryside as a whole, the highly unitary public ownership by the collectives had been enforced over virtually all means of production. After 20 years of reform, however, the farmer households, which had previously been deprived of practically all means of production, have now again acquired a considerably large amount of production means. According to the annual random surveys among more than 67,000 farmer households conducted by the Rural Random Survey Team under the State Statistical Bureau, by the end of 1984 when the household-based contract responsibility system had been put into effect for only five years, each farmer household had on average in its possession 579.95 yuan worth productive fixed assets. Calculated on this basis, the total value of productive fixed assets owned by rural farmer households throughout the country would amount to some 109 billion yuan. Towards the end of 1990, the original value of fixed assets owned by each individual household had increased to 1,258.06 yuan, meaning that the total value of productive fixed assets owned privately by rural farmer households had reached 280 billion yuan throughout the country. By the end of 1997, the original value of productive fixed assets for each household reached 3,896.56 yuan, meaning that the total value of such assets owned by the farmer households had added up to 912.027 billion yuan. In a short span of 13 years from 1984 to 1997, the original value of productive fixed assets owned by each farmer household increased by 572 percent, with the annual average increase being 15.8 percent. Taking the countryside throughout the country as a whole, the total value of productive fixed assets owned by all the farmer households has increased by 738 percent, averaging 17.75 percent each year. Both in total amount and in growth rate, the increase was indeed impressive. It is not hard to imagine how great a momentum the rapid increase in the value of fixed assets owned by the farmer households have played in promoting the development of the rural productive forces as well as the prosperity of the entire rural economy.

The key reason that the farmer households could have accumulated so huge a amount of productive fixed assets of their own is the change from the system of "fixing farm output quotas on a household basis" to the system of "all-round contract" in the rural reform. It should be said that the system of "all-round contract" differed from the commonplace responsibility system in agricultural production because it has effected a fundamental change in the units of agricultural management. This change has brought forth two achievements with institutional significance. First, it has turned farmer households into independent economic accounting units. Second, it has enabled the farmer households to acquire ownership over their products. The system of "all-round contract" did not change the nature of the collective ownership over land. But, the distribution system established on the basis of it represented a big step forward, as best described in words of the farmers, "All the rest will belong to ourselves after delivering enough to the state and setting aside enough for the collective." In the farmers' remarks, the economic interest relations are made very clear: "Delivering enough to the state" means to pay whatever taxes due to the state as agricultural producers should; and "setting aside enough for the collective" means that the collective is entitled to collect from the farmer households part of the gains from the land as the owner of the land. Besides, the farmers should also pay various fees to the collective to cover the expenses for joint management and various communal public undertakings. The saying that "all the rest will belong to ourselves" seems rather vague. Yet, its actual implication in economics is very clear. Here, there are three categories of gains. The first is the gain of the farmers from their labor as laborers. The second is the gain for the household, which, as the body of management, shoulders all the production and operation risks and of course are entitled to gains due to the manager. The third is the gains for the farmer household as the investor, because all the management costs are paid by the household although nominally the collective is the owner of land under the system of "all-round contract." Obviously, the farmer households were deprived of the right to the last two categories of gains under the system of "fixing farm output quotas on a household basis." Under the system of "all-round contract," however, the more the management risks the farmer household dares to take and the more the investment it puts in production, the larger the part of the gains it can retain for itself. Having become a management unit exercising independent accounting and making its own decisions, the farmer household has acquired full right to dispose of that part of the gains from land it is entitled to, and can then decide by itself the proportions for reproduction, consumption and accumulation respectively. The productive fixed assets owned by the farmer households have been accumulated precisely in this way.

Obviously, the productive fixed assets of the farmers were not accumulated at the expense of the interest of the state and collective. The fundamental reason was that, after the introduction of the "all-round contract" system, the farmers have become both the managers and investors in agricultural production, rather than mere laborers, and have got the right to participate in the distribution of economic surplus. It was exactly under this condition that the assets of the farmer households have increased continuously. In the past, the operational model of "all-round contract" was considered as "contracted management." In fact, it can also be regarded as "cooperative management" between the collectives and the farmer households. The land was the asset of the collective. So, the collective can be considered as the initial investor in agriculture. But, the working funds and the additional investment are provided by the farmer households in the course of production. Therefore, the farmer households can also be regarded as investors. Because the farmer households enjoy the ownership right over the products, they can guarantee "delivering enough to the state and setting aside enough for the collective" under whatever conditions, while they themselves bear almost all the management risks for agricultural production. This management model not only can guarantee the rights and interests of the state and the collective and enable the farmers to get more for more work, but also make it possible for those farmers who dare to take more risks and make more inputs for more returns. Thus, it has provided a great incentive to the farmer households. So long as one household is willing to make more input in agriculture and perform the work properly, it not only can get enough to eat and wear and get rid of poverty, but also accumulate a certain amount of assets of its own. Once a farmer household has got its own assets and is given the right to make its own decisions of investment, continuous and more profound changes will surely take place in a still broader dimension in the entire rural property relations. As said above, the two-tiered management model, which takes household-based contract management as the base and combines centralization with decentralization, is in fact cooperative management between the collectives and farmer households. Consequently, the farmer households will be able to invest the funds they have accumulated from the cooperative management in other lines of business, thus giving rise to the household-run enterprises and enterprises set by several households jointly in the secondary and tertiary industries. In turn, this has given birth to the private sector of economy in the rural areas. On this basis, the private economy of the farmer households can again join hands with other types of economic subjects, including the collective units, the state-owned units and even the foreign-funded units, for joint ventures. It is precisely in this process that widespread and profound changes have gradually taken place in the rural property relations. It is also in this process that a new pattern has taken shape first in the countryside, in which the public sector of the economy has held the dominant position while the economy under diverse forms of ownership have developed side by side.

II. Proceeding from the Reform of State Monopolized Purchase of Major Farm Products to Overall Introduction of Market Mechanism in the Entire Rural Economy

The rural economic structure was extremely ossified prior to the reform. It was mainly reflected in two respects. First, under the highly centralized management system in the people's communes, the farmer households were deprived of any right regarding production. Second, all major agricultural products were put under the system of state monopolized purchase and the market supply-demand relations could not play any role in agricultural production. Therefore, in the rural reform, while making efforts to change the management system of the people's communes, reform has been carried out in the system of state

and grain coupons that had long remained indispensable for the urban residents. In the entire course of reform featuring the implementation of the "double-track price system," the state has taken continuous and small steps to readjust the grain purchasing prices it had set to make the prices approach step by step to the prices formed by market changes in supply and demand. In addition, the state has also reduced the amount of grain to be purchased according to pre-planned quotas and gradually increased the amount to be circulated in the market. In this way, the country has also managed to gradually get rid of the "double-track price system" and marched towards the goal of setting the prices of grain according to changes in market supply and demand and giving a free rein to free circulation in the market. Although there are now still quite a few problems that should be solved through efforts to deepen the reform, China has after all tackled the major contradiction of insufficient total supply by introducing the "double-track price system" over grain.

2. Gradually Readjust and Optimize the Structure of Agricultural Production under the Guidance of Market Demand

Along with the alleviation of the contradiction regarding the quantity of grain supply, the state has also in an overall manner relaxed its control over agricultural production characterized by state unified and fixed purchasing and marketing. Under the system of planned economy and the system of the people's commune before the reform, the most common practice was to include anything that was in short supply in the list for unified and fixed purchasing and marketing by the state. This is because at that time the contradiction China confronted was a two-folded one: one the one hand, it had to come to grip with the problem of short supply and, on the other, it must keep the prices stable. Under such pressure, the state had to put all products in short supply under the monopoly of the state and had them purchased and marketed according to strict state plans. Consequently, the country had plunged headlong into a vicious circle of "the more serious the shortage, the stricter the control; the stricter the control, the more serious the shortage." At first, the system of state monopolized purchasing covered only grain and cotton, and later its coverage was gradually expanded to oil-bearing crops, sugar-bearing crops, flue-cured tobacco and silk cocoons. Then, the system of unified and fixed purchasing was extended over virtually all agricultural products, including meat, fowl, eggs, aquatic products, fruits and vegetables produced in suburban areas. The so-called fixed purchasing refers to purchases of products made first by the government in line with state-set quotas to meet the needs of the government. Only when the farmers met the needs of the government and fulfilled the government-assigned purchase quotas at government-set prices were they allowed to put their products in the market for free circulation. In fact, for most of the farm products covered by state fixed purchasing, their total output was not even enough to meet the state quotas. So, there was virtually no possibility for them to circulate freely in the market. In this sense, there was not much difference between the fixed purchasing and unified purchasing. Moreover, not only the central government could set fixed purchase quotas on agricultural products, the local governments at various levels could also do so in line with the local needs. As a result, both the variety and amount of agricultural products upon which fixed purchase quotas were imposed had kept increasing. In the 1960s, the variety of agricultural products covered under the system of unified and fixed state purchasing even exceeded 200. In 1978, the year prior to the launching of the reform drive, the list still ran over 170. In this way, agricultural products that could be put in the market for free circulation were in fact very limited both in variety and amount, and the market for agricultural products was virtually shut down.

The system of unified and fixed state purchase of agricultural products, which was carried out throughout the country, actually meant to assign agricultural produce purchasing tasks to all the rural areas. Naturally, such a practice produced a serious adverse effect on the rational allocation of agricultural resources in different places and made it very difficult for these places to bring their comparative advantage into play, thus inhibiting the development of the productive forces of agriculture. Actually, this practice also constituted a major cause for China's long-lasting short supply of agricultural products under the system of planned economy, which in turn became one of the reasons for the government to impose strict planned control over the purchasing and marketing of agricultural products. Yet, the 20-year implementation of the state unified and fixed purchasing had failed to bring any improvement to the shortage of agricultural products. To change this situation, it was imperative to first create an opportunity to achieve an unusual increase in the supply of agricultural products to alleviate the situation of short supply. Only in this way was it possible to provide the material conditions for the reform of the system of unified and fixed state purchase and marketing of agricultural products.

The introduction of the two forms of responsibility system in agricultural production, i.e., "fixing farm output quotas on a household basis" and "overall contract," provided such an opportunity. As their implementation had greatly aroused the enthusiasm of the farmers in production, the output of major agricultural products had witnessed swift increases in a short span of six years from 1979 to 1984. For instance, the output of gain increased 33.6 percent, averaging 4.95 percent per year; the output of cotton was up by 188.8 percent, averaging 19.33 percent each year; the output of oil-bearing crops went up by 128.2 percent, with an average annual growth of 14.75 percent; and the output of meat increased by 79.90 percent, with an average annual increase of 10.28 percent. Such rapid increase in the supply of major agricultural products had basically relieved the tension between supply and demand. More importantly, there appeared a certain amount of surplus of products that were formerly under strict state control for many years because of their scarcity. Because of the surplus, it was unnecessary to enforce planned control over them any more. In 1983, the State Council decided to abolish cloth coupons by which the state rationed cloth according to plan. And in 1985, the Central Committee of the Communist Party and the State Council again decided to annul the system of unified and fixed state purchasing of grain and replaced it with a system of purchase based on contracts between the departments in charge of grain and the farmer households. Meanwhile, the government also decided to abolish the system of unified and fixed state purchasing over meat, fowl and eggs and allowed livestock by-products to circulate freely in the market. Along with the continuous increase of market supply of major agricultural products, the system of unified and fixed state purchasing has been gradually removed. This has provided an important condition for magnifying the role of the market mechanism.

In fact, the nature of household-based operation in agricultural production was exactly to enable the farmer households to carry out production in line with market demand and increase their gains. Why do the farmer households seek to increase their output continuously? Why do they continue to do so after fulfilling the quotas set by the state and meeting their own needs of consumption? The answer lies in the fact that they want to sell the surplus part of the output to the market to materialize its value. Any product in short supply in the market will witness a rise in its price. Consequently, the factors of agricultural production would naturally flow to and concentrate in the production of this product, hence making the supply of this product increase. It was precisely under the guidance of the law of value that many products whose supply had long fallen short of market demand quickly became abundant. No doubt, planned economy, particularly the economy under the rationing system, arose from the shortage of commodities. Yet, because planned economy hindered the optimal allocation of the factors of production and inhibited the enthusiasm of producers, it naturally failed to provide any remedy to the shortage of commodities. Obviously, the precondition for the reform of the system of unified and fixed state purchasing and marketing is to find a way to make the supply of commodities go beyond the critical point of shortage. The reform of agricultural management system had precisely created this basic condition. Although the farmer households have to contract for fulfilling certain state purchasing quotas, their attention is turned to the needs of the market when carrying out production. This is because, after meeting the needs of the government, they can then arrange production in line with market needs so as to sell their products at good prices. This also explains how the "double-track price system" came into being in the supply of agricultural products after the introduction of the two forms of responsibility system in agricultural production. On one hand, the farmer households would make efforts to fulfill the all state-set quotas in both variety and amount, and on the other, they would also work hard to turn out products not covered in the unified and fixed state purchasing system in accordance with the needs of the market. In order to reap economic returns for themselves, the farmers naturally incline to arrange their production according to the needs in the market. Therefore, in times when commodities were in short supply, the products the farmer households turn out of their own will mainly comprise products in short supply in the market. As a result, the market supply of these products improves. When the market supply of the products amount to a certain amount, it will be unnecessary to enforce unified and fixed state purchasing and, consequently, the coverage of the unified and fixed state purchasing for agricultural products will reduce in both variety and amount gradually. Agriculture and even the entire rural economy will then shift to the track of production according to changes in market supply and demand.

Facts have proved that the belief that China is poor in agricultural natural resources and must strictly enforce planned plantation, planned purchasing and planned marketing is groundless. Let's make a comparison between 1997 and 1978. In 1997, the area sown to farming crops throughout the country increased 2.55 percent (more than 3.8 million hectares) against 1978 and the area sown to grain crops, however, dropped 6.4 percent (some 7.67 million hectares). But, the grain output increased 62 percent. Along with the increase in the grain supply, the supply of various other agricultural products had also improved as their planting area grew by 39 percent (11.33 million hectares). The development in crop farming created the basic condition for the development of animal and poultry breading as well as aquiculture. Again, the development of the animal and poultry breeding and aquiculture had made it possible for the rural labor force and funds to flow and reorganize between different industries and across different regions, thus providing an opportunity for the development of the secondary and tertiary industries in the rural areas. It is precisely because of the role played by the market forces that the structural readjustment and optimization have taken place in agricultural production and the supply of agricultural products has improved—from a long-lasting shortage to a basic balance between supply and demand, along with some surplus in years of bumper harvest. Naturally, it is relatively easy for the farmers to arrange production in line with the demand of the market when there is a general shortage in supply. Now when the shortage in amount has been basically alleviated and the problem of variety and quality has come to the fore, how to readjust and optimize further the structure of agricultural production in line with the new changes in market supply and demand has turned out to be an outstanding problem for further reform of the agricultural produce circulation system.

3. Quick Rise of Township Enterprises in Rural Areas

Before the reform, China had carried out for many years the economic system and economic development strategy of separating urban areas from rural areas and separating industry from agriculture. Prior to 1949, in China's countryside, which subsisted on a semi-self-sufficient economy, there were many household sidelines and handicraft workshops. In the small rural towns there had been large numbers of peddlers and privately owned shops. After liberation, in the socialist transformation of capitalist industry and commerce, "Leftist" radical policies were adopted towards the rural handicraft businesses and individual shop owners and peddlers. Moreover, as more and more agricultural products were listed under the system of unified and fixed state purchasing, these shops and peddlers were devoid of supply of goods, and the handicraft workshops and household-run agricultural and sideline produce processing businesses could find nothing to process. Therefore, for a long time, the industries and commerce in the rural areas were weakened.

In the "great leap forward" movement in 1958, to increase the nation's steel production and promote agricultural mechanization, the rural people's communes all over the country set up large numbers of enterprises, mainly for the building and maintenance of farm machinery. These enterprises could be considered the predecessors of the township enterprises. At that time, they were known as commune- and production brigade-run enterprises. To maintain the operational system of the national economy of the time, to prevent the rural areas from setting up various types of small industrial enterprises to compete with the large state-owned enterprises for raw materials, energy and market and, more importantly, to prevent the loss of profits from the processing industry that would inevitably lead to a reduction in the accumulation of funds urgently needed by the government for industrialization, the government had for a long time implemented policies to limit the development of non-agricultural industries in the countryside. For example, it was stipulated that the "three-locality principle" (i.e. getting the raw materials in the locality, doing the processing work in the locality and marketing the products in the locality) must be implemented in the development of commune- and production brigade-run enterprises. But, as the overwhelming part of the agricultural products that could be used as raw materials for the processing industry had been bought up by the government in the form of unified and fixed state purchases, the "three-locality principle" was actually meant to limit the development of commercial processing industry in the rural areas and put the production of the commune- and production brigade-run enterprises within the limits of self-sufficient rural economy. This practice had made the rural industrial structure characterized by "taking grain as the key link" extremely ossified. Also, it represented a restriction for the surplus labor in agricultural production to flow to non-agricultural trades and confined the ever-increasing rural labor population to the ever-diminishing farmland areas. Consequently, large amounts of rural resources were left unused and the growth of the rural economy was subjected to restrictions. So was the increase of the farmers' incomes.

The rural reform brought forth a good opportunity to reestablish the industrial structure in the rural economy. Thanks to the implementation of household-based contract responsibility system, the enthusiasm of the farmers in production had been greatly enhanced. Moreover, the rise in the prices of agricultural products had increased the economic surplus in the rural areas, which in turn had laid the material foundation for investment in other trades than agricultural production. Along with increase in labor productivity, the problem of rural surplus labor force, which had long been there under the traditional system featuring "headlong mass action" and "big-pot" practice in distribution, had quickly surfaced. The farmers wished to open up more channels of employment and have their incomes quickly increased. Against this background, the township enterprises sprang up and developed quickly. To be more specific, the rapid development of the township enterprises after the mid-1980s, in fact, called for at least four basic conditions. First, there was an increase in surplus funds in the rural areas, only in this way can the farmers and the rural collective economic organizations be able to make investments in non-agricultural industries. Second, after the implementation of the household-based contract management system, the surplus labor force in agriculture was allowed to flow freely to non-agricultural trades. Third, the Party's policies allowed the non-publicly owned sectors and diverse forms of economy to develop under the precondition that the publicly owned sector held the dominant position. And fourth, considerable progress has been made in the development of the commodity market and the market for production factors along with the deepening of the reform, thus providing an increasingly bigger room for the survival and development of the township enterprises that operate outside the state plans. In essence, it can be said that the rapid development of the township enterprises is also a result of the in-depth development of the rural reform and the role played by the market mechanism.

In 1978 before the reform, there were altogether 1.524 million commune- and production brigade-run enterprises throughout the country, with a total payroll of 28.266 million, which accounted for 9.3 percent of the total labor force in the countryside. These enterprises generated a total output value of 49.31 billion yuan, accounting for 24.2 percent of the rural total social product. Of the sum, the output value of industry was 38.53 million yuan, accounting for some 9.1 percent of the total industrial output value of the country. By the end of 1997, the number of rural township enterprises had increased to 20.149 million, of which the number of enterprises at the village level remained roughly the same as in 1978. Most of the newly established enterprises were single household-owned ones, ones set up by several households jointly, individually and privately owned ones as well as ones in various forms of joint ventures. The number of employees working in these enterprises reached 130.504 million, accounting for 28.4 percent of the total rural labor force. These employees earned 252.93 billion yuan from the enterprises and created 2,074 billion yuan of added value, which accounted for some three-fourths of the rural total social product. Now, the township enterprises have developed into a strong pillar for the entire rural economy. For quite many years, the annual growth of the township enterprises has remained higher than that of the GDP, and the average contribution made by the township enterprises to the annual growth of GDP is 3-4 percentage point. Therefore, the township enterprises have, in fact, become an important force in the development of the entire national economy. Yet, the most valuable service done by the township enterprises is that they, relying on solely the market forces, have provided more than 100 million job opportunities for the rural surplus labor force over the past 20 years. The significance of this service can never be overestimated in helping the farmers to get better off and promoting the rural socio-economic development.

III. Gradually Expanding the Rural Reform from the Economic Field to the Social and Political Fields and Strengthening the Democratic System at the Rural Grass-roots Level

Under the systems of planned economy and the people's commune, rural village officials were appointed by authorities at higher levels basically. Their major duty was to see to it that the various sorts of tasks listed in the state plans were fulfilled. On the part of the broad masses of the farmers, they found it difficult to participate in the management and supervision of affairs related to the development of the rural economy and society. After the people's commune system was abolished, the villagers' self-governing system was introduced. However, there had been little change in the practice of appointing village officials by higher authorities. When elections were held for the villagers to choose members for the village committees, all they were asked to do was to tick on the names of candidates nominated by authorities at higher levels. Moreover, in most cases they were not allowed elect those who they liked most to leading posts at their own will. To some extent, this frustrated the initiative of the farmers to manage their own affairs.

As the farmer households have got more and more power in making their own decisions in agricultural production and the market economy has developed gradually, the farmers' democratic consciousness and legal sense have also awakened. They have raised increasingly louder cries for expanding the scope of democracy at the rural grass-root level and strengthening the rural grass-roots democratic system. Under the direct leadership of Party organizations at various levels, extensive exploration has been made in developing the democratic system of village committee, which has gradually brought into being the three systems of democratic election, villagers' meeting and openness in village affairs in the rural areas.

In democratic election, important changes have taken place in two aspects: First, direct election is introduced for village committee members, that is to say, the candidates are determined through direct election participated by all villagers who have the right to vote. This has changed the former practice in which the villagers could only choose indirectly from among the candidates nominated by the authorities. As the village committee is a self-governing organization of the villagers and the village officials are also farmers living and working in the villagers, the system of direct election of village officials makes sense for the farmers to elect those in whom they have the most confidence to manage the village affairs. Second, if a village official proves to be not up to the requirements of his post, the villagers' meeting has the power to have him dismissed. This not only represents an important expression of the democratic supervision system but also an important improvement of the system of democratic election. The establishment of the system of villagers' meeting is aimed at keeping the villagers informed of major events and major affairs in the village that are related to their own interests and enabling the villagers to play a part in the decision-making process in the form of villager' meeting or meeting of villagers' representatives rather than letting a few village officials have the say. In doing so, the purpose is to ensure openness, fairness and justice in the making of decisions related to important matters. To implement the system of openness on village affairs, particularly in relation to the village finance, the village committee is required to announce to the villagers at regular intervals major events and affairs in the village that have a direct bearing on the interests of all the villagers, including the allocation of land for residence building, family planning, management and operation of collective assets, use of funds collected from the villagers, subsidies paid to village officials, money spent to entertain guests, expenditure on village public utilities, amount of funds accumulated, as well as the village's credits and debts. This not only can keep the villagers fully informed of the major village affairs but also can put village officials under supervision from the villagers. In the words of the villagers and the village officials, it is to "keep the villagers informed and keep the village officials clean." The Party and the state made a timely summary of the experience gained in the development of the rural grass-roots democratic system, and improved and institutionalized the system. In 1998, the Standing Committee of the National People's Congress adopted an amendment to the Organic Law of the Village Committee. The amendment institutionalized the three democratic systems in the form of legal stipulations, thus making the guarantee of the villagers' democratic rights more effective.

IV. Basic Experience of Rural Reform

The summarization of the experience gained in the rural reform can proceed from many perspectives. The Third Plenary Session of the 15th Party Central Committee summed up the basic experience of the rural reform over the past 20 years from the perspective of Party leadership. The author of this chapter ventures to sum up the experience by reviewing the course of the rural reform itself. In my view, the two principles that have been firmly upheld throughout course of the reform were a major reason for the smooth progress of the reform.

First, the Communist Party of China has firmly upheld the basic principle to adopt a correct attitude towards the farmers.

Throughout the reform, the Chinese Communist Party has all along taken as its basic starting point to show respect to the wishes of the farmers, protect their interests and mobilize their enthusiasm. The Third

Plenary Session of the 11th Party Central Committee ushered in the prelude to the rural reform. Although the "Decision of the Central Committee of the Communist Party of China on Certain Problems to Accelerate Agricultural Development" adopted at the session included, as it is looked today, some contents that are not readily applicable now, the two lines it particularly stressed, i.e. the ideological line to seek truths from the facts and the working line to show respects to the wishes of the people, have all along played a vital role in the entire course of rural reform. To guarantee the farmers' economic interests and to respect their democratic rights are the basic principles proposed at the Third Plenary Session of the 11th Party Central Committee in handling affairs related to the farmers. The two basic principles also indicated that the Communist Party of China had returned to the correct ideological line and working line. Ultimate goal of the Party is to do everything in the interest of the people. So in working out rural policies, the Party has persisted in giving priority to the choice of the farmers. The Party has taken the following basic criteria in judging the correctness of farmers' choices: to see whether they are favorable to the development of the productive forces, to the growth of the comprehensive national strength and to the improvement of the people's living standards. Thanks to such a correct attitude adopted by the Party, the creativeness of the broad masses of the farmers has been brought into full play. As the Party has, from the very beginning of the rural reform, taken as its basic principle towards the farmers, what the Party has done was to summarize, institutionalize and popularize the solutions to all the most basic and important problems encountered in the reform. All these solutions were creations by the farmers, such as the choice of the management subjects, the orientation of the reform and the institutional framework. Over the past 20 years of rural reform, three important achievements that are of institutional and innovative significance have been made successively in the rural reform. They are, to be more specific, the two-tiered management system of household-based contract management that combines centralization with decentralization, the rapid emergence and development of the township enterprises, and the development of the democratic system at the rural grass-roots level.

They are all great creations by the farmers under the leadership of the Party. Yet, viewed from the perspective of policy evolution, each of these great creations did not receive support and encouragement when it first appeared. It was only recognized, summarized and institutionalized when it had been proved successful. This indicates that the motive power for institutional innovation lies in the people. It also shows that the Chinese Communist Party has the ability to sum the experiences created by the people and sublime them into theories, policies and systems.

Precisely, reform means institutional innovation. Yet, whether an innovation is correct or not, it should not be judged by whether it is catered to subjective assumptions of man, still less should it be judged by whether it complies with the current institutional framework. The conclusion can only be drawn on the basis of the results of experiment. Therefore, the key for institutional innovation lies in whether it is allowed to break through the current institutional framework and make experiment. China's rural reform has given full expression to this point. The farmers not only have been allowed to make experiments, but also have been allowed to make repeated experiments on issues over which there was much controversy and about which the conclusions were not easily drawn. In other words, those who had misgivings over these issues were allowed to take their time and wait to see the final facts, that is, the results of the practice of the people. For example, at the early stage of reform, the farmers created the system of "fixing farm output quotas on a household basis" and the system of "all-round contract." For a time, heated debate broke out in the society over the road of agricultural development. Some people even described the two systems as "having gone back to the pre-1949 days overnight despite all the hard work that has been performed over the past three decades." This example shows how heated the debate was. Heated as it was, the farmers' experiments on the two systems went on. However, in a short period of only two to three years, the system of "fixing farm output quotas on a household basis" and the system of "all-round contract" won widespread acclaim and were popularized throughout the country for the convincing effects they had produced in increasing agricultural out-

is put to the production of poor quality grain, there will be a shortage in supply; but, if the production of poor quality grain is let to go on its own, it will lead to an endless cycle of "difficult grain sales." Therefore, the only way to get out of the dilemma is to increase the variety of high quality grain to replace the poor quality grain in the market with better quality grain.

At present, the agricultural produce market is beset not only with the difficulty in grain sales. In fact, most agricultural products do not sell well and their prices keep going down. This indicates that, behind the rapid growth of agricultural production in recent years, a major and universal contradiction exists, that is, undue importance has been attached to quantity while neglecting quality and the improvement of efficiency. If viewed from the perspective of system and mechanism, this contradiction will sublime to the fact that role of the market mechanism has not been brought into full play.

In the past when the supply of agricultural products fell short of demand in China, all attention and efforts were devoted to increasing the output of agricultural products. There was nothing wrong in this under the conditions at that time. However, when the problem of quantity has gradually diminished and that of variety and quality has come to the fore, we have failed to effect a fundamental change in the means to regulate agricultural production.

To some extent, to regulate the allocation of the factors of agricultural production by administrative means can indeed attain the objective of increasing the output of agricultural products. But, administrative means have often been proved helpless in improving the quality. The reason lies in the fact that the quality of products is determined by the consumers who have the right to choose after their basic demand for amount is satisfied. In other words, quality is determined by the market. When agricultural production reaches a stage at which the optimization of variety and the improvement of quality are taken as the major objectives, the allocation of factors of agricultural production must keep in step with the needs of the market. Since the reform drive was launched, profound changes have taken place in the means for the allocation of agricultural production factors in China. For instance, the shift from "taking grain as the key link" to "taking best advantage of local conditions" marks a great progress. Under the situation of universal food shortage, "taking best advantage of local conditions" might prove to be effective because it can increase maximally the amount of agricultural products. However, when the issue of quantity is basically solved, to continue to stick to the principle of "taking best advantage of local conditions" would be tantamount to only taking into consideration the conditions and wishes of the producers. Products turned out under the guidance of this principle would inevitably clash with the actual needs of the market. Therefore, at the current stage of agricultural development, it is imperative to pay more attention to the market needs on the basis of "taking best advantage of local conditions." That part of poor-quality grain, which does not sell well in the market, is largely produced under the guidance of the principle of "taking best advantage of local conditions." Although such grain does not sell well in the market, the production still keeps going on. Why? The reason lies in the incentive provided by state policy of "purchasing grain at protective prices," and that the information of market changes has not reached the farmers. When the production keeps going on as before, it will naturally result in greater and greater stockpiling. Now, the State Council has made it clear that such poor-quality grain would be removed from the list of grain to be purchased at protective prices in year 2000. With this information of market needs reaching the producers, a change is bound to take place in the structure of grain production and in the amount of supply.

The example of grain supply and demand fully indicates that, despite the fact that China's agriculture is subjected to constraints of both resources and market needs, due attention must be paid to bringing into the play the role of the market mechanism, i.e., to regulating agricultural production according to the needs in the market. The regulatory role played by the government in agriculture should be manifested mainly in two aspects. The first is the establishment of a sound market system for agricultural products. Apart from efforts in the construction of market facilities as well as the establishment of market rules and organizational setup, it is also necessary to intensify efforts in the establishment of an agricultural produce information system to provide the farmers in a timely manner with accurate and sufficient information in terms of production, supply and demand as well as prices for all kinds of agricultural products. The second is that, while giving support to agriculture, primary attention should be paid to promoting scientific and technological progress, improving the conditions for production and protecting the ecological environment – all of which are conducive to a sustained and steady development in the comprehensive capability of agriculture. It is still necessary to provide the producers with protection in price and to regulate the supply and demand of major agricultural products. Yet, in normal conditions the prices of agricultural products should be mainly regulated by the supply and demand in the market. The responsibility of the government is to protect the productivity of agriculture under any conditions. So long as the productivity is maintained at a certain level, China can certainly cope with the fluctuations between the years of bumper harvest and lean harvest with an appropriate amount of grain reserves and imports.

The complexity of the question regarding China's countryside lies in the hugeness of the rural population. Therefore, the rural development has to fulfil a dual task, i.e., guaranteeing the supply of agricultural products and at the same time helping the broad masses of the farmers to get prosperous as soon as possible. Nevertheless, the limited arable land and huge rural population forms an irreconcilable contradiction. It is simply impossible to make the rural population prosperous only by increasing the quantity and improving the quality of the agricultural products. The only way to make the rural population rich is to reduce the population size. China is no exception in front of this law. To this end, China must accelerate its pace of industrialization and urbanization and facilitate the transfer of rural population to non-agricultural sectors and townships in a massive scale. The decision adopted at the Third Plenary Session of the 15th Party Central Committee clearly pointed out that developing the small cities and towns was a major strategy to spur on the economic and social development in the rural areas. The key in the implementation of this strategy also lies in bringing into full play role of the market mechanism. On the one hand, it is necessary for the government to strengthen overall planning in regard to these cities and towns so as to save land and ensure environmental protection. On the other hand, it is necessary to make every possible efforts to bring into play the role of the market mechanism in the migration of the people, the construction of urban infrastructure and public utilities, the development of social undertakings as well as the establishment of the social security system. Only by breaking away from the old model for urban development under the system of planned economy and bringing into full play the role of the market mechanism can the strategy of developing small cities and towns be implemented smoothly. It is also in this way can the urban economy and rural economy be brought onto the orbit of coordinated development.

Notes:

(1) *Collected Works by Chen Yun 1949-1956* (Chinese edition), People's Publishing House, 1984, pp. 207-210.

(2) Bo Yibo: *Reminiscences on Some Important Policy Decisions and Events*, Vol. I, p. 191, Central Party School Publishing House, 1991.

(3) *Selected Works of Deng Xiaoping, Vol. II, 1975-1982* (Chinese edition), p. 275, People's Publishing House, 1983.

CHAPTER 4

PLANNING AND MARKET IN CHINA'S REFORM OF ECONOMIC STRUCTURE

Synopsis

In their economic reform, all socialist countries have come upon such a common problem, that is, whether the system of planned economy or the system of the market economy should be chosen as the system model for the allocation of resources. To study this problem, the theoretical circles have made pains-taking efforts. And in practical economic life, selective comparisons have been made between different models. Due to the influence of classical Marxist theory and the socialist economic practice of the former Soviet Union and taking into consideration the realities both at home and abroad shortly after the victory of its socialist revolution, China chose the system model of the planned economy after the founding of the People's Republic. For a time, this model helped amass strength domestically to ensure the construction of key projects, thus making a contribution to the development of the national economy. Yet, due to its intrinsic drawbacks, this model had failed to play an effective role in the allocation of resources, resulting in low economic efficiency and insufficient vitality of the enterprises. It had increasingly fallen short of the demand imposed by the development of the productive forces. Therefore, as of 1978, China began the great practice of reform and opening to the outside world and launched a revolutionary transformation from planning to market in its economic structure and basic mechanism of economic operation. The Third Plenary Session of the 11th Party Central Committee re-established the ideological line of emancipating the

by the People's Republic, thus to make sure that the People's Republic control the economic lifeline and the state-owned sector be made the leading sector of the national economy. With regard to private capital, for a considerably long period to come after the victory of revolution, it was necessary for us, on the one hand, to make use of its enthusiasm as much as possible to promote the development of the national economy and, on the other, adopt appropriate and flexible measures to restrict it. As for the individual agricultural sector and the handicraft sector, both of which were widely scattered, it was necessary to take cautious and gradual but active steps to guide them to develop in the direction of modernization and collectivization.

Confiscated bureaucratic capital, which was put under socialist public ownership, constituted the major part of the state-owned sector of the national economy. On the eve of liberation, bureaucratic capital roughly accounted for about 66 percent of the industrial capital of the whole country and 80 percent of the fixed assets in industrial trades as well as mining and transport industries. Under the Resource Commission of Kuomintang regime were 219 industrial and mining enterprises, which produced 90 percent of the country's iron and steel (the highest output, 928,000 tons, was produced in 1943), 33 percent of the national total output of coal (the record year was 1942 when the output reached 62 million tons), 67 percent of electricity (the record year was 1941 when the country produced a total of 6 billion kwh.of electricity), 45 percent of the national total output of cement (the highest year was 1943 when the national cement output reached 2.29 million tons), as well as all the output of petroleum and of non-ferrous metals. In addition, bureaucratic capitalists controlled all of China's financial and monetary institutions, railway and highway transportation, postal and telecommunications undertakings, aviation industry as well as 44 percent of the country's shipping tonnage, along with a dozen or so monopolistic trade companies. Thanks to the confiscation of bureaucratic capital, the strength of the socialist public-owned economic sector had increased greatly. According to available statistics, in 1949 the output value turned out by the state-owned industry accounted for 41.3 percent of the total generated by big industrial enterprises throughout the coun-

try. State-owned sector claimed 58 percent of electricity generated, 68 percent of the total output of crude coal, 92 percent of the pig iron output, 97 percent of the steel output, 68 percent of the cement output, and 53 percent of the cotton and yarn output. In addition, the state-owned sector held control over all the railways, postal and telecommunications undertakings as well as most of the modern communications and transport facilities.

Apart from the bureaucratic capital confiscated, the state-owned sector also owed its emergence and development to another source, i.e., the publicly run economy that came into being during the period of the "revolutionary base areas." Yet, the contribution from this source was insignificant. At the initial stage, the publicly run economy in the "revolutionary base areas" was developed by the army men and civilians in these base areas to meet war needs. As early as in 1927, the publicly run economy, with an obvious socialist nature, appeared in the revolutionary base areas. It mainly comprised industries for military purposes, such as weapons, ammunitions, quilts, clothing, iron casting, etc. There were also some industrial establishments turning out products for civilian use, such as coal-mining, salt and textile production, paper-making, leather processing, etc. Besides, publicly run commercial establishments and banks were established. Such publicly run economy played an important role in supporting the revolutionary wars, satisfying the needs of the people and promoting the economic development in the revolutionary base areas.

After liberation, the state had made massive investments for large-scale construction, bringing forth a large number of state-owned enterprises. In a span of 30 years, the country invested some 700 billion yuan to build more than 3000 big and medium-sized projects, resulting in bringing into being a large group of new industrial bases. By 1978, the number of industrial enterprises in China had amounted to 350,000 and the total value of fixed assets in enterprises owned by the whole people had reached 320 billion yuan, 25 times as much as that accumulated in some 100 years prior to 1949. These enterprises and industrial bases constituted the initial foundation of modern industry.

II. Formation of the System of Planned Economy

1. Historical Causes for the Adoption of Planned Economy in China

In China, the system of planned economy came into being in the First Five-Year Plan period. It was established by learning from the experience of the former Soviet Union in building socialism.

There were profound historical reasons for China to adopt the planned economic system at the initial stage. In terms of ideology, market economy was associated with capitalism while planned economy was considered a basic feature of the socialist system. Since China wanted to build socialism, it was taken for granted that it should practice planned economy. Viewed from the perspective of historical conditions at that time, the semi-feudal and semi-colonial economy passed from old China was an awful mess. So, in order to heal the wounds inflicted by the long years of war and effect a change in China's backward economic outlook, it was generally held that planned economy could concentrate human, financial and material resources for construction of key projects. From the perspective of international background, after the Great Depression in the 1930s, all newly established socialist states adopted the model of planned economy, and even some capitalist countries, such as France, also believed that planned economy could overcome the shortcomings of the market economy.

By 1957, the highly centralized and unified system of planned management was basically established in China. It covered not only to the system of control by the planning departments but also the financial system, monetary system, investment system, price system, goods and equipment circulation system, labor and personnel system as well as distribution system. In 1957, the number of industrial enterprises under direct the control of various departments of the State Council had increased from a little more than 2,800 in 1953 to over 9,300. The variety of industrial products listed under state planned control had increased from 115 to 290. And the variety of goods and materials listed under state unified allocation had gone up from a little more than 220 to over 530. In terms of national income distribution, the proportion earmarked

as state fiscal revenue had accounted for some 34 percent, of which 75 percent was put at the disposal of the central government.

2. Basic Contents of the Planned Economic System

China's planned economic system comprised mainly the following contents.

The first is the planning system of the national economy. The overall plan of the national economy must comprise plans that guide the operation of the various sectors of the national economy. In terms of time span, the national economic plan covers long-term plans, the medium-term plans (five-year plans) and short-term plans (annual plans). From the perspective of contents, it is composed of three parts – economic development, scientific and technological development as well as social development. And in terms of levels for management, it consists of state plan, departmental and regional plans as well as plans of the enterprises.

The second is the procedure and method employed to formulate the national economic plans. In mapping out national economic plans, a three-step procedure is usually adopted. The first step is that the state put down the mandatory statistics and pass them down to the various departments and localities, and these statistics will be taken by the localities and departments as the basic requirements and outlined schemes in drafting their own plans. The second step is that the various departments and localities submit the plans they have drafted according to the state-set mandatory statistics and their specific conditions to the State Planning Commission (now renamed "State Development and Planning Commission"). The third step is that, on the basis of the draft plans worked out by the various departments and localities, the state strikes an overall balance. The method of overall balancing is the basic method used in formulating the national economic draft plans. Overall balance is mainly enforced in finance, credit, foreign exchange as well as materials and goods supply.

The third refers to the organizational system of planning, including the organizational system for management of plans, division of responsibilities among the organizations for management of plans at various

levels and their mutual relations. The organizational system of management of state plans is divided into four levels – central, provincial, municipal and county.

The fourth is the management system of plans. It includes mainly the policy decision-making system in the management of plans and the regulatory system in the management of plans.

The decision-making procedure in planning was characterized by undue subjectivity and arbitrariness and was far from being institutionalized and legalized. Those who made the decisions only wield their power but not took any responsibility, and the result was naturally that they worked out the plans but not held any checks over their implementation, and laid stress on input but not paid any attention to output. Under the planned economic system, the implementation and regulation of national economic plans were mainly realized by regulating the single mandatory plans that matched the centralization of power. Economic and legal means are seldom used.

3. Major Characteristics and Shortcomings of the Planned Economy

— Allocating resources by the means of planning. The allocation of resources was mainly conducted between the various administrative departments and different regions; it was done by means of planned quotas, administrative distribution and coordination. In terms of finance, unified central control was enforced on receipt and expenditure according to state plans; and the banks only served as "cashier" institutions for all those departments in the society exercising planned control over funds.

— Direct management of enterprises by the state. The state plans were neither predictive nor guiding, but mandatory. The enterprises were not independent economic entities but affiliates to the government departments. To the enterprises, the planned quotas of the state were not for reference in their decision making but administrative assignments that must be fulfilled. The management of human, financial and material resources of the enterprises as well as their production, marketing and sales must all comply with the state planned quotas.

— Management centering around material objects. The basic content of the state plans was to reflect and control over the material activities, such as their production, circulation, distribution and consumption, as well as the balances between them. As for their movement and balance of value, it only took a secondary position.

— The government was both the owner and manager of state-owned assets; it both controlled and directly intervened in macro-economic activities.

The highly centralized planned economic system in China once played an important role in mobilizing and amassing the country's limited resources for the smooth construction of key projects and the development of a fairly comprehensive foundation for industrialization. It also played an important role in quickly changing the backward situation left over from old China.

But, along with the development of the productive forces, the drawbacks of such a planned economic system had become increasingly apparent with the passing of time. In terms of ownership, undue stress was placed on the role of the public sector, particularly that of the state-owned sector, while repelling and restricting the development of non-publicly owned sectors. In industrial management, far too many enterprises were placed under the direct control of industrial departments under the central government; the number of enterprises under the direct leadership of the central government increased from 2,800 in 1953 to 9,300 in 1957. In terms of finance, the central government took too large a share, leaving the local governments and enterprises with too small a share. With regard to the distribution of materials and goods, the variety of materials and goods, whose distribution was conducted by the State Planning Commission in a unified and balanced manner, increased from 55 in 1952 to 231 in 1957. In planned control, the coverage of direct planning expanded quickly. In the distribution system, egalitarianism prevailed, resulting in the "iron-bowl" practice in the labor system, which was characterized by enterprises eating from the "big pot" of the state, while all individual workers eating from the "big pots" of the enterprises. In foreign economic relations, the country had long isolated itself from contacts and exchanges with the external world and closed its door to the rest of the world. All these turned out to be obstacles for further development of China's national economy.

As the state exercised over-rigid control over the enterprises and retained too much power for itself in many aspects, such as in financial affairs, selection and appointment of enterprise officials, material control as well as welfare affairs, officials of the enterprises had limited power over the operation of their enterprises, particularly in such areas as production, supply of raw materials and sales of products. This situation had seriously hurt the enthusiasm of the enterprises as well as their workers and staff. Some enterprise officials had much complaints about this. In 1956, the director of a state-owned enterprise was only given the power to approve the use of 200-500 yuan of funds. Too much power was concentrated in the hands of the enterprises' superior authorities, which virtually looked after all matters related to enterprise management, thus leaving little power to the enterprise officials to make their own decisions. In a sense, the enterprises were only affiliates to the administrative institutions. It was virtually impossible for the enterprises to function as independent economic entities.

As for the relations between the central and local governments, the power for economic management and decision making was highly concentrated in the central government, while the local governments and enterprises had little power to make their own decisions. The central government exercised direct control through the various departments under it, thus cutting off the economic links between different departments and enterprises in the same region, adversely affecting co-operation along specialized lines in the region and giving rise to serious waste arising from repeated construction. Take Luoyang for example. The construction of the Luoyang Tractor Plant was undertaken by the Luoyang Engineering Bureau under the Ministry of Construction. When the construction had come to an end, most of the construction workers in the bureau stayed idle and waited to be sent somewhere else. At the same time, however, the Ministry of Metallurgical Industry was moving construction workers from another place to Luoyang for the construction of the Luoyang Non-ferrous Metal Refining Works, the Ministry of Electric Power Industry was transferring construction workers to the city from northeast China for the construction of the Luoyang Power Plant, and the Ministry of Textile Industry was also planning to build a textile mill in Luoyang and was moving engineering corps to the city. The moving of a large engineering corps naturally brought trouble to thousands of workers and their families. Once an engineering corps was moved to a new construction site, it would have to build a number of affiliated enterprises and necessary life facilities. This not only put off the construction dates and incurred serious wastes of human and financial resources, but also caused enormous difficulties to the life of the construction workers.

The Party Central Committee realized the problem of over-centralization and excessive control. In 1956, Mao Zedong made a report entitled "On the Ten Major Relationships." Drawing on the lessons of the Former Soviet Union, he summed up China's experience and stressed the importance to handle well the relations between the state, the units of production and the producers, as well as the relations between the central and local governments. He pointed out, "it is not right, I'm afraid, to place everything in the hands of the central or the provincial and municipal authorities without leaving the factories any power of their own, any room for independent action, any benefits." He also admitted that the Party and government did not have much experience at that time on how to divide power and returns properly among the central authorities, the provincial and municipal authorities and the factories.

It is an issue of vital importance for a big a country like China to handle well the relations between the central and local governments. In the early years of the People's Republic, China introduced the system of big administrative zones. Under the system, the entire country was divided into six administrative zones, each of which covered several provinces. This system was abandoned in 1954 to reinforce centralization and unification. Step by step, all major industrial enterprises were put under the direct control of the related departments of the central government. The practice had proved that depriving the local governments of the necessary power to make their own decisions would naturally affected their enthusiasm. In order to tackle the contradiction between the central and local governments, Mao Zedong pointed out, "To resolve this contradiction, our attention should now be focussed on how to enlarge the powers of the local authorities to some extent, give them greater independence and let them do more, all on the premise that the unified leadership of the central authorities is to be strengthened. This will be advantageous to our work of building a powerful socialist country. Our territory is so vast, our population is so large and the conditions are so complex that it is far better to have the initiative come from both the central and the local authorities than from one source alone. We must not follow the example of the Soviet Union in concentrating everything in the hands of the central authorities, shackling the local authorities and denying them the right to independent action."

In September 1956, the Eighth National Congress of the Communist Party of China was held. In his political report to the congress on behalf of the Party Central Committee, Liu Shaoqi said, "To improve the work of the enterprise leaders not only calls for the efforts of the enterprises but also the efforts of the state departments at higher levels. Here, it is necessary to point out such a fact, that is, more often than not the state departments at higher levels impose too rigid a control over the enterprises, thus hampering the initiative and flexibility of the enterprises and incurring undue losses in our work. It is necessary for us to delegate to the enterprises adequate autonomous power in such areas as the management of plans, management of finance, management of cadres, deployment of workers and staff, welfare facilities, etc., under the precondition that the unified leadership and planning of the state are ensured." He also pointed out, "The leading bodies of state economic departments must make earnest efforts to do a good job in those things for which they are responsible and leave alone things that have nothing to do with them. Only when the powerful leadership from the state departments at higher levels is combined with the initiative of the enterprises can we push our cause forward rapidly." These proposals were put forward in view of the situation that the central government had exercised too much and over-rigid control over the local governments and enterprises.

At the Eighth National Congress of the Party, Premier Zhou Enlai made an important speech on improving the economic system. He said, "It is necessary and possible for us to further divide the administrative power between the central government and local governments and improve the administrative system of the state according to the principle of unified leadership, stratified management, adopting methods suited to the local conditions and do what is suitable to the occasion, so as to bring the initiative of the local governments into full play."

In order to reform the economic system and make it cater to the needs of the development of the productive forces, the State Council held a national conference on the economic system from May to August in 1956. The conference examined the phenomenon of too much concentration of power in the hands of the central government, discussed about and put forward proposals on how to improve the economic system. Later, the State Council solicited opinions from various circles on these proposals. In October 1957, the Enlarged Third Plenary Session of the Eighth Party Central Committee approved in principle "Provisions on Improving the Management System of Industry (Draft)," "Provisions on Improving the Management System of Commerce (Draft)," and "Provisions on Improving the Management System of Finance (Draft)." In November 1957, the three documents were adopted at the 61st plenary meeting of the State Council. Approved in principle at the 84th meeting of the Standing Committee of the National People's Congress, they were promulgated in the name of the State Council. The general principle of the three documents for the reform of the economic system was to readjust the relations between the central and local governments as well as the relations between the state and the enterprises, and to delegate part of the power for industrial, commercial and financial management to the local governments and enterprises, with the hope to bring their initiative and enthusiasm into better play and ensure the fulfillment of unified state plans in accordance with the local conditions.

The three documents were aimed at improving the situation of excessive centralization and over-rigid control from the central government at that time. The reform programs included in them were well thought out and the steps proposed were appropriate. To take them as a whole, however, although they also touched upon the issue of enlarging the decision-making power of enterprises, they mainly focused on re-adjusting the relations between the central and the local governments. Not sufficient attention was paid to the issue of how to handle the relations between the state and the enterprises. The reform programs included in the documents were not implemented because of the coming of the "Great Leap Forward" movement shortly afterwards. In the period of "cultural revolution" (1966-1976), due to the political turmoil and the influence of the "Leftist" thinking, any correct measure adopted previously was branded "capitalistic," thus further aggravating the drawbacks of the original economic system.

From the "Great Leap Forward" movement to the Third Plenary Session of the 11th Party Central Committee, China's economic system had undergone several reforms and changes. All these, however, had failed to bring fundamental solutions to the problems and virtually no positive results had been achieved. The major problems were as follows: First, not attempt was made to step beyond the limits of administrative control and the argument was only focused on the question whether the control should be enforced by the central government or the local governments. Naturally, such argument failed to effect a change in the situation that the state imposed excessive and over-rigid control over the enterprises. Second, frequent attempts were made to centralize and decentralize enterprises. The alternate centralization and decentralization gave rise to such a vicious circle of "decontrol and retrenchment, decontrol leading to chaos and chaos leading to control." Consequently, the enthusiasm and creativeness of the enterprises and the workers were inhibited. Third, the dozens of ministries and commissions under the central government vertically extended their power into the cities. Yet, they only cared about industries, especially the heavy industries, while overlooking the development of the basic infrastructure and public utilities, service trades and agriculture. As a result, this had further strengthened the barriers between the different departments and regions as well as that between the urban and rural areas.

Section 2

Exploration in the Market-oriented Economic Reform

The crucial question in China's reform of the economic structure lies in the choice between planning and market. More than 20 years have passed since China adopted the reform and open-up policy. It can be said that the entire course China has traversed in the reform has been a process to choose between planning and market in terms of both theory and practice. The first theoretical breakthrough regarding the economic reform came in people's improved understanding of the traditional planned economic system. Along with the improvement in understanding, the drawbacks in the traditional planned economic system became increasingly apparent, and gradual steps have been taken to introduce the market elements. As a result, the market orientation has become the mainstream in the economic reform. It was not until 1992 when the report to the 14th National Party Congress affirmed that the objective of China's economic reform was to establish a socialist market economy that the market orientation was finally established.

I. Initial Exploration Prior to the Drive of Reform and Opening to the Outside World

Prior to the Third Plenary Session of the 11th Party Central Committee, China basically followed the "model of the Soviet Union" in its economic system due to the influence of the product economic theory prevalent in the former Soviet Union. At that time, the following understanding occupied a dominant position in the economic theoretical circles: Planned economy was nothing but product economy, and it manifested the essential nature of socialism; commodity, money and market were things unique to capitalism, and both the commodity economy and the market economy were established on the basis of private ownership; the market economy was in diametrical opposition to the planned economy; and possessing the attributes of an economic system, the market economy was not merely an economic means or a model to achieve the economic objectives. At that time, people's understanding of the planned economy and market economy was basically limited to the mechanism of planning and the mechanism of market. In spite of the heavy ideological fetters and the dominant position held by the "model of the Soviet Union," there arose the demand to reform the traditional planned economic system as people had become increasingly aware of its drawbacks. In both the theoretical and practical realms, the dominant tendency among those in favor of reform was to allow the market forces to play a supplementary role within the framework of the system of planning. Chen Yun, for example, drawing on the experience and lessons in socialist construction in the early years of the People's Republic, put forward the famous proposal of "three dominant's and three supplementary's,: namely, in terms of economic elements, making the state-owned and collectively owned sectors play a dominant role and allowing the privately owned sector to play a supplementary role; in terms of regulatory means of production, making planned production play the dominant role and allowing free production that was geared towards the market and kept within the limits permitted by state plans to play a supplementary role; and in terms of market development, making the markets controlled by the state play the dominant role and allowing the free markets under the guidance of the state to play a supplementary role. In a dauntless spirit, some economists took the lead in criticizing the traditional theory of planned economy and the rigid economic system. They were the forerunners to advocate the market-oriented economic reform.

As early as in 1956, Sun Yefang, a famous economist in China, pointed out that it was imperative for the socialist economy to make full use of the law of value within the framework of state plans -- to force the enterprises to reduce costs, improve management and raise economic efficiency. In 1978 when he was rehabilitated from the wrong criticisms launched against him, he once again pointed out, "Of all the laws and rules, the law of value is the most important." In his book *On Socialist Commodity Economy*, Zhuo Jiong stated, "The concentrated expression of the commodity economy is the market, while the market constitutes an expression of progress in the economic life of mankind. From the size and scale of the market, one can judge the level of economic and cultural development of a society. In human society, there is nothing more attractive to people than the market, which is both permanent and ever-lasting." However, due to the serious ideological banishment of the time, they were both wrongly criticized. In the years that followed, it had become a taboo to say that socialism could make use of the market mechanism or adopt the market economic system.

II. Gradual Advances in Theoretical Exploration since the Drive of Reform and Opening to the Outside World Was Launched

In 1978, the Third Plenary Session of the 11th Party Committee re-established the ideological line of emancipating the mind and seeking truths from facts. The session stated that it was absolutely necessary to handle China's economic issues in accordance with the objective economic laws, show respect to the role played by the law of value and conduct pertinent reforms of the traditional economic system. Since then, China's reform of the economic structure had entered a new historical era. In both theory and practice, the reform in this period has always been focused on making a choice between planning and market. The theoretical breakthrough regarding the reform of the economic structure was first reflected in people's understanding of the traditional planned economic system. In the reform, the market elements had been gradually introduced and the market orientation has been upheld as a major line running through the entire course of reform. It was not until 1992 when the report to the 14th National Party Congress affirmed that the ultimate objective of China's economic reform was to establish a socialist market economic system that the position of the market orientation was finally secured. The reform in this period can be roughly divided into the following stages:

1. 1979-October 1984: Introduction of Market Mechanism in Planned Economy

The Third Plenary Session of the 11th Party Central Committee ushered in the prelude of China's reform and opening to the outside world. The rural reform, featuring the household-based contract responsibility system, developed rapidly in the countryside and achieved great success. The commercialization and marketization of farm products brought great benefits to the peasants, thus immensely arousing their enthusiasm in production. Experimental reform of enterprises was conducted in Sichuan and some other places. The reform was characterized by enlarging the power of the enterprises in making their own decisions regarding management. In both urban and rural reforms, the primary attention was focused on lifting control within the limits allowed by state plans and gradually introducing the market elements.

Inspired by the ideological line of emancipating the mind and seeking truth from facts, which was reinstated at the Third Plenary Session of the 11th Party Central Committee, the period from 1979 to 1981 turned out to be a more lively period for the economic theoretical circles, when a heated debate broke out over the issue of "planning or market."

In April 1979, the well-known "Seminar on the Role of the Law of Value in Socialism" was held in Wuxi. At the seminar, the participants reached agreement in the following: Socialist economy was commodity economy; the means of production were also commodities; and the law of value could play a role in the socialist economy. These confirmed the status of commodity, value and the law of value in the socialist economy. At the seminar, some scholars ventured the idea that socialist economy was also market economy. Moreover, they used the term "socialist market economy." Regarding the role of the law of value, there were three opinions. First, the essential nature of the socialist economy was planned economy. However, as commodities still existed at the current stage, the socialist economy was therefore a planned economy with elements of the commodity economy, in which the law of planning played the primary role while the law of value played the secondary role. Second, the socialist economy was a planned commodity economy. Planning was subjective. Commodities were the basis and actual contents of planning, while the law of value was the fundamental economic law. Third, the socialist economy was a combination of the planned economy with commodity economy; they could "infiltrate" (each other) or remain "monolithic." It could be said that confirming the roles of the law of value and market regulation sounded clarion call for the market-oriented reform in China.

In June 1979, the government work report delivered at the Second Meeting of the Fifth National People's Congress pointed out that it was necessary for China to gradually establish a system in which the regulation through planning was combined with the regulation through the market; and that it was necessary to attach due importance to the role of regulation through the market while ensuring that the regulation through planning to play the major role. Shortly afterwards, a widespread discussion was unfolded in the theoretical circles about the relations between planning and market. The discussion centered on the slogan of "making the planned economy play the dominant role while letting regulation through market play a supplementary role." At that time, it was generally held that "market economy" was a socio-economic system and another name of capitalism, while "regulation through the market" only referred to the means of economic regulation, which had no natural connection with capitalism and could be used to serve socialism. Therefore, "regulation through market" instead of "market economy" was used in both printed documents and discussions. People's understanding of the relationship between planning and market was still limited to the specific forms of their combination – which should take the dominant position and which should play the supplementary role, and which represented the "system" and which could only play the role of a "tool" or a "means." With regard to the forms of their combination, three different proposals were put forward. One was the "monolithic theory," that is, to make a clear distinction between the planned economy and the regulation through the market, with each being allowed to play a role in its own domain. The second was the "theory of mutual infiltration." The proponents of this theory argued that planning and market could infiltrate each other and be combined. The third was the "theory of overlapping," meaning that planning and market could be overlapped, and the plans must be realized through market while the market could only play its regulatory role through planning.

In November 1979, in an interview with Frank B. Gibney, Vice-Chairman of the Compilation Committee of the Encyclopaedia Britannica, Inc., Deng Xiaoping pointed out, "We cannot say that market economy exists only under capitalism. Market economy was in its embryonic stages as early as feudalist society. We can surely develop it under socialism." His words produced widespread repercussions in the government departments in charge of economic work and the theoretical circles. Although most people in leading positions and in theoretical circles found it hard to accept the view that market economy and market mechanism should be made to play a full role in the socialist system, Deng Xiaoping insisted on his view about the market economy. In October 1985, in his interview with Henry Grunwald, head of an American delegation of senior entrepreneurs to China, he again pointed out, "There is no fundamental contradiction between socialism and a market economy. The problem is how to develop the productive forces more effectively," and "If we combine a planned economy with a market economy, we shall be in a better position to liberate the productive forces and speed up economic growth."

In September 1980, the Office of Economic Restructuring of the State Council drafted the "Initial Proposals on Economic Restructuring." The document clearly pointed out, "The socialist economy at the current stage of China is a commodity economy in which the public ownership of the means of production holds the dominant position while diverse economic elements exist side by side." It also stated that in efforts for the economic restructuring it was necessary to "make conscientious use of the law of value and shift from the unitary regulation through planning to bringing into full play the role of regulation through the market under the guidance of planning." However, due to the setbacks encountered in carrying out the reform to grant more power and profits to the state-owned enterprises as well as the disastrous effects produced by the "Western-style Great Leap Forward," some problems appeared in the national economy, such as economic confusion, increased deficits and rising inflation. Consequently, the opponents to the market-oriented reform attributed all the problems to the use of the market regulation and the law of value and voiced criticisms to the above-described correct theories.

In 1982, the report to the 12th National Party Congress formally put forward the principle of "the leading role of the planned economy and the supplementary role of market regulation." The principle meant to push forward the reform of the traditional and centralized planned economic system and allow some products to be regulated through the market without being planned, that is, let the law of value spontaneously play a regulatory role, within the limits circumscribed by the state's unified plan and in light of the specific conditions at different periods. The report says, "This serves as a supplement to planned production and circulation, subordinate and secondary to it but essential and useful nonetheless." The report also stated that, apart from enforcing mandatory plans for products and enterprises that were vital to the national economy and people's livelihood, guidance plans, whose implementation was mainly ensured by means of economic levers, could be used with regard to many products and enterprises. "But whether in mandatory planning or in guidance planning, we must strive to make it conform to the objective reality, constantly study the changes in market supply and demand, consciously make use of the law of value and such economic levers as pricing, taxation and credits, in guiding the enterprises to fulfil state plans, and grant to them varying degrees of powers to make decisions as they see fit." As for the numerous small commodities, the enterprises were allowed to arrange production flexibly in accordance with the changes in market supply and demand.

The report pointed out, "Correct application of the principle of ensuring the leading role of planned economy supplemented by market regulation is of fundamental importance to the reform of China's economic systems. We must correctly define respectively the scope and limits of mandatory plans, guidance plans and market regulation and, on the premise that a basic stability of commodity prices is maintained, gradually reform the pricing system, price control measures as well as the labor and wage systems, and establish an economic administrative system suited to China's conditions so as to ensure the sound growth of the national economy." This marked the beginning of the gradual introduction of market elements in the planned economic system as well as the beginning to study the ways and approaches to bring into play the role of market regulation in the national economy. But, the principle of ``ensuring the leading role of planned economy and making market regulation play a supplementary role" still meant to take planned economy as the fundamental feature of the socialist economy. It still stressed the role of planning and maintained that market and market mechanisms could at most play a supplementary role.

In 1982-83, "erroneous views," such as the socialist economy was commodity economy or market economy, were bombarded with criticisms, so was those which laid stress on the market mechanisms. During the campaign to combat "spiritual pollution" in spring 1983, some people suggested launching criticisms to the ideas of commodity economy and market economy and branding them as manifestations of "spiritual pollution" and "capitalist liberalism" in the economic theoretical circles. For a time, "commodity" and "market" became taboos, and commodity economy or market economy were forbidden in public discussion. Such theoretical taboos prevailed until 1984 when the Third Plenary Session of 12th Party Central Committee was held.

2. From October 1984 to 1988: The Period of Planned Commodity Economy

Along with the upsurge of reform and opening to the outside world, the state-owned sector and non-state-owned sector of the economy had achieved different degrees of development. This indicated that the non-state-owned sector, which had clearly defined property rights and competed in the market for survival, had shown greater vitality, while the state-owned sector, which operated under state mandatory plans, lacked the incentive for competition and were subjected to soft budgetary constraints, had shown little vitality and reaped poor returns. Both of them demanded for reform of the economic structure to bring into full use of the market mechanisms. In May 1984, the State Council issued the "Interim Regulations on Further Expanding the Decision-Making Powers of the State-owned Industrial Enterprises." To carry out these regulations not only called for a reform of the enterprises themselves but also a fundamental reform of the entire economic system and the mode of its operation. In October 1984, the Central Committee of the Chinese Communist Party passed the "Decision on Reform of the Economic Structure." The document clearly pointed out that the socialist economy in China was a planned commodity economy on the bases of public ownership. It stressed that full development of the commodity economy was an insurmountable stage in socio-economic development and also a necessary condition for China's economic modernization. It was necessary to act in accordance with the economic laws, especially the law of value, and make full use of the market mechanisms in developing the socialist economy. The meeting decided to carry out an extensive reform of the planned economic system. To carry out the reform, it was first necessary to break away from the traditional concept that the planned economy was directly opposed to commodity economy. The document stressed that it was necessary to conscientiously implement the law of value in the socialist planned economy. Only by developing a commodity economy was it possible to really invigorate the economy and compel the enterprises to improve efficiency and operate flexibly and adapt themselves quickly to the capricious changes in social demands. Such an objective could never be attained by merely relying on the administrative means and mandatory plans. The implementation of planned economy is complementary rather than opposed to the utilization of the law of value as well as the development of the commodity economy. It was wrong to set them opposed to each other. The decision called for narrowing down the scope of mandatory plans and enlarging that of guidance plans. Mandatory plans would be enforced on important products that were vital to the national economy and people's livelihood and must be distributed through allocation by the state, and on economic activities that had an important bearing on the overall economic situation. As for the majority of products and economic activities, guidance plans would be mapped out in accordance with specific conditions. The focus of planning work would be shifted to medium- and long-range plans and annual plans would be appropriately simplified. At the same time, it was necessary to appropriately reform the methods of planning, pay full attention to economic information and forecast, and improve the scientific level of planning.

The theory of the planned commodity economy represented an important breakthrough in the theory of socialist economy and marked the establishment of the position of the law of value in China's economic life. It indicated that the market orientation had become an inevitable trend in China's economic reform. Therefore, Deng Xiaoping spoke highly of it, claiming it as the "political economy that combines the fundamental tenets of Marxism with China's practice of socialism."

After the Third Plenary Session of the 12th Party Central Committee confirmed the development of a socialist commodity economy as the goal of China's economic restructuring, the operational mechanisms corresponding to the socialist commodity economy had not been explicitly defined. Therefore, the theoretical circles made earnest studies. The report to the 13th Natinal Congress of the Communist Party of China, delivered on October 25, 1987, further expounded on how to develop a socialist commodity economy and how to bring into full play the role of market mechanisms. The report pointed out that some of the things that had been introduced in the process of reform, such as the enlarged markets for productive means, capital, technology and labor as well as the issuance of stocks and bonds, were phenomena that were not unique to capitalism. They were bound to appear in the wake of socialized mass production and along with the development of the commodity economy, and socialism could and should make use of them, trying at the same time to minimize their negative effects in practice. The report also stated that the socialist planned commodity economy should be a system that integrates planning with the market. In this connection, the reported called for clarifying several basic concepts. First, it said, the essential difference between the socialist and capitalist commodity economy lied in the form of ownership on which they are based. The socialist commodity economy based on public ownership provided the possibility for the society to maintain a balanced growth of the national economy. The Chinese people's task was to make this possibility a reality by a judicious use of both means: regulation through planning and regulation through the market. The socialist commodity economy could not develop without the growth and improvement of the markets, so regulating through the market did not mean practicing capitalism. Second, planning should be done according to the principle of commodity exchange and the law of value. The form of direct economic control that relied chiefly on mandatory planning could meet the requirements of the development of a socialist commodity economy. It was improper to equate regulation through planning with mandatory planning. It was necessary to gradually reduce the scope of mandatory planning by such means as signing contracts in accordance with the principle of exchange of equal value, contracts by which the state would place orders for goods with enterprises, and enterprises with one another. The state should gradually shift to using mainly indirect means to control the enterprises. Third, the operating sphere of both planning and the market covered the whole society. On the whole, under the new economic mechanism "the state regulates the market and the market guides enterprises," the state would regulate the relations between supply and demand through economic, legal and necessary administrative means and create a favorable economic and social environment in which enterprises were guided towards correct management decisions. At that time, the main task in deepening the reform was to change the managerial mechanisms of enterprises, and with that end in view, to institute supporting reforms in the systems of planning, investment, allocation of materials, finance, monetary affairs and foreign trade, so as to gradually establish the basic framework for a planned commodity economy. From then on, the regulatory role of market mechanisms on economic operation had been brought into increasingly better play and the market orientation of the reform had become clearer.

After the 13th National Party Congress, a heated debate erupted in the theoretical circles over the question which should be taken as the basic mechanism, planning or the market? By then, more and more people were in favor of the view that socialist economy should be a market economy. In 1988, the economists in Guangdong Province sponsored "bimonthly symposiums on market economy at the primary stage of socialism." Papers read at the symposiums were collected in a book entitled *Market Economy at the Primary Stage of Socialism*. Participants to the symposiums expressed three views regarding the market economy. The first was that commodity economy was market economy. The second was that market economy was developed commodity economy. And the third was that market economy represented a way for resources allocation as opposed to planned economy. At the National Symposium on the Theory of Economic Restructuring and the Theoretical Symposium to Mark the 10th Anniversary of the Third Plenary Session of the 11th Party Central Committee, separately held in October and December 1988, some treatises were read and they focused on the socialist market economy. It indicated that, by then, the theoretical workers had bypassed the stage of merely taking market mechanism as a supplementary means and came to the understanding that market mechanism was an intrinsic mechanism for the operation of the socialist economy, that the role of the market and the law of value was indispensable to the socialist economy, and that the operating sphere of the market covered the entire society and it did not only exist as a supplement to planned economy.

3. From 1989-1991: Combination of Planned Economy with Market Regulation

This was a period of improvement and rectification for China's national economy. In fact, at the Third Plenary Session of the 13th Party Central Committee, held in September 1988, the Party Central Committee already made the decision to improve the economic environment and rectify the economic order as such outstanding problems as overheated economic development, excessively high hikes of prices and chaos in the commodity circulation had appeared. On November 9, 1989, the Fifth Plenary Session of the 13th Party Central Committee adopted the "Decision on Further Improving the Economic Environment, Rectifying the Economic Order and Deepening the Reform." The decision pointed out that the key question in the reform was to gradually establish an economic operational mechanism that would combine planned economy with market regulation. During the period of improvement and rectification, there should be a wider scope of planning and, therefore, it was necessary to appropriately strengthen centralization. With regard to the reform of the planning system, it stressed the necessity to appropriately enlarge the scope of mandatory plans and to take back appropriately some of power in granting approvals to new construction projects.

In the field theoretical studies, for reasons known to all, starting from the second half of 1989 some people began to equate the market-oriented reform to privitization and the market economy to capitalism. They called for a return to the planned economy centering on products and expansion of the scope of mandatory planning. For a period of time, market economy again became a forbidden zone in theoretical study. And people even were afraid to mention planned commodity economy.

The "Proposals of the Central Committee of the Communist Party of China Concerning the Formulation of the Ten-Year Plan and the Eighth Five-year Plan for National Economic and Social Development," issued on December 30, 1990, stated that it was the basic orientation in deepening the reform of the economic structure to establish an economic operational mechanism that combined planned economy with regulation through the market when efforts were made to develop a socialist planned commodity economy. It further pointed out that, to combine planned economy with regulation through the market, it was necessary to have a clear understanding of the following few points. First, planned economy could maintain, in general, a well-coordinated development of the national economy and the rational allocation of resources, while market regulation could play a role to enable the fittest survive and strengthen economic vitality. It was necessary to combine the two together and bring their respective advantages into play so as to ensure a sustained, steady and coordinated development of the national economy. Second, planned economy was not confined to mandatory planning alone; mandatory planning and guidance planning were both specific means of the planned economy. Along with the deepening of the economic reform, the improvement of the economic structure and the continuous development of the market, it was imperative to further reduce the scope of mandatory planning and appropriately enlarge the scope of guidance planing, so to bring the market mechanisms into better play. To enforce planned control, it was necessary to consciously follow the law of proportional development of the economy and the law of value, take into consideration the relations between supply and demand in the market, and regulate the economic operation through the market, which should be made to play its role within the bounds of overall state plans and law. Third, generally speaking, the role of planning should mainly manifested in the control enforced over total supply and demand, in the readjustment of the economic structure and economic layout, and in major economic activities that had an important bearing on the overall economic situation. The role of market regulation should be expressed in such economic activities as the routine management of production and technological upgrading projects of the enterprises as well as small-scaled construction projects. The document also stressed the necessity to strengthen efforts in building a market system and establishing market organizations, that is, to establish a national unified market system under the guidance and management of the state. It also pointed out that it was necessary to improve the consumer goods market, expand the productive means market and establish the markets of capital, technology, information, real estates and labor. It urged the different regions, including the urban and rural areas, to open up their doors and remove all sorts of barriers to effect a change in the situation of regional blockage and market segmentation.

In December 1990, Deng Xiaoping pointed out, "We must understand theoretically that the difference between capitalism and socialism is not a market economy as opposed to a planned economy. Socialism has regulation by market forces, and capitalism has control through planning.... If we did not have a market economy, we would have no access to information from other countries and would have to reconcile ourselves to lagging behind." During his inspection tour of Shanghai during the Spring Festival of 1991, he made a series of important speeches, preaching the similar view. In February-April the same year, the *Liberation Daily* published four commentaries by Huangfu Ping (apparently a penname) written in accordance with the spirit of Deng Xiaoping's speeches. All the four articles touched upon the emergence presence and development of market economy in China. These articles caused quite a stir throughout the country and ignited a heated debate in the theoretical circles over the question whether the market economy was "socialist" or "capitalist" in nature. At the a symposium on "Some Important Theoretical Questions in Current Economic Work of China," sponsored by the Chinese Academy of Social Sciences in July that year, the proponents of planning held that, in the process of reform and opening to the outside world, it was always necessary to pay attention to the issue about the socialist nature. Therefore, they argued, it was necessary for us to uphold the public ownership; in no way should we indulge in privatization either in name or in reform, neglect planning and develop the Western-styled market economy. In other words, they argued, the nature of "socialism" or "capitalism" should never be neglected, as it was important to avoid the danger of going astray from the socialist orientation and take the capitalist road. The proponents of the market orientation, however, proceeding from experience and lessons in China's economic construction, the international conventional practices as well as the intrinsic law in economic development, argued that commodity economy was an insurmountable stage in the development of the socialist economy. They held that the market economy, which used the market mechanism as the major means in resources allocation, had obvious advantages in terms efficiency and mechanism over the planned economy. If China wanted to realize its economic take-off and get a place in the economically powerful nations of the world, it had, besides implementing the policy of reform and opening to the outside world, to rapidly develop a market economy. Apart from this, there was no other way out.

At the meeting to mark the 70th anniversary of the founding of the Communist Party of China and at the Fourth Plenary Session of the 13th Party Central Committee, President Jiang Zeming stressed that, as means for economic regulation, both planning and market were objective requirements for the development of commodity economy on the basis of socialized mass production. Therefore, the utilization of both within certain limits should not taken as the landmark to distinguish socialist economy and capitalist economy.

To sum up, in the period from the Third Plenary Session of the 11th Party Central Committee to the eve of the 14th National Party Congress in 1992, a major change occurred, that is, the focus of people's attention had shifted from the division of power between the central and local governments to the introduction of the market mechanism, although no fundamental change took place in the rigid system of planned economy. During this period, some objectives were achieved, including streamlining government, granting more power to lower levels, reducing the scope of mandatory planning and enlarging the decision-making powers of the local governments and enterprises. As a result, market regulation can now play an increasingly significant role in the national economy, and the market forces can show its superiority in effectively allocating the resources. More importantly, more and more people have accepted the market-orientated reform. All this has laid a solid foundation for the socialist market economic system.

4. Since 1992: The New Stage of Socialist Market Economy

Practice in the reform of the economic structure has brought about a significant change in the operational mechanism of China's national economy and its socialist ownership relationships. What the people see now is that where the role of the market mechanism is brought into better play and where diverse forms of ownership exist side by side, where the economic development will be the more rapid and the economic strength will be stronger. Experience gained in both practice and theoretical exploration have made more and more people realize that both planning and market are but two different means or forms for the allocation of resources; neither of them possesses the attribute of the socialist economic system, let alone being taken as a landmark to differentiate the social systems. Then, what a road should the socialist economic reform follow – the road of planned economy or the road of market economy? And what is the nature of socialist market economy?

The persuasive thesis put forward by Deng Xiaoping in his southern China inspection tour in early 1992 put a perfect end to the long-drawn debate over "orientation of planning" vs. "orientation of market." In incisive language, Deng Xiaoping stated, "The proportion of planning to market forces is not the essential difference between socialism and capitalism. A planned economy is not equivalent to socialism, because there is planning under capitalism too; a market economy is not capitalism, because there are markets under socialism too. Planning and market forces are both means of controlling economic activities." He also said, "We should be bolder than before in conducting reform and opening to the outside and have the courage to experiment. We must not act like women with bound feet. Once we are sure that something should be done, we should dare to experiment and break a new path." He said, "The reason some people hesitate to carry out the reform and the open policy and dare not break new ground is, in essence, that they're afraid it would mean introducing too many elements of capitalism and, indeed, taking the capitalist road. The crux of the matter is whether the road is capitalist or socialist. The chief criterion for making that judgement should be whether it promotes the growth of the productive forces in the socialist society, increases the overall strength of the socialist state and raises living standards." At the same time, he stressed, "Right tendencies can destroy socialism, but so can 'Left' ones. China should maintain vigilance against the Right but primarily against the 'Left'." The remarks by Deng Xiaoping were a scientific summary of the theoretical studies and practice of China's economic reform. They have removed fundamentally the fetters on the ideology of the people, who formerly treated planned economy and market economy as basic attributes of social and economic systems. Also, they put an end to the long-drawn debate over the nature of planning and market – attaching the former to "socialism" and the latter to "capitalism."

On June 9 1992, President Jiang Zemin delivered a speech in the Party School of the CPC Central Committee. In the speech, he pointed out, "The fundamental task in speeding up the reform of the economic structure is to establish as soon as possible a new socialist economic system, while the key issue in establishing the new economic system is to acquire a correct understand about planning and market as well as their mutual relations, that is, to pay more attention to and bring into play the role of the market in allocating resources under the macro control of the state." He also said, "Numerous facts have shown that the market is an effective form for the allocation of resources and in providing the incentive. Making use of the competition and price levers, the market allocates goods and materials that are in limited supply to those links that create the best returns and brings pressure and impetus to the enterprises. Moreover, the market responds promptly to various kinds of signals. Because of these advantages, the positive role of the market in economic development has been realized by more and more people in the socialist countries. The biased understanding about the market in the past has now been abandoned."

The 14th National Party Congress, held in October 1992, made the establishment of a socialist market economic system the target model for China's economic reform and expatiated it systematically. On behalf of the Party Central Committee, Jiang Zemin stated in clear terms that the objective of China's reform of the economic structure was to establish a socialist market economic system. The report said, "Setting the right objective for the reform of China's economic structure is vital to the success of the drive for socialist modernization. Correct understanding and handling of the relations between planning and market regulation is crucial. According to conventional thinking, a market economy is peculiar to capitalism, and a planned economy is the basic feature of socialism. Since the Third Plenary Session of the 11th Party Central Committee and with the deepening of the reform, we have gradually freed ourselves from those conventional ideas and acquired a new understanding of this question. This has played an important role in advancing the reform and economic development." Practice in China has proved that where market forces have been given full play, there the economy has been vigorous and has developed in a sound way. To optimize the economic structure, to improve economic performance, to accelerate economic competition, it is necessary for China to continue to intensify the market forces."

By establishing a socialist market economic system, it means to let the market forces, under the macroeconomic control of the state, serve as the basic means of regulating the allocation of resources, to subject economic activity to the law of value and to make it responsive to the changing relations between supply and demand. The report said, "We should make use of pricing and competition to distribute resources to those enterprises that yield good economic returns. In this way, we shall provide an incentive for enterprises to improve their performance, so that the efficient ones will prosper and the inefficient ones will be eliminated." The report went on to say, "Since the market was sensitive to changes in demand, we should use it to make timely readjustment in production, as necessary. Nevertheless, we must be aware that the market has its own weaknesses and negative aspects. Macro-control of the economy by the state is therefore very important, and the way in which it is exercised must be improved. We should work hard to establish an integrated national market, and we should give more rein to market forces. We should guide the growth of the market by economic policies, regulations, planning and necessary administrative means, in accordance with objective laws." The report said, "During the process of establishing the socialist market economy, the extent to which planning is combined with market regulation and the form the combination takes may vary at different times, in different places and in different sectors of the economy. We should be bold in exploring news\ ways, dare to experiment and constantly review our experience so as to expedite the replacement of the old structure with the new." The report called on the Chinese people to further emancipate their minds, not to be get tied up in the abstract debate over what is socialist and what it capitalist, and to be aware that both planning and market are economic means, and free themselves from the restrictive notion that planned economy and market economy represent basic economic systems of the society. It stressed that the socialist market economic system was an integrated part of the basic system of socialism.

Article 15 of the Constitution of the People's Republic of China stipulates, "The state practices socialist market economy." From the high plane of Constitution, the establishment of a socialist market economic system has been made the goal model to guide China's economic reform and construction. By then, the debate over planning and the market has basically ended and the position of market-oriented reform has ultimately established. The focus in theoretical studies has been shifted from making a choice between planning and the market to what steps should be taken in establishing and improving the socialist market economic system as well as its operational mechanism. Nearly

200 years have elapsed since the founders of Marxism put forward the theory of scientific socialism. Now, the Chinese Communists have advanced the theory to establish and develop a market economic system in socialism. It represents an important contribution to and latest development of Marxism.

Section 3

Accelerate the Establishment of a Socialist Market Economic System

I. Upholding the Basic Economic System in Which the Public Ownership Holds the Dominant Position and the Economy under Diverse Forms of Ownership Develop Side by Side

China is now at its primary stage of socialism. It must develop an economy under diverse forms of ownership under the condition that the public ownership holds the dominant position. To uphold and improve the basic economic system in which the public ownership holds the dominant position while the economy under diverse forms of ownership develop simultaneously is a correct historical choice and a basic experience summarized in China's long-term practice. It is also an important contribution made by the 15th National Congress of the Chinese Communist Party of China.

An important task of the reform of the economic structure is to readjust and improve the ownership structure. Under the system of planned economy, the state-owned sector of the economy almost covered the whole society, thus giving rise to a situation in which the public ownership constituted the sole form of ownership that was allowed to exist, and resulting in that the state-owned sector being spread to thin. Therefore, it is necessary to strategically readjust the layout of the national economy and make the layout and structure of the national economy corresponding to the socialist market economy.

The guiding principle for readjusting the layout of the national economy is: The state-owned sector must hold a dominant position in important industries and key areas that have an important bearing on the lifelines of the national economy. In other areas, the state-owned sector can pull back appropriately through reorganization of assets and readjustment of structure to strengthen key projects, so as to improve the overall quality of state-owned assets as well as its power of control and influence.

1. In the Strategic Readjustment of the National Economy, the First and Foremost Question Is to Determine the Status of the State-owned Sector.

In the socialist market economy, state-owned enterprises are a special type of publicly owned enterprises. They can only be in a small number in the economy of a country, but a "well-operated and highly efficient" small number. By "well-operated and highly efficient," it means that, on the one hand, the state-owned enterprises must accomplish the social goals the state assigns to them and, on the other, they themselves must generate relatively high efficiency and are relatively competitive. In the market economy, the state-owned enterprises will mainly exist as a material means for the government to settle problems that the market forces fail to settle and to control and regulate the national economy. The state-owned sector must hold control over the lifelines of the national economy and provide guidance to the economic development. Such a guiding role of the state-owned sector should be mainly manifested in its power of control, rather than in terms of number and the amount of assets they possess.

What are the important industries and key areas that have an important bearing on the lifelines of the national economy?

In the socialist market economy, the primary objective to be achieved by the state-owned sector is to improve the public benefits in society. The state-owned sector of economy should concentrate in those industries and areas that are related to national security and social stability, influence the overall socio-economic development, control the lifelines of the national economy and provide public products. In other words, they are important industries and key areas in which the non-state-owned sectors are economically incapable and unwilling to get involved, but industries and areas that constitute the lifelines of the national economy. At the current stage of development, the so-called "important industries and key areas" should include the following: (1) areas important for national security, such as war industry, space-flight industry, money mincing and monetary control and supervision; (2), infrastructure and public utilities that show strong attributes of public products, such as water conservancy large-scaled construction projects and highways; (3) areas with the nature of natural monopoly, such as extra-large projects for the exploitation of irreproducible resources, urban water supply; and (4) areas of strategic importance in the development of the country, such as the high and new technology industry.

2. It Is Necessary to Firmly Grasp the Principle of Leaving Something Undone to Get Something Done, Strengthen Efforts in Key Areas and Pull Back from the Commonplace Areas and Improve Industrial Structure in the State-owned Sector.

Now, the state-owned enterprises can be found in all industries and trades of the national economy. This has led to a situation in which the state finance feels incapable to give support to essential projects due to a shortage of fund while a large amount of fund is spent on a large number of unnecessary projects. Therefore, it is necessary to us to, proceeding from the perspective of achieving an overall development of the state-owned sector and bringing into play its power of control over the entire national economy, readjust strategically the layout of the state-owned sector and shorten the excessively long and scattered battle line in order to gradually withdraw the state-owned capital from commonplace areas of competition to strengthen the important industries and key areas. In practical work, it is necessary to combine "advancement" with "retreat." State-owned capital withdrawn from the commonplace areas of competition should be used to support enterprises in those industries that must be protected. What form of investment (sole funding, shareholding, or share partnership holding) to be adopted for the state-owned enterprises should be determined by the particular characteristics of particular industries as well as the requirements for capital operation. Readjusting the layout of the state-owned sector should be combined with reshuffling the organizational structure of the enterprises. Energetic efforts should be made to bring into being a considerable number of large enterprises and large enterprises consortiums in industries and trades that must be protected so as to increase the size of enterprises in these industries and trades and reap economic returns from scale. In the course of readjustment, particular attention should be paid to upgrading the traditional industries with advanced technology, vigorously developing develop industries that contain high and new technology and cutting down the scale of or eliminating those outdated industries and enterprises.

3. It Is Necessary to Readjust Regional Distribution of the State-owned Sector.

While making efforts to improve the industrial distribution of the state-owned sector, it is necessary to take active steps to readjust and optimize its regional distribution, especially its distribution between the central, west and east parts of the country, so as to make the regional distribution of the state-owned sector more rational. Take industry for example. The proportion of the state-owned sector in the central and west parts of the country is over 20 percentage point higher than that in the east part for various reasons, including that the non-state-owned sectors in these regions have developed slowly and the bulk of state investments have been put in raw materials, war and energy industries in these regions. In the future, some necessary preferential policies should be adopted for the central and west parts of the country on the basis that the economy under various forms of ownership receives the same treatment, so as to ensure a marked growth in the capital owned by people there and enable these regions to attract more capital, including foreign capital and capital from the east part of the country, for local development. At present, it is necessary to appropriately relax control over the non-state-owned sectors and allow them to participate in the development of raw materials, energy and transport industries. At the same time, it is necessary to take gradual steps to improve the rules for the operation of the market economy to promote the readjustment of the state-owned sector and the regional economic development in the central and west parts of the country.

4. It Is Necessary to Further Deepen the Readjustment of the Ownership Structure through the Strategic Reorganization of the State-owned Sector.

Non-publicly owned sectors of the economy, including individually owned sector, the privately owned sector and the foreign-funded sector, constitute an important part of the socialist market economy. They will develop side by side and mix together with the publicly owned sector. The report to the 15th National Party Congress says that all forms of ownership that comply with the principle of "three favorables" (favorable to the growth of the productive forces in the socialist society, favorable to increasing the overall strength of the socialist state and favorable to improving the people's living standards) can and should be used to serve socialism. This statement has a dual meaning. First, support must be given to the development of all sectors of the economy, should it be state-owned, collectively owned or in other forms of public ownership, or non-publicly owned, as long as it is conducive to the development of the productive forces in the society. Second, any form of combination of assets and any form of organization of enterprises, so long as it is favorable to socialized mass production, should be boldly adopted for the development of the productive forces of socialism. Therefore, encouragement given to the development of non-publicly owned economic elements is necessary for the development of social productive forces. It should be permitted and receive support from the current policies.

In the strategic reorganization of the state-owned sector, it is necessary to change a large amount of property rights that are unfeasible to be controlled by the state into non-state-owned property rights and turn them into tradable property rights in pure economic sense as required by the market economy, so as to realize innovation in the enterprise system. In institutional terms, it is necessary to ensure that the property rights, in line with the requirements of market competition, flow freely between different regions, different trades, different departments and different enterprises. In other words, it is necessary to make it possible for the property rights to break through the unnecessary administrative barriers in market operation, and ultimately realize the goal of marketization in the allocation of resources.

5. As the Problems in the State-owned Enterprises Are an Concentrated Expression of All the Deep-rooted Contradictions in the Traditional System, the Strategic Reorganization of the State-owned Sector Will Be an Extremely Arduous and Complicated Process.

The completion of this process not only calls for rationally tackling the problems left over from history and readjusting the current structure of interests but also requires the support of a certain degree of political system. To view the problems in state-owned enterprises from the perspective of strategic reorganization of the state-owned sector, the essence of the reform of the state-owned enterprises does not lie in the managerial mechanism of the enterprises themselves, nor is it the simple question to help the enterprises extricate themselves from their difficulties. Rather, it is a question of how to get the government withdraw from those trades and areas that are unfeasible for it to get involved and how to establish and develop an enterprise that meets the requirements of the market economy. Therefore, it is necessary for the government to make a series of institutional arrangements to establish and improve a "withdrawing mechanism" for the state-owned enterprises by establishing a well-developed social security system and a practical state assets transfer system. It is necessary to develop a multi-tiered capital market and encourage the non-state-owned sectors to take part in the reform of the state-owned enterprises and the reorganization of the state-owned sector. And it is necessary to make active efforts to create conditions for the state-owned sector to gradually shift its functions to stabilizing economic operation, implementing the state's strategic plans and raising the efficiency of the market. The government must strengthen guidance by policies, and supervision and control according to law, so as to provide a market environment for fair competition between different economic elements.

II. Upholding the Orientation of Establishing a Modern Enterprise System in the Reform of State-owned Enterprises

1. Pushing Forward the Innovation of Enterprise System Category by Category in Line with the Demand of Establishing a Modern Enterprise System

The modern enterprise system is a basic system under the conditions of the socialist market economy. It is related not only to the survival and development of the state-owned enterprises but also to the success or failure of the overall reform of the economic structure as well as the sustained and sound development of the national economy. It is necessary for China to unswervingly push forward the reform and development of the state-owned enterprises in the direction of the modern enterprise system. In making efforts to introduce the modern enterprise system, it might be feasible to divide the state-owned enterprises in key industries that have an important bearing on the lifelines of the national economy into two main categories. One category comprises special enterprises established and governed according to special laws and regulations, and the other, ordinary enterprises standardized according to civil laws, particularly the corporate law.

Enterprises in the first category are not enterprises in the real sense. They do not operate for profits. Rather, their major goals are the social functions they are assigned. The areas in which they operate include those related to state security, such as the war industry, aeronautical and astronautical industry and money mincing, and infrastructure and public utilities that show strong characteristics of public products, such as large-scale water conservancy facilities, urban water supply facilities and highways. Such enterprises can be special corporate entities, and it is necessary for the state to impose necessary control over them, such as conducting checks over them in terms of types and quality of their products and services, their development programs and costs. At the same time, however, it is necessary to create institutional conditions to encourage these enterprises to carry out competition in management and services, so as to force them to operate according to the principles of marketization as much as possible, such as inviting and offering bids. Enterprises in the second category are competitive in nature and their major objective of operation is to make profits. They can be in areas that are naturally monopolistic, such as extra large construction projects in the exploitation of irreproducible resources, and areas that are strategically important for national development, such as high and new technological industries. The typical form of such enterprises is the corporate system, i.e. joint-stock companies and limited-liability companies.

To establish a corporate management structure featuring effective check-and-balance relations among the owners, decision-makers and executives is the core of the modern enterprise system. But, to achieve the goal of establishing an effective corporate management structure, it is imperative to expedite reform of the property right system in the state-owned enterprises so as to make the representatives of the owners of state-owned capital fall into places. Except for the tiny number of enterprises that must be monopolized by the state, it is necessary to foster and develop multiple kinds of investment subjects, gradually bring about a diversification in stock rights and form a rational ownership structure. It is necessary to improve the corporate management structure in strict accordance with the "Corporate Law" as well as its supporting regulations, clearly define the responsibilities of the congress of shareholders, the board of directors, the managers and the supervisory board, so as to form an effective check-and-balance mechanism and combine their rights and responsibilities with their interests. Under the precondition that the owners have come to place and the role of the congress of shareholders has brought into full play, it is necessary to take further steps to materialize the trusteeship between the council of shareholders and the board of directors and the commissioning relations between the board of directors and the managers, and strengthen the supervisory power of the supervisory board. It is necessary to create a new mechanism for a large number of entrepreneurs to emerge and gradually grow to maturity, rationally decide their rewards according to their contributions, study ways for the managers to hold shares of their enterprises, form incentive and restrictive mechanisms over the behavior of the entrepreneurs, and facilitate the improvement of the corporate management structure. Along with transformation towards the corporate system, it is necessary to take the formation of large enterprises and large enterprise consortiums as an important means in readjusting the organizational structure of state-owned enterprises. Taking capital as the central link, energetic efforts should be made to bring into being a large number of big enterprises and large enterprises groups that are highly competitive in the market.

Of course, it is relative to classify the enterprises as well as the trades that are suitable for them this way. Their classification should suit the times. It should be different at different stages in the development of the national economy. In the same trade, there is also the possibility to adopt different enterprise forms.

2. Establishing New Management, Operational and Supervisory Systems for State-owned Assets

To cater to the requirements of the socialist market economy and the established status of the state-owned sector, it is necessary, in reforming the management system of state-owned assets, to separate the functions of the government as managers of social and economic affairs from the functions of the government as owners of state-owned assets, and separate the functions of state-owned assets management from those of state-owned assets operation. Under the preconditions to maintain and increase the value of state-owned assets and improve the efficiency of market operation, it is necessary to clearly define the rights and responsibilities of all relevant parties and combine the rights with the responsibilities. It is necessary to study new models for the management of state-owned assets that can bring into better play the enthusiasm of the local governments. After the state-owned enterprises are disconnected with the Party, government, military and judiciary organs, the ownership over them should be exercised by state-owned investment subjects (such as large enterprise groups that are up to the necessary qualifications and newly established state-owned investment companies), so as to enable the enterprises operate in accordance with the rules of the market economy. It is necessary to establish and gradually improve the supervisory and evaluating systems for state-owned assets. The departments concerned should strengthen their auditing and financial check-up systems over state-owned investment subjects. Studies should be made to gradually open up channels and approaches for intermediary institutions in the society to evaluate the work of state-owned investment subjects.

3. Earnestly Implementing the Reform Strategy of "Focusing on Large Enterprises and Giving a Free Hand to Small Ones" and Actively Pushing Forward the Optimal Reorganization of State-owned Capital

It is necessary to combine the readjustment of the layout of the state-owned section with the strategy of "focusing on large enterprises and giving a free hand to the small ones." While making efforts to invigorate the small enterprises, attention should be paid to facilitating the development of large enterprises and large enterprise groups. It is necessary to make energetic efforts to accelerate the pace of floating reorganization of state-owned capital and promote the readjustment of the layout of the state-owned sector and the reform of the state-owned enterprises. The transfer of state-owned capital from the competitive realms to the strategic realms calls for the transfer of state-owned property rights or stock rights. The reorganization of the enterprise assets involves the readjustment of the organizational structure, change of products, mobility of workers and lay-off of redundant personnel. Particularly, it not only involves the readjustment of the existing reserves of state-owned capital but also calls for well-developed markets of property rights and stocks as well as the participation of the investors. This is bound to be long and gradual process as it requires the infusion of sufficient social funds. Therefore, in practical work, the state-owned enterprises in trades from which the state-owned capital should be pulled out can first be transformed into standard stock-limited or liability-limited companies. Those up to the required standards can be turned into listed companies either directly or through assets reorganization. When the right opportunity arrives, the state-owned stocks can be sold out for cash so to gradually reduce the proportion of state-owned stocks. Another alternative is for the enterprises to issue negotiable bonds first in society and, when the term expires, have the creditor's rights turned into stock rights. Active efforts should be made to promote the development of monetary assets management companies and, through reorganization of the enterprises' assets and creditor's rights, gradually retrieve the state-owned capital at proper opportunities after getting a clear picture of the enterprises' stocks. As for the small enterprises, they can be decontrolled and invigorated through various means, including merger, declaring bankruptcy, leasing out, contract management, joint-stock partnership and selling out.

4. Optimizing the Assets and Liabilities Structure and Establishing a State-owned Capital Increase and Infusion Mechanism

According available statistics, state-owned enterprises and enterprises with shares held by state-owned capital all encounter such problems as shortage or even serious shortage of capital funds, high debt rates and negative balance of assets and liabilities. They urgently call for the establishment of a reparatory mechanism for the infusion and increase of state-owned capital to relieve their debt burden.

In principle, the increase of capital funds should be combined with the strategic reorganization of the state-owned sector and the innovation in the enterprise system. Particular importance should be attached to bringing into play the role of the capital market. Of the state-owned enterprises that accord with the orientation of the readjustment of the layout of the state-owned sector, those enterprises that are relatively large in scale and are more competitive should be receive priority to have their capital funds increased. With regard to those enterprises that are smaller and operate in a poor manner, they can first undergo reorganization and structural readjustment, and then give them more funds to promote their development.

For these enterprises, there are several possible ways to increase investment in them and reduce their debt burdens. First, the funds they have acquired by way of ``turning allocations into loans" can be turned into state's input for capital funds. As for other loans granted to the enterprises, the creditor's rights can be turned into stock rights through consultation. And funds pooled from among the workers and staff in the enterprises can be turned into worker-staff shares through consultation. Active steps should be taken to make use of the capital market, strengthen efforts in pooling capital funds, look for new investors and work earnestly to change the operational mechanism of the enterprises. With regard to debts due to the banks, considerations can be made to establish state enterprise assets-debts trusteeship organizations and making them take the responsibility to conduct reorganization of the assets and liabilities of the enterprises entrusted to them. At the same time, part of the cash funds retrieved from the strategic withdrawal of the state-owned sector from commonplace competitive industries should be reinvested as capital funds in enterprises in industries that must be protected so as to relieve them of their debt burdens.

5. Establishing Special Organizations and Foundations to Promote the Reform and Development of State-owned Enterprises

Drawing on international experience and taking into account the actual conditions in China, special organizations should be established to be responsible for affairs related to the readjustment of the state-owned sector and the reform of the state-owned enterprises through making overall arrangements and mapping out unified plans. In practical work, these organizations should be careful to ensure a reasonable pace of progress, adopt appropriate steps and measures and sum up experience constantly. The funds retrieved from the strategic withdrawal of state-owned enterprises should primarily be used in the structural readjustment of the state-owned sector and in solving problems related to social security. Therefore, this author suggests establish a state-owned enterprise reorganization fund and a social security fund. The former is to be used for the reform and development of state-owned enterprises in industries that should be strategically strengthened, and the latter is used to establish a social security system so as to provide a social security network for the smooth progress of reform of the state-owned enterprises and to meet the basic needs of life for the laid-off workers and staff.

III. Accelerating the Transformation of Government Functions and Improving the Macro Control and Regulatory System

1. Accelerating the Transformation of Government Functions and Separating the Functions of Government from Those of the Enterprises

As the manager of social affairs, the government is duty-bound to do well in macro control and regulation. It is responsible in formulating the industrial policies and doing the organizational work for their implementation, maintaining the normal economic and social order, creating a market environment for fair competition and enforcing law strictly.

First, it is necessary to clearly divide work between the government and the market. In line with the actual progress in the marketization of the economy, it is necessary for the government to gradually withdraw from and reduce its functions in those areas that are unfeasible for it to directly intervene, and increase its functions in those areas where it is hard for the market to play a role. The transformation in the functions of the government should be mainly aimed at target to promote and improve the market mechanism, gradually cut its power to directly intervene in the micro-economic entities, and transfer those functions that should not be performed by the government to the enterprises, the market and the social intermediary institutions. In establishing and improving the market rules, while attaching importance to exercising control and supervision over the behavior of the market subjects, the government should pay more attention to ensuring equal rights between the market subjects, strengthening contractual relationships and promoting market competition. The government should focus its attention on improving the macro control and regulatory system, strengthening its power and quality of control, providing sufficient and reliable public products, and creating a sound environment for economic development.

Second, it is imperative to clarify the scope of activities and budgetary spending areas for governments at different levels under the conditions of the market economy. It is necessary to reasonably divide the power of office for governments at various levels and make it controllable so as to change the disorganized situation of overlapped power of office and functions between governments at different levels. On this basis, it is necessary to establish and improve a government responsibility system that corresponds to the power of office for government at each level so as to bring about an organic combination of power, responsibility and interests with the resources at its disposal. Attention should be paid to avoiding too wide a gap between the two, for too wide a gap between them might give rise to such problems as incompetence, rent seeking and bureaucracy. It is necessary to gradually clarify the legal basis and procedures governing the behavior of governments at different levels, improve the democratic and scientific level in policy making by governments at various levels and strengthen legal and social supervision as well as supervision of public opinion over government activities.

Third, it is necessary to strengthen the ranks of government public servants and improve the open examination and recruitment system, challenge system, and testing, promotion and punishment system. Under the preconditions to streamline government organizations, cut down redundant personnel, strengthen supervision for clean government and improve the qualities of public servants, it is necessary to raise the salaries for public servants by large margins, improve the incentive mechanism for government work and raise work efficiency.

Fourth, as the owner of the state-owned capital, the government exercises the functions as entitled to the owner. However, it should refrain from directly interfering in the management of the enterprises. On the part of the enterprises, they should hand back to the government the social functions they have shouldered.

2. Promoting Financial Reform and Augmenting the Financial Strength of the State

First, it is necessary to, taking the opportunity of the current reform of "replacing collection of fees by levy of taxes," establish a proper order in public distribution. It is imperative to earnestly sort out the numerous fees of an administrative nature under various sorts of names, call off those items that are unreasonable and turn those items that are in fact taxes into taxes.

Second, it is necessary to intensify efforts in transforming the functions of finance and establish a powerful state financial system. It is necessary to strengthen collection and management of taxes and improve the system of tax categories and rates on the basis of the reform to establish the tax-sharing system so as to ensure the sources of financial incomes for the state. Efforts should be made to study the structure of financial expenditure for the state. Normally speaking, expenditure on national security of a country, spending on the routine activities of the government, money spent in providing public products, investment in large infrastructure facilities and capital construction projects and funds invested as financial guarantee for macroeconomic control are areas of priority in the financial expenditure of the state. Therefore, it is necessary to clearly define the financial powers of the central and local governments, reasonably share out the expenditures between the central and local governments and vigorously strengthen the authority and power of macro control of the central government over financial affairs.

Third, further improve the taxation system and deepen the reform towards the establishment of the tax-sharing system. It is necessary to expand the coverage of value-added tax, speed up work in unifying the income taxes levied on domestic-funded and foreign-funded enterprises and promote fair competition among enterprises under various forms of ownership. It is necessary to improve the levy of personal income tax and consumption tax and begin to collect inheritance tax so as readjust the distribution of income and prevent the appearance of excessively large gaps in income. It is necessary to improve the export duty reimbursement policy to support the development of foreign trade. It is necessary to improve the transferred payment system and give more support to the backward regions and special trades.

3. Accelerating the Reform of the Monetary System

First, it is necessary to turn the People's Bank of China into a central bank in the real sense. Since the enactment of the "Law on the People's Bank of China," great progress has been made in the reform of the

People's Bank. In the reform, the People's Bank has made the following its primary goals: to maintain the stability of the value of RMB and a balance between money supply and demand; and enforce monetary supervision so as to effectively strengthen macro control and regulation over the monetary work. In terms of organizational setup, it has abolished the provincial and municipal branches and set up trans-provincial branches according to the division of economic regions to strengthen vertical leadership in the monetary supervisory work. On this basis, it is necessary to further strengthen its independence and authority as the central bank. With regard to macro control and regulatory means, the management system based on credit fund quotas has been abolished and the management system based on the quality of credit assets has been established to gradually dovetail with the international practice.

Second, it is necessary to conduct reform of state-owned commercial banks in line with the requirements of the standard corporate system and to ensure that the investment subjects are diversified, the banks are as enterprises and their operation follows market rules. Meanwhile, it is necessary to establish monetary assets management companies, actively study ways to "turn debts into stocks" and dissolve bank credit risks by employing methods common in the market economy. It is necessary to vigorously develop various kinds of corporate banks, allow foreign banks to set up branches in China and encourage competition under the precondition that the monetary security of the country is guaranteed.

Third, it is necessary to make energetic efforts to develop the financial market. The money market is expected to play a great role in the circulation of capital among banks. It is necessary to take active steps to develop securities markets so as to provide the enterprises with a new channel to pool funds. It is necessary to vigorously develop and codify the stock markets, improve the quality of listed companies step by step and turn the system of planned control over stock issuance into a system of selection by the market. To keep step with the strategic readjustment of the state-owned sector and the reform of state-owned enterprises, it is necessary to actively study ways and opportunities to get the

old-age pension, unemployment insurance and medical care insurance and is supplemented by social welfare, social relief and special care given to disabled servicemen and family members of revolutionary martyrs as well as jobs for demobilized servicemen. At present, major efforts should be made in the following aspects:

First, making energetic efforts to do a good in providing workers and staff laid off from state-owned enterprises with basic life necessities and create opportunities for their reemployment.

Along with the deepening of the reform of the state-owned enterprises, large numbers of workers and staff have become redundant and been laid off. It is necessary to resolutely follow the demands included in the "Circular of the Central Committee of the Communist Party of China and State Council on Making Down-to-Earth Efforts to Do Well in Ensuring the Basic Life Needs of Workers and Staff Laid off from State-owned Enterprises and Create Conditions for Their Reemployment" and other relevant documents and create conditions for their repositioning and reemployment. First of all, it is necessary to guarantee the laid-off workers with basic life necessities. To tackle this problem, the key is to have sufficient funds. The funds should be pooled from three sources—he enterprises, the society and the financial departments, with each contributing one third. It is necessary to guarantee that funds pooled in such a way are used for the set purposes. Second, it is necessary to make active efforts to ensure that the laid-off workers are reemployed (reemployment is indeed the best choice for them). To attain this goal, it is necessary to run well the reemployment service centers in the enterprises, increase fund input for vocational training and implement preferential policies adopted by the state with regard to the levy of taxes and the grant of small-sum loans. Third, it is necessary to further improve the so-called system of "three guarantees" (i.e., the reemployment service centers of the enterprises guarantee the basic life needs of the laid-off workers and staff for three years at the most; when the three-year term expires, the laid-off workers and staff still not unemployed are guaranteed unemployment allowances for another two years according to relevant stipulations; if still not employed after the two-year term, they will be guaranteed set sums of money from the civil affairs departments needed by urban residents to maintain a minimum standard of living). Fourth, it is necessary to ensure the full-amount and timely issuance of old-age pensions to the retired. Resolute measures should be taken to pursue that the enterprises turn in their payments for social security purposes. Fifth, great importance should be attached to the repositioning and reemployment of redundant workers and staff in the regions and industries as well as communities with more difficulties. By the areas with more difficulties, they mainly refer to certain areas in northeast China, northwest China and southwest China. By industries with more difficulties, they mainly include the coal-mining, non-ferrous metal, forest and military engineering industries. And by communities with more difficulties, they mainly refer to those who are relatively advanced in age, lack the necessary skills, poor in ability or physically handicapped.

Second, accelerating the establishment of the old-age, medical-care and unemployment insurance systems to provide a social security network for the reform of state-owned enterprises.

Most importantly, it is necessary to expand the coverage of the social security system to include workers and staff in enterprises under various forms of ownership into the system. Efforts should be made to improve the old-age insurance system to ensure that the pensions are issued to the retired workers and staff of state-owned enterprises in time and in full amount and make up to them the outstanding amount as soon as possible. With regard to unemployment insurance, the "Regulations on Unemployment Insurance" should be earnestly implemented. It is necessary to strengthen the collection, management and utilization of unemployment insurance funds. Meanwhile, it is necessary to do well in unemployment relief work to provide the laid-off workers with basic life necessities. In the reform of the medical care system, it is necessary to take into consideration the affordability of the workers and staff. Once the orientation of the reform is decided, the reform should be carried out with vigorous efforts.

V. Improving Legislation for the Market Economy

One important aspect of China's socialist construction is to continuously improve the socialist legal system, govern the country according to law and build a socialist country with a well-established legal system. To this end, it is imperative to implement the principle that there must be laws to go by, the laws must be observed and strictly enforced and law-breakers must be prosecuted. Efforts must be made to strengthen legislation as well as enforcement of and supervision according law, and continuously improve the legal system in line with the requirements of the socialist market economy.

In terms of legislation, it is necessary to strengthen work in the enactment of laws that codify the behavior of the market subjects so as to make enterprises under various forms of ownership operate and compete on an equal footing within the provided legal framework and enable them to get better protection for their legitimate rights and interests. It is necessary to improve legislation related to the market system and market environment so as to standardize transactions in the market and ensure that the economic and credit order remains normal. It is necessary to strengthen legislation governing the macroeconomic regulatory functions of the government so as to standardize the government's behavior and enhance the state's power and authority in macroeconomic control and regulation. In the enforcement of law, the recent amendment to the Constitution has made the socialist market economy the fundamental choice for China's basic economic system. To enforce law, it is necessary to ensure the authority of the Constitution and relevant laws. At the same time, vigorous efforts should be made to educate the people with knowledge of law and create a sound social environment in which everyone is abide by law.

It is necessary to further improve the basic property system under the conditions of the market economy. While making efforts to earnestly implement and enforce the relevant stipulations in the Constitution regarding enterprises under various types of ownership, it is necessary to adopt various effective measures to protect the legitimate property of the citizens and ensure equality for different kinds of property rights in market transaction. It is necessary to improve or annul those stipulations in various laws and regulations that contradict the basic principles embodied in the Constitution and stop acts of discrimination against and encroachment upon the rights of non-publicly owned economic sectors. It is necessary to amend or abandon laws and administrative regulations that do not conform to the economic relations now, strictly limit "legislation by different departments," and improve and codify the contract relations, credit relations and property relations under the conditions of the market economy. It is necessary to accelerate the reform of the judiciary system and eliminate as soon as possible local protectionism in law enforcement. At the same time, great efforts should be made to strengthen supervision over law enforcement. In view of the contradictions and problems encountered in judicial practice, it is necessary to gradually amend and improve the relevant laws in accordance with specified procedures and on the basis of earnestly and timely summing up experience.

CHAPTER 5

CHINA'S OPENING POLICY TOWARDS OUTSIDE WORLD

Synopsis

In its efforts to reform and open to the outside world over the past 20 years, China has undergone the historical change from the closed-door policy to opening to the outside world, and has achieved great achievements arousing worldwide attention. Summing up the basic experience in opening to the outside world over the past two decades, China has, in ideological terms, proceeded from the overall background of peace and development of the current era, persisted in taking development as the absolute principle and in upholding the principle of "three favorables" (favorable to promoting the growth of the productive forces in the socialist society, favorable to increasing the overall strength of the socialist state and favorable to raising the people's living standards) advocated by Deng Xiaoping, correctly handled the relations between opening to the outside world and reform and relations between opening to the outside world on the one hand and independence and self-reliance on the other, and maintained a sustained and steady development of the national economy in the course of opening the country to the rest of the world. In terms of strategy to open up the country, China has adopted a "gradual model" (starting from the coastal areas and then proceeding to the inland regions, first focusing on selected areas or regions and then shifting the focus to chosen industries and trades, and first making experiments in the special economic zones and then making it codified and institutionalized throughout the country) and step by step bought into being an institutionalized system to open to the outside world. In the utilization of foreign

funds, China has always made it the focus of work to absorb foreign direct investment (FDI), which has played a positive role in the economic development of the country. With regard to opening the capital market, China has remained cautious and played an important role in withstanding the disastrous effect of the financial crisis that broke out in Asia and swept across the world. In foreign trade, China has, to cater to the needs of opening to the outside world, carried out a series of market-oriented reforms of its foreign trade system, which has greatly enhanced the enthusiasm of the export enterprises. In the mix of export products, China has made full use of its advantages in resources by making the labor-intensive products the bulk of products for export, thus greatly enhancing the competitiveness of its products in the international market. Finally, in face of opportunities and challenges posed by the economic globalization and in the course of making efforts to join the World Trade Organization (WTO), the Chinese government has taken international competition as the core, adopted active and down-to-earth steps and played a more and more important role in the international economy.

To implement unswervingly the policy of opening to the outside world is an important component of Deng Xiaoping Theory; it is also a basic state policy of China in its efforts for socialist modernization. Now, China has turned out to be a developing country that has made most use of foreign investment. By the end of 1998, the accumulated total amount of foreign investment China had actually used reached US$407.248 billion. Foreign-funded enterprises, which have been developing quickly, have become an important force for the sustained growth of China's economy. China has reaped marked achievements in foreign trade. Over the past two decades, the annual average growth of foreign trade has remained around 15 percent, much higher than the annual average growth rate of 9 percent for the gross domestic production (GDP). In terms of total volume of imports and exports, China was ranked the 32nd in the world in 1978. In 1998, it had jumped up to the 9th. Practice over the past 20 years has fully proved that reform and opening to the outside world is the road for China to get rich and prosperous and attain its goal of modernization.

Why has China reaped such great achievements in its drive of reform and opening to the outside world over the past two decades? Much valuable experience needs to be summed up. What is more urgent, however, is for us to sum up the basic experience gained over the past 20 years in opening up the country to the rest of the world in face of the negative aftermath caused by the Asian financial crisis over the past few years and of the new situation brought about by the economic globalization to our drive to open up to the outside world. This is extremely important for China when it is stepping into the 21st century.

Section 1

Historical Background and Basic Features of China's Opening Policy

I. Peace and Development Are the Two Major Themes of the Present Era; the World Today is an Open World; and the Economic Construction of Any Country Cannot Be Independent of the Development in the World.

Deng Xiaoping is the chief architect of China's drive of reform and opening to the outside world. With extraordinary political courage and insight, he timely seized the opportunity and, basing himself on the objective laws governing the development of the world economy, clearly pointed out that the world today was an open world and the development in any country could not possibly be independent of the trend of development in the world. Therefore, he repeatedly told the Chinese people that the development of China could not be separated from that of the world. Socialist system can be established in one country or a couple of countries. But, the socialist construction can in no way be separated from the world. Closing the country to international intercourse is bound to lead to failure. China is an important member of the international community and is now in an international political and economic system in which the mutual relations are getting increasingly closer and the mutual influence is getting increasingly more profound. The world and its development are the international background and condition for China's socialist construction, and so China's development cannot be independent of or separated from the tide of the world. Meanwhile, in the development of the world, the existence and development of China cannot be overlooked. Based on the accurate analysis of the situation and trend of economic development in the world and firmly grasping the two major themes of development in the present era, China has unswervingly made opening to the outside world one of its long-term basic state policies.

The world today is an open one, and no country can disassociate itself from the economic system of the world and seek rapid development by closing its doors. One important reason for China's long-drawn backwardness in history was to close its doors to external exchanges. Deng Xiaoping pointed out that it was impossible now for any country to seek development by closing its doors to the outside world. We have paid dearly, so did our forebears. China's experience has repeatedly testified that, to develop the productive forces and get rid of poverty and backwardness as soon as possible, it is necessary to open the country to the outside world, be bold to assimilate all the fruits made by all civilizations in human history, including those created in the capitalist society and make full use of foreign and domestic resources and markets, so as to make China's economic development echo with the progress in the world more closely and mix into the world economy that is now in the course of integration. International experience has also proved that all countries or regions that boast relatively rapid development are open economically. So, opening to the outside world is the inevitable result of economic development in the modern world.

To go with the trend of economic development in the world, China has unswervingly implemented the basic state policy of opening to the world. This is in fact a question of great strategic significance for China to achieve a prolonged, sustained and steady development in its economy and society. Just as Deng Xiaoping pointed out, if the opening policy was not changed in the first half of the next century, there would be no need to change it 50 years later when the exchanges with the rest of the world further expand.

II. Development Is the Absolute Principle. It Is Necessary to Emancipate the Mind, Adopt the Attitude of Seeking Truth from Facts in Any Adjustment of the Open Policy, and Uphold the Most Fundamental Criterion of "Three Favorables" to Promote China's Economic Construction.

To shift from the closed-door policy to opening to the outside world, there is bound to be a profound emancipation of the mind. Cutting off the country from the outside world and the implementation of the system of planned economy for a long time had fettered the people's mind and limited their vision. The Third Plenary Session of the 11th Party Central Committee held in 1989 set right the previous wrongs, reestablished the ideological line of emancipating the mind and seeking truth from facts and resolutely established opening to the outside world as a long-term basic state policy. This represented an important change in China's strategy for economic development. Any move China has made in the course of opening up the country to the outside world, from the adoption of the open policy to the making of every important decision, was a result of emancipating the mind, seeking truth from facts and changing in ideas. Along with the widening of the scope of the opening-up drive, people's understanding of this policy has been increasingly enhanced, which, in turn, has turned out to be great driving force to further enlarge the scope of the drive.

An important experience of China is to guide the opening-up drive with the Deng Xiaoping Theory. The drive to opening to the outside world not only has produced a widespread and profound impact on the Chinese economy but also effected a great clash in people's long-held ideas. It was precisely to combat the "Left" tendency to label everything either "capitalist" or "socialist' that Deng Xiaoping put forward the principle of "three favorables" and made it the fundamental criteria in judging any work done. This had removed the ideological hindrance for efforts to open to the outside world. In order to make socialism to fully display its advantages, it is necessary for China to boldly assimilate all the fruits of civilization created by mankind and draw on the advanced forms and methods of management developed in all countries, including the developed capitalist countries. Proceeding from this strategic guiding ideology, Deng Xiaoping repeatedly stressed that "development is the absolute principle"; that opening to the outside world not lead to capitalism, nor would it do us any harm; that our doors had not opened wide enough and they should be opened wider; and that opening to the outside world was a long-term policy, it would not change.

In the course of China's drive to open up to the outside world, some negative things have appeared. This is inevitable. Also, there is nothing strange that people come up with some misgivings and raise some questions. A successful experience China has gained is to grasp the true essence of Deng Xiaoping's strategic thinking and comprehensively and objectively analyze the advantages and disadvantages in opening up to the outside world. For instance, after the Asian financial crisis, the negative influence produced on China's economy by the international economic fluctuations has gradually appeared and expanded. Consequently, some people have come up with worries about the increasing dependence of China's economy on foreign trade and the policy of opening up to the outside world. With regard to this situation, it is necessary for us to be aware that China has a big domestic market and there is much room for the economy to maneuver, and it is possible for us to mitigate the negative influence of the international economic fluctuations through readjusting the economic structure, improving the macroeconomic control and regulation and strengthening international economic cooperation. The world economy is of an open type and it can never do to give up efforts in further opening up to the rest of the world under the pretext that the country's economy has affected by international economic fluctuations. Again for example, in the utilization of foreign investment, some other people think that too many enterprises have been established and operated with foreign direct investments and foreign investment has come into the country too rapidly.

ket economic system, which is featured with market-based resource allocation in a global context. Opening to the outside world is a flat denial of autarky and it would bring about fundamental changes in the highly concentrated planned economy in terms of the scope and forms of resource allocation. In the process of opening, the traditional economic system will inevitably pose various barriers. To meet the requirements of opening, comprehensive reforms should be carried out in various aspects of China's economic system.

Selection of the contents and steps of opening should be favorable to the consolidation and development of reform and economic construction. For a transitional economy, the most important function of opening is to accelerate reform. The open policy plays an invaluable role in the transition from a planned economy to a market one. In China's case, one of the most successful experiences is promoting reform by opening to the outside world. Firstly, opening has enhanced people's awareness of reform. Since reform readjusts the old production relations and the existing interest distribution pattern, it would inevitably threaten the old power pattern and vested interest groups, and in return would meet with all kinds of ideological obstacles. In such a situation, opening can serve as an impetus to reform. When the people get in touch with the international community on all fronts, they may find the traditional mechanism incongruent with the working rules of the international economy. This would impel people to reexamine the old economic mechanism, show more initiatives in reform and become more reform-oriented. Secondly, opening is favorable to maintaining a correct reform direction. During the reform, people may be caught in a dilemma. On the one hand, people may feel that a certain reform is favorable to the development of the market economy. On the other hand, they are uncertain whether the reform is of a capitalist nature. This perplexity results from a lack of thorough understanding of the capitalist system and the market economy. At the time when China first opened to the capitalist world, what we had before us was a world of market economies that had undergone hundreds of years' development and reached a rather high level of development. Game rules of the market economy have been gradually perfected and become an organic part of the capitalist system. Only by opening-up can we distinguish commonality of market economy from the defining features of a capitalist society. By doing so, we can better comply with the operational laws of the market economy and avoid detours. Thirdly, opening to the outside world is favorable to drawing on the experience and lessons of other transitional economies. Learning from the successful experience of those transitional economies may speed up our reform whereas learning from their failures may make us avoid repeating the same mistakes or reduce losses. Fourthly, opening provides opportunities for learning from other developing countries. Many developing countries or regions have adopted all sorts of reform measures for developing the economy, many of which can serve as early experiments for China, and supply China with precious references. It is just on the basis of experience and lessons from other countries that China has unswervingly advanced its reform in the past two decades.

IV. Combine Opening up with Self-reliance to Ensure the Stable and Sustained Growth of the National Economy

Opening up is a practical step integrating a country's economy into the world's economy, thus strengthening the interdependence between China's economy and that of the rest of the world. Therefore, we must properly handle the relations between further opening up and self-reliance. Self-reliance is one of China's basic guidelines in its economic construction, which is decided by China's actual conditions. Mr. Deng Xiaoping pointed out that China's affairs should be dealt with according to China's actual conditions and by relying on China's own strength. (*Selected Works of Deng Xiaoping*, Vol. I, p. 372) In other words, we must bear it in mind that opening up is just a means to an end, rather than an end in itself. Our purpose is developing productive forces through opening up. It's also wrong to take opening as simply relying on foreign aid for everything, or even for fulfilling modernization. Self-reliance does not reject opening but serves as a foothold. Without this foothold, opening up would be like water without a source and a tree without roots. As a means for strengthening self-reliance, opening may reinforce weak links in the national economy and promote the national economic strength as a whole.

To develop China, we must start with our basic conditions, go our own way and base our foothold on our own ability. Self-reliance does not mean excluding everything blindly, nor doing everything by relying on our own strength and starting from scratch. Taking initiatives in further opening up for development shows the confidence and ability of a nation and is the true meaning of self-reliance. Every country or nation has experienced a long course for developing its own culture, technology and level of productivity, which can not be either replaced or copied blindly by any other country. However, no county or nation can develop economically, technologically or socially totally independent of other countries or nations. Creatively learning from other countries through opening is not only congruent with the spirit of self-reliance, but also a shortcut to enhancing the capacity for independence. Just as President Jiang Zemin pointed out, "Being self-reliant and self-independent is by no means building our country with the doors shut for the rest of the world, but rather aims at raising opening to a new height." ("Proper Handling of Some Important Relations in the Socialist modernization Drive"—A Speech Delivered at the Closing Ceremony of the Fifth Plenary Session of the Fourteenth Party Central Committee, September 28, 1995.)

Section 2

China' s Strategy of Gradual Opening

To implement a gradual opening strategy is a successful experience based on China's actual conditions and an important feature of China's economic transition. China's gradual opening strategy is mainly manifested in its step-by-step popularization of successful experience from experiments, according to the requirements and level of national economic development as well as on the basis of weighing gains and losses. China has successfully followed a road of gradual opening, which is compatible with the overall strategy of reform.

I. Regional Opening in China Started from Coastal Regions and Expanded to the Inland Areas in all Fields and at Various Levels, Bringing about Benefits to Both Regional and National Economies.

China's experience in the past two decades of opening shows that, in a global economic system predominantly featured with mutual dependence, one country can more effectively build up the strength to fend off all kinds of international risks and expand potentials for economic development through broadening and deepening opening and enhancing the level of participating in international division of labor and international exchanges. China has followed a distinctively gradual approach in its opening, that is starting from coastal regions and then expanding to the inland areas with different focuses in different stages.

Roughly speaking, China's opening has experienced several stages of development. In the first stage, which was between 1979-1983, some major actions were tried out. As a first step, campaigns were launched to unify people's understanding of opening, emancipate the minds of the public and get rid of the traditional idea of "being free from any foreign and domestic debts." Freed from the old ideological shackles, China started to borrow from developed countries and attract foreign businesses to invest directly in China. In July 1979, the central government granted Guangdong Province and Fujian Province special policies and more flexibility in order to bring into full play the advantages of the two provinces as the home town of many overseas Chinese and neighbor of Hongkong and Macao. Then according to China's actual conditions and with reference to the successful experience in setting up export processing zones and free trade zones in other countries, four comprehensive special economic zones were set up in Shenzhen, Zhuhai, Shantou and Xiamen with special policies and economic systems.

The second period was from1984 to 1987, during which more importance was attached to the special economic zones (SEZs). On his inspection visit to the SEZs, Deng Xiaoping fully affirmed the policy of setting up SEZs and pointed out that more SEZs should be set up, especially in some port cities. In April 1984, the central government decided to open 14 port cities, including Tianjin, Shanghai, Guangzhou, Zhanjiang and Beihai. In February 1985, some 61 cities or counties in the Pearl River Delta, Yangtze River Delta and southern Fujian were set up as coastal economic development zones. In the early 1986, the size of the SEZs in Zhuhai, Shantou and Xiamen was expanded. In May 1986, the State Council organized a guiding group to coordinate with affairs concerning foreign investment in China and issued in October 1986 the "Provisions on Encouraging Foreign Investment," for the purpose of protecting the legal rights of foreign-funded businesses, fully taking advantage of the low costs in labor and land use in China, and better attracting foreign investment.

The third stage is between 1988-1991, during which more coastal regions were opened. Based on the achievements already made and the international trend of development, the central government extended the coastal economic opening regions to Liaodong Peninsula, Shandong Peninsula and other places. In April the same year, in the First Meeting of the Seventh National People's Congress, a decision was approved to turn Hainan Province into China's largest special economic zone. In April 1990, China decided to develop and open Pudong New Development Area in Shanghai, to which were granted the preferential policies for special economic zones. In 1991, the State Council approved the establishment of bonded areas in Shanghai, Shenzhen, Shantou and Tianjin Port as tax-free bases for foreign trade, cargo storage, export-oriented processing and transit trade.

The fourth stage began in 1992, during which an all-round and multileveled opening pattern with focal points gradually took shape. Inspired by Deng Xiaoping's talks made on his south China inspection tour, China's opening drive progressed on all fronts. The central government systematically proposed the "Four-Along Opening Strategy," which was along the coast, border, Yangtze River and railways as part of the "Continental Bridge" linking Europe with Asia. To be specific, emphasis was given to the coastal regions from Bohai Bay to Beihai Bay, the border areas in Xinjiang, Inner Mongolia and Heilongjiang with members of the CIS and those in Yunnan and Guangxi for business with South Asia and Southeast Asia, Pudong Development Zone for stimulating the overall development of the Yangtze River valley downstream from Chongqing City, and the railways from Lianyun Port and other ports to the Altai Mountain Pass in Xinjiang.

Starting from regional preferential policy in the 1980s, China has, in its opening course, experimented with special economic zones which have served as a showcase of reform and opening to the outside world and expedited the emergence of provinces like Guangdong as regional economic powers. In the early 90s, the central government made a timely strategic decision to open and develop Pudong in Shanghai. Since then, Pudong had played a leading role in pulling up the economy of the Yangtze River Delta or even the entire Yangtze River valley, which replaced Guangdong to become the fastest-growing region. In the late 90s, in order to boost the opening of the vast territories of inland China and closing regional gaps, the central government granted preferential policies to inland regions as well, which marked a new era of opening and development for provinces in central and western China.

II. Integrate Regional Opening with Industrial Opening and Gradually Shift the Focus of Opening from the Former to the Latter

In the initial stage of opening, China took the strategy of gradual spreading of regional opening to close the gap between different regions and distribute benefits of opening to most parts of the country. Along with the progress of regional opening, China has adopted the strategy of opening the primary and secondary industries first and the tertiary industry later. Since 1990s, China began shifting its focus to industrial opening in order to attract foreign funds, expedite economic restructuring and industrial upgrading, and improve the internal quality and competitiveness of its economy.

Considering such things as the unbalanced development and different risk-resisting capacities between industries, China gave priority to opening many sectors in the primary and secondary industries at the initial stage, while allowing foreign investment to go to a few sectors of the tertiary industry. Since 1992, China further expanded the field for

tering economy within the Zone. In applying these preferential policies, we must pay attention to the following. First, preferential policies should be written into the law as soon as they become mature so as to keep the stability of policies. Secondly, the pioneering nature of reform should be given due attention to. Therefore, policies concerning foreign investment in fields like land leasing, retailing, banking and insurance must be experimented and proved to be successful in the SEZs before they could be applied elsewhere. Thirdly, the time limit of preferential policies should be emphasized. Some favorable policies only serve to initiate the construction and development of SEZs and they should be no longer in effect after the achievement of the policy goal. Fourthly, preferential policies shall not be granted only in terms of regions, but according to industries as well. At the initial stage of development and construction, it is more convenient to operate and easier to attract industrial capital with regional preferential policies. When industries have reached a certain level, the focus of preferential policies should be shifted to support industrial development, since it can direct investment to basic and hi-tech industries that are necessary to promote national economic quality.

In November 1993, the Third Plenary Session of the Fourteenth Party Central Committee approved the "Decision on Some Issues Concerning the Establishment of a Socialist Market Economic Structure," which mapped out a comprehensive blueprint for a socialist market economic system, defined the fundamental steps to promote reform, opening up and modernization drive, and marked significant breakthroughs in guiding ideology. Since early 1994, China put forth major reforms in taxation, banking, foreign exchange, foreign trade, investment, price, and circulation systems. In order to construct a market environment with standardized and fair competition across the country, SEZs were required to put the interest of the country above everything else and carry out the reform policies mentioned above. This reduced the differences in policies between the SEZs and other regions, especially in taxation and foreign exchange regulation systems. With the implementation of nationally unified macroeconomic policies, the SEZs had to reorient themselves for development. For this reason, the central government made necessary readjustment and improvement on the policies for the SEZs. Such readjustment is helpful for the SEZs to establish a socialist market economic system before other regions and meet the requirements of international practice. It also helps to produce more complete and more standard systems and policies, and create an environment of fair competition.

In spite of the readjustment on the policies in SEZs, China will by no means change its fundamental policy to set up SEZs, but go on with it. Generally speaking, China's SEZs has two functions. First, it serves as an experimental site for reform, a growth point for development, and a source of radiation effect. Second, it is China's special economic form to use international economic resources. These two functions take on different features at different stage in the SEZ construction. As long as these special functions exist, SEZs should exist and develop. President Jiang Zemin pointed out during his inspection tour in Guangdong, that we should unswervingly carry out the construction of SEZs to a higher standard. He also stressed that the central government's determination to develop SEZs will never change, nor will its basic policies for the SEZs change, nor will SEZ's position and role in the nationwide reform and transformation drive change.

Section 3
Achievement and Prospects of Utilizing Foreign Capital in China

International capital flow plays a more and more important role in the global economy, which has impact not only on the speed, but also on the form and quality of economic growth in every country. At present, China is in the period of transition from the planned economy to the market economy. Utilizing foreign capital is an important means of making use of two kinds of resources and two markets. During its opening to the outside world for the past two decades, China has always attached great importance to the absorption of foreign direct investment

Structural Changes in the Utilization of Foreign Capital (%)

	Percentage of loans	Percentage of FDI	Percentage of other forms of capital
1985	57.8	35.7	6.5
1995	21.5	77.9	6.6

Since 1992, China has become the country with the second largest amount of FDI in the world for four consecutive years. According to the statistic analysis of the Report on Overseas Fundraising by Developing Countries issued by the International Bank for Reconstruction Development (IBRD) in 1996, the amount of FDI attracted by the developing countries had more than doubled from 1991 to 1995, of which, 66 percent was absorbed by the Eastern Asian regions and FDI in China accounted for 40 percent of the total in all developing countries. It is estimated that the amount of foreign capital coming from member states of the APEC accounted for 72 percent of total used in China, of which, FDI made up as much as 93.2 percent.

Since 1996, attracting FDI has entered a period of readjustment and improvement. By the end of 1996, more than 283,820 foreign-funded enterprises had been approved in China; contracted investment had reached US$469.39 billion and US$176.595 billion of this had been put to use. The percentage of FDI in China's national fixed assets and GNP gradually increased from 2.9 percent and 1.1 percent in 1991 to 10.4 percent and 5.2 percent in 1996 respectively. During this period, multinational corporations entered our country one after another and investment centered on such areas as major cities and the Yangtze River Delta. At present, of the 500 biggest multinational corporations in the world, about 200 of them have invested in China.

During this period, the form of FDI had also experienced the following changes: (A) change from starting up new enterprises to mergers; (B) change from general mergers to selective mergers (mainly focused on large SOEs and well-performing enterprises); (C) change from scattered mergers to concentrated mergers, i.e., foreign investors deliberately merge with the SOEs in the same area or leading enterprises in the same sector across regions; (D) change from stock-partnership to controlling stakes. Powerful multinational corporations often required that enterprises hold controlling shares and products be sold domestically. Foreign share holders generally achieve a controlling position in businesses through three ways, i.e., investing in joint ventures, purchasing stocks and increasing capital; (E) change from export of capital to export of brands of commodities. Foreign brands either directly replaced Chinese brands or purchased Chinese brands and in turn they were ignored; (F) change from joint ventures to solely foreign-funded enterprises. In recent years, the number of projects, the amount of contracted investment and amount of actual investment of solely foreign-owned enterprises have all exceeded those of joint ventures.

II. The Role of FDI in China's Economic Development

China's successful attraction and utilization of foreign capital has played an important part in speeding up its economic construction and enhancement of the overall level of its economy.

1. Impact on the aggregate volume of economy

The statistics showed that the scale of the actual foreign investment, the sum of FDI and other kinds of foreign investment (the same as follows) had a strong and fairly long-standing connection with the growth of GNP. This indicated that the increase of actual foreign investment evidently pushed on the corresponding growth of GNP.

2. Impact of the Open Economy on the Supply and Demand and Investment of Domestic Capital

In the 1980s, the increase speed of China's financial expenditure surpassed that of income. Therefore, the supply and demand of capital was tight. Meanwhile, the supply of foreign currency was not sufficient and the current account of the international balance of payments was in deficits. Under this circumstance, the supply of foreign loans and introduction of foreign investment, in a sense, alleviated the short supply of domestic capital and at the same time supported the rapid growth of economy. With the enlargement of its scale, the percentage of foreign

was that the FDI has slightly declined for the recent one or two years. More importantly, China was faced with a new challenge to attract foreign investment due to the change of the international economic situation. Since 1990s, with the quickened integration of China's economy with the international economy, the domestic market has changed into a stage for international competition and the competition in the domestic market one of capital strength and technological innovation. During this period, China will be confronted with greater competition pressure with regard to attracting foreign investment.

Confronted with the new pressure of international competition, under the condition of upholding the open-door policy, China issued policies to stimulate domestic consumption so as to maintain the steady and sustained increase of the economy. Besides, China managed to eliminate the negative effect on the economic growth caused by the decline of export and the slight reduction of foreign investment. Meanwhile, the Chinese government has adopted different kinds of measures to broaden the channels of export and to make effective use of foreign investment. It can be said that this is a wise decision of the Chinese government. China enforces the policy of opening to the outside world according to the actual situation of China. Broadening channels of domestic consumption, China, according to national macro-economic tasks, has adopted a lot of measures to make effective use of foreign investment as well.

1. Further broadening the Field and Scope of Foreign Investment

From Jan. 1, 1998, some preferential policies concerning exemption of tariffs and value-added taxes have been enforced to stimulate and support foreign investment and imported facilities for domestically funded projects. During the recent one or two years, more and more foreign-funded financial institutions and insurance companies were approved to enter China. At present, foreign banks approved to conduct RMB business have increased to twenty or so. On the whole, China has made further progress in its width and depth of opening to the outside world.

2. Create an Environment for Foreign-funded Enterprises and Domestic Enterprises to Compete on Equal Footing

This mainly includes the following two respects: equal policy and equal system. As far as the policy is concerned, some practice and experience of joint ventures can be borrowed by the domestic enterprises when they join funds, co-operate and merge with other enterprises or purchase other enterprises, preferential policies for foreign businessmen can also be granted to top domestic enterprises, conditions of attracting businessmen and investment should be made known to the public, and domestic and foreign investors should be treated equally without discrimination. As far as the system is concerned, only with the removal of system barriers to the development of domestic enterprises and the acceleration of SOE reform, could enterprises have incentives for achieving long-term development and avoiding short-term behaviors. As long as barriers between different regions and departments are broken, the unreasonable limit on restructuring the ownership of state assets is removed, and the reasonable circulation of resources governed by the law of market is promoted, a group of powerful enterprises and enterprise groups will take shape as quickly as possible. Moreover, they will further develop and survive in the competition with the multinational corporations.

3. Further Strengthening the Guidance of the Direction of the Foreign Investment

With regard to the growth pattern of the Chinese economy, foreign investment should be guided in such a way that it can introduce advanced technology, encourage hi-tech industries, enhance the R & D of those foreign funded enterprises stationed in China, promote the system transition of SOEs and facilitate the development of central and western regions of China. In recent years, China has already accumulated some good experience, for example, requiring multinational corporations to establish joint ventures and technology development centers in China; demanding foreign companies to transfer the latest products to branches operating in China; giving priority to projects which invested in central and western regions of China. In a word, through effective guidance of

export dramatically reduced the trade surplus. Take the first half of 1999 for example, from January to May, the total volume of China's export was US$67.6 billion, a 7.9 percent drop from the same period last year while the volume of import reached US$60.5 billion, a 15.3 percent increase from the same period last year. This reduced China's trade surplus by US$0.18 billion and the role of export in the economic growth changed from positive to negative. Furthermore, because of the increased instability of international trade market and international financial market, the reform of future foreign trade system will be more difficult than that of any other periods in the past.

Under such new circumstances, the reform of Chinese foreign trade system is confronted with dual tasks. On the one hand, it should serve the needs of national macroeconomic development and promote export through various policy measures, including restructuring the export commodities, improving the forms of trade, diversifying the import and export markets, and rectifying unreasonable charges in foreign trade. Moreover, efforts should be strengthened in negotiating with trade protectionism according to international practice to protect the normal export of our country. Meanwhile, according to the changing international landscape in foreign trade, the export drawback rate should be adequately raised to boost the export of those commodities that have high competition potentials in the world market or have close connections with industry. On the other hand, according to the principle of "equal treatment to domestic and foreign companies," reform of the foreign trade system should be advanced hand in hand with the reform of the economic system under the context of overall opening. The principle of "equal treatment to domestic and foreign companies" should be fully reflected in legislation or amendments to laws and regulations to encourage competition on equal footing. In addition, the reform of foreign trade system should be carried out together with the reform of legislative and administrative systems. Within the framework of a regulated free trade system, foreign trade management should be opened on full scale and finally complete the transition from a system of administrative examination and approval to a system of legal registration to meet the needs of enterprises and the principles of international trade organizations.

Section 5
China's Opening to the Outside World in Face of Economic Globalization

With the acceleration of the global economic integration process and the intensification of opening to the outside world, the potential uncertainties and risks of an open economy would increase. Especially after the Asian financial crisis that swept across the whole world, international economy is now faced with the harshest threat since the beginning of the second half of the century at the end of the century. People have come to a better realization of the mutual relationship, mutual infiltration, mutual influence and mutual dependence of all nations in the open economy. Economic globalization has become an unavoidable reality. Faced with this reality, how to harmonize with the development of the world economy by taking a more conscious and more active attitude is an important subject facing China's opening to the outside world.

I. Influence of the Asian Financial Crisis on China's Opening to the Outside World

Since the beginning of this century, very few regional economic crises have attracted such a worldwide attention as the one that hit Asia in 1997. The Asian financial crisis appeared to be a financial problem, but was actually a result of paradoxical movement of demand and supply in real economy and production, and readjustment in industrial structures. This financial crisis did not create destructive influence to the Chinese economy. For one reason, RMB is inconvertible in capital transaction. For the other, the capital market has not been opened to the foreign capital. The more important reason, however, is that China has accumulated considerable economic strength in the twenty years of reform

market. At the same time, it also occurs under the condition that the rapid development of new technological revolution represented by information technology and the coming of knowledge economy provides unprecedented convenience for the economic exchange among all nations of the world. As long as the law of socialized production exists, the pace of technological innovation will not stop and the trend of economic globalization cannot be held back. This is the inexorable trend of social progress as well as that of social economic development. In the face of the economic globalization, and with this as the basic foothold for the formulation of policies, we can integrate China's economic development into the mainstream of world economic development.

Economic globalization is fundamentally an international industrial restructuring led by advanced nations and mainly propelled by multinational corporations. The industrial restructuring in the economic globalization has not only resulted in a complete transfer of some industries, but more importantly a transfer of some links in the production chain within the same industry. In most cases in the past, due to the limitation of various technological conditions, the division of labor in industry and adjustments in the industrial structures were conducted within the border of a single country. With the further expansion of the market and closer relations of international economic exchange, it takes more money and time to conduct industrial restructuring within one single country than doing it through the process of economic globalization. In western countries such as the United State, where investment and trade are relatively more open, the economic transition is now going from the industrial economy to knowledge economy due to their fulfillment of readjustment and optimization in the whole world. They have, therefore, maintained a strong momentum of economic growth.

At present, against the background of economic globalization, structural readjustment has already become a theme of the world economy. Both developing and developed countries are trying hard to find their shares of division of labor and positions in the new international economic environment so as to determine their own competitive advantages. Generally speaking, the opportunities brought about by the economic globalization for China are reflected in several ways. First of all, it expanded the space for the application of resources. For example, things from the traditional elementary products and raw materials to appropriate applicable technology and production equipment, from high and new technology to advanced business management knowledge, from direct investment of the foreign capitalists to loans and funds from different sources and different kinds are all available in the world market. Appropriate use of these resources can produce huge enormous profits, which can be turned into direct productive force. Secondly, globalization has also provided an applicable and expanding international market. The wide coverage and multivalent property of the international market has made it possible for China's commodities, labor or service to get into it through comparative advantage, which has created conditions for China to look for comparative advantage. Thirdly, China itself possesses a huge economic scale and market potential, which is very attractive to other countries and regions. This, in turn, creates opportunities for China to make use of international resources. Such external economic effects prove to be an important opportunity to China, a country that is undergoing the process of transition.

The process of economic globalization is often accompanied by a blind market leading force and a high degree of uncertainty. Freedom of economy and trade is a preferred slogan of economic powers in international economic relations. We should take a cautious attitude to the further intensification of opening to the outside world.

First, economic globalization brings harsh challenges and threats apart from benefits and opportunities. One of the basic principles is that the globalization of world economy also means a universality of market economy in the scope of the whole world. China's opening to the outside world to participate in international cooperation also means that it must compete under the rule of market economy in the world. To a great extent, it is a competition of perfection degree of the market economic system and a competition of the international competitive power of a nation's enterprises. For a developing country like China that is undergoing the transition to market economy, it is an arduous test if it wishes to stand firm in the competition and develop itself.

ficiaries. More specifically, liberalization in agricultural trade will not threaten "food security." Even if the import quotas for agricultural products are cancelled, the rate of food self-sufficiency in 2005 would still be maintained at over 92 percent. Considering the scale economy and the monopolistic nature of the auto industry, the negative influence on the auto industry and employment will be less than expected if China enters into the WTO and the declining rate in the output and employment will be around 12 percent. The competition brought along by trade liberalization would reduce the number of auto manufacturers by 27 percent, but the size of auto companies would expand, which is helpful for raising their efficiency and competitive edge in the international market. Due to the impact of the entry into the WTO in the agricultural sector, the actual household income in rural areas, in spite of the transfer of some rural labor to non-agricultural sectors by 2005, would be 2.1 percent lower than it would be if China does not enter into the WTO. However, the actual household income in urban areas would increase by 4.6 percent.

Besides, China's entry into the WTO will cast great influence on the export market of labor-intensive products and the import market of primary agricultural products in the world. The international market share of garment products made in China will rise by 10 percentage points, thus reducing the market shares of other countries. The increase in the export of land-intensive primary agricultural products in China can hopefully exceed that of Japan in 2010 to turn China into the largest import country of agricultural products.

The influence brought about by China's entry into the WTO to economy determines the orientation of its domestic policy readjustments, which can be summarized as follows. (1) The policy of industrial readjustment will provide support to capital and technology intensive industries to offset the unfavorable impact brought about by trade opening on these industries to stimulate the upgrading of the industries. (2) The policy of tax readjustment will strengthen the function of redistribution of tax revenues to slow down the expansion of possible income differences and prevent social instability related to this. (3) It will create conditions necessary for the transfer of agricultural labor force.

The flow of agricultural labor force into the secondary and tertiary industries and from rural areas into urban areas is a precondition as well as the chief challenge for the realization of industrialization and modernization in China. In a relatively long period of time, this task will be more formidable than the reemployment problem now facing state-owned enterprises. China's accession to the WTO will ensure the entry of labor-intensive products into the international market. (4) It will promote a relatively high savings rate to secure and attract more inflow of foreign capital.

From the perspective of near future, we should start from the background of globalization to optimize the commodity structure of export and participate in international trade on all fronts. The basic direction is to occupy those technology-intensive parts of the industry with high added value according to our comprehensive strength and comparative advantages and transfer labor-intensive production with low added value to other countries, rather than occupying the entire industry. Secondly, long-term cooperative relationship should be established with transnational corporations in trade investment. This is the focal point in China's utilization of foreign capital to develop trade. On the basis of this, we should facilitate the development of China's transnational business through various means. Besides, we should actively participate in multilateral and regional cooperation in economy and trade. Particularly we should try our best to participate in the formulation of the new rules and regulations for international trade and investment. In the liberalization process of trade investment initiated by the multilateral or regional economic organizations, we should safeguard the interest and benefit of the developing countries and try our utmost to establish a fair and rational new order of international economic trade on the basis of balanced rights and obligations.

IV. In Response to the Economic Globalization, Keeping International Competitive Advantage at the Core to Correctly Determine the Role of the Government

In the next 10 to 20 years, China will be faced with the double challenge of industrialization and globalization. Effort being made to enter the WTO is a specific manifestation of such a challenge. In this process, the economic functions of the government are of crucial importance.

According to the conclusion of a latest research project, the main challenges imposed by the economic globalization on the development of the economic roles of governments of developing countries can be summarized as follows. Firstly, under the situation of globalization of the product market and massive entry of multinational corporations, the key to extending the production scope and upgrading industrial and import structures lies in how the government should help domestic enterprises enter new sectors of production and improve the competitiveness of the new products. The second is how the government should strengthen the control over capital flow, maintain flexible policies on exchange rates and establish a sound domestic financial system. The third is that with the impact of external factors (such as the deterioration of trade conditions, sharp decline of external demand, unfavorable changes in foreign interest and exchange rates), we should emphasize the role of the government in income redistribution. The focal point is how the government can reduce the negative influence brought about by external factors on the low-income social stratum to prevent this social stratum from becoming a source of social instability and spread benefits gained from international competition to a larger number of people by means of taxation, transfer payments and establishment of a perfect social security system.

China's economy is now undergoing a transformation from agriculture-based rural economy to industry-based urban economy and from the planned economic system to the socialist market economic system. This is the basis on which the government determines its economic role. Problems and difficulties arising in the course of economic transformation are undoubtedly the focus of the government's work. Only a healthy and perfect economic internal system can leave more flexibility for the government to respond to economic globalization.

The result of economic globalization is bound to be an unprecedented intensification of international competition. China enjoys the following advantages in the international competition. First of all, it has a domestic market with huge potentials. This is the fundamental factor that distinguishes the economy of a big country from that of a small one. As long as the domestic market is unified and competitive, the enormous market scale will provide sufficient market conditions for improving the international competitiveness of newly emerging industries. Secondly, it has a virtually unlimited supply of cheap labor. This will ensure China's competitive advantage of labor-intensive products for a long period of time. Thirdly, it has a high savings rate. This will provide a foundation for huge investments needed for rapid economic development. Fourthly, overseas Chinese all over the world and international trade and financial centers such as Hong Kong will play an extremely important intermediary role in foreign economic activities. All these advantages are the objective basis upon which China has benefited from international competitions over the past twenty years, and they will also be the basis upon which China continues to benefit from international competition in the future.

Reference:

(1) Ji Chongwei, Fang Sheng and Sang Baichuan: "China's Opening to the Outside World at the Turn of the Century – Basic Experience from the 20 Years' Opening to the Outside World," carried in *Reform,* 1, 1999.

(2) Fang Seng: "Cognitive Problems on Raising the Level of Opening to the Outside World," *People's Daily,* November 5, 1998.

(3) Liu Shanzai: "Important Achievements and Basic Experience in China's Opening to the Outside World," *Management World*, No. 2, 1999.

(4) Wu Jinglian: *Contemporary Economic Reform in China: Strategies and Implementation*, Shanghai Far East Press, January 1999.

(5) Jiang Chunze, Chen Yaoting and Lei Da: *China's Transition of Economic System in International Comparison*, Wuhan Press, December 1997.

(6) Qi Yuan: *Twenty Years of China's Opening to the Outside World,* Zhongzhou Ancient Books Press, December 1998.

(7) Yin Jiqing: *Twenty Years of Reform in Foreign Economic Trade in China*, Zhongzhou Ancient Books Press, December 1998.

(8) Zhang Zhuoyuan, Huang Fanzhang and Li Guang'an: *Review of the Twenty Years in Economic Reform and Future Prospects,* China Planning Press, Sep-

tember 1998.

(9) Li Shantong, Zhai Fan and Xu Lin: "Analysis of Influence of Entry into WTO on China," carried in *China Development Study – Selections of Research Reports in the Development Center of the State Council*, ed. by Ma Hong and Wang Mengkui, China Development Press, May 1999.

(10) Xiong Xianliang: "How the Chinese Government Responds to the Challenge of Economic Globalization," carried in *China Development Study – Selections of Research Reports in the Development Center of the State Council*, ed. by Ma Hong and Wang Mengkui, China Development Press, May 1999.

(11) Ma Hong and Wang Mengkui: *China's Economic Situation between 1998 and 1999 and Future Prospects*, China Future Press, April 1999.

(12) Zhou Zhenhua: *System Transformation and Economic Growth – Analysis of China's Experience and Canonical Forms*, Shanghai Sanlian Bookstore, Shanghai People's Press, January 1999.

(13) Di Yinqing and Zheng Gang: "Strategic Thinking Concerning the Entry into the WTO," carried in *Studies in Contemporary Economy*, No. 5, 1999.

(14) Lin Ling, Tang Jie and Feng Subao: "China and the Integration of Global Economy," carried in *Opening Pioneering*, Nos. 2-3, 1998.

(15) Research Project Team of Chinese Society of Macro Economics, State Planning Commission, "Studies Concerning China's Strategic Problems in International Investment and Fund Raising in the Course of Economic Development at the Turn of the Century," carried in *Management World*, No. 1, 1999.

(16) Jiang Xiaojuan: "Utilization of Foreign Capital and the Formal Transformation of Economic Growth," carried in *Management World*, No. 2, 1999.

(17) Guo Shuqing: "Economic Globalization and China's Opening to the Outside World," carried in *International Economic Editorial*, Nos. 5-6, 1999.

(18) Zhou Jianming: "Towards a Better Understanding of the Trend of Economic Globalization and a Higher Level of Opening to the Outside World," carried in *Shanghai Economic Studies*, November 1997.

CHAPTER 6
THE REFORM OF CHINA'S MACROECONOMIC ADMINISTRATIVE SYSTEM

Synopsis

The transition from the old and highly centralized planned economic system to a socialist market economic system in China has brought along great changes in its macroeconomic system. The defects of the old system are mainly twofold. The first is the over-centralization of the administration power, which has hampered the initiative of local governments and enterprises. The second is the egalitarian income distribution system, which is characterized with "everyone eating from the same big pot" or "everyone getting the same reward or pay as everyone else regardless of one's performance in work." Under this egalitarian income distribution system, enterprises and their employees had no material interest concern about the results of their production and operation. Therefore, China's economic reform started from eliminating these two defects: giving away part of the economic administration power to local governments, enterprises and the market; separating the government from enterprises and abolishing the egalitarian income distribution system to create a favorable environment for fair competition among enterprises. Meanwhile, efforts have been made to establish a macroeconomic regulatory system that is in compliance with a market economy. The fiscal and tax system has been reformed and a new system dividing taxes between the central and local governments has been created, which have brought along ini-

tiatives of governments at all levels to manage financial affairs. The income distribution pattern has been readjusted through the fiscal and tax system reform, which has made it possible to follow the principle of giving first priority to efficiency with enough consideration of equity. Moreover, reforms of the financial system have strengthened the role of the central bank in maintaining the national currency stability and an effective financial supervision. Commercialization-oriented reforms of specialized banks have led up to a substantial and steady development of the financial market. On top of all these, the unremitting efforts to curb inflation, to guide the national economy for a "soft landing," to expand domestic demand and to drive up the economic growth have been continuously consummating the macroeconomic regulatory system in which planning, the public finance and the finance are beginning to play mutually coordinated and supportive roles.

Section 1

The Basic Orientation for the Reform of the Macroeconomic Regulatory System

I. Breaking Up the Highly Centralized Administration System, Simplifying the Administration and Delegating Power to Local Governments and Enterprises

Highly centralized administration system is one of the most important features of the traditional planned economic system. The basic theoretical grounding for the formulation of this administration system is that China had established public ownership of the means of production. This should enable the government, which was regarded as the center of management for all social and economic activities, to directly allocate labor and resources in accordance with the demand of the society and realize the equilibrium between demand and supply. Out of this consideration, the whole society was regarded as one big factory, the production planning was unified, the procurement and marketing were monopolized by the state, and their needed labor and personnel were also assigned by the government. It was then believed that this system could dissolve the capitalistic contradiction between socialization of production and private ownership of means of production, and the contradiction between the uncontrolled expansion of production capacity and the limited demand that depended on the purchasing power of the great masses of the people. It was also firmly held that this system could avoid periodic economic crises and realize long-term and steady economic development.

In the early years after the founding of the People's Republic of China, this highly centralized administration system played an important role in concentrating the whole nation's capacity to construct a number of industrial and transportation projects, which laid down a foundation for China's industrialization. In the first Five-Year Plan period, though our national economic strength was very weak, we simultaneously constructed 156 important projects mainly because of the highly centralized system of administration. The successful development of the atomic bomb, hydrogen bomb and artificial satellite in the 1960s as well as the great economic achievements in the 30 years before the start of the reform could all be regarded as the results of bringing the advantage of socialism into full play under the highly centralized system of administration, which made it possible to concentrate strength to accomplish a few big endeavors.

However, with the expansion of the economic scale and the development of the productive forces, this highly centralized system of administration started to show more and more disadvantages. The most important one is that localities have too little power over economic management and the enterprises almost became 'beads of the abacus" that were moved at will by the government. This seriously hampered the initiative of localities and enterprises. Moreover, constant changes and diversification of social demand requires continual readjustment of the production structure in order to meet the demand. Nevertheless, the ever changing and diversifying demand cannot be precisely forecasted or exactly calculated. For this reason, it is never possible to put the enormous and ever changing social production into one unified plan. If one tries to do this impossibility, he or she is doing an exacting but unrewarding task. "Planning cannot catch up with changes," which is a common phenomenon. More often than not, over centralized planning leads up to monotonous mix of products, slow progress in technology and distortion of industrial structure. Additionally, due to interventions of political factors, centralized planning made the national economy to experience one big fluctuation after another and prevented the economic development to reach the planned target. Practice has proven that this highly centralized system of administration has hindered the development of the productive forces.

In 1978, the Third Plenary Session of the Eleventh Party Central Committee restored the Party's sound ideological line, conducted in-depth analysis of the disadvantages of the existing economic system and explicitly pointed out the following. "The realization of the four modernizations requires the expansion of the social productive forces by a large margin, which in turn requires changes in the current production relations, superstructure, administration methods, modes of behaviors and ways of thinking that are incompatible with the growth of productive forces in many aspects. These changes will constitute a profound revolution." Thus, this plenary session of the CPC Central committee decided on the orientation, principles and major tasks of the ensuing reform. From then on, the reform of China's macroeconomic administration system set off the process of continuous important breakthroughs and mutual advancement of perceptual knowledge and practice. For the purpose of simplifying administration and delegating decision-making power, the following reforms have been carried out:

1. Granting Farmers with Decision-making Power in Agricultural Production

China's reform started in the rural areas. Due to the fact that the area of land per capita is too small, agricultural production is still based on manual labor and the output depends to large extent on the initiative of the farmers. Therefore, the reform of the rural economic system should be, in the first place, to change the over-concentration in land operational decision-making power and production planning. As a result, this reform abrogated the system of people's communes, changed the managerial system characterized with three-level ownership in land utilization—the commune, the production brigade and the production team, with the production team being regarded as the foundation, started to pursue a land utilization system featured by household contract responsibility linking remuneration to output and brought about the combination of household operation with unified operation of the collective. This change delegated the decision-making power over agricultural production to rural households. Before 1979, the state issued mandatory plans for 25 major agricultural products, specifying the sown area and total output for them in different regions. In 1985, mandatory agricultural production planning was called off and the output of major agricultural products started to be regulated by guidance plans or the market. Now, the state is encouraging the farmers to produce grains and guiding them to readjust the grain structure through purchasing at protective prices all the grain that the farmers are willing to sell. Transferring the operational decision-making power to households has greatly aroused farmers' initiative in production. From 1978 to 1984, the annual total grain output of the whole country increased from 304.8 million tons to 407.3 million tons, representing an annual growth of 4.95 percent; and the annual amount of grain per capita grew from 318.7 kilograms to 395.5 kilograms, marking an average annual growth of 3.66 percent. This helped solve the problem of feeding the entire population once for all. In 1996, the annual total grain output of the whole country reached 504.5 million tons, and the annual grain per capita reached 414.4 kilos. This means that, if a year sees a bumper harvest, China will have more than enough grain to consume.

2. Enlarging the Decision-making Power of Local Enterprises

In 1984, the Third Plenary Session of the Twelfth Party Central Committee made the "Decision on the Reform of the Economic Structure" and, consequently, the reform spread from the rural areas to urban areas. With the expansion of the decision-making power of local enterprises as the focus, reforms in macroeconomic aspects, such as planning system, material supply system, labor and remuneration system, financial system, commercial and trading system, pricing system and the system of public finance and taxation, were all launched. These reforms resulted in an important step forward in changing the situation of the over-centralization of the administration power of the old economic system. In 1978, the State Council promulgated the "Provisions on Expanding the Operating and Managerial Decision-making Power of State-owned Industrial Enterprises," and later the "Law of Industrial Enterprises Owned by the Whole People," and in 1992 the "Regulations on Reforming the Operating Mechanism of Industrial Enterprises Owned by the Whole People," all of which gradually expanded the decision-making power of enterprises. The decision-making power granted to the enterprises covers production and operation decision-making, product and labor services pricing, product marketing, goods and materials procurement, import and export rights, decision making regarding investment, utilization of retained profits and disposal of assets operated by them, establishment of sub-branches, etc. Such power granted to the enterprises has strengthened their vitality and enabled them to move forward in the direction of independent management, being solely responsible for their gains and losses, bearing their own risks and seeking development on their own. Moreover, the fact that the government gave back the power that should be with enterprises created some conditions for shifting the role of the government.

3. Turning to the Market Matters It Can Handle Better

Under the traditional planned economic system, the government undertook many things that should have been regulated by the market. For example, prices should be formulated through market competition. Only in this way, can prices serve as demand signals as well as the means for competition and can the market play the basic role in allocating resources. Nevertheless, the government priced the overwhelming majority of goods before the reform, and in the total volume of retail sales in the whole society. Of the total income from sales of means of production and the total volume of agricultural and sideline products purchase, 97 percent, 100 percent and 92 percent were priced by the government respectively. Now, the mechanism for the market to form prices has basically established. In the total volume of retail sales in the whole society, the market regulates the prices of 92.5 percent of the goods, in the total income from sales of the means of production, the market regulates 82.1 percent of the goods, and in the total volume of agricultural and sideline produce purchases, 79 percent are regulated by the market. In addition, some matters that can be handled by intermediary organizations have now been handed over to them.

4. Expanding the Economic Administration Power of Local Governments

China has a large population and is vast in territory. The area and population under the jurisdiction of a province are as large as that of a country in Europe. Therefore, it is one of the most important purposes of the reform to mobilize the initiative of the local governments in doing the organizational work for economic construction, encourage them to take better advantage of the favorable conditions in the regions they administer to develop their respective advantages and unique economies under unified national planning and the guidance of the policies of the central government. Before the reform, local governments had very limited power over economic administration. In the process of the reform, their power has got gradually expanded.

A lot of administration power in production, investment, pricing, foreign trade, labor and remuneration, science and technology and social development that used to rest with the central government has now been gradually handed over to local governments. In terms of investment scale, the State Planning Commission reviews and approves large and medium-sized fixed capital investment projects while other departments of the central government or the local governments review and approve smaller projects. In terms of funding requirements, the State Planning Commission was responsible for reviewing and approving projects each of which needed an investment of more than 10 million RMB before 1985. As of 1985, it only took responsibility for examining and approving projects each of which needs an investment of more than 30 million RMB. From 1987, any investment project in energy, transportation and raw material industry to be approved by the State Planning Commission must have an investment demand of more than 50 million RMB. In order to meet the needs of reform and opening up to the outside world, the central government also gradually expanded the investment approving power of local governments in coastal areas. In 1985, the State Council make public a decision stipulating that, if a capital construction project in either Guangdong or Fujian province needs less than 200 million RMB and no help is called for from the central government, it can be approved by the provincial governments after a feasibility report was prepared and submitted to it. In 1988, the State Council made another decision. According to this decision, the Hainan Provincial Government was given the power to grant approval to any construction project requiring an investment of less than 200 million RMB, if conditions for its construction, production, product marketing and foreign exchange needs could be met by the province itself, and if the province was capable of paying back the loans they borrowed. Secondly, if an export-oriented productive project planned to export 70 percent of its products, which did affect the national export quotas, the provincial government could approve it no matter how large the investment requirement was. In 1992, the Sate Council published still another decision, which stipulated that, for an above-norm non-productive project in Pudong of Shanghai, only the project proposal needed to be approved by the State Planning Commission or the State Council itself, the feasibility report and the construction-starting report for the project could be approved by the Shanghai Municipal Government though both the reports were required to be submitted to the State Planning Commission for the record. For a large and medium-sized productive project, which called for less than 200 million RMB, was in compliance with the industrial policy of the central government and did not need the central government to create the conditions for its construction, the Shanghai Municipal Government could approve its feasibility and construction-starting reports after the project proposal was approved by the State Planning Commission.

In order to meet the requirements for expanding the reform and opening toward the outside world, the central government also granted special policies to some areas. In 1985, the State Council stipulated that, a non-productive project in Guangdong and Fujian Provinces that was to be solely funded by foreign investors could be approved by the provincial governments no matter how large the investment requirement was. If a technology introduction project was to be funded with foreign exchanges raised independently by the provinces and requires less than 10 million US dollars, the provincial government concerned could approve it. From 1988 onward, a productive project in Tianjin, Shanghai, Guangdong, Fujian, Beijing, Liaoning, Hebei, Shandong, Jiangsu, Zhejiang, Guangxi or any of the special economic zones, which would be funded by Sino-foreign joint ventures or Sino-foreign partnership enterprises, which requires less than 30 million US dollars, which was in compliance with the state industrial policy and did not need the central government to create conditions for its construction, production and foreign exchange requirements, and the product of which to be exported did not affect the national export quotas, could be approved by the provincial, municipal or regional government concerned. A project in such infrastructure as energy, transportation and telecommunications and in tourism facilities to be funded by foreign investors in Hainan Province could be approved by the provincial government no matter how large the investment requirement was if conditions for its construction and operation did not need to be created by the central government. Other foreign funded investment projects or projects for which the foreign exchange needed would be borrowed and repaid by the province on its own could also be approved by the provincial government if the total investment of each did not exceed 30 million US dollars, the conditions for its construction and operation did not need to be created by the central government and if the export of its products did not affect the national export quotas. The provincial or regional government concerned could also approve similar projects in the provinces and autonomous regions of the hinterland if the investment requirement did not exceed 10 million US dollars each.

In consideration of the special positions and roles of key cities in the economic development, the central government made 14 key and coastal open cities economically independent from their respective provincial governments in terms of planning. From February 1983 to February 1989, the State Council in succession approved Chongqing, Wuhan, Dalian Harbin, Guangzhou, Xi'an, Qingdao, Ningbo, Xiamen, Shenzhen, Nanjing, Chengdu and Changchun to be independent from their respective provincial governments in the national planning and gave them the economic administration power of provincial governments. As such, their economic and social development plans were directly submitted to the State Planning Commission. In order to divide more rationally the economic responsibility and administrative power among the central, provincial/regional/municipalities and districts/county governments, the central government made a decision in July 1993 that, the positions of provincial capital cities independent from their respective provincial governments was to be rescinded except for that of Chongqing, Shenzhen, Dalian, Qingdao, Ningbo and Xiamen. Nevertheless, they could continue to implement the preferential policies offered to coastal open cities.

In order to mobilize the initiative of governments at all levels to manage money matters and to break up the highly centralized budgeting system that was characterized with unified revenue and unified spending, the central government started to implement a local public financial responsibility system known as "separation of revenue and spending, dividing revenue responsibilities among all levels of the government," "Dividing Taxes, Checking and Ratifying Revenues and Spending, Sharing Revenue Responsibilities and Spending Constraints Among All Levels of the Government". However, in minority nationality regions, prominently less developed areas, coastal open cities and cities economically independent from their provincial governments, special budgetary administration system was practiced. Meanwhile, a township budgetary administration system was established and consummated.

In March 1985, the State Council promulgated "Regulations for Implementation of the Policy of Dividing Taxes, Checking and Ratifying Revenues and Spending, Sharing Revenue Responsibilities and Spending Constraints among All Levels of the Government." This document stipulated different taxes to be collected by different levels of the government and started to change the old method of dividing revenue sources on the basis of the subordination relationship between enterprises and different levels of the government. This was a significant step forward to a complete implementation of the tax division system.

In July 1988, the State Council issued a "Decision on Methods for Local Governments' Fulfillment of Their Responsibilities for the Public Finance." In accordance with this decision, the whole country was classified into 37 different types of areas that would implement different financial responsibility systems, including progressive revenue increase responsibility system, total revenue sharing system, total revenue sharing system when the total revenue is more than the planned, progressive revenue turnover increase responsibility system, revenue turnover quota system and subsidy quota system, etc. These methods gave considerations to the different realities of different areas and are conducive to solve the problem of disparity in revenue sources among different areas. Since the base of revenue as the responsibility of and the spending budgetary constraint on a level of government was to remain unchanged for several years, this decision is conducive not only to the expansion of the local government's decision-making power and but also to the mobilization of their initiatives in increasing revenue and saving expenditures. Nevertheless, this reform was not based on a rational design of classification of taxes but on the subordination relationship between the government and enterprises. Moreover, the categorization of spending was based not on "factor method" but on the "base method"; the substantial part of the increased revenue will go to the local public finance. Along with the economic development, the proportion of the revenue of the central government would become lower.

Although the above reforms played a positive role in breaking the highly centralized fiscal system and in strengthening the local financial capacities, some problems became increasingly evident. First of all, the fiscal system was not standardized and well-regulated, failing to reflect the principle of equity and efficiency. Secondly, the ensuing fiscal responsibility system was likely to lead to regional protectionism and blockade, which was unfavorable for the formation of a unified national market. Thirdly, the fiscal system and tax system was incongruent with each other. Local governments sometimes went beyond their power to reduce or exempt taxes, leading up to heavy losses of the state revenue. Fourthly, such a system could hardly reverse the trend of decreasing proportion of the total revenue in GNP and decreasing proportion of the Central Government's revenue in the total revenue. Consequently, the state's financial capability of macroeconomic regulation would be unavoidably undermined. These problems could be better resolved only through a tax division system.

The major purposes of pursuing a tax division system are the following two. The first is to establish a standardized income distribution relationship between the central and local governments so as to ensure a balance between the financial power and authority of office at various levels of the government; realize an organic combination of responsibility, power and interest; and eliminate the arbitrariness in the distribution of the financial sources among the different levels of government. The second is to gradually increase the proportion of the total revenue in GNP and that of the central government's revenue in the total state revenue to an appropriate extent so as to strengthen the ability of the Central Government in macroeconomic regulation.

The implementation of the tax division system roughly includes the following five steps.

1) Expenditure of the government at different levels is determined on the basis of the specification of their duties and responsibilities. The expenditure of the central government includes such items as capital construction investment, investment in technical transformation and new product development in enterprises under its direct administration, and geological prospecting investment. Other expenditures to be paid out of the central government's public finance include cost of national defense, cost of armed police, cost of diplomacy, aids to other countries, repayment of both the capital and the interest of domestic and foreign debts owed by the central government, cost of public security organs, procuratorial organs and people's courts, and operating expenses of such undertakings as cultural activities, education, health care and science. Expenditures out of local governments' public finance include local capital construction investment, cost of technical transformation and new product development conducted in enterprises under their ad-

ministration, expenses of supporting the agriculture, expenses of urban maintenance and construction, cost of such undertakings as local cultural activities, education, health care and science, cost of local governments' administration, cost of local public security organs, procuratorial organs and people's courts, part of the cost of armed police, cost of people's militia, price subsidies and other relevant costs.

2) The fiscal revenue is distributed to different levels of the government on the basis of their respective duties and responsibilities and scope of expenditure, and in accordance with the principle of consistence of financial power with duties/responsibilities as well as of consistence between revenue and expenditure.

The fixed sources of the public finance of the central government include tariff, consumption tax and value-added tax collected by the Customs, consumption tax, income tax from enterprises and companies under its direct jurisdiction, income tax from non-banking financial institutions, revenue (including business tax, income tax, profit and urban maintenance and construction tax) from head offices of railway and insurance companies and banks, profit from enterprises and companies under its direct administration. Besides the already-paid 20 percent drawback of export duties by foreign trade companies, local public finance will be responsible for all the export tax reimbursement incurred thereafter.

Fixed revenue sources of the local government include business tax (excluding that from head offices of railway, insurance companies and banks), income tax from enterprises and companies under its jurisdiction (excluding income tax from non-banking financial institutions), profit turnover from local enterprises and companies, individual income tax, urban land use tax, fixed-assets investment orientation regulation tax, arable land taking tax, deed tax, inheritance and assignment tax, land appreciation tax, and revenue from compensated use of state-owned land.

Revenue shared by the central and local finance include value-added tax, resources tax and securities transfer tax. 75 percent of the value-added tax is distributed to the central public finance while the other 25 percent go to the local public finance. Resources tax is divided according to types of resources, with tax from marine oil resources going to the central public finance and that from other resources to the local public finance. The securities transfer tax, on the other hand, is equally divided between the central and local public finances.

3) The base for revenue and expenditure of the local public finance has been reasonably determined. The fiscal and tax system reform in 1994 set the revenue and expenditure of the local finance in 1993 as the base for measurement.

4) The revenue turnover to the central government and the subsidies from the central to the local government has been scientifically appraised and ratified. On the condition that the central public finance holds a dominant portion of the total revenue, the policy of returning part of the revenue turnover or transfer payment from the central government to local governments should be pursued.

5) Authorities for collecting taxes set aside as the sources of the central government's revenue (known as state taxes) and those for collecting taxes as the sources of the local government's revenue (known as local taxes) have been separately established in compliance with the tax division system. Central taxation authorities are responsible for collecting those shared taxes as well as central taxes, with set proportions of the shared taxes returned to local governments later. And local taxation authorities are responsible for collecting local taxes.

The implementation of the tax division system has achieved the expected effects. The state revenue has witnessed significant growth in successive years and the proportion of the revenue of the central government in the total revenue has started to grow. With further specification of the duties and responsibilities of the central government and of those of local governments, the revenue distribution relationship among different levels of the government is being standardized. This has laid down a solid foundation for the establishment and stabilization of a rational relationship between the central and local governments and for bringing the initiatives of the localities into full play under the unified leadership of the central government.

II. Breaking the "Big Pot" of the State and Introducing Com-

petition Mechanisms

One of the main features of the old macroeconomic system was that enterprises could eat from the same "big rice pot" provided by the state. The success in breaking up this old system and creating mechanisms for competition among enterprises so as to bring their initiatives in production, operation and new product development has marked a breakthrough in the macroeconomic system reform.

Posing most difficulties to the reform was the traditional ideology and customary habits. For decades, state-owned enterprises have been used to relying on the care of the government, producing whatever and whatever amount in accordance with the national plan. Their products were allocated and transferred by the government, their profits were handed over to the government, their needed fund was applied for from the government, and the government assigned their employees. Consequently, enterprise management was confined to the management of production process. Through long years' practice of such a centralized system, state-owned enterprises had become "caged tigers" that had neither competitiveness nor ability to survive. They were plagued with problems of poor adaptability to the market demand, shortage of R & D capability, backward management and over redundancy. In the face of competition from foreign-funded companies, joint ventures and township enterprises, they were bogged down in a very awkward situation. This led some foreign economists to the conclusion that China did not have enterprises in the true sense. On the other hand, the government set up a lot of departments to administrate enterprises. These government departments undertook nearly all the operating and managerial activities, which not only stifled the vitality of enterprises, but also distracted government's attention and efforts from solving problems in macroeconomic regulation and the development of public utilities. The consequence was the dislocation of the government role and the role of enterprises.

In order to break the "big pot" of the government available to state-owned enterprises and push them to the market, the State Council issued in 1979 "Stipulations on State-owned Enterprises' Retention of

Part of Their Profits." In accordance with this document, state-owned enterprises were allowed to establish their own production development fund, employee welfare fund and staff award fund with their retained profits. In 1981, various profit retaining and profit/loss responsibility systems started to be implemented to build up a link between economic performance and benefits of enterprises and their employees. These systems prompted employees to care for the economic performance of their enterprises out of the consideration of their own material benefits and bored a little hole in the "big pot."

In order to stabilize the profit distribution relationship between the state and enterprises and to overcome the defects of the existing profit turnover system, efforts have been made to explore for ways of gradually introducing income tax into profit distribution. In 1983, the State Council ratified and referred to all governmental organs the "Provisional Measures for Converting Profit of State-owned Enterprises into Tax" submitted by the Ministry of Finance and income tax started to be collected across the country in June that year. Large and medium-sized enterprises with any profit should pay income tax at the rate of 55 percent of their profit. Profit after tax was partly delivered to the state and partly retained by the enterprise. This was the first step of converting profits into tax.

The second step of the reform known as "converting profit into tax" was taken in September 1984. By categorizing the original industrial and commercial tax into a number of new taxes according to the respective natures of taxpayers and levying an income tax of 55 percent on the profits of large and medium-sized enterprises with any profit, income tax was started to be calculated and collected from state-owned enterprises in accordance with the newly designed eight graduated rates of their extra profit. In addition, adjustment tax rates were checked and ratified separately according to the different situations of different enterprises. Meanwhile, after the start of the levy of income tax, enterprises should be fully responsible for their own profits and losses and the state would not appropriate any fund to them. The criteria for judging whether an enterprise was a small one were loosened to an appropriate degree and enterprises continued to be required to repay loans before paying tax and to set aside part of their profits as contributions to two types of funds. The second step of the reform for the purpose of converting profit into tax has greatly increased the financial strengths of enterprises, strengthened their vitality, improved their capability to develop themselves and stabilized the sources of the state revenue. Nevertheless, due to the fact that the income tax rate was too high and that different enterprise had different adjustment tax rates, the ensuing situation was described as "whipping the fastest ox." More seriously, the stipulation requiring enterprises to repay their loans and set aside part of their earnings as contributions to two types of funds before paying taxes further complicated the relationship between the government and enterprises.

During the process of converting profit into tax, some enterprises and sectors continued to practice the income distribution system referred to as profit-loss responsibility system. This included profit turnover's progressive increase responsibility system, input and output responsibility system, profit-loss responsibility system practiced in loss-making and marginal profit-making enterprises, profit sharing system practiced in civil aviation and post-telecommunication industries, total input and output responsibility system practiced in oil and petrochemical industry and in the Ministry of Metallurgical Industry, and the output responsibility system practiced in the National Nonferrous Metal Corporation.

The fiscal and tax system reform in 1994 eliminated adjustment tax, contributions to the above-mentioned two types of funds and various responsibility systems, unified the income tax rate for domestic enterprises and started to implement a proportional tax rate of 33 percent. For enterprises with a narrow profit margin, preferential income tax rates of 27 percent and 18 percent were granted within a certain period of time. This reform was a major step towards in breaking the government's big rice pot from which enterprises used to ladle their food and in creating fair competition among state-owned enterprises.

III. A Macroeconomic Regulatory System Was Established and Consummated

The process of reforming the macroeconomic regulatory system has been a combination of destruction and construction. Sometimes destruction came before construction, sometimes the vice verse is true and while in other case destruction and construction happened at the same time. If the above-mentioned simplification of administration, decentralization of decision-making power and breaking of the big rice pot can be regarded as destruction of the old macroeconomic regulatory system, it is imperative to establish and consummate a new macroeconomic regulatory system that is capable of meeting the requirements of a socialist market economy.

1. Market Economy Needs Macroeconomic Regulation

The Fourteenth National Congress of the Communist Party of China (CPC) in 1992 put forward the reform target of constructing a socialist market economy, bringing reform into a new era. In 1993, the Third Plenary Session of the Fourteenth Central Committee of the CPC passed "Decision on Some Issues Concerning the Establishment of a Socialist Market Economic Structure." The decision outlined the framework of a socialist market economic system that should be established, highlighted the objective requirements of changing the government's roles and establishing and consummating a healthy macroeconomic regulatory system, and discussed the absolute necessity of such a sound system. The major tasks of macroeconomic regulation include maintaining overall economic equilibrium, promoting the optimization of economic structures, guiding the national economy to develop in a sustained, rapid and healthy way, and advancing overall social progress. Macroeconomic regulation shall mainly rely on economic means and large steps forward shall be made in in-depth reforms of the taxation, financial, investment and planning systems to strengthen the comprehensive coordination in economic operation. Planning should make clear the objectives and major tasks of the national economy and the social development in addition to the required supportive economic policies. The central bank should aim at the stability of the value of the national currency as the priority target by readjusting money supply and maintaining international balance of payments. The public finance should focus on readjusting the economic structure and income distribution in the society through budgeting and taxation. Monetary and fiscal policies should be utilized in coordination with industrial policies to maintain a basic equilibrium between the aggregate demand and aggregate supply to promote a coordinated economic and social development.

A market economy needs macroeconomic regulation, which is determined by its objective laws. Under market economic conditions, the law of value prevails in all economic activities and the allocation of means of production depends on value movement. Compared with allocation of resources by administrative means under the traditional planned economic system, allocation of resources by the law of value is far more effective and efficient. Nevertheless, market is by no means omnipotent. It has inherent shortcomings of spontaneity and blindness. The market itself can not solve problems in such areas as maintenance of the aggregate equilibrium, income distribution and social security. Macroeconomic regulation has to make up for the dysfunction of the market and its inherent shortcomings. In addition, without a stable economic and social environment, the market can hardly function well. If an economy rises and falls dramatically and prices keep jumping up and down, the lever of the value shall not play the normal role. Macroeconomic regulatory policies of a developing country have extremely important roles to play in implementing strategies of catching up with developed countries. Only by effective macroeconomic regulation, can economic policies capable of promoting sustainable, healthy and rapid economic development be formulated and correct development strategies be implemented. The necessity of macroeconomic regulation has been proven by both developed economies and newly emerging economies. All market economies have their own unique macroeconomic regulatory systems. The most important reason for the rapid economic development of new industrialized countries is their formulation and implementation of correct development strategies in addition to their microeconomic vitality. Our country has a large population but a weak economic basis and unbalanced regional development. Only by implementing macroeconomic regulatory policies can we bring market competition into correct play, coordinate various contradictions in the process of the economic development, maintain the stability of our macroeconomic situation and create a good macroeconomic environment for the realization of our modernization.

2. Improving the Macroeconomic Regulatory System

The transition from the traditional planned economic to a socialist market economic system calls for the establishment of a new type of macroeconomic regulatory system. From 1992 when the reform target of establishing a socialist market economic system was proposed until now, we have kept exploring for effective means of macroeconomic regulation in the practice of cubing inflation and expanding domestic demand to establish and consummate an effective macroeconomic regulatory system. As a result, great changes have been achieved in both reform and development.

Under the guidance of Deng Xiaoping's talks given on his south China inspection tour and the spirit of the Fourteenth National Congress of the Communist Party of China, the step of China's economic development and reform was obviously accelerated in 1992. In the first half of 1993, China's GDP, total value of industrial output, value of fixed assets investment and total value of retail sales of consumer goods grew by 13.9 percent, 25.1 percent, 61 percent and 21.6 percent respectively, compared with the same period of the previous year. These striking indexes were clear signs of economic overheating. The major problems identified were as follows. The first was that, aggregate demand was growing too fast that it had largely exceeded the aggregate supply. The second was the irrational economic structure. With the rapid expansion of stock market, futures transactions and real estate industry, the development of infrastructure and basic industries lagged far behind. The most outstanding contradiction was the constraint of transportation as a bottleneck on the economic development. The third problem was the chaotic situation in the financial sector characterized with unregulated massive fund-raising and short-term loans, uncontrolled establishment of financial institutions, overheating in establishing development zones, and overheated real estate development. All these further deteriorated the unbalance between the aggregate demand and aggregate supply and further distorted the economic structure. The fourth problem was resulted from various irrational tax exemptions, reductions and evasions, which led up to large-scale drainage on the revenue. The fifth one was the unbalance between import and export, with export increasing by 4.4 percent and import 23.2 percent, resulting in drastic devaluation of RMB and great pressure on keeping international balance of payment.

In order to resolve the above-mentioned problems in the economic life and prevent further deterioration of the overall economic situation, the CPC Central Committee opportunely issued a "Circular on Strengthening and Improving Macroeconomic Regulatory Methods" in late June 1993. Then a number of macroeconomic regulatory measures were taken.

In the financial sector, fund-raising activities in violation of state regulations were prohibited, issuance of various types of bonds and particularly the issuance of local policy bonds were put under strict control, unauthorized financial institutions were ordered to be closed or integrated into authorized ones within deadlines and black market of priced securities was forbidden. In addition, money supply was strictly controlled. The People's Bank of China stopped lending to non-banking financial institutions, started to retrieve within deadlines loans lent in violation of relevant regulations, raised deposit and loan interest rates twice in succession, and cancelled the right of provincial branch offices of all banks to increase or decrease loans by 7 percent. It was also stipulated that any fund-raising should not offer an interest rate higher than that of the T-bonds in the same period in order to give priority to the issuance of treasury bonds and bonds for key projects construction.

In terms of financial and taxation administration, tax collection and supervision were strengthened, tax exemptions and reductions out of ultra vires authorization were removed, policies of exempting and reducing contributions to "Energy and Transportation Fund" and "Budget Readjustment Fund" were all declared invalid, the too rapid growth of institutional purchasing power was controlled, budget for meetings was cut by 20 percent, and study tours and investment attracting activities by way of exhibitions in other countries were also strictly controlled.

In terms of foreign exchange administration, stipulations for foreign exchange turnover were consummated, overseas investments and other types of capital outflow were strictly scrutinized and approved, hundreds of millions of US dollars were sold at foreign exchange markets home and abroad to exercise a large-scale intervention in prices of foreign exchanges, the circulation of foreign currencies at the domestic market was restricted, and speculations in foreign exchanges was forbidden.

In order to control the scale of the investments in fixed assets, ongoing projects were checked up, new projects were put under rigid review and approval procedures, and the real estate market regulation was strengthened.

In order to control price hikes, it was forbidden to increase the prices of commodities and services regulated by the state; local price readjustments were suspended; and the food risk fund and non-staple food readjustment fund were established.

The above macroeconomic regulatory policies achieved their planned effects. The economic overheating was basically put under control, financial order took an obvious turn for the better, with illegal fund-raising, money-lending and establishment of financial institutions basically put under control, and with half of the short-term loans illegally lent retrieved. Measures taken to check up real estate and development zones effectively curbed speculations and economic bubbles. The stock market became stable and the heat in real estate industry started to cool down.

In order to consolidate the above achievements and enable the existing macroeconomic regulatory system to meet the requirements of the socialist market economic system, the CPC Central Committee and the State Council resolutely launched a series of important reforms of the macroeconomic regulatory system in such areas as taxation, financial management, and foreign exchange and price administration systems in 1994. In spite of the broad coverage and difficulties and risks involved in this big endeavor, all the reforms progressed smoothly, owing to sufficient preparation, good implementation and coordination of mutually supportive measures and correct handling of new problems arising in the process. As a result, the timely establishment of the new macroeconomic regulatory system consolidated and expanded the accomplishments of the macroeconomic regulation and control. In 1995, a series of relevant macroeconomic regulatory measures were taken to curb inflation. Among the major measures taken, the first was the implementation of an appropriately tight fiscal and monetary policy: the scale of investment in fixed assets continued to be under control, new projects were held under strict control, bank loans for investment in fixed assets were strictly controlled in accordance with the national plan, and on-going projects were checked up. Secondly, fund for consumption was controlled to prevent it from growing too rapidly, and salary increase; arbitrary bonus and subsidy distributions were all prohibited. Thirdly, the circulation order was streamlined and prices were regulated and supervised, and the major role of state-owned trading enterprises and supply and marketing cooperatives in stabilizing the market and controlling prices was emphasized. Important goods reserve system and price risk fund were established at both the central and local levels to strengthen the state's capability of regulating the market. In order to strengthen agriculture, governors' "rice bag" responsibility system, mayor's "vegetable basket" responsibility system, the related price control target responsibility systems and urban non-staple food supply bases were established to guarantee adequate supply of food and vegetables. Moreover, import was utilized to readjust the domestic supply capacity. Finally, market regulations were promulgated to standardize pricing behavior at the market and strengthen supervision of prices.

The macroeconomic regulation in the several consecutive years not only promoted a sustained, rapid and healthy development of the national economy but also effectively solved such outstanding problems of overheated investment, excessive consumption growth, financial disorder, too much money supply and unduly high inflation. As a result, China's economy successfully achieved a "soft landing" and started to move on an appropriately rapid and relatively steady track. The successful macroeconomic regulation ensured the fulfillment of the Eighth five-year Plan, making those five years a period with the fastest economic growth and the least fluctuation since the founding of the new

China and created a good start for the Ninth Five-Year Plan period.

In the advent of the successful economic "soft landing," the problem of demand shortage occurred. To make things worse, the Asian financial crisis broke out in the second half of 1997, touching off a massive craze of currency devaluation and drastic foreign trade reduction in China's neighboring countries and regions, which had serious impact on China's economic development. As a response to such a situation in order to maintain the sustained and rapid economic growth, China's central government resolutely decided to adopt the policy of expanding domestic demand early 1998. Treasury bonds worth 100 billion RMB were issued and bank loans worth the same amount were provided to support agriculture, forestry and water conservancy projects, transportation, telecommunication and urban and rural power networking projects, state-owned grain reserve warehouses' construction projects, economical housing projects and ecological and civil capital construction projects in urban areas. In 1999, the effort in expanding domestic demand was further strengthened, active fiscal policies continued to be followed, and more treasury bonds were issued to support the on-going infrastructure projects, technological transformation in enterprises, environmental protection projects and construction of schooling facilities to meet the requirements of the expansion of university enrollment. In the first half of 1999, the central bank took measures to increase money supply. From 1998 to the second half of 1999, it lowered the interest rates by wide margins on four consecutive occasions, rescinded its control over the size of loans by commercial banks, increased re-loaning to rural credit cooperatives and extended the floating range interest rates for loans to small and medium-sized enterprises. In order to increase the supply of the basic money, the central bank improved the deposit reserve system, expanded open market transactions of treasury bonds and financial bonds, and strengthened its operations at the money market. With the support of these measures, the national economy has managed to maintain a relatively high rate of growth despite the steadily dropping commodity prices in the past over 20 months.

The macroeconomic regulatory system has been continuously improved from the time of curbing inflation to the time of expanding domestic demand. The coordinated and mutually supportive operation of the three regulatory means of planning, public finance and finance has enhanced the efficiency of macroeconomic regulation. To summarize the macroeconomic regulatory system and its operational mechanism in the past years, the following features are predominant.

(1) Macroeconomic Regulating Target System Was Scientifically Determined by Annual Planning.

In the first place, macroeconomic regulation must have well-defined targets. Then all the regulatory means can operate around the targets in a mutually supportive and efficient way. At the end of each year, the central government would hold economic working meetings, analyzing the economic situation, suggesting targets and related policy measures for economic development in the next year, and formulating a draft annual plan for discussion by the annual meeting of the National People's Congress. The core of the annual plan includes eight macroeconomic regulatory targets. They are rate of economic growth, total investment in fixed assets, limits of price hikes, total volume of import and export, state revenue and expenditure, money supply, registered urban unemployment rate and population growth rate. These eight indexes impact and constrain each other, which constitute an overall reflection of the actual operation of the national economy. In-depth analysis and scientific forecast of the trend of economic development are the basis for setting the eight targets feasibly. The draft plan is usually discussed in great detail by the State Planning and Development Commission and other relevant departments and then finalized by the State Council with sufficient consultation with experts. After its approval by the National People's Congress, the plan would take on legal force, obliging various government departments and authorities to go all out for its fulfillment. In this sense, the annual plan is the basis for macroeconomic regulation and for the coordination of various regulatory means.

(2) Regulatory Measures Were Opportunely Adopted in Response to New Situations in the Operation of the National Economy.

Unexpected situations often occur in the process of the economic operation. The macroeconomic regulatory system should be able to detect and track these new situations in order to opportunely readjust policy orientations for the purpose of fulfilling the macroeconomic regulatory goals. In the event that the economy is heavily influenced by unexpected factors, targets for macroeconomic regulation may have to be revised accordingly; the revised macroeconomic regulatory goals need to be approved by the Standing Committee of the National People's Congress. Whether the macroeconomic regulatory system can correctly respond to unexpected situations is a test of its efficiency.

The eruption of the Asian financial crisis in the second half of 1997 created strong negative impact on China's export. Since 1998, the state has employed a series of regulatory measures to offset the negative impact. These measures include the implementation of an active fiscal policy, issuance of treasury bonds, strengthening infrastructure construction, the policy of encouraging private investment, improving the financial services for small and medium-sized enterprises, raising salary, subsidies to temporarily laid-off workers, unemployment benefits and living security line, readjusting prices, stopping unreasonable fee collection, providing consumption loans to stimulate consumption, accelerating urban and rural housing system reform to cultivate housing industry into a new economic growth point, expanding university enrollment, raising the rate of export tax drawback, strengthening export credit support, expanding the areas in which foreign investors are allowed to invest, granting more preferential policies to attract foreign investment, etc. The timely adoption of these measures has played an important role in solving the problem of insufficient demand and in maintaining the sustained, rapid and healthy economic development. Judging from the present situation, we can say that a set of effective means for curbing inflation and for enabling economic soft landing have been found. Nevertheless, no effective means for expanding domestic demand, for increasing private investment and for encouraging consumption still remain to be looked for.

(3) Fiscal, Monetary, Investment, Consumption, Export and Income Distribution Policies Have Been in Close Coordination.

The various economic levers for macroeconomic regulation constitute a unified and interrelated whole. They work best when they are well coordinated with each other. During the process of curbing the inflation from 1993 to 1996, monetary policies played a larger role. While on the one hand, fiscal policies have played a larger role in the efforts of stimulating domestic demand and driving up the economic growth in the past few years. However, in view of the continuing price downfall and the deteriorating deflation in the past two years or so, monetary policies should have played a larger role. For example, a much more important purpose of exercising active fiscal policies and promoting the construction of key projects by T-bond issuance is to bring along more bank lending, more private investment and higher consumption growth. Nevertheless, active fiscal policies implemented in the recent two years have failed to achieve the expected stimulating effect. This has greatly weakened the expected effects of the policies for expanding domestic demand.

(4) Macroeconomic Regulatory Policies Sometimes May Fail to Be Effective.

Macroeconomic regulatory policies do not always arrive at expected targets. Sometimes, regulatory and control measures meet with very prominent effects and in some cases they do not work at all. From the implementation of macroeconomic policies in recent years, policies designed to control demand have in general worked very well. While on the other hand, those for stimulating demand and for increasing efficient supply, though having worked well in the time characterized with shortage of supply, have met with relatively much larger difficulty to reach their designed goals under the condition of buyers' market. For instance, the central bank has lowered the interest rates for seven times on running in the hope that consumption and investment could increase. To the dismay of policy makers, individual savings deposits still keep rising vigorously with weak market sales and little investment desire. For another example, the central bank wanted bank loans to be increased by increasing basic money supply. However, owing to the constraint of insufficient effective market demand, money supply could not increase as expected and it was also difficult to see any meaningful increase of bank lending. This is a problem that has never occurred since the founding of the People's Republic. This fact shows that the implementation of regulatory policies needs other supportive policies and policy transfer mechanisms as well as a favorable economic and social environment. Otherwise, a regulatory policy can hardly receive desired social response. As a new problem in macroeconomic regulation, regulatory failures deserve further study.

Section 2

Reform of the Planning System

The reform of the planning system in the past two decades has made great progress. This reform can be divided into two periods. The first period is from 1978 to 1993, with a focus on reforming the highly centralized planning system whereas the second period is from 1993 to date. This has been an era of innovations in planning system, planning contents and planning methodology for the purpose of establishing a new planning system that accommodates the requirements of a socialist market economy.

I. Major Contents of Reform of the Planning System Prior to 1993

Before 1993, China's planning system reform was mainly reflected in greatly reducing plans of mandatory nature and improving plans of the nature of guidance, making plans of the nature of guidance gradually become the major form of planning and enabling the market to play a larger role in a wide range of areas.

1. Production Planning

Before 1979, the state made mandatory plans on the production of 25 kinds of major agricultural products, including sub-plans on the output and sown area for these agricultural products in every region. After the Third Plenary Session of the Eleventh Party Central Committee, mandatory planning was gradually reduced, which was no longer in existence by 1985. At the end of 1993, the state administered only the total output of nine kinds of agricultural products, including grain, cotton, oil-yielding crops, sugar, tobacco, meat, aquatic products, afforestation area and natural rubber.

The state mandatory planning in industrial production was reduced year by year as the following table shows.

Industrial Products Administered by the State Planning Commission by Mandatory Planning

Year	Number of Industrial Products Produced under Mandatory Planning	Percentage of the Value of the Total National Industrial Output (percent)
1980	120	40
1985	60	20
1992	59	11.7
1993	36	6.8

From 1985, the state continued to administer by mandatory planning only the volume of key materials transported by rail, volume of boat freight by enterprises under the direct leadership of ministries and handling capacity of major coastal cities. It started to administer by guidance planning the volume of road haulage, handling capacity of other ports, volume of barge freight, total cargo transportation turnover by civil aviation and business volume of post and telecommunication.

2. Commodity Circulation Planning

There were 256 types of commodities under the unified allocation by the State Planning Commission in 1979. This number was reduced to 20 or so in 1985 and 19 in 1990. Though this number remained the same as in 1992, the percentage of commodities in terms of value under unified allocation decreased by a large margin. In 1993 this number came down to 12.

In 1979, the number of first-category commodities purchased and dispatched in accordance with the state planning was 65. This number was reduced to 23 in 1987 and further down to 15 in 1993. Among the 15, 13 were purchased and dispatched by mandatory planning while 2 by guidance planning.

Changing Proportions of Key Materials under Unified Allocation in GDP (%)

Year	Steel Products	Timber	Cement	Coal
1979	77.1	85.0	35.7	58.9
1984	62.3	44.4	24.1	49.0
1990	41.6	30.7	13.1	50.4
1991	40.7	25.9	11.0	52.5
1992	34.3	19.5	6.9	49.5
1993	19.9	9.9	4.5	49.2

3. Price Regulation

The purpose of the pricing regulation reform was to bring back the role of the market in the formation of prices. In 1992, the State Price Control Administration lifted price controls over 571 types of products and delegated to provincial authorities the power to control the prices of 22 kinds of products. By the end of 1992, the State Administration of Commodity Prices and other relevant central authorities directly controlled the prices of only 89 means of industrial production, down from 737 at the end of 1991. Among the 89, only 33 were priced by the state. In 1993, the control over the prices of most of steel products and 200 million tons of coal under unified allocation was also lifted. Towards the end of 1992, the State Administration of Commodity Prices and other related central authorities only directly controlled the prices of nine kinds of agricultural products, five of which were priced by the state while the other 4 priced with reference to the state guidance plan. In 1993, both the purchasing and selling prices of all types of grains were basically liberalized. By the end of 1992, only 5.9 percent of the goods in the total volume of retail sales of the whole society, 12.5 percent of the total sales of agricultural products sold by farmers and 18.7 percent of the total sales of means of production sold by industrial enterprises were priced by the state.

4. Foreign Trade

In 1980, more than 900 kinds of export commodities were under the coordination and control of the State Planning Commission. This number was reduced to 31 in 1985 and 29 in 1991. In 1993, the "Provisional Regulations on Export Commodity Administration" was put into force. The total number of export commodities under the administration of the state by way of export quotas and licenses was 138. Among the 138, planned quotas controlled 38, initiative quotas 54, ordinary licenses 54 and passive quotas 38. The proportion of export commodities under the control of licenses in the total volume of export was reduced from 66 percent to 30.5 percent.

5. Social Development

The State Planning Commission used to make the overall national labor and wage plan, specifying the total employment and total amount of wages for the whole country, issuing labor and wage plans to different sectors and departments in different regions that were owned by the whole people, and promulgating separate wage quotas for state organs, institutions and enterprises for quantitative control purposes. In 1993, formerly promulgated labor and wage quotas were reformed and some new quotas taking the whole society into account were added, linking the number of employees and the payroll to GNP and indexes of economic performance. At the same time, the coverage of the issued plans extended from the total number of employees and the payroll of organizations owned by the whole people to those of organizations of other types of ownership. Except for the stipulation that payroll increase should not exceed the planned quotas, other quotas were not distributed among the levels of the governments. They were issued only for monitoring and guiding purposes. Local plans for changing rural permanent residence into urban permanent residence were submitted by provincial and municipal planning commissions to the State Planning Commission. After being balanced in consideration of the overall national situation, they were included in the national plan and then issued separately to different regions as directive plans.

Education started to be administered by both mandatory and directive plans. That is to say, part of the enrollment plan is mandatory and part of it is directive. To be more specific, the state only gives directive plans to each region for the number of students who are trusted by employers to be educated in higher learning institutions and those who are self-sponsored.

The plans for health care, culture, broadcasting, film production, TV work, physical culture, social security, etc., though all included in the national plan, are only directive plans.

With the great-scale reduction of the areas administered by mandatory state plans, the number of areas under local administrations by mandatory plans is also obviously reduced.

II. The Planning System Reform since 1993

With the continuous deepening of the economic system reform during the Eighth Five-Year Plan period and particularly after 1993, the planning system reform entered a stage of institutional innovation, the major purpose of which is to establish a new planning system that complies with a socialist market economy. During this period, the following progress has been made:

1. The Scope of Coverage by Mandatory Planning Has Been Gradually Reduced

(1) Production

In the area of agricultural production, all the mandatory plans were abolished in 1985 and the state now only issues directive plans for nine kinds of major agricultural products, including grain, cotton, oil-yielding crops, sugar-yielding crops, tobacco, meat, aquatic products, area of qualified, afforestation and natural rubber. In the area of industrial production, the number of industrial products produced under the state mandatory planning was further reduced from 36 in 1993 to 12 in 1998. The value of these 12 kinds of industrial products takes up only 4.1 percent of the national total industrial output.

(2) Commodity Circulation

As mentioned before, the number of goods and materials that were allocated by the State Planning Commission through a unified plan was already reduced to 12 in 1993, from which this number has been further reduced. Since 1998, only part of five kinds of productive means, such as crude oil, refined oil, coal, natural gas and automobiles, were distributed by a unified plan.

(3) Price Regulation

Mechanisms with which the market mainly determines prices have been established. At present, the prices of almost all commodities and services are determined by the market, except for those few monopolistic public utilities and crucial commodities that concern the lifeline of the national economy and people's basic livelihood and that are not suitable for market competition. In 1996, the value of goods whose prices were regulated by the market came up to 92.5 percent of the total retail sales in the whole society, the value of goods which were priced in accordance with the state guidance was as low as 1.2 percent, and that of the goods which were priced by the government was only 6.3 percent. Among the means of production, only such crucial goods as petroleum, electric power and chemical fertilizers were priced by the government and the prices of the rest were all regulated by the market. To be more exact, the value of means of production whose prices were determined by the market amounted to 81.1 percent of the total sales of means of production, the value of those means of production whose prices were determined in accordance with the state guidance was as small as 4.9 percent, and that of those means of production which were priced by the government was only 14 percent. In the total volume of agricultural and sideline products purchased by the government, 79 percent were priced by the market, 4.1 percent was priced in accordance with the government's guidance, and only 16.9 percent was priced directly by the government.

(4) Investment in Fixed Assets

Investment decision-making power of enterprises and local governments has been further expanded. To date, the value of investment in fixed assets planned by the central authorities has been lowered to 20 percent of the total across the nation.

(5) Foreign Trade and Foreign Exchanges

In 1994, mandatory plans for the total volume of imports and exports were completely cancelled. At the same time, enterprises' autonomy over foreign trade was further expanded. Import and export quotas and the number of import and export licenses were both reduced. The operational areas of important and export enterprises were liberalized. Except for a few kinds of important or special commodities, the state started to mainly use such economic levers as foreign exchange rates, tariffs, and interest rates and export credit and legal means to readjust foreign trade. And the average tariff level has come down from 43.2 percent in 1992 to the present average level of 17 percent. In 1994, China successfully abolished the dual foreign exchange administration system and unified the then two existing exchange rates, and established a nationally unified foreign exchange market among banks and a floating exchange rate for RMB on the basis of market supply and demand. On December 1, 1996, China declared its acceptance of the obligations stipulated in Article 8 of the "IMF Treaty" and put into effect the convertibility of RMB in current accounts three years earlier than promised.

2. The Methods for Balancing and Coordinating the Overall Economic Size and Important Economic Structures Have Been Improved.

In the process of the formulation and implementation of annual plans, the calculation of the value of the national economy and the coordination and allocation of the financial resources of the whole society have been strengthened to maintain a better equilibrium between basic factors of production and key commodities. The balance and coordination of aggregates of economic components and their major structures are divided into the following seven different levels of equilibrium: At the first is the equilibrium between the aggregate demand and the aggregate supply. At the second is the equilibrium between the total volume of financial resources and important economic structure. At the third is the equilibrium between the total volume of all the residents' disposable cash income and the use structure. At the fourth is the equilibrium between financial resources of investment in fixed assets and the investment orientation. At the fifth is the equilibrium between the supply and demand of major agricultural products, energy, basic raw materials and essential means of agricultural production. At the sixth level the equilibrium between labor demand and labor supply in the whole society. And at the seventh level is the calculation and coordination of the overall price level and important price structures. In the process of improving the work to balance and coordinate the aggregates of economic components and their major structures, the planning authority has strengthened its ties with related economic regulatory authorities, which has played an important role in macroeconomic regulation.

3. The System of Planned Target Indicators Has Been Reformed.

Since 1995, planned targets have been roughly classified into three categories according to their nature and functions: targets of macroeconomic regulation, anticipated target indicators, and targets in allocating public funds and all the other resources available in the whole society. However, as a special way of macroeconomic regulation and public resources allocation by the state in the process of the transition from the old economic system to a new one, a very small number of planned target indicators still remain mandatory.

4. A State Goods Ordering System Has Been Gradually Established and Improved.

In 1994, the state started to establish a goods-ordering system. In 1995, the government continued to practice the system under which orders for the following 4 type of goods such as rubber, cars, tyres, and raw iron are placed by the state. On the basis of summing up the experience in this experiment, a system under which the state places orders for some important good has been gradually standardized. And a unified state-goods-ordering system has been established step by step to cover important agricultural products, means of agricultural production and basic industrial products.

5. A State Plan Reporting and Information Disclosure System Has Been Established and Consummated.

In 1993, the state started to try out the formulation of annual planning reports, which reflected the change of planning's function and strengthened its policy nature. In 1995, the state further standardized the nature, categorization, contents, forms of plans, and their formulation, promulgation and implementation, leading to relatively complete set of annual planning reports. In addition to this, it was also required to submit reports on special topics about prominent contradictions and most serious problems in the annual economic development. In 1995, the state started to implement a publicizing system for planning reports.

A macroeconomic information disclosure system has been consummated. In 1997, the State Planning Commission started to successively release information on the production, capacity-building, market demand, prominent contradictions, serious problems with the development, and the policy orientation in the power, coal, oil refinery, ethylene, transportation, steel and non-ferrous metal industries. The purpose of these information releases is to guide the microeconomic players' investment behavior.

6. Inter-period Macroeconomic Regulation Has Been Well Exercised in the Implementation of Plans.

On the basis of strengthening the monitoring, anticipation and early warnings of the macroeconomic and market operations, inter-period regulation was carried out at an appropriate degree. The major purpose of inter-period regulation is to readjust the amount and orientation of the flow of the financial resources of the whole society, guarantee the need of key projects for construction fund, maintain an equilibrium between the demand and supply of sensitive goods, handle the problems in production, construction, transportation, domestic trade, and foreign trade and economic cooperation that need to be coordinated by planning departments, fight natural calamities and help the people to tide over natural disasters, and deal with other unexpected situation.

7. The Important Role of Planning in Guiding the Readjustment, Optimization and Upgrading of Economic Structure with Industrial Policies Has Been Strengthened.

Since 1994, the State Planning Commission, together with relevant departments of the central governments, has strengthened studies of the overall industrial policy and special industrial policies. "The Outline of National Industrial Policies in the 1990s" and "Industrial Policies for the Auto Industry" have been approved and promulgated by the State Council for implementation. In December 1997, the State Planning Commission promulgated "Catalogues of Industries, Products and Technologies Encouraged by the State to Develop." Meanwhile, the newly revised "Guiding Catalogues of Industries for Foreign Investment" and "Water Resources Industrial Policy" were also promulgated, the latter of which is the first industrial policy in China's basic industries.

8. The Medium- and Long-term Planning Has Been Further Improved.

In order to meet the requirements of the development of a socialist market economy, the planning system has been gradually shifting shift its focus to medium and long-term planning. This is favorable not only for short-term allocation of resources by the market, for making better use of the advantage of planning in long-term allocation of resources, and for promoting a an organic combination of planning and the market and the mutual complementation of their respective advantages. In order to scientifically formulate the "Ninth Five-Year Plan" and the "Long-Range Objectives Through the Year 2010," the contents and methods of planning have been further improved. 1) Studies on medium and long-term development strategies have been strengthened, which has made the "Ninth Five-Year Plan" a strategic plan laying down a solid foundation for entering the next century. 2) Forecasts of the long-term market environment, trends of the world's economic development and technological advances have been strengthened, leading up to the implementation of sustainable development strategies and the promotion of the transition from extensive growth mode to an intensive growth mode. 3) Planning has become comprehensive with clear focus. In-depth studies and careful planning for the priorities have been conducted in key areas and issues that have important impact on the overall situation. Great importance has been attached to the formulation of plans for social development, particularly the formulation of plans for the development of education, medi-care, population, science and technology, environmental protection, urban public utilities, poverty alleviation and social security system. 4) Major macroeconomic target indicators in the in the Ninth Five-Year Plan have been well calculated, balanced and coordinated, and the economic growth rate and the investment scale in the Ninth Five-Year Plan period have been rationally determined. 5) New ways for promoting the organic combination of the market with planning have been further explored in the process of formulating the long-term plans. 6) Links between medium/long-term plans, industrial policies and state-owned land streamlining plans, those between medium/long-term plans and annual plans, and those between the overall plan and special plans and policies were well bridged. All these links have formulated a complete system for the implementation of the state medium and long-term development strategies and plans.

Section 3

Reform of the Fiscal and Taxation System

China's fiscal and tax system reform started from the delegation of power and the concession of profits to local governments and enterprises. Such a reform changed the system of unified collection of revenue and coverage of expenditure under the traditional old economic system, gradually overcame the malpractice of over unification and administration of too many areas, and greatly stimulated the initiatives and creativeness of local governments and enterprises the economic development. Particularly since the Fourth Plenary Session of the Fourteenth Party Central Committee, the reform of the fiscal and taxation system has achieved many breakthroughs in accordance with the reform targets of establishing a socialist market economic system, some crucial relationships in the fiscal distribution have been basically straightened out, and a fiscal system framework capable of meeting the requirements of the socialist market economy has been basically established. The fiscal system reform has changed the old administration mode of over centralization, unified collection of revenue, and unified coverage of expenditure, successfully achieved the transformation from the fiscal responsibility system to a taxes dividing system, and initially established a multi-level fiscal system with taxes dividing system as the foundation. The reform of the taxation system has broken the unitary tax structure formed under the traditional planned economic system, expanded the areas under taxation regulation, and established a new turnover tax system with value-added tax as the mainstay and consumption and business taxes as supplements. Meanwhile, the income taxation system has also been established and consummated. The reform of the budgeting system has been changed the traditional sing-entry budgeting and a double-entry budgeting system including both current account budgets and construction budgets has been initially practiced.

I. Transition from a Compound Fiscal and Taxation System to a VAT-based Tax-sharing System

After two steps of the "conversion of profits into taxes" in 1983-84, the original industrial and commercial tax was broken into four parts, namely, product tax, value-added tax, business tax and salt tax. The state also levied resources tax on mining enterprises. In addition, local taxes such as urban maintenance and construction tax, property tax, vehicle use tax and urban land use tax started to be collected one after another. In order to meet the needs of China's economic system reform, a number of new taxes were established and started to be collected. By the year of 1993, China's tax category had already numbered 32 and a compound tax system had been established with turnover tax and income tax as the mainstay and the other taxes as supplements.

Since the establishment of the fiscal responsibility system and the two steps of the 'conversion of profits into taxes, China's fiscal and tax system reform has made quite significant breakthroughs. Nevertheless, the current system still can not meet the requirements of the socialist market economic system in some respects. The first problem is the uneven distribution of tax burdens, which is rather unfavorable to fair competition among enterprises. For, income tax system was designed in accordance with the nature of ownership of enterprises and enterprises of different ownership pay their income tax at different rates. Turnover tax system was designed for the purpose of readjusting irrational and unreasonable planned prices. Its has many rates the differences of which are rather wide. Secondly, it greatly complicated the income distribution relationship between the state and enterprises. This relationship is far from being standardized and can not guarantee stable sources of the state fiscal revenue. Thirdly, the proportion of the central fiscal revenue in the total national fiscal revenue was getting increasingly lower, leading up to a mismatch between the financial capacity of the central government and its duties and responsibilities, weakening its capability of economic regulation. Fourthly, both the scope and strengths of regulation by taxation was not sufficient and the land and financial markets could hardly be regulated by taxation. Fifthly, the implementation of different tax rates for domestic and foreign-funded enterprises caused more and more serious contradictions. There also appeared some confusion in the operation of the fiscal and taxation system.

In order to solve the above problems, the central government decided to deepen the fiscal and tax system reform. The guiding principles of the fiscal and taxation system reform in 1994 were to unify tax laws, rationalize tax burdens, simplify the taxation, divide up power reasonably, straighten out income distribution relationships, guarantee state revenue and establish a tax system meeting the needs of the socialist market economic system.

The reform of the turnover tax system changed the traditional practice of adopting differentiated tax rates for different tax categories on the basis of products. The replacement is a tax system that levies value-added tax on both production and circulation. The purpose of the reform was to establish a turnover tax system with the value-added tax as the major component while business tax and consumption tax as supplementary. To be specific, the original industrial and commercial tax is converted into value-added tax, business tax and consumption tax at the rates of 55 percent, 35 percent and 10 percent respectively. The new turnover tax system is composed of value-added tax, consumption tax and business tax. Value-added tax is universally levied on production and circulation including wholesales and retail sales, while consumption tax is levied on a few kinds of consumer goods and business tax levied on sales of services and real estate on which value-added tax is not levied. Value-added tax is levied only on the newly added value created by taxpayers in their productive and operational activities. The areas on which value-added tax is levied include production, wholesale, and retail processing/manufacturing of imported materials, and repair and replacements. The basic rate of value-added tax is 17 percent with a low-grade rate of 13 percent. The low-grade rate applies only to basic food and means of agricultural production. Products for export are usually exempted from value-added tax. In terms of value-added taxation administration, a system was established in which the tax is not included in the price and special invoices are used that specify the due tax. For small taxpayers whose annual sales are small and that do not have complete and perfect accounting, their value-added tax is collected on the simple basis of their annual sales at stipulated rates. The reform of the value-added payment system includes special registration of value-added taxpayers, the use of special value-added invoices, and the auditing of both the seller and the buyer. In this way, an effective taxation checking system was established.

The new consumption tax is levied on eleven kinds of consumer goods, including cigarette, alcohol, cosmetics, expensive jewelry, motorcycles, cars, diesel and kerosene, etc. Consumption tax is collected either as a percentage of the total sales or at a rate to be determined by the price. The price according to which a consumption tax rate is determined is the price excluding value-added tax but including consumption tax. On the basis of levying value-added tax universally on all goods, business tax is levied only on a small number of operational activities. These activities include services, assets transfer and real estate sales. Organizations and individuals conduct taxable operations, transfers and sales pay business tax at stipulated rates and according to the total amount of their operating income. The business tax rate in transportation, building industries, post and telecommunication, cultural

the requirements of the state budgetary administration, neither could it exert effective supervision over the flow of funds from the public finance. Therefore, establishing a budgetary administration system at both the central and provincial levels became a matter of priority on the agenda.

China's double-entry budget system has followed the following principles. First of all, the double-entry budgeting-oriented system reform should be consistent with the ultimate goal of establishing a socialist market economic system. With the deepening of reform, various economic components in China have achieved considerable development. Correspondingly, macroeconomic administration of state-owned enterprises has changed from direct administration to indirect regulation and regulatory means have changed from administrative ones to economic and legal ones. As an important means of macroeconomic regulation, the state budget planning must be adapted to such changes. Secondly, the reform should be favorable for reflecting the dual role of the socialist state. China is a socialist country with public ownership as the mainstay. The state has not only the role of the social and economic administrator and the role of the owner of state-owned assets. In other words, the state public finance should guarantee not only the normal operation of state apparatus, but also the maintenance and appreciation of the value of state-owned assets. Thirdly, the reform should be favorable for straightening out the income distribution relationship between the fiscal authorities and the other departments of the central government. There are large budgetary funds in China. The double-entry budget should gradually take them into the scope of its regulation. Fourthly, the reform should strengthen the budgetary constraining mechanisms, reflecting the characteristics of being scientific, simple and clear and realistically showing the amount and orientation of the flow of fiscal funds. Fifthly, the reform should facilitate reform initiatives in other related aspects. Sixthly, the reform should be favorable for legal construction concerning the administration of the State public finance.

III. An Important Step in Reforming the Fiscal and Tax

System—Conversion of Fees into Taxes

Over a long period of time since the launch of the economic reform and opening-up toward the outside world, the mainstream in China's fiscal and tax system reform has been "decentralization of power and concession of profits." In this process, the central government established the fiscal responsibility System for local governments and the government set up the contact operations responsibility system for enterprises. However, due to the increasing decentralization of financial decision-making power and continuing expansion of the government organs, the public finance has been under mounting pressure. And local governments at all levels have found it more and more difficult to pay for the growing number of government employees and to meet the financial requirements of the economic development. In recent years, some local authorities have gone beyond their power to collect fees under various decent names and such trends of unreasonable fee collection have been intensifying. Statistics show that fee collection and fund-raising nationwide in 1996 amounted to over 360 billion RMB (not including social security fund), about 46 percent of the state revenue in that year. Among the fees local governments have been collecting and funds to which they have been asking for contributions, about 80 percent of them were unauthorized. According to the estimation based on a survey, the factual ratio between the total amount of fees and fund-contributions collected and the state revenue is 1:1.

Fee collection and fund-contribution requirement are products of the transition from the old economic system to the new one. To some extent, they have played a certain positive role in fundraising by local government at all levels for the purpose of pushing forward economic construction and social development. However, the current fee-collection and fund-contribution requirements have gone far beyond the original intention and led up to a series of problems. The first is the increase of the burden on enterprises. According to a survey of 300 key enterprises nationwide by the State Economic and Trade Commission, unreasonable fees and fund contributions of various kinds they have been paying take up 20 percent of their pretax profits, almost equal to their net profits. Secondly, the tax base is seriously eroded. The tax base shrinks in proportion with the amount of fees paid and fund-contributions made, directly reducing the size of the state revenue. Thirdly, one of the purpose of fee collection is support inefficient and redundant departments and institutions, which has made it possible for government organs to continuously expand. Investigations show that 30-40 percent of the fees and fund contributions are used to pay government employees. In some places, 100 percent is used to this end. Besides the high cost of fee collection, this has resulted in overstaffing of government organizations and low efficiency of government work. Fourthly, fee collection and fund-contributions have also encouraged blind investments. A handsome part of the fees and fund contributions are used for the repeated construction of "small but comprehensive" and "large and comprehensive" projects, aggravating the already-unbalanced economic structure. Fifthly, corruption is fostered. Large amounts of fees and fund contributions out of budgetary supervision provide an important source of "small treasuries" of many local governments and authorities, which has led up to chaotic income distribution and prevalent corruption. Therefore, it is imperative to "convert fees into taxes" by further reforming the fiscal and tax system and in accordance with the requirements of the development of the socialist market economy.

The overall objective of "converting fees into taxes" is to establish a state revenue distribution system with tax revenue as the mainstay and a small number of regulatory fees as supplements. More specifically, it is designed to reduce the proportion of non-tax income in the state revenue to the current level of many other countries and raise the proportion of state revenue in GDP to about 20 percent.

Conversion of fees into taxes is an important move in promoting the development of the national economy and social development. First of all, it is helpful for raising the proportion of state revenue in GDP and strengthening the state's capacity of macroeconomic regulation. Due to the widespread unreasonable fee collection and fund-contribution requirements in recent years, the financial capacity based on the state revenue has been rather limited. Converting fees into taxes will help bring the large amount of government income dispersed within different departments of the central government and local governments at all levels into the state revenue, thus enabling the state to amass the necessary financial capacity to better support the economic and social development in accordance with the overall target of macroeconomic regulation. Secondly, it is conducive to the rule of law over taxation administration and standardization of the order of revenue distribution. At present, a large part of the fees collected and fund contributions required has the nature of taxes. To convert these fees fund contributions into taxes can legalize their collection and further straighten out the income distribution relationship between the government and enterprises and that between organizations and individuals. Furthermore, these income distribution relationships will be under the supervision by the whole society to realize legal and standardized administration. Thirdly, it is helpful for punishing corruption and building an efficient and corruption-free government. Under the conditions of developing a socialist market economy, the government income should mainly come from taxation. It should not rely on fees and required fund contributions. Only by converting fees into taxes, can government gray income be eliminated, creating conditions for an efficient and corruption-free government.

"Conversion of fees into taxes" concerns the following. First, fees and fund contributions of a tax nature will be converted into taxes. Road maintenance fee, auto purchase surcharge, water and passenger transport surcharges and road construction fund contributions will be converted into fuel tax; mineral resources compensation fee, radio administration fee and water resources fee into resources tax; education surcharge, rural education development surcharge, local education surcharge and local education fund contribution into education tax; urban public utilities surcharge, urban drainage charge and municipal works auxiliary projects charge will be integrated into municipal works maintenance and construction tax. Fees levied on road use and on vehicles have been determined as the breakthrough point of the reform of "converting fees into taxes." The collection of these fees shall be standardized first to accumulate experience on the basis of which the conversion of the other fees will follow one after another. Secondly, fees levied on some services that are not part of the government's due responsibilities and functions and should be provided through the market will be replaced by business charges, which in turn become taxable in accordance of relevant laws. Government's fee collection should be practically distinguished from business charges. Institutions that are self-sustained by collecting charges on the services they provide and those that have to get subsidies from the public finance to make up for the difference between what they collect and what they spend should be gradually transformed into companies or intermediary organizations. Thirdly, collection of a small number of fees can be kept, but measures shall be taken to work out perfect and standardized regulations. The administration of the collection of the regulatory fees infeasible to be converted into taxes and that of their uses shall be clearly separated. Unreasonable fee collections and fund contribution requirements are strictly forbidden and collection of new fees and fund contribution requirements are suspended during the rectifying period. And the collection of all unreasonable fees under all sorts of pretexts shall be resolutely abolished.

Although a lot of progress has been made in China's fiscal and tax system reform, there is still a long way to go compared with the requirements of the economic and social development. To be more exact, the current fiscal and tax system and fiscal situation can not meet the requirements of further development of the national economy and the social development. In view of the rapidly changing economic environments both at home and abroad, China's fiscal and tax system reform is still confronted with many new problems and arduous tasks. Nevertheless, we are convinced that under the correct leadership of the CPC Central Committee headed by President Jiang Zemin, the reform will be further deepened. With the deepening of the overall economic reform, the state fiscal situation will surely be fundamentally improved, which will provide stronger support for the development of the national economy.

Section 4

Reform of the Financial System

The guideline for the reform of China's financial system is to meet the requirements of the construction of a socialist market economy, be consistent with the basic economic system in which the public ownership is the mainstay and multi-types of economic components develop side by side, comply with the multi-leveled economic development and unbalanced regional development, enable the financial sector to play a better role in the macroeconomic regulation of the national economy and in the optimization of allocation of resources, facilitate the prevention of financial risks and the stabilization of the financial order, be favorable for the adaptation to the trend of financial globalization, and promote a sustainable, rapid and healthy development of the national economy. The ultimate target of the reform is to establish (1) a macroeconomic regulatory system operated by the central bank that independently formulates and implements monetary policies; (2) a financial organizational system with the separation of policy finance from commercial finance, with the state-owned commercial banks as the mainstay and with the coexistence of multi-types of financial institutions; (3) a unified and open financial market system that facilitates ordered competition and strict administration.

I. Establish a Strong Central Banking System to Strengthen Financial Supervision and Regulation

The primary task of deepening the financial system reform is to streamline the People's Bank into a real central bank and establish a strong central bank regulatory system. There are four separate objectives as follows. First of all, the responsibilities of the central bank should be clarified. The People's Bank of China is the central bank, enjoying the exclusive rights of currency issuance. It regulates and administrates all the financial institutions and financial activities nationwide and runs the national treasury on behalf of the government. According to the "Law of the People's Bank of China," the People's Bank of China has eleven obligations and responsibilities that can be basically summed up into the following six categories: (1) formulating and implementing monetary policies and maintaining the stability of the value of the national currency; (2) supervising and regulating all the financial institutions in accordance with relevant laws to maintain a legal and healthy operation of the financial sector; (3) maintaining the normal operations of the payment and liquidation system; (4) holding, managing and operating the state's foreign reserves and gold reserves; (5) managing the state treasury and other financial businesses on behalf of the government; and (6) representing the Chinese government to conduct international financial activities. All the business of all the subsidiaries of the People's Bank of China at all levels should be put under unified administration. Branch organizations of the central bank have the following 7 functions: (1) financial administration and supervision; (2) surveys and statistic analysis; (3) readjustment of the horizontal money supply; (4) management of the state treasury; (5) cash allocation; (6) management of foreign exchanges; and (7) inter bank clearing.

The monetary policy system has been be reformed and consummated. In the "Decision on Some Issues Concerning the Establishment of a Socialist Market Economic Structure," it stated that the main mechanism the central bank relies on to readjust and regulate money supply should be changed from the control of credit scale to the application of such monetary policy instruments as the rate of deposit reserves, the central bank's re-lending rates and open market operations. The ultimate objective of the monetary policies is to maintain the stability of the value of RMB and prevent inflation, thus facilitating economic development.

The improvement of the administration of the lending scale of the state-owned commercial banks is an important step forward in the reform of the macro financial regulation and control system towards the requirements of the socialist market economy. Approved by the State Council, the People's Bank of China decided to cancel the quota control of the lending scale of the state-owned commercial banks from January

1, 1998 and to gradually start administrating and supervising commercial banks by means of assets-liability ratio and risk forecast. This was an important measure to implement the spirits of the national conference on financial work, and to deepen and accelerate the reform of the financial system, marking an important change in the mode of macro financial regulation in our country. Monetary policies refer to all guidelines and strategies taken by the central bank to regulate money supply for achieving the purpose of macroeconomic regulation.

Strengthening financial supervision is the need for maintaining a normal operation of the financial sector and the foundation for an effective implementation of monetary policies. The major objectives of financial supervision and regulation is to maintain safety and liquidity of the assets of financial institutions and their capacity of paying debts to protect depositors' interests, uphold the order of the financial sector and the safety of the financial system, and ensure fair and efficient competition in the financial market place.

The reform of the People's Bank's supervisory and administrative system is an important measure in strengthening the financial supervision. In accordance with a decision made by the CPC Central committee and the State Council, the People's Bank of China started reforming its administrative system in October 1997. As a result of the reform, the original 31 branch offices in the 31 provinces, municipalities and autonomous regions were replaced by nine trans-provincial branch offices. In the provincial capital cities without branch offices, financial supervision offices were established. The rights and obligations of the headquarters of the central bank, its trans-provincial branch offices, central sub-branch offices and sub-branch offices are all clearly defined, which has strengthened the supervisory and regulatory role of branch offices at all levels. This reform has reinforced the authority of the central bank in carrying out monetary policies, strengthened its independence and impartiality in performing its roles in financial supervision and regulation, and facilitated the improvement of the professional quality of the central bank's staff as administrators and supervisors.

II. A Diversified Banking System Has Been Established That

Has Guided the Sound Development of Non-banking Financial Institutions

Since the launch of the overall economic reform and opening-up toward the outside world, China's banking system has changed from a unitary banking system into a diversified banking system with the central bank as the leader, the solely state-funded commercial banks as the mainstay and the coexistence of joint stock and regional commercial banks and various types of financial institutions. Through the diversification of financial institutions and the introduction of competition mechanisms, the economic performance and the quality of services of all the banks have gradually improved.

1. National Policy Banks Have Been Established.

Policy finance is indispensable for any country in the period of economic development. It is essentially a financial instrument with which the government and the financial sector permeate and make use of each other. On the one hand, policy finance is a transformed means of state revenue distribution. While on the other, revenue distribution makes use of a financial instrument to legalize the operation of fiscal fund. Policy finance is an important tool for the government's macroeconomic regulation and economic intervention. At the same time, it is not only a regulator that plays the regulatory function of the government but also a player at the macroeconomic market operates money business. Therefore, the establishment of independent policy banks is instrumental in the formulation of different interest groups and a better restrictive mechanism.

According to the stipulations in the related documents issued by the State Council, our country's policy banks are independent legal persons. They are independent accounting entities that are autonomous, managed as if they are enterprises with the operating goal of breaking even. As financial institutions, policy banks have the same function of credit intermediaries as commercial financial institutions do. On the other hand, they are special financial institutions that have special and close relations with the government. As banks, no matter how large policy functions they have, they must have the nature of financial enterprises. Therefore, policy banks first of all must exist as "real banks." They should implement the economic policies of the government with banking instruments rather than instruments for revenue distribution, offering relief or rationing.

Policy finance has inherited some of the behavioral features of the traditional planned financial system. The means of its allocation of financial assets and of its operational readjustments both have features of planning. Nevertheless, the precondition for its planning features is that they do not harm market mechanisms. Its positioned role is to make for the niche left by commercial finance and to overcome the defects and negative part of the market. Its operating mechanism is not the same one as that of the traditional planned financial system. It is not a subordinate to or administrative means of the government. Rather it is a secondary financial driver meeting the requirements of macro regulation. With the support of relevant laws and regulations of the government, policy finance will operate and develop in parallel with commercial banks. Nevertheless, commercial finance is the mainstay of the financial system while policy finance is designed to play complementary roles.

2. Specialized Banks Have Been Converted into real Commercial Banks.

With their policy business detached and taken away, the original state-owned specialized banks (Industrial and Commercial Bank of China, Agricultural Bank of China, Bank of China and People's Construction Bank of China) have been transformed into commercial banks. These commercial banks have made important steps forward in striving for intensive operations by strengthening their internal management, making efforts to prevent financial risks, reinforcing their unified corporate system and strengthening their unified management of and strict supervision over the operations of their subsidiaries.

The core of the reform of the commercial banking system is to develop mechanisms with which they can enjoy autonomous management, bear full responsibility for their own profits and losses, promote self-development on their own and constrain their behavior out of their own will. Since 1994, the State Council has emphasized many times that solely state-funded commercial banks should no longer issue policy loans, paving the way for the reform. State-owned commercial banks should improve their profitability by increasing income and lowering cost in legal ways. Except for the Agriculture Bank of China, the other state-owned commercial banks should place the business focus in large and medium-sized cities. And those branch offices of theirs that have small volumes of business and are making losses for a long period of time should be either closed or integrated into others for downsizing and cost reducing purposes. They should strengthen the administration by their first-level legal persons, establish and consummate their internal control mechanisms, increase their capital funds through various channels, raise and keep a sufficient capital ratio, separate and transfer part of the bad debts formed in the past to the operation of special organs and establish strict lending quality control mechanisms so as to promote the quality of their assets to the level of banks in medium-developed countries.

3. The Management Mechanism of Rural Credit Cooperatives Has Been Reformed in Accordance with the Principle of the Cooperative System

Rural credit cooperatives constitute the basis of China's rural finance and their management system reform has overwhelming importance for China's agricultural development. Currently, a lot of problems exist in rural credit cooperatives, the root reason of which is the deviation of their operations from the principle of the cooperative system. The cooperative system can meet not only the requirements of the household contract responsibility system, but also the requirements of modern agricultural production. At present, it is rather difficult to increase farmers' income only by raising the prices of agricultural products. And the conflict between farmers' small-scale production and the demand of the large domestic market has been getting more and more serious. Therefore, it is necessary to link the production; processing, sales and financial services closely together to overcome the conflict between household based small-scale agricultural production in rural areas and the huge domestic market. The profits from the processing and sales of agricultural products should be returned to farmers according to the amounts of agricultural products they have sold in order to increase their income and promote their purchasing power for industrial products. To this end, rural credit cooperatives should be run as cooperative financial organizations that are managed democratically by their voluntary shareholders and mainly provide financial services for their members. In this way, rural credit cooperatives will substantially promote the development of the rural economy.

4. Various Types of Non-banking Financial Institutions Have Been Gradually Developed.

Insurance companies securities companies, trust and investment companies and financial companies attached to enterprise groups are important components of China's financial system. In particular, securities companies and trust and investment companies have played an important part in the development of China's capital market. The appearance and the development of the capital market and the growth of securities financing year by year are important accomplishments of the reform of the financial system. The proportion of direct financing in a country depends mainly on enterprises' credibility, economic performance and fundraising capability. Effective and regulated expansion of direct financing will not reduce the aggregate amount of capital of the whole society, but rather lighten the pressure on banking credit and reduce banks' risk. The central bank should continue to assist relevant authorities in pushing forward the shareholding system-oriented reform of enterprises, appropriately accelerate the development of the capital market and gradually increase the proportion of direct financing. Trust and investment companies should be reformed according to the principle of "regarding trust as the mainstay, separate management of different lines of work, increasing scale of operation and exercising strict supervision." In early 1980s, local governments and enterprises had the desire to put their money into the management of financial institutions for larger returns, owing to an increase of their disposable capital. To meet this need, non-banking financial institutions such as trust and investment companies were established. Owing to an overestimation of market demand for trust business, too many trust and investment companies were approved and established. Some trust and investment companies invested their short-term trust deposits in the overheated real estate industry. To make things worse, the administration of and the supervision over trust and investment companies were far from sufficient. These have put many trust and investment companies into extremely difficult situation. The lesson is that trust and investment companies should adhere to the operating principle of "managing others' financial matters according to the entrustment of others," completely separate their trust business from their securities business, expand the scale of their operations and exercise strict supervision. Financial companies attached to enterprise groups should utilize the long-term idle funds of the subsidiaries of their own groups for technological upgrading. They should never act like commercial banks whose major business is short-term financing.

5. The Financial Sector Has Been Opened Wider to the Outside World.

Financial institutions established by foreigners in China constitute an important component of China's financial sector. The principles for upgrading the level of opening the financial sector to the outside world are as follows. The first is fair competition and mutual benefit. The introduction of foreign financial institutions can facilitate the reform and development of China's financial sector and at the same time promote domestic financial institutions' capability of participating in international competition, thus expanding China's trade and economic cooperation with other parts of the world. Secondly, China's trade and economic cooperation with other countries are the basis for the opening of its financial sector to the outside world. And the level of the openness of the financial sector should accord with the size of international trade and economic cooperation. Thirdly, the level of the openness of the financial sector should correspond with our country's capability of regulating and supervising financial institutions. And strict market entry requirements must be specified in order to introduce only sound foreign financial institutions with good credibility, sufficient financial strengths and high management capacity. Fourthly, equal national treatments should be given to foreign financial institutions in terms of taxation, service provision, and regulation and supervision. In 1979, the Japanese Long-term Credit Bank established an office in Beijing, the first foreign financial institution in China. So far, offices of foreign banks in China have numbered 175, with a total assets value of US$35.4 billion and foreign exchange loans of US$27 billion, about a quarter of all foreign exchange loans in China. Nine insurance companies from eight countries have set up twelve business offices in China, ten of which have already started their business.

III. The Financial Market Has Been Improved and Standardized and the Foreign Exchange Administration System Has Been Reformed

Practice has shown that the establishment and development of a sound financial market is of vital importance for optimizing resources allocation, promoting fund collection and circulation, improving the efficiency of the use of funds, raising funds for long-term uses and establishing a modern enterprise system.

The financial market is generally composed of two parts: money market and capital market. The Capital market, which includes stock market, bond market, fund market and medium and long-term credit market, refers to the part of the financial market where securities financing is carried out and medium and long term loans whose terms are longer than one year can be obtained. As funds raised from this part of the financial market are mainly used for expanded reproduction, it is known as the capital market. As an important part of the capital market, the securities market possesses great potential of securing medium and long-term capital through issuing stocks and bonds, with public stocks and bonds circulating freely on the secondary market. The monetary market is the part of the financial market where short-term funds are raised and circulated. It includes inter-bank short-term loans market, bill market, counter-purchase market and short-term credit market. The capital market and monetary market are both places of transactions between buyers and suppliers of funds. Although they are both "reservoirs" for amassing funds and "distribution stations" for allocating funds, they have clear division of functions. Generally speaking, long-term capital is raised from the capital market while short-term capital from the money market. With the continuous expansion and diversification of the financial market in our country, a monetary market with inter-bank short-term loan market and foreign exchange market as the mainstay and a securities market with transactions of stocks and treasury bonds as its main business have been gradually formed.

The reform of our country's financial market is oriented to the establishment of a unified and open financial market system characterized with orderly competition and strict administration. The targeted new financial market will have the following characteristics. It will be a unified market but have multi-level operations. The high level of the financial market will allocate resources throughout the country while its medium and low level will allocate resources within a region. The new financial market system will expand the capacity of both the monetary market and the capital market. Funds will be pooled through financial instruments rather than through administrative appropriations as in the past. Under the strict supervision of the central bank, the operation boundaries of all players that enter the financial market will be clearly defined and their market entry qualifications and behavior will be standardized. Two-way flow of funds at the same level of the market and one-way flow of funds among different levels will coexist so that the state can control the direction of fund flow and keep a basic equilibrium of the monetary market. In the capital market, the primary market is strictly controlled while the secondary market is properly opened up. Under the regulation and control of the central bank, a basic equilibrium between the two markets has been maintained.

Developing the securities market is an inexorable requirement of the establishment of the socialist market economic system. A sound securities market featuring healthy development, good order and safe operation is of vital importance for optimizing the allocation of resources, readjusting economic structures, raising more funds from the whole society and facilitating the development of the national economy. Strengthening supervision and regulating operations are important conditions for the healthy development of the securities market. The central government has decided to establish a nationally unified supervisory system over the transactions of securities and futures, stipulating that China Securities Supervision Committee should be responsible for supervising and regulating securities and futures nationwide. This is a major move in reforming the securities supervision and regulation system.

The enactment and implementation of the "Law of the People's Republic of China on Securities" serves as a milestone in the establishment of a legal infrastructure for the securities market in China. This law stipulates the norms of behavior at the securities market, reflects the common interests of investors, brokers and issuers as well as the will of the state, and has binding force to all the participants. Among a series of regulations, special attention has been given to the following principles. (1) The principle of transparency, equity and fairness must be adhered to. (2) Both the issuance and transactions of securities must abide by the law. (3) On one hand, investor's legal rights and interests must be protected by legal means while on the other hand their awareness of risks must enhanced. (4) Behaviors such as inside transactions, cheating and manipulation of the market must be forbidden. (5) While strengthening the supervision and regulation of the securities market, supervisors and regulators also must abide by the law, improving the transparency of their work and subjecting themselves to supervision. (6) All the relevant organizations responsible for different links of the issuance and transactions of securities must fulfil their legal obligations and responsibilities and ensure the truthfulness, precision and completion of the information on securities' issuance and transactions. (8) All illegal behaviors must severely punished, the market order must be maintained and the interests of the general public must be protected. Upholding these principles is highly necessary for maintaining a standardized and orderly securities market and for promoting its steady and healthy development.

In the situation in which both development and reform are being speeded up, it is imperative to further reform the foreign exchange administration system. The objective of the reform is to maintain the stability of the value of RMB and gradually make it an internationally convertible currency. In the "Decision on Some issues Concerning the Establishment of a Socialist Market Structure," it was pointed out that a floating and regulated foreign exchange rate system and a unified and standardized foreign exchange market should be established to gradually enable RMB to become a convertible currency. China has followed to maintain the stability of the weighted-average exchange rates between RMB and other major currencies in the world. In 1994, major reforms were carried out in the foreign exchange administration system and successfully combined the dual foreign exchange rates. In December 1996, RMB became convertible in current accounts earlier than the planned time. The inter-bank foreign exchange market and the foreign exchange purchase and settlement system among banks were established, the practice of foreign exchange retention and turnover has been rescinded, and mandatory planning for foreign exchange earning and spending was canceled. The state started to exert macro regulation and control of the balance of international payments through legal and economic means. The issuance and circulation of Foreign Exchange Certificates were stopped. At the same time, the control of foreign exchanges in capital accounts has been gradually loosened for the purpose of the final realization of the full convertibility of RMB including capital accounts. Practice has shown that these reform measures are conducive not only to the control of the aggregate amount and structure of foreign debts but also to the protection of foreign investors' interests. Therefore, they have commonly commended by the international community.

Since the start of the reform and opening toward the outside world, especially in the recent few years, China's financial system reform has made remarkable progress especially. The opening of the financial sector to the outside world has been expanded, financial supervision has been strengthened and financial services have been improved. These accomplishments have played an important role in improving macroeconomic regulation and control, curbing inflation, promoting economic development and maintaining social stability. Nevertheless, we should be keenly aware that a host of problems still exist in the financial sector. Though we effectively curbed inflation and accumulated a lot of experience in this area, the current financial system cannot meet the needs of further development of our national economy or the requirements of the newly changed domestic and the international situations due to the more complicated external environment of our country's economic development. The current deflation has led up to continuing downfalls of prices, serious shortage of money supply, sluggish growth of investment in the whole society and a flat consumption market. Therefore, active measures should be taken to strengthen the role of monetary policies in facilitating economic growth. While preventing and dissolving financial risks, a credit incentive mechanism must be established. State-owned commercial banks not only should emphasize the safety and reliability as the top priority, but also should attach importance to the feasibility and market prospects of the projects for which the loans are issued, thus improving the efficiency, economic performance and liquidity of their financial resources.

CHAPTER 7

THE RELATIONS AMONG REFORM, DEVELOPMENT AND STABILITY IN CHINA

Synopsis

The proper handling of the relations among the reform, development and stability is a basic experience for the smooth advance of China's economic transition and the striking achievements we have made in this regard. In this chapter, the author focuses on this experience to make explorations from many aspects.

In Section 1, the author explains the significance of handling properly the relations among the three, and points out this basic strategic idea was proposed in a step-by-step manner after the Third Plenary Session of the Eleventh Party Central Committee. It is the summary of both the positive experience and negative lessons we have drawn from the socialist construction in China. At present we are facing a series of complicated relations among the reform, development and stability. Only by properly handling their relations can we take hold of the overall situation to guarantee the smooth development of the economy and the society. It is the inevitable choice for resolving the primary contradictions of the current stage in China.

Sections 2, 3 and 4 are the main body of this chapter. In this part, the author expounds from three aspects the basic experience in properly handling the relations among the reform, development and stability in the new historical period in accordance with the rich experience gained in the practice of the past twenty years' reform and opening. The author points out that as long as we firmly take development as the aim, the reform the driving force

and stability the guarantee and incorporate the speed of development with the reform drive and the society's capability adapting itself to the changes, the economic development and system transition can be smoothly pushed forward without disrupting social stability. This is a new experience gained from the great undertaking of building socialism with Chinese characteristics after the Third Plenary Session of the Eleventh Party Central Committee.

In section 5, looking forward in the future, the author analyses the new challenges to be faced by our reform, development and stability in the early 21st century. The author also makes exploratory and policy-oriented suggestions on how to promote development, deepen the reform and maintain stability in the new situation.

Section 1

Significance of Correctly Handling the Relations Between Reform, Development and Stability

I. Relations Between the Reform, Development and Stability

The strategic idea of correctly handling the relations between the reform, development and stability was proposed step by step after the great strategic decision has been made at the Third Plenary Session of the Eleventh Party Central Committee to shift the focus of work of the Party and the country to socialist modernization construction. In the new historical period, we shall develop economy and push forward the reform; in the meantime, we shall maintain stability. So it is inevitable and self-evident for us to be faced with the problem of how to handle the relations among them. However, in the 1980s, the advance of the reform, the development of economy and the maintenance of stability were discussed and practiced as three separate key problems. As for the proper handling of the relations among the three, no complete proposition has ever been made. At that time, the internal relations of the three were understood from the angle of their respective importance.

At the Third Plenary Session of the Eleventh Central Committee, convened in December 1978, decisions were made to shift the focus of the work of our Party and our country to economic construction and it was proposed that the basic task of our Party and our country was to develop the productive forces. This marked a great turning point after the founding of New China. Deng Xiaoping pointed out insightfully, "The key for China to solve all problems is to depend on its own development." With this as the turning point, development was put in a central position.

China must carry out reform in order to develop. The reform started from the countryside and was successful. At the Third Plenary Session of the Twelfth Party Central Committee in October 1984, decisions were made to carry out reform on the urban economic system as well. Based on the understanding that reform is the second revolution in China, the strategic idea was proposed to "guide the overall development with reform." So, reform was put on the top of the agenda.

In 1989, along with the development and deepening of the reform, the former interest pattern and the operation order of the former systems were under threat and various social contradictions became salient. In order to guarantee the smooth advance of the reform and development, Deng Xiaoping stressed again that stability was of great importance and even noted, "To maintain stability is the overriding task."

Although all these discussions expounded on the significance of the reform, development and stability, they only emphasized their respective importance instead of touching upon the relations between them. The explicit and complete proposition on the proper handling of the relations of the three was not made until the 1990s.

In 1992, marked by Deng Xiaoping's talks during his south China inspection tour and the Fourteenth National Congress of the CPC, the reform and opening to the outside world and the modernization drive of China entered a new stage. With the rapid development of economic transition and the national economy as well as changes in the structures of industries, enterprises, urban and rural areas and benefit allocation, the importance of correctly handling the relations between reform, development and stability became ever the more prominent, due to the salient contradictions caused by the readjustment of the interest relations. The third generation of leaders of the Central Committee headed by President Jiang Zemin upheld and applied creatively the Deng Xiaoping theory; and explicitly put forward the guideline to take hold of the overall situation through carrying out reform and opening, expediting development and maintaining stability. In accordance with the new situation and the newly emerged problems, President Jiang Zemin pointed out that the relations among reform, development and stability was a key issue when he expounded in 1995 the major relations concerning the overall situation in China's socialist construction. After that, proper handling of the relations among the three was included as the basic guideline of the Party in the resolution adopted at the Fifth Plenary Session of the Fourteenth Party Central Committee. This is a new experience gained from building socialism with Chinese characteristics since the reform and opening of China.

II. Summary of the Experience and Lessons in the Practice of China's Socialist Construction.

Deng Xiaoping's thinking on the reform, development and stability was put forward after a close observation of the practice in the two decades and more before the reform and opening if we view it from a broader historical background.

It was declared at the Second Plenary Session of the Seventh Party Central Committee in March 1949 that the victory of the Chinese revolution was only the first step made in a "10,000-*li* Long March" and large-scale economic construction would be conducted in the future. As a matter of fact, work was done according to this guideline in the first few years after the founding of New China. It was clearly pointed out at the Eighth National Congress of the CPC in September 1956 that after the reform on the socialist reformation of the ownership of the means of production, "the contradiction between the proletariat and the bourgeoisie had been basically resolved" and "the main contradiction in China has become one between the needs of the people to establish an advanced industrial country and the reality of a backward agricultural one, between the needs of the people for rapid economic and cultural development and the state in which the present economic and cultural development falls short of the people's needs. This contradiction was, in nature, one between the advanced social system and the backward productive forces. Unfortunately, in the twenty years or more afterwards, under the guidance of the ultra "Left" thought, class struggle was made the "central link," and the focus of our Party and our country's work was never shifted to economic construction. Therefore, the superiority of socialism was given little chance to display its advantage; the productive forces developed slowly, unstably and uncoordinatedly and people's livelihood was not improved much. According to statistics, compared with 1952, the total output value of industry and agriculture grew by 8.1 times, the national income grew by 4.2 times, but the national consumption per capita only doubled in 1980. It shows that the speed of the improvement of people's living standard was much slower than that of the other two. The improvement of people's livelihood was not in conformity with the work they had done. Especially during the ten-year "cultural revolution," the country and the people suffered a lot and it caused a lot of disasters. Deng Xiaoping profoundly summarized the bitter lessons learned from "taking class struggle as the key link" and pointed out that our basic mistake was that we had not concentrated on economic construction. Therefore, he noted that we must "concentrate on developing the social productive forces and this is the most fundamental for us to bring order out of chaos."

During the 20 years before the Third Plenary Session of the Eleventh Party Central Committee, the social productive forces of China developed slowly, lacking in stability and coordination. This is because rigid systems under the planned economy fettered the development of the productive forces besides the damages caused by the "Left" lines and policies based on the assumptions about the "class struggle."

The premises of the planned economic system we practiced before the reform are the "two assumptions." One was that the state was able to get all sorts of information about social production and social needs and central planning authorities could process the information in a timely manner and making the correct decisions. The other was that all the means of production were owned by the whole people and the whole society was a community without different interests. However, China's socialist economic practice shows the above mentioned premises are not available. First, the social needs are various and changeable, so it is impossible for central planning authorities to know everything clearly. In addition, science and technology develop very fast with changing social production, making it unrealistic to cover everything in state plans. Rejection of the market mechanism will inevitably fetter the development of the productive forces. Second, under the conditions of socialism, there exist not only the state-owned or collectively owned sectors of economy, but the private sector as well. Therefore, it is impossible for all enterprises to share the same material interests. To exclude market competition and its incentive and binding mechanism will inevitably stifle the vitality and vigor of production. So, if we proceed from the above-mentioned premises and the practice planned economic system that is obviously not in conformity with the reality of China, it will certainly result in low efficiency of economic operation. This explains the long standstill of China's national economy before the adoption of the reform and open policy. Just as Deng Xiaoping said, "This situation forced us to make a decision to carry out the reform at the Third Plenary Session of the Eleventh Party Central Committee in December 1978," and "If we do not carry out the reform, our modernization drive and socialism will be doomed."

Stability is closely connected with economic development and structural changes. Before the Third Plenary Session of the Eleventh Party Central Committee, China had suffered dearly from social instability. The first time was during the period from 1958-1960, when China launched the "Great Leap Forward" movement, placing one-sided and unrealistic emphasis on high-speed growth of industrial and agricultural production and construction. (In agriculture, it was proposed that the grain production targets set in the Twelve-year Agriculture Development Program be achieved within three to five years, or even within one or two years. And in industry, it was suggested to accomplish the goal of catching up with or even surpassing Britain within three years in steel output, rather than fifteen years as previously planned.) The relations of production were subjected to drastic changes and became incompatible with the level of the productive forces. The collective ownership in the form cooperatives was rapidly changed into the commune ownership in the rural areas. As a result, public canteens were opened and the ultra-Left policy of "eating free" was implemented. At the same time, the privately owned plots of land and household sidelines and rural fairs were abolished. The "Great Leap Forward" and the "people's commune" movement caused great damages to the industrial and agricultural construction as well as social instability. The second time was during the "cultural revolution." The damages caused by the "Left" ideological line and the two counter-revolutionary cliques led by Lin Biao and the "Gang of Four" caused nationwide turmoil, greatly disrupting the economic construction and social life. The national economy was pushed to the brink of collapse and the political and a most serious damage was caused to social stability since the founding of the People's Republic.

The Third Plenary Session of the Eleventh Party Central Committee decided to shift the focus of work of the Party and country to socialist modernization, thus ushering in a new epoch for China's modernization drive. Over the past 20 years, our Party has made achievements that aroused worldwide attention in development, reform and stability and accumulated rich experience in handling the relations between the three in accordance with the wise decisions and policies made by Deng Xiaoping, such as "Development is the absolute principle," "The reform is the second revolution in China" and "To maintain stability is the overriding task," etc. Over the past 20 years, although constant changes have taken place both at home and abroad and the country has been subjected to great pressure and challenges in various aspects, China has firmly adhered to the policy of deepening reform, ensuring development and maintaining stability. In the late 1980s, in particular, when the former Soviet Union disintegrated and drastic changes occurred in East Europe, there was a loud cry in the CPC, demanding to place a campaign against "peaceful evolution" at the top of the agenda. In such a complicated situation, the Central Committee of the CPC remained sober-minded and realized that although there were complicated reasons for the changes in the former Soviet Union and East Europe, the fundamental one was the problem that relations between reform, development and stability had not been tackled properly. Based on such understanding, the Central Committee of the CPC did not loosen confidence in reform, development and stability. Rather, it called on people throughout the country to "seize opportunities, deepen the reform, expand opening, promote development and maintain stability." Thanks to the correct decisions and policies of the Central Committee of the CPC, China turned disadvantages into advantages, difficulties into driving forces and challenges into opportunities.

In a word, the practice of China's socialist construction, especially in the 20 years' reform and opening, proves convincingly that correctly handling the relations between the reform, development and stability is crucial in bringing under control the overall situation and guarantee the smooth development of the economy and the society. Otherwise, we will have to suffer and pay a high price. This is the profound summary of both the experience and lessons gained from China's socialist construction.

III. Inevitable Choice of Resolving the Main Social Contradictions at the Present Stage in China

The main social contradiction in China at present is one between the ever-increasing material and cultural needs of the people and the backward social production. This is decided by the objective forces at the primary stage of socialism, such as the development level of productive forces, changes in different stages and the characteristics of the economic system. Such a contradiction is not one that production comparatively lags behind people's needs in a general sense. Instead, it includes specific social and historical contents. According to the general law governing the development of human society, socialism, as an advanced social system superior to capitalism, is established on the basis of the highly developed productive forces of a capitalist society. However, the social productive forces of China are very backward in spite of its socialist system, due to special social and historical conditions. The backwardness here is obvious not only in comparison with developed countries, but also in terms of the necessary material and technological foundations for socialist modernization. It is just in these two senses that the sharp contradiction between the backward social production and the ever-increasing needs for material and cultural development of the people was formed and it has constituted the main contradiction at the primary stage of socialism. We should not solve this contradiction by class struggle. On the contrary, we can only do so by greatly developing the social productive forces. This is the correct way to resolve the main contradictions at the present stage in China.

In contemporary China, in order to develop the productive forces, we need to solve the problems concerning the development of the productive forces (for instance, the application of science and technology in production, the adjustment of industrial structure, etc.) on the one hand. More-over, we shall conduct reform to remove the obstacles to the development of the productive forces by abolishing the production relations and superstructure that can not adapt themselves to the development of the productive forces. This is the emancipation of the productive forces. The reform is the direct driving force and solid foundation for development. Just as what Deng Xiaoping said, "The adherence to the reform and opening decides the fate of China" and "The significance of the reform is to lay a good foundation for the sustained development in the next decade and the first fifty years of the next century."

However, smooth reform and development can only be realized in a stable social environment. The history of the world economy development shows that during structural and system transition, the economic structural imbalance and social riots can easily take place. An American scholar Hintinton discussed this in his book *The Political Order in a Changing Society*. According to him, for the transition from US$500 to US$3000 in the per-capita national income, social riots will certainly take place if the process takes a very short period of time. Based on this statement, it may be concluded that, in a transitional period with high-rate economic growth, only by properly handling the relations among the reform, development and stability can we realize the coordinated development of the economy and the society, maintain the stability of macro-economy, upgrade the industrial structure and complete the transition smoothly. If a stable situation does not exist and the country is plunged into confusion, it would be difficult to push forward the reform, achieve development and satisfy the material and cultural needs of the people.

In this regard, the transition of the former Soviet Union and East European countries left us valuable lessons. Because they carried out radical reform and neglected economic development and social stability, the economy went steadily downhill by a big margin, and unemployment rate soared high for a long time. This further led to social disorder, even today, there is constant turmoil in some countries. We should ponder deeply on and draw on these lessons.

The practice in former Soviet Union and China shows from different perspectives that the relations of the reform, development and stability must be properly handled, for both system and structural transitions mean to readjust the former interest pattern. In this process of interest readjustment, the normal operational order of the former system must be changed whereas some new factors will give rise to or intensify the contradictions between the new and the old forces. The changes in the normal order and the intensification of the contradictions between the two forces may lead to social turmoil. At present and in a period afterwards, there will be complicated reasons for the problems and contradictions in the social and economic life. Some problems are merely legacies from the old system, some are derived from the "system vacuum" in the transitional process and still some are caused by the friction between the old system and the new one when the new system has just been established and the market is not well developed. Under such circumstances, we must adhere to development, reform and stability and properly handle the relations among them in order to realize the transition smoothly.

In short, pushing forward the reform and development in political and social stability while realizing social stability through reform and development is the inevitable choice for us to resolve the main social contradictions in China at present.

Section 2

Reform as the Driving Force

—One Basic Experience in Correctly Handling the Relations Between Reform, Development and Stability

Over the past two decades, under the guidance of the Deng Xiaoping theory, the Communist Party of China has led a reform that is unprecedented in width and depth in China's history and solved a series of major problems concerning the reform theoretically and in practice, including the nature and objectives of the reform and criteria for appraising the results of reform.

I. Unity Between "Second Revolution" and "Self-improvement of the Socialist System"

The understanding of the nature of the economic system reform surging forward with great momentum in China is vital in properly handling the relations among reform, development and stability.

"The nature of the reform is the same with our revolution carried out in the past, that is, to remove the obstacles preventing social productive forces from developing and free China from poverty and backwardness. In this sense, the reform can be called a revolutionary change." Deng Xiaoping noted explicitly, "The reform is the second revolution of China." The nature of the reform since 1979 is to reform the planned economic system copied from the former Soviet Union, formed under the guidance of the "Left" trend of thought and which had greatly fettered the development of the productive forces.

The core of setting the objective pattern of the economic system is to handle properly the relations between planning and market. Five suggestions have been made on the reform objective pattern: a) the planned economy as the mainstay with market regulations as supplements (1980); b) the planned commodity economy (1984); c) a system with the internal unity of the planned and market economy (1987); d) combination of the planned economy and the marked regulation (1989);

e) socialist market economic system (1992). With the development of reform and the gradual freedom from the fetters of the traditional ideas of the planned economy, the exploration into the reform objective pattern has become deeper and increasingly mature. Based on knowledge gained and testified in practice, it was put forward at the Fourteenth National Congress of the CPC that the objective of the reform is to establish a socialist market economic system. According to this objective, China's economic system reform will not only call for a better regulatory role of the law of value and market mechanism, but also enable the market mechanism to play a fundamental role in resources allocation and economic operation. Over the past twenty years, China's economic system reform is, on the whole, market-oriented, in spite of twists and turns in understanding the relations between planning and market. Even under the circumstances of domestic political turmoil and drastic changes in the former Soviet Union and East Europe, China had stood firm in carrying out its market-oriented reform.

The fundamental reform of the economic system inevitably calls for the reform on other systems to meet the requirements of the socialist modernization construction. Over the past two decades, the Communist Party of China well grasped the fundamental nature of the reform as the second revolution and pushed forward the reform in many fields—economy, science and technology, education, culture and politics. Though reform, the productive forces have been emancipated, which greatly promoted the social and economic development.

As far as its fundamental nature and role in emancipating productive forces fettered by the old system are concerned, the reform is the second revolution of China. However, it differs from the first revolution aimed at overthrowing the old government and the old social system carried out in the years before 1949. The reform undertaken in China since 1979 has been carried out on the premise of adhering to the basic system of socialism and therefore is self-improvement and self-development of the socialist system. This is reflected in the following ways. 1) The leading party is the party in power—the Communist Party of China instead of other parties or political organizations. 2) The majority of participants in reform are from the working class and the broad masses of the people instead of other classes and social forces. 3) The reform targets at the links and aspects in China's existing production relations and superstructure that are incompatible with the development of the productive forces, rather than fundamentally changing the whole socialist system. 4) The purpose of the reform is to emancipate and develop the productive forces instead of overthrowing the existing political power. 5) The function of the reform is to reform the traditional planned economic system and other systems so as to give full play to people's creativity and initiatives and further invigorate the socialist economy and every aspect of social life instead of fundamentally changing the basic social form of China. Over the past two decades, China has consistently adhered to the correct direction of the reform—the unity of "second revolution" and "self-improvement of the socialist system." This has constantly deepened the reform, developed the productive forces, improved people's life, stabilized political and social situation and eventually embarked China on the course of thriving progress.

II. Taking "Three Favorables" as the Sole Criteria to Evaluate the Reform

China's economic system reform is an unprecedented great undertaking. In this historic transition, however, what should be the criteria for evaluating the reform? This is a question faced by all transitional countries, but only answered by China in explicit language.

It was Deng Xiaoping who answered this question. Oh his south China inspection tour in 1992, he pointed out sharply, "The reason some people hesitate to carry out the reform and the open policy and dare not break new ground is, in essence, that they are afraid it would mean introducing too many elements of capitalism and, taking the capitalist road. The crux of the matter is whether the road is capitalist or socialist. The chief criterion for making that judgment should be whether it promotes the growth of the productive forces in a socialist society, increases the overall strength of the socialist state and raises living standards." This wise conclusion on the criteria for making judgment on the reform is of great significance for further emancipating the mind and pushing forward the reform.

What should be pointed out is that these criteria are not Deng Xiaoping's own ideas, instead, they are the collective ideas of the Party. In the autumn of 1992, the "three favorables" were written down in the report of the Fourteenth Party Central Committee as the fundamental criteria for evaluating whether the reform is successful or not. In spite of disagreement from a few people to these criteria and proposal for other criteria, the Party reiterated and emphasized the importance of adhering to the criteria of "three favorables" at the Fifteenth National Congress of the Party. This is an important contribution made by the Party to the theory concerning China's economic system reform.

The "three favorables" are a product derived from Deng Xiaoping's theory of establishing socialism with Chinese characteristics and the sharp ideological weapon to analyze and understand the new things emerging during the process of reform and opening. The problem of the shareholding system is a typical example.

In the 1980s, the shareholding system appeared in some places of China where the reform had begun earlier and aroused controversies. Some people thought that the shareholding system meant private ownership and hence privatization whereas others did not take the equity structure into consideration and simply equated the shareholding system with the public ownership, no matter who contributes the capital and controls the stocks. Still some people suggested analyzing the shareholding system. They thought it was one of the organizational forms of capital socialization and its nature should be decided by the specific equity structure. Due to these different opinions, it was very hard to promote the shareholding system for quite a long period of time. In 1992, Deng Xiaoping made a speech on his south China inspection tour. He explicitly put forward the criteria of "three favorables" which fundamentally removed the obstacles to the shareholding-oriented reform. He also made specific and clear instructions on stocks and securities. He noted, "Are securities and the stock market good or bad? Do they entail any dangers? We allow people to reserve their judgment, but we must try these things out. If they prove feasible after one or two years of experimentation, we can apply them elsewhere. Otherwise, we can put a stop to them, either all at once or gradually, totally or partially. What is there to be afraid of? So long as we keep this attitude, everything will be all right, and we shall not make any major mistake."

From then on, experiments of the shareholding-oriented reform advanced smoothly. By the end of 1996, 9200 state-owned enterprises were transformed into joint stock companies with limited liabilities, with capital stocks of 600 billion yuan and 150 billion yuan raised from the society. Although some of the enterprises practicing the shareholding system are net yet standardized, on the whole, the shareholding system has played an active role in promoting the economic development of China, especially in the enterprise system reform and shift of the operational mechanism.

There are still many similar examples. Practice shows that the criteria of "three favorables" provide us a sharp ideological weapon to analyze the complicated issues arising in the process of the reform. Making correct use of this weapon is of great significance in pushing forward China's economic system reform.

According to the practice of China's economic system reform, we must pay attention to the following three points so as to correctly understand and apply the criteria of "three favorables." Firstly, we should stick to the objectiveness of the criteria and shall not replace it with any subjective criterion. Secondly, we should link these criteria with adhering to socialism (Deng Xiaoping pointed out explicitly, "The chief criterion for making that judgment should be whether it promotes the growth of the productive forces in a socialist society and increase the overall strength of the socialist state.") So we shall not deviate from the premise of adhering to socialism, otherwise the criteria of "three criteria" would lose their own value. Thirdly, we should have an overall understanding of the "three favorables," especially the internal connections between them.

The criteria of "three favorables" are a united and complete whole. Among them, the first one, that is "favorable to promoting the growth of the productive forces," is the basis. For one thing, the development of the productive forces is the precondition and basis of all social developments. The increase of the overall strength and rising of people's living standards will depend on the development of production. Secondly, the important demonstration of the superiority of socialism is to make the social productive forces to develop at a speed never reached by the old society. The second criterion, favorable to increasing the overall strength of the socialist state, is the natural extension and logic result of the first one and they are closely related, for the development of the productive forces is the source of the increase of the overall strength. We will not be able to promote the overall strength of our nation without the development of the productive forces. The third criterion, favorable to raising people's living standards, is the ultimate purpose of the first and the second criteria, because the superiority of the socialist system can only be shown by the fact that social productive forces develop at a speed never reached by the old society to gradually meet the ever-increasing needs of the people for material and cultural life. So, we should understand the criteria as a complete and whole system.

In short, the criteria of "three favorables" can help push forward reform, develop the productive forces and maintain social stability. They are the standards for properly handling the relations among the reform, development and stability.

III. A Gradual Approach

There are two different ways in the world to transform a planned economy into a market economy. One is the shock therapy and the other is the gradual model. China has taken a gradual approach since the 1980s.

The so-called gradual approach refers to the accumulative and marginal evolution model of transition to a market economy. Compared with shock therapy, the gradual reform approach appears more mild. China's "gradual" reform approach has the following features.

1. Proceed from Rural Areas to Urban Areas

Agriculture is the foundation for developing the national economy, especially in China. At present, the rural population accounts for 80 percent of the total in China. Without a proper incentive mechanism for farmers, agriculture will not be able to boost the rapid development of the national economy. Rural areas are featured with collective economy, which, compared with the dominating state-owned economy in urban areas, is a comparatively weaker link which can be easily broken first. This decides that China's economic system reform would inevitably start in the rural areas. After the Third Plenary Session of the Eleventh Party Central Committee and under the guidance of the reform and opening policy, millions of farmers were greatly inspired. The household responsibility system created and started by the farmers in Fengyang County, Anhui Province was affirmed and supported by the Central Committee of the CPC. Then the rural reform focusing on the household responsibility system developed rapidly and vigorously. In the four years from 1979 to 1983, historical changes took place in China's countryside and agriculture changed from solely collective operations into collective plus household operations, with rural households as important units of agricultural production. After the system of fixing farm output quotas for each household and the system of a household being solely responsible for their own farming operations were recognized as responsibility systems by No.1 Document of the Central Committee of the CPC in 1982, the household responsibility system became very popular across China. By the end of 1983, the rural households involved in the responsibility system accounted for 98 percent of the total.

The reform in the rural areas greatly pushed forward the development of agricultural productive forces, and in the meanwhile, set an example to the reform of the whole economic system. Marked by the "Decision on the Reform of Economic Structure," adopted by Party Central Committee in October 1984, the main battlefields of China's reform on economic structure began to shift from the rural areas to the urban ones. In this sense, China's "second revolution," like the "first revolution" led by the CPC, took the same road of "surrounding the cities from the countryside"

2. Proceeding from Coastal Areas to Inland Areas

China's economic system reform has been running in two parallel lines: one is from the countryside to the cities and the other is from coastal areas to inland regions. In July 1979, a decision was made by the Central Committee of the CPC and the State Council to set up special economic zones (SEZS) in Shenzhen, Zhuhai and Shantou in Guangdong Province and Xiamen in Fujian Province. The "specialty" of these zones is shown in the following five aspects: a) absorption and utilization of foreign funds for construction; b) market regulation of economic activities; c) Preferential taxation system for enterprises in the SEZs; d) larger scope of authority of the local government in economic regulation; e) more flexible policies for import and export. By doing so, an opening was made inside the planned economy.

After the establishment of the four SEZs, the Party Central Committee and the State Council decided in 1984 to open fourteen coastal cities and Hainan Island and to establish economic and technological zones in some cities. Over the past decade and more, the economy in the coastal areas developed rapidly. According to statistics up to 1992 when the Fourteenth National Congress of the CPC was held, the total value of GDP in these areas reached 1280.6 billion yuan, accounting for 53.3 percent of the national total; GDP per capita reached 2,775 yuan, 32 percent higher than the average of the country.

Based on the development of the coastal areas, the Fourteenth Party Congress put forward the guideline of "opening the coastal areas, major river valley regions and border areas." China has successively opened 13 inland border cities, 6 cities in river valleys and 18 capital cities of provinces, forming a pattern of an overall opening from coastal areas to inland regions.

3. Starting with the Development of the Non-state-owned Sector, Such as Village and Township Enterprises, Private and Foreign-funded Enterprises, to Bring About a Situation in Which the Public Ownership Makes up the Mainstay while Economic Elements under Diverse Forms of Ownership Develop Side by Side.

Since the 1950s when China conducted socialist transformation on agriculture, handicraft industry, and capitalist industry and commerce, the trend of centralization in ownership and operation had been rather strong,. Particularly when the "Left" line was prevalent, the non-state-owned economy was severely buffeted. After the reform and opening, a breakthrough was first sought to make in the non-state-owned economic field in 1980. This strategy of developing outside the state-owned economy had greatly promoted the development of non-state-owned economy and the high-speed growth of the whole national economy. In 1997, the output value of the non-state-owned industries reached 8470.5 billion yuan, accounting for 74.5 percent of the total value of the whole industry. The assets value of industrial enterprises expanded rapidly. In 1997, the asset value of industrial enterprises with independent accounting in China amounted to 10,343.9 billion yuan, among which that of the non-state-owned economy reached 4,433.2 billion yuan, accounting for 42.8 percent of the total. It was just because we started with encouraging the development of non-state-owned economy and introducing market economy outside the planned one that a competitive group was formed outside the state-owned one and finally made the state-owned economy itself change.

4. Proceeding from "Policy Readjustment" Featuring Decentralization of Power and Concession of Profits by the Government to Enterprise System Innovation and the Strategic Restructuring of the Entire State-owned Sector in the Course of SOE Reform

China's SOE reform has been carried out in three steps. The first step began in the early 1980s, which expanded the autonomy of enterprises, especially in profit distribution, so that enterprises can gain certain benefits. The second step began with the adoption of the "Decision on the Reform of Economic Structure" at the Third Plenary Session of the Twelfth Party Central Committee in October 1984, featuring the separation of ownership from operation. On the premise that the state retains ownership over enterprises, the right to operation was delegated to lower levels. The third step began with the experiment on establishing a modern enterprise system after the Fourteenth National Congress of the CPC. According to the standards of "clear property right, specified rights and obligations, separation of government from enterprises and scientific management," standardized corporate reform was carried out in large and medium-sized SOEs to transform them into legal person entities and player competent in market competition. At the same time, the state-owned economy and SOEs were strategically restructured according to guideline of "grasping the large enterprises while letting go the small ones." Through this gradual method, SOEs based on the planned economy were gradually transformed in line with the requirements of the socialist market economy.

5. Practicing the "Double-track System" First and Then Unifying Them and Implementing a Unitary Market Economic System When Conditions Are Ripe

This is an important creation made by China in its gradual reform to realize the economic transition and it is best shown in the reform on prices. The former price system in China was in a state of disorder due to the long-time neglect of the law of value, so the reform on it must be carried out. However, two different approaches are available. One is to liberalize prices at one time; the other is to take a steady and step-by-step approach. China took the latter for the following reasons. Firstly, the pricing system reform must be in line with market development. Since the former is a rapidly changing variable while the latter a slowly changing one, it is unrealistic for market development to adapt itself to the pricing system reform. Secondly, the pricing system reform should take the characteristics of different industries and products into consideration for choosing to carry out the policy of liberalization or regulation or combination of the two. Thirdly, the pricing system reform should consider various economic, political and social factors. For the above reasons, China did not take the first approach. Instead, it practiced "a double-track system" for a period of time and then gradually changed to a unified market system. This is most typical in the price reform of industrial capital goods. The "Notice on Liberalizing the Prices of Over-Produced Industrial Capital Goods and Those Sold by the Producers Themselves" was jointly issued by the State Administration of Commodity Prices and the State Bureau of Materials and

Equipment in January 1985. According to this document, the prices of the products within the state planning shall be strictly consistent with state pricing and shall not be changed as prices outside the planning. The prices of industrial capital goods sold by the producers themselves or over produced shall no longer be confined within 20 percent of the fixed prices as previously stipulated. These products can be sold at prices slightly lower than those in the local market to play the role of market and price regulation. By doing so, the prices of industrial capital goods follow the "double-track system," i.e. the combination of the state pricing system and the market-regulated price system. The double-track system plays a certain role in breaking the unitary state pricing system. After the implementation of the double-track system, the gap between the two different prices of the same product widened rapidly, and the market-regulated prices started to take the lead. With the development of the market economy, the two systems were gradually united into the market-regulated price system. As a result, the prices of goods in the market have become to reflect the law of value and the supply and demand in the market.

6. First Pushing Forward the Economic Structural Reform, Maintaining Economic Development and Social Stability to Distribute More Benefits to People and Then Carrying Out the Political Reform and Reforms in Other Fields at a Proper Time

How to deal with the relations between the reform on economic system and that on political system is very important in the proper handling of the relations among the reform, development and stability. In the 1980s, some people suggested that the political system reform be implemented first and the economic system reform next. The guideline of the Central Committee of the CPC shows that the establishment of socialism with Chinese characteristics needs reform on not only the political and economic systems, but also the educational, management and other systems. However, these reforms must be conducted according to a proper order of priorities, which is a very important aspect of the gradual reform. The economic system reform would develop the market economy under socialist conditions, emancipate and liberalize the productive forces and promote the sustained, rapid and healthy development of the national economy. All these can benefit the people immensely. On such a basis, the political system reform can be conducted with better results. China's practice shows that following such an order is the correct choice. If China had chosen to carry out the political system reform first, it would not have made such great achievements today.

It is not accidental for China to take a gradual approach for its reform. There are profound reasons for doing so.

China's economic system reform is not just making some amendment to or improvement of the former economic system. Instead, it is the second revolution carried out within the basic economic system of a socialist society. Since it is a revolution, it is reasonable for the leaders guiding the process to move in a cautious way and avoid reckless radical measures. Moreover, the reform would inevitably change the existing pattern of interest relations and therefore needs to win understanding and support from the society. These considerations have contributed to the adoption of the gradual approach in advancing the reform in China.

There are objective reasons as well. The complicated national situation, the arduousness of reform and political stability also call for a gradual approach. China is a populous country with huge territories and unbalanced regional economic development. There are great disparities in the level of social and market development between the cities and the countryside, between the coastal areas and the interior areas and between the state-owned economy and non-state-owned economy. This decides that we must take a gradual approach instead of starting all at once. Judging from the internal connections of the economic system reform, each part is closely connected with others. While all parts form an integrated whole, a breakthrough must be made somewhere correctly. In the 1980s, reform proceeded in such a way that it made breakthroughs in those weak parts of the planned economy while avoiding "biting on the hardest bones," which were those parts most strictly controlled under the planned economy. This would inevitably involve a gradual process. Besides the economic reasons, there is also the requirement of politics. When Deng Xiaoping met with the US ex-president J. Carter, he pointed out, "The main objective for China is to develop and get rid of backwardness so as to strengthen its national power and improve its people's livelihood. Doing such things needs a stable political environment. Without a stable political environment, we can achieve nothing." Had a radical approach been taken, the society and the people would not have been capable of adapting themselves to the changes and there could have been social riots. In short, it is an inevitable and correct choice for China to take a gradual approach in the reform.

Through twenty years' practice, it has become more and more obvious that it is proper and correct to take the gradual approach, although the two systems may coexist for a longer period of time and some new contradictions may arise during this period. This approach has greatly promoted the rapid growth of the economy, won universal understanding and support from the society and well maintained social stability. Therefore, the gradual approach is in conformity with China's state conditions.

Section 3

Development as the Focus —Second Basic Experience in Correctly Handling the Relations Between Reform, Development and Stability

Over the past two decades, China has made world-acclaiming achievement in its economic and social development. The GDP soared from 362.4 billion yuan in 1978 to 7,955.28 billion yuan in 1998, an increase of 5.38 times according to comparable prices. In 1995, China reached the target of quadrupling the GDP of 1980 five years ahead of the plan. In 1997, China quadrupled the GDP per capita set forth in the Nine Five-year Plan three years in advance. The population of China had an increase of 250 million from 1981 to 1997. It's a real wonder for

China with such a large population increase to quadruple its GDP per capita in only 17 years. The rapid development of production enabled us to bid farewell to the time when life necessities were supplied in quotas. Now most people have adequate food and clothing and are on the road to a more comfortable life. The bank balance of the people all over the country soared from 21.1 billion yuan by the end of 1978 to over 5900 billion yuan by the end of June 1999, an increase of 280 times. Experts from the World Bank once made the comments that "China has achieved within the time of only one generation what other countries have achieved with the efforts of several generations."

Over the past 20 years, China made great progress in its economic and social development because it has resolutely and fruitfully pushed forward the reform, greatly emancipated the productive forces fettered by the old system and unswervingly placed economic construction at the center of its work. This is another basic experience in handling the relations among the reform, development and stability in China.

I. Upholding Economic Construction as the Focus and Setting the Route, Phases and Strategy for Development

After the decision was made at the Third Plenary Session of the Eleventh Party Central Committee to shift the focus of work to the modernization drive, Deng Xiaoping warned the whole country time and again that we should draw on historical lessons and should never deviate our work from economic construction. He pointed out, "If we deviate from this center we will run the risk of losing material basis. All of our other work should be conducted around it without causing any disturbance and distraction. We had very bitter experience in this regard in the past 20 years," and "We must not idle away any single day from the first year of the 1980s on and should concentrate on the modernization drive." Since we have done like that in the past 20 years, we have avoided many detours in our economic and social development.

China's economy has developed at a very rapid pace since the reform and opening. This is inseparable from the correct setting of the route, phases and strategy for development by the Party and the state.

Over the past 20 years, the most valuable experience in our modernization drive is that we proceed from the reality of China and take our own road. Since western counties started industrialization process and market economy several hundred years ago and have accumulated rich experience, China must attach great importance to learning from and drawing upon their experience. However, we must not copy their experience even if they have been proven successful in their practice. The core of proceeding from the reality of China and taking our own road is to take our road with Chinese characteristics. We have discarded the planned economic mode taken by the former Soviet Union in which the heavy industry took up unduly high proportions while agriculture and the light industry lagged far behind and market economy was expelled. We have also refused to take the road of industrialization taken by Western capitalist countries and their economic system based on the private ownership. Our experience gained in the past 20 years fully shows that the road we take is one with Chinese characteristics and is an absolutely right one. Only by adhering to socialism can China develop and only by proceeding from the reality of China and taking our own road can China really adhere to socialism.

Since 1980s, the Party and the state have made correct judgment on which stage of social development China is in on the basis of summarizing historical experience and analyzing the reality in China. They reiterated that China is in a primary stage of socialism, which will take at least one hundred years to go through. This is the most fundamental reality. It is just because of understanding of such a reality that China's policies have played a great role in pushing forward economic and social development.

While setting the correct development route and phases, we must formulate correct strategy for development. In the early 1980s, Deng Xiaoping proposed the well-known "three-step" strategy. The first two steps, which should be finished by the end of the 20th century, include quadrupling the GNP from 1980 and ensuring the people adequate food and clothing and a relatively comfortable life. For the last step, which should be finished in 30 to 50 years in the 21st century, the objective is to catch up with medium-developed countries, ensure the people a comparatively rich life and basically realize modernization. This strategy was put forward on the basis of summarizing the past lessons of unrealistic economic development, deep analysis of the major trend of the global economic development and the basic national conditions of China. The practice in the past 20 years proves that this strategic objective is grand and realistic as well, and it has become the guideline for the action of the whole Party and people all over the county.

II. Strengthening and Improving Macro Regulation, Maintaining Macro-economic Stability

The maintenance of macro-economic stability is the basic condition for the sustained, rapid and healthy development of the national economy and the important guarantee for maintaining social stability. The economy of China has grown rapidly since the reform and opening. The average annual increase of GDP from 1979 to 1998 is 9.7 percent. This is because we pushed forward the market-oriented reform, constantly expanded and strengthened the role of market mechanism and invigorated micro-economic units. It is also because we gave play to the role of the "visible" hand while we strengthen the role of the "invisible" hand and maintained the stability of macro-economy through strengthening and improving macro-regulation.

During economic transition, many uncertain factors would cause fluctuations of the economic growth. We must strengthen and improve macro regulation to maintain the rapid economic growth and avoid inflation. This is particularly so in the process of liberalizing the prices of commodities and services, for these prices will rise spontaneously. If investment and consumption demands get out of control in such a situation, serious inflation is easy to be triggered off, resulting in the rocketing of commodity prices. In order to curb inflation, the investment and consumption demands must be under control. But the over-control of the demand will bring about the toboggan of the economic growth. For example, in the early 1980, the economy grew at an accelerating rate, with a growth rate of 5.3 percent in 1981, 9 percent in 1982, 10.9 percent in 1983, 15.2 percent in 1984 and 13.5 percent in

1985; at the same time, the demand for investment and consumption grew too fast and the prices rose. After taking some measures to control the demand, the growth rate of economy dropped to 8.9 percent. However, the problem caused by system factors of the rising demand had not been resolved, so in 1987 and 1988, the growth rate rose to 11.6 percent and 11.3 percent respectively, and serious inflation took place. In 1988 and 1989 the retail price index of the commodities in the whole society rose 18.5 percent and 17.8 percent respectively over the previous year. So in the last quarter of 1988, we began to improve the economic environment and rectify the economic order, reduce investment and control the demand. In 1990 and1991, price increase rate dropped to 2.1 percent and 2.9 percent respectively. In the meanwhile, the economic growth rate dropped to 4.1 percent and 3.8 percent in 1989 and 1990 respectively, only one third of the average growth rate from 1984-1988.

In the 1990s, on the basis of summarizing historical experience, China's macro regulation started to adapt to the demand of the market economy and closely link with the deepening of the reform. So macro regulation in this period was more mature and efficient than that conducted in the 1980s. For example, owing to the super high increase of investment in 1992, 1993 and 1994, the growth rate of the economy reached 14.2 percent, 13.5 percent, 12.6 percent respectively. During the three years, the investment in fixed assets in the whole society increased 44.4 percent, 61.8 percent and 30.4 percent respectively. Serious inflation took place again. The retail price index of commodities rose to 13.2 percent (1993), 21.7 percent(1994) and 14.8 percent (1995). In the second half of 1993, the central government took a series of measures of strengthening macro regulation to deal with the overheating in real estate and development zones, the disorder in financial sector, the over-growth in fixed assets investment and the inflation caused by it. Then the government carried out a few reforms in macroeconomic filed, curbing inflation successfully and the price increase rate dropped gradually, 6.1 percent in 1996 and 0.8 percent in 1997. At the same time, the economic growth rate slowed down as well, 10.5 percent in 1995, 9.6 percent in 1996 and 8.8 percent in 1997 respectively. The economy did not plummeted as a result of the macro regulation, instead the "soft landing" was realized. This success story under market economic conditions has won high praises from the rest of the world, for how to bring a serious inflation under control without damaging economic growth is a very tough problem to all countries. For China, a country in economic transition, it is particularly difficult to realize the "soft landing" of its economy.

The experience to realize the " economic soft landing" is mainly as follows:

a) Combining the control over demand with the increase of supply. The above-mentioned inflation was mainly caused by the rapidly rising prices of the investment goods and the land for construction brought about by the super high increase of the investment in fixed assets. Then the prices of consumption goods also escalated. In the meantime, the unbalance in supply and demand of some important agricultural produce such as rice also caused the rise of food prices, which aggravated the inflation. Statistics showed that the commodity retail prices increased by 21.7 percent in 1994, 60 percent of which was caused by the rise of food prices. In view of the main reasons of inflation, measures were taken to deepen the reform of the financial system to strengthen the control over sources of investment. As a result, the growth rate of investment dropped year by year until it was back to the normal growth level, i.e. 17.5 percent and 14.8 percent in 1995 and 1996 respectively. On the other hand, investment was increased to reinforce agriculture. The bumper harvest in agriculture for several consecutive years after 1995 brought down the prices of agricultural produce effectively, which played an important part in lowering the general level of commodity prices.

b) Combining macro regulation with the deepening of reform. Since 1994, China reformed its financial, taxation, banking, foreign trade, foreign exchange, investment and pricing system vigorously in accordance with the defects existing in the macro-economic management system to meet the demands of the socialist market economy. These reforms turned out to be successful and guaranteed the enforcement of the macro regulation measures.

c) Macro regulation was carried out mainly through economic means, and at the same time, supplemented by necessary administrative means. In 1992, the pace of the reform and opening speeded up significantly after the Fourteenth National Party Congress. In order to adapt to the changes in the economic system, macro regulation was mainly conducted through economic means so that it could play an effective role. On the other hand, many aspects of the old system were still functioning, due to the special period of economic transition. The overheating in development zones and real estate and the swelling in investment, etc. were largely caused by the administrative actions of the government. Relying on economic means alone without the supplements of necessary administrative means was not sufficient in solving these problems effectively and efficiently.

Since 1998, in order to maintain the stability of macro-economy, the problem of deflation and the shortage in demand must be resolved. Owing to the impact of the Asian financial crisis, duplicate construction in previous years and shrinking domestic demand, the retail price index of commodities had dropped for 20 consecutive months from October 1997 to May 1999. Meanwhile, export decreased, supply of industrial and agricultural products generally exceeded market demands, domestic funds sat idle and the deposits in financial institutions kept increasing. These caused the reduction of enterprise profits, aggravation of the loss-making situation of enterprises, flat income increase of farmers in spite of increased agricultural output, weakened consumption in both urban and rural areas and low investment incentives for collectives and individuals. In the first half of 1998, aiming at the above-mentioned problems, the central government took a series measures to expand investment and stimulate export and domestic demand, but these measures were not very effective. In the first quarter of that year, GDP increased by 7.2 percent from the same period last year; in the second quarter, the increase dropped to 6.8 percent. The government therefore decided in the second half of 1998 to implement an active fiscal policy by issuing T-bonds of 100 billion yuan, couple with another 100 billion yuan in bank loans. These bonds and loans were mainly invested in infrastructure construction, such as agricultural water conservancy, transportation, telecommunications, urban public utilities and electric grid improvement, etc. As a result, economic situation was improved. In the third quarter of 1998, the growth rate of GDP rose to 7.6 percent, the fourth quarter 9 percent, and that of the first quarter of 1990 rose to 8.3 percent. However, owing to its limited scope of pulling effect, the investment in infrastructure failed to stimulate private investment and domestic consumption significantly. In the second quarter of 1999, the momentum of the growth of investment and consumption began to slow down, with export falling, demand shrinking and signs of deflation developing. To solve these problems, the central government decided to take new measures, including issuing an additional 60 billion yuan in T-bonds on the basis of 150.3 billion yuan of budgetary deficit and T-bonds set at the beginning of the year and properly readjusting the investment direction. Besides the infrastructure, investment would be increased for key sectors, key enterprises, key products, science and technology and education. The central government would also take measures to encourage non-governmental investment, increase the income of public servants and increase the income of those with lower income so that the demand for consumption will be stimulated. These measures would play an active part in dissipating signs of deflation, increasing demand and improving economic growth in the second half of 1999 and even in 2000.

The practice since the reform and opening, particularly in the 1990s, proves that while the market is playing the basic role of allocating resources, macro regulation should be strengthened and improved to maintain the balance between the gross demand and gross supply and the stability of the Renminbi (RMB) through timely fiscal and monetary policies as well as other measures. This is of great importance to the deepening of the reform, expansion of opening, promotion of development and maintenance of stability.

III. Upholding Opening to Promote the Reform, Development and Stability

Opening to the outside world is a basic national policy of China and an important part in constructing socialism with Chinese characteristics. Deng Xiaoping once said, "Opening to the outside world is of great significance. It is impossible for any country to develop by isolating itself from the rest of the world and with its door closed. Neither can it develop without enhancing its associations with other countries or without introducing the advanced experience, advanced science and technology and funds from developed countries" and "China must open its door if she wants to develop, to get rid of poverty and backwardness."

Opening to the outside world is key to the reform, development and stability. First, opening itself is a kind of reform and it is the inevitable choice for establishing a market economic system. The market economic system is an achievement of human civilization and shall be shared by mankind. In the process of opening, China has proceeded from its own realities and drawn on the experience of developed countries, including enterprise system innovations, operation of the capital market and financial sector and macro-regulation under the market economic conditions, so as to promote the economic system reform.

Opening is also indispensable for promoting development. China must open to the outside in order to realize industrialization and modernization and to develop market economy. The development of human society shows that development of the productive forces is closely connected with the expansion of market. The development of human society is a process in which market constantly expands beyond the boundaries of regions and even of countries to gradually form regional market, national market and international market. Besides, opening can serve as an important driving force for the high-speed economic growth through various ways, including developing foreign trade, introducing advance technology and promoting labor exchanges.

China's opening has developed vigorously and made striking achievements since 1997, especially since the Fourteenth National Party Congress. Foreign trade developed very fast: the total volume of imports and exports increased by an annual average of 15 percent, obviously higher than the economic growth rate of China and the growth of world trade in 1998. The total volume of imports and exports of

China's foreign trade amounted to US$323.9 billion, accounting for 3 percent of the world total and ranking the eleventh in the world. The volume of foreign fund used doubled: the average annual increase of foreign fund really used is 32.1 percent, among which the direct foreign fund used increased 57.1 percent annually in average from 1991 to 1996. By the end of 1998, the total volume of foreign funds used in China was US$406.9 billion with the total amount of direct foreign investment US$265.6 billion. Opening expanded from the coastal areas to the interior areas, and the pattern of an all-round opening has taken shape. This has not only promoted the development of regional economy, but also played an irreplaceable role in promoting the growth and improvement of the quality of the national economy as a whole.

Opening promoted economic development and social stability. During the Eighth Five-Year Plan period, every percentage point increase in exports brought about 0.2 percentage point increase in GDP. In 1998, foreign investment was 17 percent of domestic investment in fixed assets; the industrial output value of foreign-funded enterprises accounted for 19.9 percent of the total nationwide; export of foreign-funded enterprises amounted to 44 percent of the total; and 5.78 million people were employed by foreign-funded enterprises. This demonstrates that the development of foreign-funded enterprises has played an important role in promoting the economic growth and social stability in China.

To bring the role of opening into better play, China must do well in the following three aspects.

1. Expanding Foreign Trade by Improving Efficiency

Promoting the rapid development of foreign trade is an important task of opening to the outside world. From the structural perspective, China's foreign trade growth mainly depends on the export of labor-intensive products and competitive prices while in terms of the mode of trade, processing trade and the trade by foreign-funded enterprises rose very quickly. Since domestic enterprises and specialized foreign trade companies generally lack competitive advantages in fund supply, technology, management and services, foreign trade, export in particular, forcing management and optimizing structure, and serve as "windows" and "experimental areas" for China's reform. The central and western regions should raise their opening and economic development to a new level through their own efforts and necessary support from the rest of the country. While expanding regional opening, China has timely raised the issue of expanding opening in terms of sectors and carried out preferential policies accordingly, thus better integrating regional opening with sectoral opening.

Section 4

Stability as the Guarantee —Third Basic Experience in Correctly Handling the Relations Between Reform, Development and Stability

Political and social stability is the precondition for reform and development. In the 100 years and more before the founding of new China, China had been in chaos caused by wars and social upheavals; the country was in poverty, the people had nothing to depend on for their living. The ten-year "Cultural Revolution" again plunged China in all kinds of hardships. Historical experience has proven time and again that reform and opening would end up in nothing without economic and social stability. Deng Xiaoping pointed out repetitively that "In order to conduct modernization drive whole-heartedly, we must maintain and develop a united, stable and active political situation in the first place," "Without stability, it is impossible for us to undertake the course of socialist construction, let alone other things." and "Without a stable environment, we can achieve nothing. We may even lose what we have achieved." Over the past 20 years, China has created a stable social environment, in which remarkable achievements have been made.

I. Giving Top Priority to the Stability of the Overall Situation

It is crucial to maintain the stability of the overall situation in order to maintain social stability. Over the past 20 years, China has accumulated a lot of experience in this regard, which mainly includes the following.

1. Properly Handle the Major Problems Concerning the Overall Situation

The political movement that centered on class struggles and lasted for more than 20 years caused a lot of wronged, false and erroneous cases. To redress these cases was the loud call from the whole Party and people all over the country, as well as the requirement for maintaining the stability of the overall situation. After the Third Plenary Session of the Eleventh Party Central Committee, numerous wronged cases were redressed, including the case of "Hu Feng Reactionary Group" (1955), "the Rightists" wrongly classified (1957), the "Rightist Opportunism" wrongly charged (1959) and a lot of wronged cases in the "cultural revolution," especially the cases of Liu Shaoqi, Peng Dehuai, Tao Zhu and other Party and state leaders. Additionally, some measures were taken to readjust social relations, for example, the labels on landlords and rich peasants were removed, the class status of the former industrialists and businessmen was changed without exception to cadres and workers and intellectuals were declared a part of the working class, etc. All these acts played an important rote in resolving the contradictions left over by history and promoting social stability. In order to correct the "Left" mistakes from roots, it was necessary to completely clarify the confusion between right and wrong caused by the "Gang of Four." This would naturally involve the mistakes made by Mao Zedong in his later years. The correct appraisal of Mao's merits and demerits was a problem having bearing on the overall situation. In view of this, the Central Committee of the CPC took very prudent attitude, scientifically analyzing and criticizing the mistakes made by Mao Zedong in his later years while affirming the historical position of Mao Zedong and the system of Mao Zedong Thought. So the thinking of the whole Party and people all over the country was unified.

Over the past 20 years, China has also handled properly some major

and Political Reform

In the past 20 years, the reform in China has mainly been concentrated on its economic system. However, the political system reform has also been carried out in some areas. The ideological line of emancipating minds and seeking truth from facts, and the political line of centering on economic construction formulated at the Third Plenary Session of the Eleventh Party Central Committee actually marked the start of the reform of the political system.

On August 18,1980, Deng Xiaoping delivered an important speech entitled "On the reform of the System of Party and State Leadership." He analyzed various defects existing in China's political system and set forth the aim, principle and contents of the reform on it. This speech proved to be a programmatic document guiding China's reform in this regard. In 1986, he pointed out in another article entitled "On Reform of the Political Structure," "In the reform of the political structure, our general objectives are as following: (1) to consolidate the socialist system, (2) to develop the socialist productive forces and (3) to expand socialist democracy in order to bring the initiative of the people into full play." At the same time, he pointed out that the objectives of the political structural reform were to ensure the continuing vitality of the Party and the state, eliminate bureaucratism and increase efficiency, and stimulate the initiative of grass-roots units.

According to the general objectives, China carried out active exploration and reform in improving the people's congress system, the system of multi-party cooperation and consultation led by the Communist Party of China and developing socialist democracy and politics. The First Meeting of the Fifth National People's Congress held in 1978 adopted the Constitution, which stipulated that the National People's Congress was the highest organ of state power. In 1982, the Fifth Meeting of the Fifth National People's Congress made some amendments to the Constitution, with many new contents added and the power of the Standing Committee of the National People's Congress was expanded. The National People's Congress Standing Committee was given the authority of making laws except for the most fundamental ones. Some specialized committees were added to the Standing Committee for studying, discussing and drafting up relevant proposals. In the past 20 years, the National People's Congress and its Standing Committee enacted 339 laws altogether. Local people's congresses and their standing committees also enacted over 6,000 local laws and regulations, thus formulating a fairly comprehensive system of laws and regulations, including civil law, criminal law and administrative procedure law, which provides the basis for developing the rule of law. Besides legislative power, the National People's Congress and its Standing Committee also exercise power in decision-making, personnel appointment and removal and supervision. Furthermore, the Communist Party of China has constantly proved the multi-party cooperation system and the system of political consultation in practice. Democracy at the grass-roots level in both cities and the countryside has been vigorously developed. Over the past 20years, the political structural reform has played a very important role in developing socialist democracy, mobilizing the initiative of the broad masses of the people and promoting the development of the productive forces.

China has followed the principles below in conducting the political structural reform: a) proceeding from China's realities instead of copying political systems from the West and practicing multi-party election system; b) advancing reform in an orderly and a step-by-step manner. Deng Xiaoping pointed out: When we judge whether the political system, political structure and policies of a state are right or not, we have three criteria in mind: The first is whether the political situation of that country is stable; the second is whether it can strengthen national unity and improve people's living standards; and the third is whether the productive forces can be developed in a sustainable way. Some counties carried out the political structural reform alone without developing the productive forces and reforming the economic structure. Worse still, they did not pay due attention to the influence exerted by the political structural reform on the political situation in the country and the stability of the society. As a result, the reform gave rise to great social upheavals, even led to the disintegration of the country, leaving behind profound lessons.

other hand, if the strength is too strong, the interests pattern will suddenly become unbalanced, leading to social instability. The experience of China in keeping the balance can be summarized as follows. a) Reform measures should be carried out at a proper time on the basis of a correct assessment of the situation and consideration of the possible impact on various aspects of the society. If the condition is not ripe, actively create favorable conditions and wait for the proper time to come. This may seem to slow down the reform process, but reform would proceed smoothly and turn out not to be slow at all with social stability and the support from people. b) Emphasis should be placed on preventing "all-round campaigns." If all-round campaigns are launched, the interests of all sides would be affected. Although each single reform measure may not be very strong in itself, the forces created together could lead to chain reactions which would exceed social adaptability. c) A compensation mechanism should be established. Under the traditional system, a low-salary system was practiced in cities and towns. The salaries of employees did not include housing, medical care, and educational expenses for children while in the countryside, the price of agricultural produce was comparatively low because the price parity had not been rationalized. In view of such conditions, China's reform has compensated the employees in the cities and towns for their salaries and the peasants for their selling prices of agricultural produce so as to pay the debts in the past. d) A new social security system should be established. With the deepening of reform and acceleration of the industrial restructuring, the number of laid-off workers from SOEs has increased and the low-income group in the cities and towns become larger in recent years. To resolve the problem, China has established a basic life security system with Chinese characteristics for the laid-off workers from SOEs, an unemployment security system and the lowest life security system for people living in the cities and towns. And with the economic development, the standards for these systems will be raised accordingly. Through the three security systems, the basic life of the laid-off SOE workers and the low-income group will be guaranteed and social stability will be maintained.

Opening has played an important role in introducing foreign funds, advanced technologies, management experience, bringing the comparative advantages of China into full play, increasing employment opportunities and promoting economic growth. This has been proved by the practice in the past 20 years. So we must unswervingly expand opening. However, in the process of opening, there exists the problem of properly handling the relation between the extent of opening and social stability, which is best shown in how to handle the relation between opening and safeguarding the national economic security. Practice shows that strengthening the power for sustained development of the national economy and enhancing global competitiveness are key to safeguarding the national economic security. In the past 20 years, we did not ensure security with a closed door. Instead, we gave play to our comparative advantages, participated in international division of labor and exchanges and made use of the markets at home and abroad. In this way, we could consider China's survival and development from a global strategic angle and take the whole issue of development, competition and security into consideration.

Section 5

New Situation Faced in Reform, Development and Stability at the Turn of the Century and Tentative Ideas on Properly Handling Their Relations

I. The New Situation Facing China at the Beginning of the 21st Century

At the turn of the century, China's reform, development and stability are faced with new situations as well as new challenges both domestically and globally.

First, the revolution of science and technology in the world is developing by leaps and bounds and the era of knowledge economy has arrived. The striking progress of science and technology has been the major driving force in the 20th century pushing forward economic de-

technology upgrading while attaching importance to the development of electromechanical industry, high-tech industry and science, technology and education. The economy of China has grown at an average speed of 10 percent annually since the reform and opening, owing to the expansion of the aggregate economic volume and readjustment of the industrial structure. Obviously, the existing economic structure could hardly support a relatively rapid economic growth in the 21st century, nor could it provide a basis for improving economic efficiency and competitiveness by a wide margin. The strategic industrial restructuring should be aimed at structural upgrading. With the ever strengthening of the position and role of heavy industry in economic growth, the development of equipment industry represented by electromechanical industry is urgently needed. In the future economic development, the structural basis for economic growth will shift from the resource industry dominated by energy and raw materials to high processing, high technology and high value-added industry with electromechanical industry as the mainstay. While speeding up industrialization, we shall speed up the development of information industry and promote the information-based development of the national economy.

To shift the focus from developing the eastern coastal areas to quickening the economic development in the central and western regions. After entering the 21st century, the disparities in economic development and living standards between the eastern coastal areas and the central and western regions of China would probably enlarge at the beginning and then gradually diminish. Therefore, it is necessary to foster new economic growth points in the central and western regions, increase the investment in infrastructure in these regions and promote on this basis the coordinated and integrated economic growth across regions so as to narrow regional disparities.

To shift the focus of economic growth in the near future to sustainable development. At the beginning of the 21st century, the contradictions between the economic development and the protection of resources and environment in China will become more acute. So we must further pursue a resources-saving development strategy and adopt a system of compensated use of resources, increase input in environmental protection and greatly develop environmentally-sound industries and take active measures to harness environmental pollution by tree planting, soil conservancy and desertification control so as to realize the coordinated development of economy, society and environment.

2. Reform

At present, the economic system reform in China has entered a stage in which the toughest problems are to be tackled. To deal with those hardcore problems inherited from the past and the old economic system, it requires more determination, more careful planning, more solid steps and more forceful measures.

First, we shall continue adjusting and improving the ownership structure and speed up the reform on SOEs. We shall actively explore the forms for realizing the public ownership and speed up the development of a mixed ownership system. We shall also restructure the state-owned economy, push forward the enterprise system reform and establish the modern enterprise system while actively developing collective and private economies.

Second, various kinds of markets shall be further developed, especially the capital market, to better play the role of allocating resources. In the reform of nearly 20 years, the commodity markets in China developed very fast while the factor market, especially the capital market, developed rather slowly. Recent study showed that the degree of factor marketization in China was 36.57 percent in 1997 whereas that of capital marketization was 17.2 percent. Therefore, development of the capital market (including securities market and property rights exchange market, etc.) shall be treated as a matter of top priority in the next-step reform. Developing the capital market can facilitate the restructuring of the state-owned assets, push forward the establishment of market systems and promote the distribution system reform and the expansion of the opening to the outside world. Now the capital market in China is not large in scale and there is substantial room for its development. Since the development of capital market may lead to deepened reform on many aspects, it should be dealt with as a strategic issue. At the same time, we shall further improve and develop the land market, labor market and technology and information market.

After setting the objectives of the reform, we shall make correct assessment of the situation in accordance with these objectives, seize the opportunity and unswervingly push forward the reform. During this process, we will go deep into the practice and make investigation, summarize experience and pay attention to the methodology guiding the reform. We shall guard against impetuosity when tacking difficult hard-core problems, loss of focus when the scope of reform is expanded, advocating unrealistic slogans when setting targets for each campaign and overgeneralization when popularizing the experience gained from the reform or correcting some local mistakes.

Thirdly, the political system reform shall be advanced in accordance with the deepening of the economic system reform. On August 18, 1980, in his important speech "On Reform of the System of Party and State Leadership," Deng Xiaoping spoke clearly on the guiding thinking and basic ideas about the political structural reform. He said that the purpose of political restructuring was to overcome bureaucratism, develop socialist democracy and stimulate the initiative of the people and of the grass-roots units. Over the past 10 years and more, with the deepening of the economic structural reform, there has been an increasing demand for corresponding reform in the political structure. Since the political structural reform is different from the economic structural reform in nature and complexity, it should be advanced in a determined but cautious manner. The reform should be carried out in an orderly way under the leadership of the Party in line with China's realities instead of copying the any model from the West.

3. Stability

In the process of pushing forward the development and reform, it is inevitable and normal to see some elements of instability. This is nothing to be alarmed about. As long as factors influencing the overall situation are dealt with and systemic or structural sources of instability are removed in time, the long-term stability of China can be safeguarded. Economic stability is not only an important aspect of the social stability, but the basis for maintaining political and social stability as well. Currently, the following problems can influence the overall stability economically:

(1) Eliminate Financial Risks and Maintain Financial Stability

Finance is the core of modern economy and the most important part in economic operation. To guarantee the security of the banking system, healthy development of the securities market and standardized operations of the insurance industry is closely related to the reform, development and stability. At present, the size and proportions of bad loans in state-owned commercial banks and non-banking financial institutions are on the rise, with payment crisis and financial disturbances looming large. Lowering profits and increasing losses for banks and other financial institutions will intensify the contradictions in the payment of the central finance and increase the pressure on inflation. Flow of international capital, especially speculative capital, still threatens the safety of the domestic financial market and system. Under such circumstances, we must pay great attention to maintaining financial security in China. At present, it is necessary to maintain the stability of Renminbi and the foreign exchange rate; actively reform the state commercial banks to strengthen control over credit assets; further improve the insurance system for deposits in commercial banks to safeguard the interests of depositors and the security of the banking system; increase the favorable balance under current account to keep sufficient national foreign exchange reserves and rationally control the scale and structure of foreign debt; carry out financial opening with prudence, monitor and control the flows of foreign capital; improve the quality of bank capital, increase capital funds of the bank, reduce bad assets; and actively foster and strictly monitor and control capital market to prevent over-speculation.

(2) Alleviate Pressure of Employment to Dissolve the Risks of Unemployment

At present, employment in China is in a grave situation, with considerable risks lurking. On the one hand, the accumulated unemployed population from past years and the newly added work forces each year in cities and towns need jobs. And the employment pressure is just aggravated with large-scale reemployment programs of the laid-off SOE workers and transfer of the surplus rural labor to non-agricultural industries, as a result of industrial restructuring. On the other hand, the social security system is not yet well-established in China, which increases the risks in employment and reemployment. Judging from the developing trend, the expansion of opening and changes in the international market will also bring about risks to employment. Therefore, we should put the issue of employment and reemployment high on the agenda and maintain necessary economic growth. While upgrading industrial structure, importance should be attached to labor-intensive industries, especially to giving support to the development of the medium-sized and small enterprises, non-state-owned economy and the tertiary industry that can absorb more employees. Moreover, we shall develop rural economy in an all-round way, actively develop village and township enterprises, guide the multi-channel transfer and orderly movement of the surplus labor in the countryside to avoid the abrupt increase of trans-regional flow of labor. In the reform of SOEs, redundant employees shall be properly and actively channeled out and arranged by the reemployment programs. The social security system shall be perfected whereas education and on-the-job training systems shall be vigorously enhanced to improve the quality of the work forces, creating favorable conditions for expanding employment.

(3) Pay Attention to Effect of Capital Accumulation to Prevent Income Polarization

At present, the disparity in the income distribution of the social members is becoming improperly greater. The number of urban poor is on the rise, gray and illegal income comes in large amounts with low transparency and little effective control. Closely connected is the constant swelling of underground economy, which is the soil for breeding corruption and social instability. Without active and efficient measures to stop the trend, hidden income will take up larger proportions and the social income distribution will further get out of control. In this way, it would be more difficult for the state to regulate income disparity, and in the end the negative effect on social stability would become greater. In the process of economic transition, we should pay special attention to the accumulation effect of capital, that is the rich will become richer by using his capital to get more social wealth. Through income distribution and taxation policies, the state shall regulate income levels and take measures to safeguard the basic living standards of the low-income group to prevent unduly great disparities and polarization in wealth, thus guaranteeing the realization of the objective of common prosperity in the present stage.

Acknowledgement

China's basic policy of reform and opening to the outside world was decided in the late 1970s and early 1980s, which ushered in the prelude for its transition from the planned economy to the market economy. This strategic change has stimulated its economic growth. From 1978 to 1996, the average annual increase of the country's GDP remained at 9.9 percent while the growth in 1997 and 1998 was 8.8 percent and 7.8 percent respectively. Over the past 20 years, China's economy witnessed the fastest growth throughout world and the achievement has won worldwide acclaim.

Now, China has reached a critical stage in its reform of the economic structure. Therefore, it is of great significance for China to systematically sum up the experience and lessons in the economic transition over the past two decades. This is bound to expedite the establishment of the socialist market economy and its corresponding operational mechanisms that are conducive to raising the economic efficiency. In this sense, summing up the experience is also an urgent task that we should accomplish as soon as possible.

Based on the above understanding and in line with a suggestion by Mr. Chen Jinhua, Vice Chairman of the National Committee of the Chinese People's Political Consultation Conference and Board Chairman of China (Hainan) Institute of Reform and Development, the institute brought together a group of renowned experts and scholars to compile this book on the eve of the 50th anniversary of the founding of New China. Here, we would like to extend our thanks to all the renowned experts and scholars involved in the project, including Mr. Chen Jinhua, who personally wrote the "Introduction." They readily accorded our request and wrote the articles. Their efforts will, no doubt, make this book authoritative and appreciated by a wide readership. We would also like to express our special thanks to Mr. Wang Mengkui, director and research follow of the Center of Development Studies under the State Council, for being the chief editor and personally writing the "preface" to the book. Our thanks also goes to other contributors, including Mr. Zhou Shulian, research fellow of Institute of Industrial Economics under the Chinese Academy of Social Sciences, and Wang Yanzhong, Ph.D. in economics of the Institute of Industrial Economics under the Chinese Academy of Social Sciences; Mr. Zhang Zhuoyuan, research fellow of Institute of Economics under the Chinese Academy of Social Sciences (Chapter II); Mr. Chen Xiwen, chief and research fellow of Rural Department of Center of Development Studies under the State Council (Chapter III); Mr. Gao Shangquan, director-general of China Society for Reform of Economic Structure, and Director and Professor of China (Hainan) Academy of Reform and Development (Chapter IV); Mr. Chi Fulin, executive director and professor of China (Hainan) Academy of Reform and Development and vice chairman of China Society for Reform of Economic Structure (Chapter V); Mr. Zheng Xinli, vice secretary-general and research fellow of State Development and Planning Commission (Chapter VI); and Mr. Lin Zhuomu, executive deputy director and research fellow of Macro-economic Research Institute of State Development and Planning Commission, and Mr. Chang Xiuze, research fellow of Macro-economic Research Institute of State Development and Planning Commission (chapter VII).

The book is published in both English and Chinese editions. The English translators are Feng Qi, Wan Hua, Feng Jun, Zhou Quanfa, Gao Huali, Chen Mingfen and Huang Shengtai, and they also deserve our heartfelt thanks. We would like to thank Mr. Li Zhenguo of the Foreign Languages Press for polishing the English text of the greater part of this book. We would also like to express our special thanks to the Germany Technical Cooperation Company (GTZ) for their financial help and the Foreign Language Press for their warm support in the publication of this book.

China (Hainan) Institute for Reform and Development

March 2000

图书在版编目（CIP）数据
中国经济转轨二十年：英文 / 王梦奎主编. —北京：
外文出版社，2000. 6
ISBN 7-199-02610-0

I. 中… II. 王… III. 经济体制改
1979-1999—英文 IV. F121

中国版本图书馆 CIP 数据核字（

英文版责编　李振国
中文版责编　刘文渊　刘春英
封面设计　蔡　荣
英文翻译　殷仲仪　冯　奇

外文出版社出版
（中国北京百万庄大街 24 号）
邮政编码 100037
中国国际图书贸易总公司发行
（中国北京车公庄西路 35 号）
北京邮政信箱第 399 号　邮政编码 100044
2000 年（大 32 开）第 1 版
2000 年第 1 版第一次印刷
（英）
ISBN 7-119-02610-0 / F• 79 (外)
06500 (平)